flattery
Self-examination
CARNALITY
CONTENDING
Church Attendance
Hate
Rebuking
MuRMuRING
LEADING
praise
MINISTRY
Prayer

Modesty
conversation
watching
benevolence
LOVE
Bitterness
FELLOWSHIP
JUDGING

Fear
BACKBITING
FASTING
COUNSEL
communication
FRUGAL
hospitality
giving
LAUGHTER

WARFARE
Forgiveness
VANITY
Unity
SINGING
confession
TRUSTING
EDIFICATION
SEPARATION
Vengeance
THOUGHTS
reading & studying
TEACHING
Witnessing
Meditation

Volume 2
DAILY STRENGTH 2
DEVOTIONS FOR BIBLE BELIEVING STUDY

Douglas D. Stauffer
Andrew B. Ray

Bonus: Includes weekly Bible study tips

ISBN 978-1-942452-27-0

Scripture quotations from the King James Bible need no permission to quote, print, preach, or teach. For clarity, all scripture is in italics with reference and any emphasis in bold print. Any deviation from the King James Bible is not intentional.

For more information, contact:

McCowen Mills Publishers
Dr. Douglas D. Stauffer, President
6612 Hickory Way Lane
Knoxville, TN 37918
(866)344-1611 (toll free)
Website: *www.BibleDoug.com*
Email: *Doug@Bible.com*

LTB Publications
Dr. Andrew B. Ray, Pastor
5709 North Broadway Street
Knoxville, TN 37918
(865)688-0780
Website: *www.LearntheBible.org*
Email: *pastorray@LearntheBible.org*

Acknowledgements

The authors would like to express their deepest appreciation to the following:

Most preeminently, the precious Lord Jesus Christ for His saving and sustaining grace.

Those who invested the time and effort into our spiritual development, along with the men and women who have been persecuted and sometimes put to death for the faith and their trust in the Saviour and His word.

Our devoted wives for their constant support, encouragement, and understanding through our years of marriage and ministry together. They are truly God's *second* greatest gift to each of us *(Romans 6:23)*.

Mrs. Lois Barnes for her many hours of proofreading and grammatical suggestions.

Mr. Rick Quatro and Mr. Jonathan Judy for their invaluable assistance in formatting the book text.

Mr. Tom Rood for his creativity reflected in an impressive cover design.

Lastly, the members of Antioch Baptist Church, Knoxville, TN for their faithful support and encouragement during this long process of writing our second devotional book.

Recommendation

"Many find the Lord's command *six days shalt thou labour,* combined with *study to shew thyself approved unto God,* a bit overwhelming. In such a busy age, even the most sincere Christians often find it difficult to dig into the Bible as deeply and consistently as they should or would. Just as millions have benefited from pastors' sermons, countless others have been aided by devotional works produced by gospel ministers. This is such a work, and it carries with it the bonus of having been produced by men who love and believe every word of God's holy scripture. These daily readings will provide guidance, instruction, and encouragement to the church of God."

Pastor James Knox
THE BIBLE Baptist Church
DeLand, Florida
www.jamesknox.org

Author Biographies

Dr. Douglas D. Stauffer is an internationally recognized authority in the field of Bible history and defense. He is a prolific author, having written eleven books along with many writings published in Christian periodicals. Because of his biblical expertise, *Oxford University Press* commissioned Dr. Stauffer to work as one of two contributing editors for the notes on the *New Pilgrim* King James study Bible.

Immediately, following high school, Doug served a four year tour of duty in the USAF. Upon discharge, he returned to Pennsylvania to attend *The Pennsylvania State University,* graduating with a BS degree in accounting. A few months later he began attending Bible college.

While attending Bible college, Dr. Stauffer passed the CPA exam. He then worked as controller of several organizations. In 1994, he gave up his work as CFO of a multimillion dollar company along with managing his own firm when God began dealing with him about dedicating his time more fully to the ministry. Since that time, he has earned his ThM and PhD in Religion from *International Baptist Seminary.*

Along with being a frequent guest speaker on radio and television, he has served ten years in pastoral ministries and logged thousands of hours teaching in churches and at the college level. Dr. Stauffer currently serves as an evangelist and president of *Partners for Truth Ministries.*

Doug and his wife Judy are blessed with two children, Justin and Heather.

Dr. Andrew B. Ray is the pastor of Antioch Baptist Church in Knoxville, Tennessee. He has a heart for the Lord, His word, the church, the family, as well as the next generation. He spends countless hours counseling and obediently declaring "all the counsel of God." As a diligent student of the scriptures, he earned his Doctor of Theology degree and faithfully preaches and teaches at the church, as well as the Bible institute.

Before becoming pastor in May 2007, Dr. Ray served as assistant pastor for four years at Antioch Baptist Church under Dr. David F. Reagan. Upon Dr. Reagan's death, Andrew was unanimously voted as pastor of Antioch Baptist Church.

Bro. Ray is the author of *The Fingerprint of God* along with a four year series of devotional books called *Daily Strength: Devotions for Bible-Believing Study.* He has also written several gospel tracts and is currently serving as an editor for a songbook that incorporates scriptural songs, bringing back original lyrics altered or removed by modern hymnals.

God has blessed Bro. Ray and his wife Lula with five children: Noah, Hannah, Sara, Charity, and Isaac.

How to Use This Book and an Admonition to the Reader

Two vital admonitions for personal use of the scriptures entail reading *(1 Timothy 4:13)* and studying *(2 Timothy 2:15)* the Bible. Yet, far too many Christians allow books and other materials to supersede their personal interactions with God's word. This devotional series should never usurp either of these crucial commands and God-given admonitions. Rather, the role of this volume serves to assist, expand, and help focus personal or group Bible study.

NOTE: The heading at the top of each page has a box to check when you complete any particular study followed by a place for entering the *completion date*. This book is intended to be more like a springboard to launch the student deeper into the most precious book ever written. It is not intended to be an end-all to Bible study. Each devotion consists of five component parts.

I. Scripture Passage

The first section before the *Introductory Thoughts* presents the relevant scripture. Be sure never to skip over the reading in its entirety of each *Scripture Passage*. If you are using the book to lead others in Bible study, make sure to read and meditate on the passage and its context ahead of time though you may want to break the passage into shorter segments while teaching. The devotion will be completely ineffective when the *Scripture Passage* has been overlooked or discounted in any way.

II. Introductory Thoughts

The *Introductory Thoughts* immediately follow the *Scripture Passage*. Apart from the scripture, this section communicates the heart of the devotion. Read it carefully and completely, taking time to examine each referenced scripture. If you are leading a study for others, it is not necessary to read this section verbatim to them. Instead, study the contents ahead of time and use it as a guide for your words and thoughts. Doing so will increase the study's effectiveness and add a personal element to the study.

III. Devotional Thoughts

The *Devotional Thoughts* section serves to make the study more personal by offering some questions to stimulate self-examination. The first section in the series of questions or thoughts is geared toward younger children.

However, older children, teens, and adults may also find these thoughts helpful. Feel free to skip this first portion if there are no young children in the study group. If you are studying alone, be sure to take the time to consider each thought or question to see how it might improve your walk with the Lord. If you are leading or studying with a group, this section should help provoke discussion and prayerful consideration.

IV. PRAYER THOUGHTS

Prayer Thoughts serve to guide the reader to thoughtfully going to the Lord with specific prayer requests. Be sure to pray as God leads. Prayer should always be a matter of the heart so you should never merely repeat the written words. If you are studying as a group or as a family, you could take time for prayer requests followed by one person leading the group in prayer. You could also dedicate some time for each member to pray. Remember that this prayer time can offer a great opportunity for teaching children the importance of prayer.

V. SONG

The final section, *Song*, is self-explanatory. Some of the songs will be unfamiliar but each has been prayerfully chosen. Each of these songs will eventually be included in a single songbook. Though some individuals and families might shy away from the thought of singing out loud in a group or alone, it was historically common for people to sing together during times of study. Follow the "song" link at *www.DailyStrengthDevotions.com* for many of the lyrics and tunes of the recommended songs.

Table of Contents

Week 1	Church Attendance	1
Week 2	Backbiting	9
Week 3	Benevolence	17
Week 4	Bitterness	25
Week 5	Carnality	33
Week 6	Communication	41
Week 7	Confession	49
Week 8	Conversation	57
Week 9	Counsel	65
Week 10	Contending	73
Week 11	Edification	81
Week 12	Fasting	89
Week 13	Fear	97
Week 14	Fellowship	105
Week 15	Flattery	113
Week 16	Flattery (con't)	121
Week 17	Forgiveness	129
Week 18	Frugal	137
Week 19	Giving	145
Week 20	Giving (con't)	155
Week 21	Hate	163
Week 22	Hospitality	171
Week 23	Laughter	179
Week 24	Judging	187
Week 25	Leading	195
Week 26	Love	203
Week 27	Love (con't)	211
Week 28	Meditation	219
Week 29	Ministry	227
Week 30	Modesty	235
Week 31	Murmuring	243
Week 32	Praise	251
Week 33	Prayer	259
Week 34	Prayer (con't)	267
Week 35	Teaching	275
Week 36	Reading and Studying	283
Week 37	Reading and Studying (con't)	291

Week 38   Rebuking 299
Week 39   Rebuking (con't) 307
Week 40   Self-Examination 315
Week 41   Separation 323
Week 42   Singing 331
Week 43   Thoughts 339
Week 44   Trusting 347
Week 45   Trusting (con't) 355
Week 46   Unity. 363
Week 47   Vanity. 371
Week 48   Vengeance 379
Week 49   Warfare. 387
Week 50   Watching 395
Week 51   Witnessing. 403
Week 52   Witnessing (con't). 411
Scripture Index 419

1

Church Attendance

Church Attendance—found 117 times in 114 verses; Note: This study is geared more to the attendance of church services, but the information given here will assist in a study of the word *church*.

Variations: church, churches

First usage: *Matthew 16:18* (church)

Last usage: *Revelation 22:16* (churches)

Defined: The word *church* designates not a meeting place, but the people who meet in that place.

Interesting fact: Though it was certainly not the same as the New Testament church, the assembled Jews who marched through the wilderness are called *"the church in the wilderness" (Acts 7:38).*

Bible study tip: Some Bible studies are more complex because no single word or phrase offers a well-rounded study. In such cases, the student must broaden the scope of study. It is important to note that Bible study takes time and dedication. Those unwilling to invest the hours in studying the scripture should not expect to glean the benefits associated to dedicated study.

Sunday, Day 1—Church Day (no devotional)
Monday, Day 2—*Christ's Custom*
Tuesday, Day 3—*Forsaking Assembly*
Wednesday, Day 4—Church Night (no devotional)
Thursday, Day 5—*Missed Blessings*
Friday, Day 6—*Behaviour in the House of God*
Saturday, Day 7—*The Joy of Attendance*

Day 1: Church Day

Acts 2:46 *And they,* **continuing daily with one accord** *in the temple, and breaking bread from house to house, did eat their meat with gladness and singleness of heart,*

47 Praising God, and having favour with all the people. **And the Lord added to the church daily such as should be saved.**

Day 2: (Monday)
Christ's Custom

Luke 4:16 *And he came to Nazareth, where he had been brought up: and,* **as his custom was,** *he went into the synagogue on the sabbath day, and stood up for to read.*

INTRODUCTORY THOUGHTS

In His earthly ministry, the Lord Jesus Christ perfectly fulfilled the will of His Father. Today's passage calls attention to one of the areas in which He accomplished that will. It was the Saviour's custom (or habitual habit) to locate and attend the local synagogue on the Sabbath day. What purpose did this custom serve? The incarnate Son of God had no need of the fellowship and spiritual blessings derived from attending places of worship, yet His faithfulness to do so clearly testifies to the importance of faithful church attendance for those who know the Lord. For the nation of Israel, the Sabbath or seventh day of the week served as the most important day. Christians in the New Testament meet weekly on the Lord's Day or the first day of the week *(Acts 20:7)*, yet the application of assembling together remains constant. Unless providentially hindered or physically confined, there should never be any question where the Christian will be at church time. Unlike the Saviour, we need the fellowship of God's people along with the spiritual admonitions received from faithful church attendance.

DEVOTIONAL THOUGHTS

- **(For children):** Christ set the example for us to be in God's house at the appropriate times. After Christ returned to heaven, His followers continued this practice *(Luke 24:52-53)*. God also wants us to follow the examples set before us and be faithful to His house.
- **(For everyone):** Is it your custom to be at church at the appointed times? Are people surprised if you are missing, or have they become accustomed to your inconsistency and instability?
- How many services a week does your church have? How many of those services do you normally attend? Are you providentially hindered from attending some services? If so, do you attend as many as the Lord allows?

PRAYER THOUGHTS

- Ask the Lord to help you develop a custom of faithful church attendance.
- Ask God to show you the importance of attending services.

SONG: *FOOTPRINTS OF JESUS*

Day 3: (Tuesday)
Forsaking Assembly

Hebrews 10:25 Not forsaking the assembling of ourselves together, as the manner of some is; but exhorting one another: and so much the more, as ye see the day approaching.

INTRODUCTORY THOUGHTS

Each week, hopefully several times a week, a body of like-minded believers to which you belong assembles for the purpose of worshipping and glorifying God. According to scripture, we are not to forsake this assembling of believers. In fact, we are to gather more frequently as we see the coming of the Lord drawing nigh. In a day when more churches are cancelling Sunday evening and midweek services, Bible-believing Christians ought to counteract the trend by finding ways to assemble with other believers more frequently. Early believers assembled on a daily basis *(Acts 2:46)*. Maybe this is less convenient during our day and time; but nonetheless, we certainly should be careful not to forsake the times already appointed for assembling together. Determine to be in your place the next time the saints assemble.

DEVOTIONAL THOUGHTS

- **(For children):** God's people repeatedly disobeyed God's word. He allowed them to be taken out of their land. They missed the house of God and when allowed to return, promised God they would not forsake His house *(Nehemiah 10:39)*. Are you taking the command to go to God's house for granted?
- **(For everyone):** Would you attend if your church added additional services? If not, why? What does this say about the condition of your heart and the priorities in your life?
- Do you faithfully attend revival meetings at your church? Do you go for prayer meetings or Bible studies? Are there times when you should be there, but you forsake the assembly?

PRAYER THOUGHTS

- Ask the Lord to help you see that He is soon coming.
- Ask God to give you the desire to assemble with other believers.

SONG: *SWEET HOUR OF PRAYER!*

Day 4: Church Night

*Acts 11:26 And when he had found him, he brought him unto Antioch. And it came to pass, that **a whole year they assembled themselves with the church**, and taught much people. And the disciples were called Christians first in Antioch.*

Day 5: (Thursday)
Missed Blessings

*John 20:24 But **Thomas**, one of the twelve, called Didymus, **was not with them when Jesus came.***

INTRODUCTORY THOUGHTS

Nothing testifies more to the regrets of missed blessings than Thomas' absence when the risen Saviour met with the disciples. Of all the times to forsake a meeting of believers, Thomas will be known for missing this meeting until the Lord comes. The Bible does not disclose why he was not with the other believers, but we do know what special event he missed – the presence of the risen Lord. Although the Lord Jesus will not visibly or physically show up in our church services, missing a service could cause us to miss His presence in a very special way. For instance, a lost sinner could get saved, or a brother or sister who had wandered from the Lord could find repentance. Maybe something for which you have faithfully prayed was to be answered during the service. Regardless of what might take place, missing the service will mean missing wonderful blessings, some of which can never be recovered. The one service you take for granted could be the very one that God meant to be most special for you.

DEVOTIONAL THOUGHTS

- **(For children):** David greatly desired to be in God's house *(Psalm 27:4)*. He loved to think about God and get his questions answered. He longed to learn God's word *(Psalm 27:11a)*. When God gives the pastor a special message for us, we need to be present to hear it.
- **(For everyone):** What could happen if you invited someone to visit church and then did not show up on the day that he or she visited? How would you feel if a friend got saved and you were not there to encourage him or her?
- Some things in life cannot be undone. Thomas could not go back and change the fact that he was missing when the Lord showed up. What blessings are you willing to miss simply because of a lack of faithful church attendance?

PRAYER THOUGHTS

- Ask God to show you the importance of attending each service.
- Ask the Lord to remind you of blessings you would have missed.

SONG: *A DAY IN THY COURTS*

Day 6: (Friday)
Behaviour in the House of God

1 Timothy 3:15 But if I tarry long, that thou mayest know how thou oughtest to **behave thyself in the house of God**, *which is the church of the living God, the pillar and ground of the truth.*

INTRODUCTORY THOUGHTS

The word *church* is frequently and almost exclusively used to refer to the building where the saints meet. A careful study of the scripture reveals that the church actually consists of the people. However, this passage also teaches that there is a proper behaviour when and where the saints assemble. It is a holy time meant to be accompanied by sobriety. In fact, believers are instructed that everything is to be done *"decently and in order" (1 Corinthians 14:40)*. As we approach the time of preaching or instruction, we should be ready to hear and slow to speak *(Ecclesiastes 5:1-3)*. During the invitation, as the Lord moves in our hearts to repent and do right, we should pay [keep] what we vow [promise] *(Ecclesiastes 5:4-7)*. Always keep in mind that the house of God is the pillar and ground of the truth and we should treat it as such.

DEVOTIONAL THOUGHTS

- **(For children):** Samuel was not in a church service when he said, *"Speak; for thy servant heareth"*; yet it would be good for us to respond to God in that fashion when we meet with God's people. Samuel listened to God and was able to tell Eli what God said. Can you tell dad or mom something that you remember about the pastor's message?
- **(For everyone):** How do you behave when you go to the house of God? Do you take the gathering of saints as a holy time or as a time to see what people are wearing or as a time to laugh and only have fun?
- What are some ways we can show respect when we gather together with other believers at the place of worship? How can our behaviour affect the world's opinion of the house of God?

PRAYER THOUGHTS

- Ask the Lord to teach you how to behave around other believers.
- Ask God to give you a sobriety concerning His work and worship.

SONG: *O LORD, 'TIS MATTER OF HIGH PRAISE*

Day 7: (Saturday)
The Joy of Attendance

Psalm 122:1 I was glad when they said unto me, Let us go into the house of the LORD.

INTRODUCTORY THOUGHTS

David was a man after the heart of God *(1 Samuel 13:14; Acts 13:22)*. He loved the Lord and it repeatedly showed in his life. Even on the occasions when he failed the Lord, he repentantly sought the Lord. In fact, one of the greatest manifestations of David's love for the Lord manifested itself in his love for the house of God. In our passage, David spoke of the overwhelming gladness he had when contemplating a trip to God's house. He received great joy in knowing that it was there that he could meet and fellowship with God whom he so deeply loved. As born-again believers, we have many reasons why we should long to meet with the saints of God in worship. We too should rejoice when others say, *"Let us go unto the house of the LORD."*

DEVOTIONAL THOUGHTS

- **(For children)**: Read *Psalm 84:2, 4*. David loved to go to God's house. The things he learned there helped him to have joy in his life every day. Are you regularly happy about going to church?
- **(For everyone)**: Do you feel as though you *"have to go"* to church or that you *"get to go"* to church? Is church attendance a burden or a joy? Do you find gladness in knowing you get to meet with the Lord?
- What are some reasons David could find joy in going to the house of the Lord? What are some reasons we should find joy and gladness in attending church?

PRAYER THOUGHTS

- Ask God to give you a longing for His house.
- Ask the Lord to help you have the right spirit when attending the place of worship.

SONG: *TAKE THE WORLD, BUT GIVE ME JESUS*

Notes: _____

_____

_____

_____

_____

_____

_____

_____

_____

_____

_____

_____

_____

Quotes from the next volume

(VOLUME 3, WEEK 1)

Subject: Aging

The strength of any people will be determined by how they deal with two people groups: their young and their old.

From youth, man is bent toward sin. As he ages, the source of temptation may change, but the fact that he is tempted remains constant.

Many believers have wasted precious years of youth succumbing to the youthful lusts of which Paul warned Timothy, while others have fought the good fight in their youth, only to regretfully compromise in their waning years.

2
Backbiting

Backbiting—found four times in four verses

Variations: backbiteth, backbiting, backbitings, backbiters

First usage: *Psalm 15:3* (backbiteth)

Last usage: *2 Corinthians 12:20* (backbitings)

Defined: to speak evil of another in his or her absence

Interesting fact: Backbiting and talebearing have many similar attributes. The Lord finds this sin so reprehensible that He emphasized this truth by using two identical verses in Proverbs. *"The words of a talebearer are as wounds, and they go down into the innermost parts of the belly"* **(Proverbs 18:8; Proverbs 26:22).**

Bible study tip: It is a good practice when studying a compound word to consider all the parts that make up the word. However, this does present its own set of difficulties. Be careful not to allow this practice to sidetrack your present study. If you see something of interest in the study concerning the component parts, make a note to return and study those things at a later date. This will enable you to complete your present study without being sidetracked with additional material.

Sunday, Day 8—Church Day (no devotional)
Monday, Day 9—*The Backbiting Tongue*
Tuesday, Day 10—*How Will We Be Found?*
Wednesday, Day 11—Church Night (no devotional)
Thursday, Day 12—*Biting and Devouring Until Consumed*
Friday, Day 13—*An Angry Countenance Drives Away Backbiters*
Saturday, Day 14—*The Sins of a Reprobate Mind*

Day 8: Church Day

James 4:11 Speak not evil one of another, brethren. He that speaketh evil of his brother, and judgeth his brother, speaketh evil of the law, and judgeth the law: but if thou judge the law, thou art not a doer of the law, but a judge.

Day 9: (Monday)
The Backbiting Tongue

Psalm 15:1 LORD, who shall abide in thy tabernacle? who shall dwell in thy holy hill?

2 He that walketh uprightly, and worketh righteousness, and speaketh the truth in his heart.

3 He that backbiteth not with his tongue, nor doeth evil to his neighbour, nor taketh up a reproach against his neighbour.

INTRODUCTORY THOUGHTS

The words that so flippantly slip from our tongues are often used by the Devil as weapons to wound others. When we think of biting something, we think of using our teeth; yet *backbiting* employs the tongue. *Backbiting* is the act of saying something disparaging about someone without regard to the harm caused to that person. Today's passage demonstrates that the Lord considers backbiting a detestable act; so much so, that David said the backbiter would not abide in the Lord's tabernacle. According to James chapter 3, the tongue kindles a great fire *(James 3:5)* and is a world of iniquity *(James 3:6)*. The Bible proves that the quaint phrase used as a child, *"sticks and stones may break my bones, but words will never hurt me"* is both untrue and unscriptural. Instead, the tongue is *"full of deadly poison" (James 3:8)*. Backbiting wounds its victims – wounds which sometimes fester for years under the surface!

DEVOTIONAL THOUGHTS

- **(For children):** Backbiting is saying mean things about a person while the person is not present. In doing so, we tend to make ourselves look good by making others feel unhappy with the person about whom we are talking.
- **(For everyone):** When speaking to others, do you find yourself speaking ill of others? Do you say things that could personally harm others or hurt their testimony? Are the things that you say about others generally uplifting or destructive?
- Have you ever had anybody say true things about you but unnecessary and brought about harm to you? How did you feel when they said those things? Should this cause you to think before doing the same to others?

PRAYER THOUGHTS

- Ask the Lord to help you to use wisdom when speaking of others.
- Ask God to help you avoid being a part of the destructive sin of backbiting.

SONG: *YIELD NOT TO TEMPTATION*

Day 10: (Tuesday)
How Will We Be Found?

*2 Corinthians 12:20 For I fear, lest, **when I come, I shall not find you such as I would**, and that I shall be found unto you such as ye would not: **lest there be** debates, envyings, wraths, strifes, **backbitings**, whisperings, swellings, tumults:*

21 And lest, when I come again, my God will humble me among you, and that I shall bewail many which have sinned already, and have not repented of the uncleanness and fornication and lasciviousness which they have committed.

INTRODUCTORY THOUGHTS

The apostle Paul was troubled greatly by the behaviour of the Corinthian believers. Due to their carnality, he could not speak to them as he would mature believers *(1 Corinthians 3:1)*. Not only was Paul troubled by their actions during his absence, but also feared their condition when they would again meet face-to-face. He warned the believers that he would not be pleased if he found them guilty of such sins. Among the other shortcomings, Paul expressly mentioned their backbiting ways. The hope was that the Corinthian believers would repent of these grievous sins and simply do right. These admonitions should make believers reflect on the fact that the Lord Jesus could also come at any moment. How would He find us? Would we too be guilty of *"debates, envyings, wraths, strifes, backbitings, whisperings, swellings,"* and *"tumults"*?

DEVOTIONAL THOUGHTS

- **(For children):** *Romans 14:12* says we will one day explain our actions to God. This includes our speech. He knows everything we have ever said *(Psalm 139:4)*. Our words should be said in the name of the Lord *(Colossians 3:17)* and to His glory *(1 Corinthians 10:31)*.
- **(For everyone):** How pleased do you think the Lord is when we allow our words to devour other brothers and sisters in Christ? Do you believe the Bible when it says that you will answer for these things at the coming judgment?
- Have you said things about someone that you should not have said? Have you brought harm to another person with your words? What have you done to make this right?

PRAYER THOUGHTS

- Ask God to remind you of people you have hurt with your words.
- Ask God to help you say only those things He wants you to say.

SONG: *DRAW ME NEARER*

Day 11: Church Night

1 Peter 2:1 Wherefore laying aside all malice, and all guile, and hypocrisies, and envies, and all evil speakings,

2 As newborn babes, desire the sincere milk of the word, that ye may grow thereby:

3 If so be ye have tasted that the Lord is gracious.

Day 12: (Thursday)
Biting and Devouring Until Consumed

Galatians 5:15 But if ye bite and devour one another, take heed that ye be not consumed one of another.

INTRODUCTORY THOUGHTS

If you bite and chew your food enough times it will break down into small pieces and disappear into your stomach. In our passage, the apostle Paul informs us that our relationships with others bear the same truth. If we bite and devour one another, we will eventually consume each other. Many believers have quit attending the house of God and given up on serving the Lord because Christians have allowed their words to devour and consume. Just as food can only withstand so many bites before it is fully consumed, other believers can only take so much backbiting before weakened beyond their willingness to withstand. As the people of God, we are responsible for strengthening each other and surely will answer to God for any backbiting.

DEVOTIONAL THOUGHTS

- **(For children):** God tells us to speak evil of no man *(Titus 3:2a)*, especially not those of our church family *(James 4:11a)*. God wants our speech to instruct and to help improve others in their service toward the Lord *(Ephesians 4:29)*.
- **(For everyone):** Have you ever known someone who quit serving the Lord because of harm caused through backbiting? Did they seem strong in the beginning and able to withstand the criticisms?
- Ultimately, every individual will stand responsible for his or her walk before God. Yet is it possible that backbiters will also hold some responsibility for causing others to be consumed?

PRAYER THOUGHTS

- Ask the Lord to strengthen you when others seek to do you harm.
- Ask God to help you strengthen and encourage those who have been slandered.

SONG: *MAKE US KIND AND TENDER-HEARTED*

Day 13: (Friday)
An Angry Countenance Drives Away Backbiters

*Proverbs 25:23 The north wind driveth away rain: so doth **an angry countenance** a backbiting tongue.*

INTRODUCTORY THOUGHTS

Some Bible teachers have erroneously suggested that anger is a sin. But God actually commands His people to be angry, yet further instructs them not to allow that anger to push them to respond sinfully *(Ephesians 4:26)*. If a man can be angry without sinning, then anger is not a sin. In fact, anger used in a righteous manner can accomplish many things for the Lord. One of the benefits of anger is found in today's passage. A good, healthy, angry countenance can serve as the best remedy to keep people from backbiting others while in your presence. The reason people backbite others is because they have an audience for their vitriol. If we would express our displeasure, the backbiting would cease. Try it out! The backbiting tongue will cease the moment you respond with an angry countenance.

DEVOTIONAL THOUGHTS

- **(For children):** If one of your friends speaks against another person, you can tell him that you don't want to hear it and that he should go talk directly to that person. Try to find something kind and nice to say about the person being discussed.
- **(For everyone):** Do you find that your ear is often the recipient of a backbiting tongue? Do others find comfort in telling you the bad news about others? How do you react when people backbite others while in your presence?
- What could you say to someone in order to let him know that backbiting others is not at all acceptable to you? How could you let that individual know that God is not pleased with his words?

PRAYER THOUGHTS

- Ask the Lord to give you wisdom when dealing with backbiters.
- Ask God to help you prevent the backbiting that happens in your presence.

SONG: *BLEST BE THE TIE THAT BINDS*

Day 14: (Saturday)
The Sins of a Reprobate Mind

Romans 1:28 *And even as they did not like to retain God in their knowledge,* **God gave them over to a reprobate mind,** *to do those things which are not convenient;*

29 Being filled with all unrighteousness, fornication, wickedness, covetousness, maliciousness; full of envy, murder, debate, deceit, malignity; whisperers,

*30 **Backbiters**, haters of God, despiteful, proud, boasters, inventors of evil things, disobedient to parents,*

31 Without understanding, covenantbreakers, without natural affection, implacable, unmerciful:

*32 Who knowing the judgment of God, that they which commit such things are worthy of death, not only do the same, but **have pleasure in them that do them.***

INTRODUCTORY THOUGHTS

Men often separate sins into categories of what they consider big and little sins. Murder and adultery are often classified as big sins, while little sins might include things like pride, "white" lies, or backbiting. Yet a closer look at Romans chapter 1 suggests that God's viewpoint of sin varies greatly from ours. According to the scripture, a person given over to a reprobate mind is capable of all of these sins. Furthermore, the passage tells us that those *"which commit such things are worthy of death"* **(Romans 1:32)**. Imagine that! The Lord views backbiting as a sin just as wicked and vile as murder. Not only does the Lord find the backbiter guilty, but also judges those who *"have pleasure in them"* that do the backbiting and other such sins.

DEVOTIONAL THOUGHTS

- **(For children):** David wanted his words to be acceptable in God's sight *(Psalm 19:14)*. However, harming an individual with our words is not acceptable to God. Backbiting is as serious to the Lord as physically harming someone or disobeying our parents.
- **(For everyone):** How much do you think God hates backbiting? Do you think He is just as angry with us when we listen to backbiting as He is when we are guilty of doing the actual backbiting?

- Would you have thought that God would list backbiting with murder, fornication, and hating Him? Does this reflect the importance of avoiding this wicked sin?

PRAYER THOUGHTS

- Ask the Lord to give you the same hatred for backbiting that He has.
- Ask God to help you find no pleasure in saying or listening to harmful words.

SONG: *WHAT THEN, SHALL CHRISTIANS SIN*

Notes: _____

_____

_____

_____

_____

_____

_____

_____

Quotes from the next volume

(VOLUME 3, WEEK 2)

Subject: Aging (con't)

Respect is not inherited, but must be earned.

Wisdom comes from the Lord, and He distributes wisdom irrespective of one's age.

In many ways, though not entirely, youth should be spent in learning, middle age in doing, and old age in teaching.

Why would you be robbed of today's joys by worry concerning troubles and sorrows that may never come to pass?

3

Benevolence

Benevolence—found one time in the Bible. Note: This study focuses on the need for assisting others during times of need.

Variations: benevolence

Only usage: *1 Corinthians 7:3*

Defined: a disposition to do good unto others

Interesting fact: Men may focus their accolades upon those who are rich, but the Lord pays special attention to the poor *(Psalm 10:14; Psalm 12:5; Psalm 14:6; Psalm 68:10; Psalm 69:33; Psalm 140:12).*

Bible study tip: Bible students should take care in approaching Bible study with preconceived notions. Do not assume to understand a passage in light of its common or historical interpretation because many times man's traditions have overly influenced these positions. Do not take as fact a philosophy based upon the modern thoughts of men. Remember that the Lord says, *"For my thoughts are not your thoughts, neither are your ways my ways, . . . For as the heavens are higher than the earth, so are my ways higher than* *your ways, and my thoughts than your thoughts"* **(Isaiah 55:8-9).**

Sunday, Day 15—Church Day (no devotional)
Monday, Day 16—*Take Advantage of Every Opportunity*
Tuesday, Day 17—*Distributing to One's Necessities*
Wednesday, Day 18—Church Night (no devotional)
Thursday, Day 19—*Caring for the Poor Saints*
Friday, Day 20—*A Man Unwilling to Work*
Saturday, Day 21—*Good to Be Liberal*

Day 15: Church Day

Acts 20:35 I have shewed you all things, how that so labouring ye ought to support the weak, and to remember the words of the Lord Jesus, how he said, **It is more blessed to give than to receive.**

Day 16: (Monday)
Take Advantage of Every Opportunity

Galatians 6:10 As we have therefore opportunity, let us **do good unto all men, especially unto them who are of the household of faith.**

INTRODUCTORY THOUGHTS

As opportunities present themselves, we ought to *"do good"* unto others. Scripturally speaking, we have a basic duty to help *"all men,"* but our foremost responsibility should be directed toward those *"who are of the household of faith."* Regardless of our heart's desire, the Lord knows there are times when we cannot help those in need. This fact should never be used as an excuse when we have a genuine opportunity, as the good that we might do to others does not always merely involve financial help. Acts chapter 3 offers an example of Peter and John who were faced with such a situation. Peter responded, *"Silver and gold have I none; but such as I have give I thee"* **(Acts 3:6).** Where these men lacked any monetary opportunity to help the lame man, they fulfilled their responsibility by imparting help in the way that God had especially enabled them.

DEVOTIONAL THOUGHTS

- **(For children):** As children, we don't have much money to help others; but there are things we can do to make someone's day better: make a homemade card, say a kind word, tell him you will pray for him, quote a Bible verse, draw him a picture, etc.
- **(For everyone):** Do you know anyone with a need that you could help meet? What efforts have you taken to be a blessing to that person or family during their time of need?
- We cannot help everyone, yet we can help some of those with particular needs. Why would the Lord put the emphasis on helping others who are saved? What are some ways in which you can help your brothers and sisters in Christ?

PRAYER THOUGHTS

- Ask the Lord to show you ways to help others.
- Ask God for opportunities to help others.

SONG: HE WAS NOT WILLING

Day 17: (Tuesday)
Distributing to One's Necessities

Romans 12:13 Distributing to the necessity of saints; given to hospitality.

INTRODUCTORY THOUGHTS

James encouraged believers to provide *"those things which are needful to the body,"* specifically mentioning food and clothing *(James 2:15-16)*. Paul's epistles also repeatedly mention that we ought to help our brothers and sisters in Christ. Yet, this does not make believers responsible for every want or desire that another believer may have. Rather, we are supposed to distribute *"to the necessity of saints."* In order to be obedient, it is important to identify what the Bible considers as a necessity. According to *1 Timothy 6:8*, men ought to be content with *"food and raiment."* It makes sense that these two things are man's only true necessities. Therefore, as brothers and sisters in Christ, we should assist others in these areas as the need arises.

DEVOTIONAL THOUGHTS

- **(For children):** How could you as a child help other children who need clothing and shoes? Try taking care of your clothes and shoes like your mom tells you. When you outgrow this clothing, it will still be good enough to give to another child who may have need of them.
- **(For everyone):** Why is it important that we are only responsible to help others with their necessities? What items do people often consider to be necessities that the Bible excludes from this list?
- When was the last time you helped a brother or sister in Christ who needed food or clothing? How did you feel knowing that you were able to help? Could the Lord trust you to help again?

PRAYER THOUGHTS

- Ask the Lord to give you a willing heart to help others.
- Ask God to meet the needs of His people and to do so through you.

SONG: *IS THY CRUSE OF COMFORT WASTING?*

Day 18: Church Night

Proverbs 19:17 He that hath pity upon the poor lendeth unto the LORD; and that which he hath given will he pay him again.

Day 19: (Thursday)
Caring for the Poor Saints

Romans 15:25 But now I go unto Jerusalem to minister unto the saints.

*26 For it hath pleased them of Macedonia and Achaia **to make a certain contribution for the poor saints** which are at Jerusalem.*

27 It hath pleased them verily; and their debtors they are. For if the Gentiles have been made partakers of their spiritual things, their duty is also to minister unto them in carnal things.

INTRODUCTORY THOUGHTS

During the first century, hard times had come upon the believers in Jerusalem. Some specific time of trial, persecution, or tribulation had put them in a difficult situation. The Bible offers specific guidance as to when to assist others who have fallen on hard times. Believers in other cities saw the need and determined to make "*a certain contribution for the poor saints*" at Jerusalem *(Romans 15:26)*. This contribution was either a monetary donation or a material contribution as the Bible says the assistance was "*in carnal things*" *(Romans 15:27)*. Today, this would be akin to one body of believers assisting another body of believers, or one individual assisting another individual. Whatever the case, we ought to help others when a real need arises and it is in our power to assist them.

DEVOTIONAL THOUGHTS

- **(For children)**: Tabitha was a woman full of good works and almsdeeds. She made coats and garments for the poor widow women and the saints of God. God wants us to do for others when they need our help. What can you do to help others?
- **(For everyone)**: Do you know of someone who has fallen on hard times? What have you personally done to help? Would the Lord have you to do more?
- Why is it important for believers to help other believers? What does this demonstrate to the world about those who are saved? How can this help the world learn what it means to be a Christian?

PRAYER THOUGHTS

- Ask the Lord to show you when others are in need.
- Ask the Lord to teach you to love helping others.

SONG: *LORD, THOU LOVEST THE CHEERFUL GIVER*

Day 20: (Friday)
A Man Unwilling to Work

*2 Thessalonians 3:10 For even when we were with you, this we commanded you, that **if any would not work, neither should he eat.***

11 For we hear that there are some which walk among you disorderly, working not at all, but are busybodies.

12 Now them that are such we command and exhort by our Lord Jesus Christ, that with quietness they work, and eat their own bread.

INTRODUCTORY THOUGHTS

It has always been the will of God for a man to work in order to support his family. God adamantly and emphatically says, "*if any provide* *not for his own, and specially for those of his own house, he hath denied the faith, and is **worse than an infidel" (1 Timothy 5:8).*** Though this truth may seem harsh to some people, God's expectations and guidelines always serve a greater purpose. Therefore, it is never God's will to financially assist someone who **will not** work though completely capable and available. There may be times when people cannot legitimately work and have a need for help; but we disobey the Lord when we help those who have needs resulting from laziness. Our last lesson showed that the Bible defines food as a necessity; but if a man will not work, he does not even deserve the necessities of life provided to him through the generosity of others.

DEVOTIONAL THOUGHTS

- **(For children):** Learn to be a good worker like the ant *(Proverbs 6:6-8)*. A good worker will have plenty to eat *(Proverbs 28:19a)*.
- **(For everyone):** Laziness results from rebellion towards God and His word. Even prior to man's fall in the garden in Eden, God gave the first man a job to do. Why should we refuse to help those who will not help themselves by working?
- Are you currently helping someone who refuses to work? Do you realize that both he and you are in direct rebellion against God's specific commands? Will you repent and do right? In doing so, you may take away this man's crutch and force him to admit that his lack of the necessities of life have resulted from sin.

PRAYER THOUGHTS

- Ask the Lord for wisdom as to when to refuse helping others.
- Ask the Lord to help you obey His word.

SONG: *DO THE NEXT THING*

Day 21: (Saturday)
Good to Be Liberal

*Proverbs 11:25 **The liberal soul shall be made fat**: and he that watereth shall be watered also himself.*

INTRODUCTORY THOUGHTS

The word *liberal* is one of the most overused and misused words in modern language. We often use the word to refer to those who have weaker morals or those who may have a particular "left-leaning" political agenda. Most often the word is used as a negative connotation by those who are traditional or more conservative. The Bible paints a much different picture of the word's usage and application. Someone who is *liberal* willingly and graciously helps others. When others are in need, he gives above and beyond to meet that need. According to our passage, "*The liberal soul shall be made fat.*" This means that the person who helps others will often receive blessings in return. This truth is confirmed in *2 Corinthians 9:6* where the Bible says, "*He which soweth sparingly shall reap also sparingly; and he which soweth bountifully shall reap also bountifully.*"

DEVOTIONAL THOUGHTS

- **(For children):** The Lord will not allow our willingness to help others go unrecognized. Read *Proverbs 19:17*; *Proverbs 22:9*; *Proverbs 28:27* and *Psalm 41:1*.
- **(For everyone):** Are you liberal in your giving toward the needs of others? Has the Lord richly blessed you because of your willing heart to help others?
- Do you find joy in helping those in need? Do you help others merely to receive a reward or because you love the Lord and want to obey His word?

PRAYER THOUGHTS

- Ask the Lord to give you a liberality in your giving.
- Ask God to give you a heart of concern for those in need.

SONG: *GIVE OF YOUR BEST TO THE MASTER*

Notes: _____

_____

_____

_____

_____

Notes: _____

_____

_____

_____

_____

_____

_____

_____

_____

_____

_____

_____

_____

_____

_____

Quotes from the next volume

(VOLUME 3, WEEK 3)

Subject: Carefulness

Worry and faith are at opposite ends of the spectrum and cannot coexist within the life of the believer.

Prayer serves as the greatest remedy for a day consumed by worry and fears.

Worry and anxieties offer no solution to the problems faced in life.

4

Bitterness

Bitterness—found in all of its forms a total of sixty-nine times in sixty-five verses

Variations: bitter, bitterly, bitterness

First usage: *Genesis 27:34* (bitter)

Last usage: *Revelation 10:10* (bitter)

Defined: As it pertains to feelings ingrained in man, it is a deep-rooted and sharp affliction.

Interesting fact: Naomi suggested that she be called *Mara (Ruth 1:20)*, a name meaning *bitter (Exodus 15:23)*, after feeling as though the Lord had dealt with her *"very bitterly."*

Bible study tip: One does not need to know the original languages of Greek and Hebrew to understand the Bible. When God desires for man to know the definition of a less familiar word, He includes the definition in the context of that word's usage. For example, *Exodus 15:23* demonstrates this truth when it says, *"they were bitter: therefore the name of it was called Marah."* Marah means bitter here as further confirmed in the book of Ruth with Naomi.

Sunday, Day 22—Church Day (no devotional)
Monday, Day 23—*What Is Bitterness?*
Tuesday, Day 24—*A Root of Bitterness*
Wednesday, Day 25—Church Night (no devotional)
Thursday, Day 26—*Bitterness of Soul*
Friday, Day 27—*Put Away All Bitterness*
Saturday, Day 28—*A Mouth Speaking Bitterness*

Day 22: Church Day

*James 3:14 But **if ye have bitter envying** and strife **in your hearts, glory not**, and lie not against the truth.*

Day 23: (Monday)
What Is Bitterness?

*Isaiah 38:17 **Behold, for peace I had great bitterness**: but thou hast in love to my soul delivered it from the pit of corruption: for thou hast cast all my sins behind thy back.*

INTRODUCTORY THOUGHTS

A good Bible student often incorporates many of the same tactics as a good detective. Defining Bible words involves such a task. No single verse specifically defines the word *bitterness*. Yet, a careful study of a few verses will help to bring the pieces together and to provide understanding. According to Isaiah, *bitterness* and *peace* are at opposite ends of the emotional spectrum *(Isaiah 38:17)*. Proverbs associates the word *bitter* directly to the word *sharp (Proverbs 5:4)*. And, lastly, the word *bitter* is connected to the word *affliction (2 Kings 14:26, Lamentations 1:4)*. Using these scriptural clues, a good student will understand bitterness to be a *sharp affliction*. Additionally, consider the connection between the words *bitter* and *bite*, making bitterness a sharp affliction with bite. Bitterness always begins on the inside of an individual and, as we will learn, eventually works its way to the outside for others to see.

DEVOTIONAL THOUGHTS

- **(For children):** When others do or say something unkind to us, God wants us to make up with them. When we stay angry day after day, we will end up doing something for which we will be sorry and God calls this bitterness. *Ephesians 4:26-27* is a good rule to follow.

- **(For everyone):** Do you ever notice anger building up on the inside? What is it that makes you so angry? Does it cause you to be rude to those around you? This anger is very likely connected to bitterness.
- Are you bitter? Can you remember a time when that feeling did not exist? What do you think brought this bitterness into your life? Are you willing to turn this over to the Lord and let Him remove the bitterness from your heart and life?

PRAYER THOUGHTS

- Ask the Lord to remove the bitterness in your heart.
- Ask God to help you recognize bitterness when it rears its ugly head.

SONG: *COME, O THOU ALL-VICTORIOUS LORD*

Day 24: (Tuesday)
A Root of Bitterness

*Hebrews 12:15 Looking diligently lest any man fail of the grace of God; lest any **root of bitterness** springing up trouble you, and thereby many be defiled;*

INTRODUCTORY THOUGHTS

Bitterness grows from within man much like the root of a plant. If left alone to fester, bitterness will eventually spring up; and when it does, it will *"trouble you."* Unfortunately, bitterness is not frequently identified during its infancy. It hides inside the individual with little evidence of its existence. As time passes, our enemies (the world, the flesh, and the devil) feed that bitterness and it begins to spring forth. As it does, it may begin to alarm or even shock us. For instance, we may yell at someone for no apparent reason. Something insignificant can even ruin our entire day. If we are not careful, we can grow increasingly comfortable with our newfound trouble and attitude. As alluded to in the scripture, the solution for bitterness can be likened to the removal of a plant by its roots. Bitterness continues to grow unless removed at its source – from the roots.

DEVOTIONAL THOUGHTS

- **(For children):** Joseph's brothers were jealous of him. One day they saw him coming, and just the sight of him made them angry inside. This is bitterness. They planned to kill him but instead sold him into slavery.
- **(For everyone):** Bitterness often finds its root in one or a couple of incidents. What is the root of your bitterness? Do you remember the time when anger began festering in the depths of your heart?
- Have you ever pulled a plant up on the surface only to have it grow back? This is like bitterness. We may fix the current issue, but the problem will not be solved until the root is completely removed.

PRAYER THOUGHTS

- Ask the Lord to keep bitterness from growing inside of you.
- Ask the Lord to help you find the root of any bitterness that continues to trouble you.

SONG: *IF I THY SPIRIT GRIEVE*

Day 25: Church Night

*Jeremiah 4:18 Thy way and thy doings have procured these things unto thee; this is thy wickedness, because **it is bitter**, because **it reacheth unto thine heart**.*

Day 26: (Thursday)
Bitterness of Soul

*Job 10:1 My soul is weary of my life; I will leave my complaint upon myself; **I will speak in the bitterness of my soul**.*

INTRODUCTORY THOUGHTS

The Bible repeatedly mentions the bitterness of soul *(1 Samuel 1:10; Job 3:20; Job 7:11; Job 10:1; Job 21:25; Isaiah 38:15)*. Job testified to speaking in the bitterness of his soul—weary of his life *(Job 10:1)*. Hannah *"was in bitterness of soul"* *(1 Samuel 1:10)* when she spoke to the Lord concerning her desire to birth a son. Interestingly, the Book of Job contains the majority of references to bitterness of soul. It is hard to imagine any mortal man enduring more afflictions of the soul than Job.

He was afflicted so deeply, he cursed the day that he was born *(Job 3:1)*. Eventually, his bitterness of soul won out and caused him to sin against the Lord. Hannah, however, spoke to the Lord in bitterness of soul and God rewarded her for her faithfulness.

Devotional thoughts

- **(For children):** Esau cried bitterly when he learned Jacob had stolen his blessing. He hated Jacob. Instead of going to God with his problem, he comforted himself by planning to kill Jacob. Jacob found out and had to leave home. Our bitterness when left to itself will always turn out bad.
- **(For everyone):** Are you in bitterness of soul? Do you allow that bitterness to drive you to the Lord or draw you away from Him? In the end, Job mishandled his bitterness. What will you do to insure that your bitterness does not blossom into something ugly?
- Bitterness that is given to the Lord can be turned into a blessing (i.e., Hannah). Will you give your bitterness to Him or allow it to grow inside of you causing you to sin against Him?

Prayer Thoughts

- Ask God to identify bitterness in your soul.
- Ask God to give you strength to yield your bitterness to Him.

SONG: *DOES JESUS CARE?*

Day 27: (Friday)
Put Away All Bitterness

*Ephesians 4:31 Let all bitterness, and wrath, and anger, and clamour, and evil speaking, **be put away from you**, with all malice:*

Introductory Thoughts

The believer is to allow no place for bitterness within his life. The book of Ephesians directly associates bitterness with the sins of wrath, anger, clamour, evil speaking, and malice. Each of these sins grieves the Spirit of God and ought to grieve the believer. As such, Christians are admonished to put away all bitterness. As bitterness shows itself in the depths of our hearts, we ought to immediately seek the Lord and plead for His help in removing it by its root. In a similar passage *(Colossians 3:8)*, we are admonished to *"put off"* many of these other sins mentioned. Always keep in mind that bitterness does not edify the believer or those around him, nor does it glorify the Lord. Simply choose to obey God by putting away and putting off bitterness.

DEVOTIONAL THOUGHTS

- **(For children):** Read *Ephesians 4:32* and *Colossians 3:13*. We are to be like our Lord. He is our greatest example. We must put away bitterness. God is never bitter against us. He is always ready to forgive. Even on the cross, He prayed for His enemies rather than allowing bitterness to spring up *(Luke 23:34)*.
- **(For everyone):** When the Bible speaks of putting away bitterness, it does not mean for you to hide it away in your heart. Instead, it means that we are to turn it over to the Lord and allow Him to completely remove it from our lives. Will you put away bitterness?
- How does bitterness affect you? How does it affect those around you? How does it affect your relationship with the Lord? Does bitterness bring about anything good?

PRAYER THOUGHTS

- Ask the Lord to give you strength to put away *"all bitterness."*
- Ask God to show you the effect your bitterness has upon others.

SONG: *WOUNDED SIN, NOW DIE IN ME!*

Day 28: (Saturday)
A Mouth Speaking Bitterness

Romans 3:14 Whose mouth is full of cursing and bitterness:

INTRODUCTORY THOUGHTS

The Bible says that *"out of the abundance of the heart the mouth speaketh"* *(Matthew 12:34)*. This means that the words proceeding out of our mouths originate in our hearts. When we speak bitter words, it is because there is bitterness within our hearts. David likened bitter words to arrows that pierce the flesh *(Psalm 64:3)*. Our words ought to be *"seasoned with salt"* *(Colossians 4:6)*; instead, we often allow our words to pierce through others. We tear people down rather than building them up. Why is this? Because we have a root of bitterness growing inside that finds its way from our hearts into and out of our mouths. Those who demean others generally do so because they are bitter. Attempts to justify this behaviour are fruitless because the Lord knows the root of the problem stems from our heart.

DEVOTIONAL THOUGHTS

- **(For children):** Joseph's brothers hated him so much that they didn't have a kind word for him. The Bible says they *"could not speak peaceably unto him."* Yet, he reacted the way God wanted him to. He forgave his brothers and *"spake kindly unto them."* He promised to take care of them when there was very little food. Joseph is a good example from whom we can learn much.
- **(For everyone):** Do you allow your words to tear others down? Why do you think you do this? Will you admit that you often do so in demonstration of some root of bitterness that exists within your own soul and life?
- Explain how our words are likened to arrows? Can you think of people that you have pierced with your words? Have you apologized to them and sought the Lord's help in removing the bitterness at the heart of the problem?

PRAYER THOUGHTS

- Ask the Lord to show you the bitterness of your heart.
- Ask the Lord to help your words be seasoned with salt.

SONG: *LORD, I'M COMING HOME*

Notes: _____

_____

_____

_____

_____

_____

_____

Notes: _____

_____

_____

_____

_____

_____

_____

_____

_____

_____

_____

_____

_____

_____

_____

_____

_____

Quotes from the next volume

(VOLUME 3, WEEK 4)

Subject: Appetite

Every Christian should bow his head and give God thanks for His provision before partaking of any meal.

Regardless of what the modern doctors, scientists, or latest fad diets prescribe, the Bible clearly states that God does not intend for His people to abstain from eating meat.

Gluttony remains one of the most misunderstood sins in the Bible.

5

Carnality

Carnality—found in all of its forms fifteen times in fourteen verses

Variations: carnal, carnally

First usage: *Leviticus 18:20* (carnally)

Last usage: *Hebrews 9:10* (carnal)

Defined: having to do with something physical, earthly, or pertaining to the flesh

Interesting fact: Five times the Bible makes a specific contrast between that which is carnal and that which is spiritual *(Romans 7:14; Romans 8:6; Romans 15:27; 1 Corinthians 3:1; 1 Corinthians 9:11)*. The Bible frequently associates the number *five* with death. For instance, one of the five contrasts of that which is carnal and that which is spiritual says, *"For to be carnally minded is **death**; but to be spiritually minded is life and peace" (Romans 8:6)*.

Bible study tip: Biblical numerology is an interesting study, but we must be careful not to allow our authority to shift from the plain teachings of scripture to something derived by an obscure connection to numbers or biblical numerology. Do not allow a fascination with the types, pictures, symbols, and numbers in scripture to overtake the literal, historical, and doctrinal truths taught.

Sunday, Day 29—Church Day (no devotional)
Monday, Day 30—*What Is Carnality?*
Tuesday, Day 31—*Carnality Stunts Growth*
Wednesday, Day 32—Church Night (no devotional)
Thursday, Day 33—*The Carnal Mind*
Friday, Day 34—*The Actions of Carnal Men*
Saturday, Day 35—*Our Weapons Are Not Carnal*

Day 29: Church Day

*Romans 8:8 So then **they that are in the flesh cannot please God.***

Day 30: (Monday)
What Is Carnality?

*Romans 7:14 For we know that the law is **spiritual**: but I am **carnal**, sold under sin.*

Introductory Thoughts

The Lord frequently uses comparison and contrast to provide insight for discovering biblical definitions. For instance, our text verse contrasts the *carnal* with the *spiritual*. This truth is not limited to our text as *1 Corinthians 3:1* also sets forth this teaching and contrast. In a related study, the Bible repeatedly contrasts the *spirit* and *flesh (Isaiah 31:3; Matthew 26:41; John 3:6; John 6:63; Galatians 5:17)*. By considering these truths together, we find that the Lord defined a *"carnal mind" (Romans 8:7)* as someone who is *"in the flesh" (Romans 8:8)*. Based upon these verses and others, we understand the word *carnal* to mean that which is earthly, natural, or fleshly.

Devotional Thoughts

- **(For children):** People love to go to the zoo and there is nothing wrong with going; however, if you go on Sunday morning, where would the Lord rather you be? Spiritually speaking, being *carnal* means doing that which comes to you naturally rather than obeying God. For instance, Eve ate a piece of fruit from a certain tree. Though fruit is healthy and Eve was hungry, God had already told her not to eat of that tree.

- **(For everyone):** *"God is a Spirit: and they that worship him must worship him in spirit and in truth"* **(John 4:24).** Since God wants man to worship Him in this fashion, we know that being carnal opposes God's expectation and demands. What does God want us to understand concerning carnality and worship?
- Do you think God cares about man's carnality? Do you think He is at all pleased when we walk in a carnal manner? How important should walking after the Spirit become for every sincere Christian?

Prayer Thoughts

- Ask the Lord to show you when you are walking after the flesh.
- Ask God to teach you to worship Him in spirit and in truth.

SONG: MY HEART'S THE SEAT OF WAR

Day 31: (Tuesday)
Carnality Stunts Growth

*1 Corinthians 3:1 And I, brethren, **could not speak unto you as unto spiritual, but as unto carnal, even as unto babes in Christ.***

Introductory Thoughts

A Christian's carnality hinders his true potential for service to the Lord. Additionally, carnal living also prohibits the future spiritual growth God intends for every Christian to experience. *1 Corinthians 3:1* provides two connections between carnality and Christian growth. First, carnality indicates that an individual has not previously matured in his walk with the Lord. As such, the apostle Paul said the Corinthian believers were carnal, as babes in Christ. Secondly, carnality stunts the future spiritual growth intended by God in every Christian's life. Paul confirmed this truth by stating that he had some things he wanted to tell the believers at Corinth. He pointed out that their carnality convinced him that they were unable to receive what he would like to say.

DEVOTIONAL THOUGHTS

- **(For children):** A baby has to eat every day to grow–first drinking milk, then eventually eating meat. God wants us to feed on His word daily (by reading, learning, and doing it) so we can grow *(1 Peter 2:2)*. We learn the easier parts first (milk), followed by the more difficult parts (meat).
- **(For everyone):** Think back over your Christian life. Have you grown in the Lord? Are you currently growing? Are you as mature in the Lord as you think that He would have you at this point in your Christian walk?
- Do you recognize anything in your life that the Lord would like to correct but your carnality impedes your development? Do you readily receive truth from God's word and adjust your actions accordingly?

PRAYER THOUGHTS

- Ask the Lord to help you grow daily.
- Ask God to help you receive His truth and conform your life to it.

SONG: *MORE ABOUT JESUS*

Day 32: Church Night

*Romans 8:5 For **they that are after the flesh do mind the things of the flesh**; but **they that are after the Spirit the things of the Spirit.***

Day 33: (Thursday)
The Carnal Mind

*Romans 8:6 For **to be carnally minded is death**; but to be spiritually minded is life and peace.*

*7 Because **the carnal mind is enmity against God**: for **it is not subject to the law of God, neither indeed can be.***

INTRODUCTORY THOUGHTS

God desires for each of His children to walk in the Spirit and be spiritually minded. Yielding our minds to carnality violates God's will. In fact, *"to be carnally minded is death" (Romans 8:6)*. When we give our minds over to the flesh, we die spiritually. We also miss out on the things that tend toward *"life and peace" (Romans 8:6)*. According to scripture, *"the carnal mind is enmity against God"* **(Romans 8:7)**. The word *enmity* is associated with the word *enemy* demonstrating that a carnal mind is the enemy of God and His will. In fact, the carnal mind not only *will not*, but *cannot* be subject to God's law **(Romans 8:7)**. Christians who are actively walking after the Spirit are the only ones faithfully obeying the Lord.

DEVOTIONAL THOUGHTS

- **(For children):** The Israelites asked God to deliver them from Egypt. The Lord did and led them to a good land. He took special care of them along the way. The people were not satisfied and could only think of the food they ate in Egypt. They wanted to return to Egypt. God was not at all pleased with their carnal minds *(1 Corinthians 10:5)*.
- **(For everyone):** What are some things you allow to occupy your mind that tend toward death? How can you occupy your mind with those things that tend toward life?
- Is your mind subject to the law of God? Is the Lord able to deal with you through His word? Are you convicted as you read the words from the pages of your Bible?

PRAYER THOUGHTS

- Ask the Lord to help you to be more spiritually minded.
- Ask God to give you *"life and peace."*

SONG: *LET NOT MY LIFE IN SIN BE PASSED*

Day 34: (Friday)
The Actions of Carnal Men

*1 Corinthians 3:3 For ye are yet carnal: for whereas **there is among you envying, and strife, and divisions, are ye not carnal, and walk as men?***

4 For while one saith, I am of Paul; and another, I am of Apollos; are ye not carnal?

INTRODUCTORY THOUGHTS

Carnality becomes increasingly difficult to hide. Eventually, it clearly manifests itself in our daily actions. The carnality of the Corinthian believers showed itself in their relationship amongst their body of believers. They began to envy one another, eventually leading to strife and divisions amongst the group. When Paul learned of their failings, he knew carnality was at the root of the problem. Another action openly revealing the carnality of the people was their relentless desire to associate themselves with particular Bible teachers. They assumed an association with someone as well respected as Paul or Apollos would give them a spiritual boost among other believers. Considering their actions, Paul knew these believers were *"yet carnal."*

DEVOTIONAL THOUGHTS

- **(For children):** As the firstborn son of Isaac, God gave Esau certain rights and privileges. He was to become the spiritual leader and head of the family. One day he grew very hungry and sold his birthright to his brother Jacob for *"one morsel of meat"* **(Hebrews 12:16)**. His carnality caused him to despise *"his birthright"* **(Genesis 25:34)**.
- **(For everyone):** Is your life filled with envy, strife, and divisions? Are you always looking for someone to follow in order to gain a perceived spiritual advantage? If so, this indicates a level of carnality.
- What are some actions that you think might indicate carnality? Do you exemplify any of those traits? Are you willing to repent of your carnality and seek the Lord's help?

PRAYER THOUGHTS

- Ask the Lord to deliver you from the sins of carnality.
- Ask Him to bring it to your attention when you bear the marks of carnality.

SONG: *LET THOSE WHO THINK THEY STAND, BEWARE*

Day 35: (Saturday)
Our Weapons Are Not Carnal

*2 Corinthians 10:3 For though we walk in the flesh, **we do not war after the flesh**:*

*4 (For **the weapons of our warfare are not carnal**, but mighty through God to the pulling down of strong holds;)*

INTRODUCTORY THOUGHTS

We are to *"fight the good fight of faith"* *(1 Timothy 6:12)*. This battle makes it imperative that we understand *"we do not war after the flesh"* *(2 Corinthians 10:3)*. Unlike many of the cults, we do not use physical weaponry in our attempts to accomplish the will of God. No physical sword or weaponry can convert the lost to Christ; however, the Bible does instruct us to use the sword of the Spirit *(Ephesians 6:17)*. In like manner, we do not have to resort to using physical weaponry to bring about our desired results during the spiritual battles. Instead, we flee to God's throne to find grace to help in time of need *(Hebrews 4:16)*. We must insure that we do not carelessly allow ourselves to believe that the spiritual weapons are inferior to carnal weaponry. The Bible enforces this thought by reminding us that our weapons are *"mighty through God to the pulling down of strong holds"* *(2 Corinthians 10:4)*.

DEVOTIONAL THOUGHTS

- **(For children):** If you want to play instead of doing your chores, but clean up your room anyway because you remember God said to obey, then you are using God's word as a weapon against sin. Our fights with others and with ourselves should be done using God's word. Jesus gave us a great example when He quoted Bible verses to the Devil as he tried to get Him to do wrong.
- **(For everyone):** To what do you resort when you need help in your Christian life? Do you go to your Bible and pray to find the answers you need? Does this help you to get victory over sin?
- The spiritual weapons given to us from God are called *"mighty"* weapons in the Bible. How often do you use the weapon of prayer? How often do you use the sword of the Spirit to convince the lost?

PRAYER THOUGHTS

- Ask the Lord to help you faithfully use your weapons.
- Ask God to help you see the might of His weaponry.

SONG: *TO ARMS, YE SAINTS, TO ARMS!*

Notes: _____

_____

_____

Notes: _____

_____

_____

_____

_____

_____

_____

_____

_____

_____

_____

_____

Quotes from the next volume

(VOLUME 3, WEEK 5)

Subject: Appetite (con't)

Food is one of the necessities to sustain life. Yet, over the centuries, man's need for food has been a source of great temptations.

A believer should be controlled only by the Lord. At no point should a man be led by the cravings of his body, even that of his appetite.

Two of the greatest treasures in godly homes involve time spent at the family altar and the supper table. Both help to develop a cohesive family unit and an unbreakable bond.

6

Communication

Communication—found in all of its forms fourteen times in fourteen verses

Variations: communicate, communicated, communication, communications

First usage: *2 Samuel 3:17* (communication)

Last usage: *Hebrews 13:16* (communicate)

Defined: to impart to another, or to make common

Interesting fact: Generally speaking, communication involves taking that which is personal or private to someone else and making it common or sharing with another. The communication can be words *(2 Samuel 3:17)* or material possessions *(1 Timothy 6:18)*.

Bible study tip: When seeking to define a Bible word, begin with a broader definition encompassing more of the scriptural usage. Once you have this definition, you can then find the specifics and differences in usage throughout scripture. Use the context of the passage to determine which usage the passage incorporates.

Sunday, Day 36—Church Day (no devotional)
Monday, Day 37—*How's Your Communication?*
Tuesday, Day 38—*Your Manner of Communication*
Wednesday, Day 39—Church Night (no devotional)
Thursday, Day 40—*Evil Communications Corrupt*
Friday, Day 41—*Put Off Filthy Communication*
Saturday, Day 42—*Communicating Your Faith*

Day 36: Church Day

Ephesians 4:29 Let no corrupt communication proceed out of your mouth, *but that which is good to the use of edifying, that it may minister grace unto the hearers.*

Day 37: (Monday)
How's Your Communication?

Matthew 5:33 Again, ye have heard that it hath been said by them of old time, Thou shalt not forswear thyself, but shalt perform unto the Lord thine oaths:

34 But I say unto you, Swear not at all; neither by heaven; for it is God's throne:

35 Nor by the earth; for it is his footstool: neither by Jerusalem; for it is the city of the great King.

36 Neither shalt thou swear by thy head, because thou canst not make one hair white or black.

*37 But **let your communication be, Yea, yea; Nay, nay: for whatsoever is more than these cometh of evil.***

INTRODUCTORY THOUGHTS

Our verbal communications involve the words that spring forth from our mouths. No doubt, the Lord considers these communications important and we should too. In today's passage, the Lord gave some specific insights concerning His expectations of our communication. First, He wants our communication to be short and to the point – *"let your communication be, Yea, yea; Nay, nay"* (**Matthew 5:37;** see also **Proverbs 10:19; Ecclesiastes 5:3, 7)**. Second, our word should be validated without the necessity of certifying it with vows, oaths, and swearing. In the context of the passage, the Lord Jesus forbade swearing *"by heaven" (**Matthew 5:34**)*, *"by the earth" (**Matthew 5:35**)*, or *"by thy head" (**Matthew 5:36**)*. When we swear by these things, we put ourselves in danger of condemnation *(**James 5:12**)*. Let your nay be nay and your yea be yea!

DEVOTIONAL THOUGHTS

- **(For children):** God asked Adam if he had eaten of the forbidden tree from which God said not to eat. Instead of just saying, "Yes," Adam used many words to try to make his sin seem less bad *(**Genesis 3:11-12**)*. God doesn't want us to cover up what we've done with our many words.
- **(For everyone):** Do you find it necessary to back up your words with godless swearing or can your word be trusted? Do you say things like, *"I swear on my mother's grave"* or *"cross my heart and hope to die"*?
- The Lord wants our words to be few and faithful. Do you find it necessary to speak voluminous words as a cloak for your lack of truthfulness in your communication?

PRAYER THOUGHTS

- Ask the Lord to help your words be few and faithful.
- Ask God to clear your mouth of worldly, godless language.

SONG: *TAKE MY LIFE, AND LET IT BE*

Day 38: (Tuesday)
Your Manner of Communication

Luke 24:17 *And he said unto them, **What manner of communications are these that ye have** one to another, as ye walk, and are sad?*

INTRODUCTORY THOUGHTS

The Lord Jesus had been brutally killed on the cross; however, many of His disciples remained unaware of His subsequent resurrection. Luke chapter 24 picks up the narrative as two of His followers walked along talking about the events of His crucifixion. Though not immediately recognized, the Lord showed up in the midst of their communications. The Lord asked them, *"What manner of communications are these that ye have one to another, as ye walk, and are sad?"* When they told Him of the content of their communications, the Lord rebuked them for their lack of faith in the prophecies of old *(Luke 24:25)*. The two disciples on the road to Emmaus did not expect the Lord Jesus to show up in the midst of their communication, but He did! Would your communication be any different if you believed Christ could "show up" in the midst of your discussion?

DEVOTIONAL THOUGHTS

- **(For children)**: *1 John 3:20* tells us that God *"knoweth all things."* He hears everything we say and even knows what we are going to say before we say it *(Psalm 139:4)*. Let your words be such that God will be pleased with what you and others discuss.
- **(For everyone)**: What would happen if the Lord showed up in the middle of your communications with others? Would He rebuke you for the content of your conversation?
- It is possible, if not probable, that the Lord Jesus will show up when you are in the middle of a conversation. If He were to show up in the midst of your speaking, about what would you want to be talking?

PRAYER THOUGHTS

- Ask God to help you have the right manner of communications.
- Ask the Lord to help you think before you speak.

SONG: *LORD, MAKE ME BOLD TO OWN MY FAITH*

Day 39: Church Night

Ecclesiastes 5:7 For in the multitude of dreams and many words there are also divers vanities: but fear thou God.

Day 40: (Thursday)
Evil Communications Corrupt

1 Corinthians 15:33 Be not deceived: evil communications corrupt good manners.

INTRODUCTORY THOUGHTS

The opening words of our passage express a desperate warning that is increasingly neglected today. The Devil has convinced many Christians that the content of their daily conversations has no bearing on their spiritual walk. The Bible, however, speaks to the contrary. In fact, the Lord sounded the warning *"be not deceived."* Why? Because quite simply: evil communications corrupt good manners! Christians who desire to serve the Lord and please Him easily can be derailed by choosing to surround themselves with those using evil communications. It is very important to speak righteous things and surround ourselves with those who carry themselves in a Christlike manner.

DEVOTIONAL THOUGHTS

- **(For children):** King Solomon loved God and was very wise, but surrounded himself with people who did not love God. When he was old, his heart was turned to false gods *(1 Kings 11:4)*. We must be very careful when choosing our friends lest they cause us to fall away from the love we have for the Lord.
- **(For everyone):** With what kind of people do you surround yourself? Do they speak of the Lord and of His goodness, or do they speak of the world and its deceptive pleasures?
- Evil communication speaks not only of cursing, but also of things that place doubt upon God's word and His work. Do you surround yourself with people who believe the word of God?

PRAYER THOUGHTS

- Ask God to help you to have the right communications.
- Ask the Lord to give you friends who speak right things.

SONG: *LIVING FOR CHRIST*

Day 41: (Friday)
Put Off Filthy Communication

*Colossians 3:8 But now ye also **put off** all these; anger, wrath, malice, blasphemy, **filthy communication out of your mouth**.*

INTRODUCTORY THOUGHTS

A basic definition of communication involves *making things common*. When we speak to others, we express what is in our minds and hearts making those thoughts common with others. The Bible warns the believer in **Ephesians 4:29** to *"Let no corrupt communication* *proceed out of your mouth, but that which is good to the use of edifying, that it may minister grace unto the hearers."* The words that come out of our mouths should edify or build up others, not demean and degrade them. They should be strengthened by what we say. Keep in mind that corrupt communications weaken the believer *(1 Corinthians 15:33)*. This is why Christians are instructed to put off all *"filthy communication" (Colossians 3:8)*.

DEVOTIONAL THOUGHTS

- **(For children)**: *Psalm 34:13a* says, *"Keep thy tongue from evil."* We should say good things to others with our mouths. We can't do this by ourselves *(James 3:8)*. God has to help us *(Psalm 141:3)* by setting a watch about our mouths and helping us to keep it shut.
- **(For everyone)**: Do your words edify or corrupt others? Do you allow filthy things to come out of your mouth or does all of your language bring glory to God?
- What are some things that you could say to others that would edify them? How could your words help a brother or sister in Christ better serve the Lord?

PRAYER THOUGHTS

- Ask the Lord to help you edify others.
- Ask the Lord to give you wisdom in your communications.

SONG: *BELOVED OF THE LORD*

Day 42: (Saturday)
Communicating Your Faith

Philemon 6 *That the communication of thy faith may become effectual* *by the acknowledging of every good thing which is in you in Christ Jesus.*

INTRODUCTORY THOUGHTS

We communicate those things which we think are important. If we find something that we genuinely enjoy, we want others to know about it so that they too can enjoy it. Is there anything more important or better than knowing Jesus Christ? Apparently, Philemon communicated his faith to others around him, partly through his actions, but likely through his willingness to speak of his love for the Lord and faith in the Lord. As believers, the Lord has given us a tremendous opportunity to speak to others about our wonderful salvation and the many benefits experienced daily. Paul said of the believers at Rome that their faith was spoken of throughout the whole world *(Romans 1:8)*. It is our duty and privilege to communicate what the Lord has done for us with others.

DEVOTIONAL THOUGHTS

- **(For children):** When Jesus walked on this earth, He healed many people in need. One man was so grateful, he wanted to stay with Jesus. Read Jesus' answer to him in *Luke 8:39*. This was more needful. We need to tell others what the Lord has done for us.
- **(For everyone):** What are the most common topics in your conversations with others? Do you speak of the Lord often or find Him seldom the topic of discussion? Do you speak to others about their need for salvation or for fellowship with the Lord?
- Do those around you know that you are saved? Do they know that you love the Lord? If not, why not? Is it possible that you are not communicating your faith like you should?

PRAYER THOUGHTS

- Ask God to give you boldness to communicate your faith.
- Ask the Lord to give you a burning desire to speak of Him.

SONG: *TELL ME THE OLD, OLD STORY*

Notes: _____

_____

_____

_____

_____

_____

_____

_____

Notes: _____

_____

_____

_____

_____

_____

_____

_____

_____

_____

_____

_____

_____

_____

Quotes from the next volume

(VOLUME 3, WEEK 6)

Subject: Appetite (con't)

The Bible says that man cannot be drunk with wine and be filled with the Spirit.

No believer should be deceived into believing that he can fill himself with the world's drink and God's Spirit.

Many carnal believers have attempted to justify their desire for alcohol with *1 Timothy 5:23*, but a careful look at the scriptures proves that they wrest (or twist) the scripture to their own destruction *(2 Peter 3:16)*.

7

Confession

Confession—found in all of its forms forty-seven times in forty-four verses

Variations: confess, confessed, confesseth, confessing, confession

First usage: *Leviticus 5:5* (confess)

Last usage: *Revelation 3:5* (confess)

Defined: making that which is hidden or unknown (at least to the eyes of men) known by openly admitting it

Interesting fact: *John 1:20* contains only thirteen words. This short verse contains the word *confessed* twice. Between the two instances of the word *confessed*, the Bible provides insight as to the definition of *confession*. *"And he confessed, and denied not; but confessed, I am not the Christ" (John 1:20)*. Denying the truth is the opposite of confessing.

Bible study tip: Coordinating conjunctions (i.e., for, and, yet, but, etc.) are often used to compare or contrast two words or thoughts. Their use often provides insights into the definition of biblical words. Remember that *"Every word of*

God is pure" (Proverbs 30:5), including even the seemingly insignificant coordinating conjunctions.

Sunday, Day 43—Church Day (no devotional)
Monday, Day 44—*What Is Confession?*
Tuesday, Day 45—*True Confession Causes Action*
Wednesday, Day 46—Church Night (no devotional)
Thursday, Day 47—*Confessing Your Sins*
Friday, Day 48—*Confessing Your Faults*
Saturday, Day 49—*Confession as a Means of Worship*

Day 43: Church Day

Joshua 7:19 And Joshua said unto Achan, My son, **give,** *I pray thee,* **glory to the LORD God of Israel, and make confession unto him;** *and tell me now what thou hast done; hide it not from me.*

Day 44: (Monday)
What Is Confession?

Psalm 32:5 I acknowledged my sin unto thee, and mine iniquity have I not hid. I said, I will confess my transgressions unto the LORD; and thou forgavest the iniquity of my sin. Selah.

INTRODUCTORY THOUGHTS

The Bible always serves as the best source for adequately defining a Bible word. According to *Joshua 7:19*, *confession* is connected to the act of telling what a person has done—refusing to keep it hidden. Joshua told Achan to give *"glory to the LORD God of Israel, and make confession unto him; and tell me now what thou hast done; hide it not from me."* *Psalm 32:5* identifies *confession* as acknowledging a matter—refusing to hide it. Additionally, *Proverbs 28:13* defines *confession* as the opposite of covering one's sin. In *John 1:20*, the word *confessed* appears twice with a defining phrase in between— *"and denied not."* In the same manner, *Acts 19:18* demonstrates that those who *"confessed" "came . . . and shewed their deeds."* The scriptural evidence points to confession as the willingness to make known that which could otherwise be private, personal, or hidden. Keep in mind that regardless of one's willingness to confess, nothing can be hidden from the Lord.

DEVOTIONAL THOUGHTS

- **(For children):** God asked Cain where his brother Abel was. Cain said he did not know. Cain knew exactly where Abel was and so did God *(Proverbs 15:3)*. Cain did not want to tell God because he was trying to hide what he had done to his brother, but it is impossible to hide anything from God.
- **(For everyone):** What are some things that believers ought to be willing to confess (hint: *Romans 10:9*; *1 John 1:9*)? How important is confession in your life?
- We are generally quick to make known things that ought to be kept quiet and slow to confess things that should be confessed. Are you willing to make known the right things?

PRAYER THOUGHTS

- Ask God to help you understand the importance of confession for your life and the life of your family.
- Ask God to help you confess the right things and never consider hiding anything from God.

SONG: *LORD, FORGIVE! MY FAITH RENEW!*

Day 45: (Tuesday)
True Confession Causes Action

Proverbs 28:13 He that covereth his sins shall not prosper: but **whoso confesseth and forsaketh** them shall have mercy.

INTRODUCTORY THOUGHTS

Many people claim to confess their sins; yet, confession not followed by action remains fruitless. Several verses in the word of God indicate the truth of the matter. Consider the next four examples: (1) Confession of sin is connected to forsaking sin *(Proverbs 28:13)*; (2) Confession of sin is followed by recompense of the trespass *(Numbers 5:7)*; (3) Solomon connected confessing sin with turning from it *(1 Kings 8:35)*; (4) Confession is followed by doing the Lord's pleasure *(Ezra 10:11)*. True confession involves much more than simply receiving the Lord's forgiveness; it involves making wrongs right. True confession is never accomplished by merely opening one's mouth and spouting forth some meaningless words. True confession always produces change in the confessor.

DEVOTIONAL THOUGHTS

- **(For children):** Jesus forgave a woman that had done wrong but also told her to go and *"sin no more" (John 8:11)*. When the children of Israel wanted God to deliver them from the Philistines, Samuel told them they must put away their strange gods, which they willingly did *(1 Samuel 7:3-6)*. We too must be willing to give up sin in order to have the right relationship with the Lord.
- **(For everyone):** Do you find yourself often apologizing to the Lord for sinning against Him, yet failing to demonstrate any outward signs of the necessary true repentance?
- If true confession is most often followed by action, when is the last time you truly confessed your sins to the Lord? Are you willing to confess them now?

PRAYER THOUGHTS

- Ask God to show you the unconfessed sins in your life.
- Ask the Lord to help you confess and forsake those sins.

SONG: *ETERNAL SPIRIT, WE CONFESS*

Day 46: Church Night

*Ezra 10:11 Now therefore **make confession unto the LORD God of your fathers, and do his pleasure***: and separate yourselves from the people of the land, and from the strange wives.

Day 47: (Thursday)
Confessing Your Sins

*1 John 1:9 **If we confess our sins, he is faithful and just to forgive** us our sins, **and to cleanse** us from all unrighteousness.*

INTRODUCTORY THOUGHTS

Because of certain false teachings, there remains a great deal of confusion concerning the matter of confessing sins. However, when we accept the Bible as our sole authority, the confusion dissipates and disappears. Our earlier study showed that actions must follow confession, but to whom should we confess? Some religions falsely teach that we confess our sins to man, but this is simply untrue. The Bible requires that man confess his sins to the Lord. This truth is confirmed repeatedly throughout the word of God. Our First John passage teaches this, but the Bible provides several additional witnesses *(Psalm 32:5; Joshua 7:19; 2 Chronicles 30:22; Ezra 10:1; and Daniel 9:4, 20*, for instance). Our next study delves into the subject of Christians confessing something to men, but confession of sin or sins must be made solely to God.

DEVOTIONAL THOUGHTS

- **(For children):** What should you do if you stole a toy from a friend and then lied about it? God wants you to confess your sin to Him. Simply name the sin and give God the details of what you are going to do about it. You might say to God: "Lord, I stole Tommy's car; and when Mom asked me about it, I lied and told her I did not do it. Please help me to do the right thing."
- **(For everyone):** Do you waste time and strength confessing your sins to other people instead of taking them directly to the Lord? How is *a man* going to help you get forgiveness from *the Lord*?
- Confessing your sins to the Lord restores fellowship that might otherwise remain hindered. What do you think happens when we fail to confess our daily sins to the Lord?

PRAYER THOUGHTS

- Ask the Lord to help you to be faithful in confessing your sins.
- Ask God to show you that confession is to be made to Him only.

SONG: *MY HEART, MY LIFE, MY ALL I BRING*

Day 48: (Friday)
Confessing Your Faults

*James 5:16 Confess **your faults one to another**, and pray one for another, that ye may be healed. The effectual fervent prayer of a righteous man availeth much.*

INTRODUCTORY THOUGHTS

A careful study of our text helps to eliminate the controversy concerning confession. We have already seen that the Bible teaches that confession of *sins* is to be made only to God. Yet, our passage tells us to confess one to another. Yet, the Bible stipulates that the confession involves one's *faults*. The difference between sins and faults is quite simple. A *fault* is not a *sin*, but rather an area of weakness that could lead to *sin*. We do not profit from confessing our *sins* to each other or even to "religious leaders." However, the Bible reveals the benefits derived from confessing that we covet the prayers of others to help overcome our areas of weakness. Perhaps, these brothers and sisters in Christ will fervently pray and even lend support and advice. This is why it is important to confess our sincere desire for their prayers. Unfortunately, misapplication of this passage to bodily healing has caused confusion. The context involves healing in areas of spiritual weaknesses, not simply a need for the body to be healed.

DEVOTIONAL THOUGHTS

- **(For children)**: Confessing your faults means you ask friends to pray for you so that you won't sin. Yet, it is unnecessary to offer them the details discussed in the previous study associated with confessing our sins to God. Using the scenario mentioned yesterday as an example, you might say to your friend, *"Pray for me that I would be happy with my own toys and that I would always tell the truth."*
- **(For everyone)**: Do you have a *"fault"*? Do you have a brother or sister in Christ from whom you can seek prayer for strength in this area? What are some other ways he or she can support you concerning this fault?
- Think of some things that might help you understand the difference between a *sin* and a *fault*. How can people help you with a *fault*, while they cannot help you with a *sin*?

PRAYER THOUGHTS

- Ask God to give you some caring believers who will pray for you.
- Ask God to help you see the difference between a *sin* and a *fault*.

SONG: *WHAT HATH THE SAVIOUR DONE FOR YOU?*

Day 49: (Saturday)
Confession as a Means of Worship

Nehemiah 9:1 Now in the twenty and fourth day of this month the children of Israel were assembled with fasting, and with sackclothes, and earth upon them.

*2 And the seed of Israel separated themselves from all strangers, and **stood and confessed their sins, and the iniquities of their fathers**.*

*3 And they stood up in their place, and read in the book of the law of the LORD their God one fourth part of the day; and **another fourth part they confessed, and worshipped the LORD their God**.*

INTRODUCTORY THOUGHTS

Any person who truly loves the Lord has a strong desire to worship Him. Yet, we frequently fail to realize the various opportunities of worship. The Bible closely connects *worship* to the word *worth*, much like the word *praise* is closely connected to the word *appraisal*. When we *worship* the Lord, we declare what we think about His *worth* to us. Perhaps, you never considered that true confession of sins to a holy God declares God's worth to you. We see this in our passage when confession and worship are mentioned together *(Nehemiah 9:3)*. When we confess our sins to the Lord, we are telling God that we desire His fellowship more than we desire *the pleasures of sin (Hebrews 11:25)*.

DEVOTIONAL THOUGHTS

- **(For children):** By confessing your sins to God, you are telling Him that you believe He is holy; He is the true and living God, and the only One who can forgive sin. You are also admitting that only He knows all that you've done *(Jeremiah 16:17)*. Confession is truly a very important part of worshipping God.
- **(For everyone):** Do you sufficiently love God enough to obey Him in the matter of confession of sins? Would you rather hold on to your sin rather than to enjoy unhindered fellowship that God so freely offers?
- What are the sins in your life that currently remain unconfessed? Are you willing to take that to the Lord right now and declare His worth by confessing those sins?

PRAYER THOUGHTS

- Worship the Lord by confessing your sins.
- Ask the Lord to give you a deeper love for Him.

SONG: *WHILE HERE I LIVE, I LIVE TO THEE*

Notes: _____

_____

_____

_____

_____

_____

_____

_____

_____

Quotes from the next volume

(VOLUME 3, WEEK 7)

Subject: Bereavement

Death takes place when the soul *(Genesis 35:18)* and the spirit *(Genesis 25:8)* leave the body.

When a loved one passes away, mourning serves as an important part of the healing process. Believers should never sorrow in the same fashion as the world *(1 Thessalonians 4:13)*, yet mourning is acceptable and proper when grieving the death of someone.

Believers understand that the separation of death is only temporary. For this reason, believers should find great hope when losing a loved one who knew the Lord. This loss serves as another reason to look forward to the joys awaiting us in heaven.

8

Conversation

Conversation—found twenty times in as many verses

Variations: conversation

First usage: *Psalm 37:14*

Last usage: *2 Peter 3:11*

Defined: the manner in which a man conducts himself in the world

Interesting fact: Out of the twenty occurrences of the word *conversation,* only two of them are found in the Old Testament, both in the Psalms *(Psalm 37:14; Psalm 50:23).* One of these speaks of those that *"be of upright conversation" (Psalm 37:14),* and the other speaks of *"him that ordereth his conversation aright" (Psalm 50:23).*

Bible study tip: The English language is a unique language in the way in which it borrows many of its words from several other languages. *Etymology* refers to the study of the history of words. When studying Bible words, it can help to study the history of the word—both how it came into the English language and how it has been historically used within the English language. Keep in mind that the manner in which a word is used in the Bible more than likely will match its historical usage rather than its modern usage. This is a common problem associated with any living language compounded by the fact that man continues to warp the once rich language of English.

Sunday, Day 50—Church Day (no devotional)
Monday, Day 51—*A Conversation—Without Words*
Tuesday, Day 52—*Change Your Conversation*
Wednesday, Day 53—Church Night (no devotional)
Thursday, Day 54—*The World's Conversation*
Friday, Day 55—*A Desirable Conversation*
Saturday, Day 56—*An Example to Follow*

Day 50: Church Day

***Psalm 50:23** Whoso offereth praise glorifieth me: and to **him that ordereth** his **conversation** aright **will I shew the salvation of God**.*

Day 51: (Monday)
A Conversation—Without Words

***1 Peter 3:1** Likewise, ye wives, be in subjection to your own husbands; that, if any obey not the word, they also may **without the word be won by the conversation** of the wives;*

INTRODUCTORY THOUGHTS

Modern usage of the word *conversation* generally limits the definition to two people involved in a dialog. However, the Bible frequently uses the word *conversation* in a different sense. In fact, our passage reveals that a conversation can occur without words. Several other verses confirm connecting works to a man's conversation (*James 3:13; 1 Peter 2:12*). The Bible's use of *conversation* can involve something that others can observe (*1 Peter 2:12; 1 Peter 3:2*) and consider (*Hebrews 13:7*). Obviously, a man's conversation is more complex than a simple discussion held between two or more persons. Scripturally speaking, our conversation reveals how we live our lives in front of others. Though this world would apply conversation only to what we say, God never intended for its usage to be limited to that single aspect.

DEVOTIONAL THOUGHTS

- **(For children):** Lot lived among the wicked people of Sodom. He was troubled every day by what he saw and heard. The Bible calls the people's actions and speech *"filthy conversation" (2 Peter 2:7-8)*. Unlike many others, we should constantly strive to live a good conversation before others.
- **(For everyone):** What kind of a testimony do you display before your friends, family, and coworkers? Do they see you as a person who loves the Lord and seeks to live holy, or one who loves the world and lives carelessly?
- In what ways could your conversation include what you say? In what ways does your conversation include much more than the words that proceed forth from your lips?

PRAYER THOUGHTS

- Ask the Lord to give you a good conversation.
- Ask God to help you win others through your conversation.

SONG: *WEEP FOR THE LOST!*

Day 52: (Tuesday)
Change Your Conversation

*Ephesians 4:22 That ye **put off concerning the former conversation** the old man, which is corrupt according to the deceitful lusts;*

INTRODUCTORY THOUGHTS

The Bible teaches us that *"if any man be in Christ, he is a new creature"* *(2 Corinthians 5:17)*. Following salvation, a man's life should display visible changes as he seeks to put off his former conversation. According to scripture, that former conversation fulfilled *"the desires of the flesh and of the mind" (Ephesians 2:3)*. By the grace of God, change is possible because every believer has been redeemed from his *"vain conversation"* *(1 Peter 1:18)*. The apostle Paul is a great example. Before meeting the Lord on the road to Damascus, Paul's conversation or lifestyle involved mercilessly persecuting the church *(Galatians 1:13)*. In his new life with Christ, he immediately began preaching the very faith he once destroyed *(Galatians 1:23)*. When a person truly places his faith for salvation in the finished work of Christ, his conversation will change accordingly.

DEVOTIONAL THOUGHTS

- **(For children):** Zacchaeus was a tax collector who charged people more money than he should. When he met the Lord, his life changed. He gave half of his money to the poor; and any person he cheated, he paid back four times as much as he took from them *(Luke 19:8)*. Likewise, our conversation should change after we are saved *(Isaiah 1:16)*.
- **(For everyone):** Has your conversation changed since you trusted Christ as your Saviour? Can people see a notable difference in the way in which you now live?
- When is the last time you examined your conversation to see if it bears evidence of your new life in Christ? What has changed since you trusted Christ?

PRAYER THOUGHTS

- Ask the Lord to help you put off the former conversation.
- Ask the Lord to help your conversation reflect your salvation; your outward lifestyle needs to match what God has done inwardly.

SONG: *AMAZING GRACE!*

Day 53: Church Night

Philippians 3:20 For our conversation is in heaven; from whence also we look for the Saviour, the Lord Jesus Christ:

Day 54: (Thursday)
The World's Conversation

*2 Corinthians 1:12 For our rejoicing is this, the testimony of our conscience, that **in simplicity and godly sincerity**, not with fleshly wisdom, but by the grace of God, **we have had our conversation in the world**, and more abundantly to you-ward.*

INTRODUCTORY THOUGHTS

God is as equally concerned with what we do as to how we do it. It is not only important that we have the right kind of conversation, but that our conversation be based on *"simplicity and godly sincerity."* In other words, our conversation should be genuine and never extravagant.

People behave for different reasons. Sometimes those reasons are godly, yet at other times they reflect ungodliness. Anyone can feign a good conversation for a short period; however, only with the Lord's help can one's motives consistently match his actions. Paul not only sought to have his conversation right before the Lord, but also desired a genuine change of heart to bring forth the proper conversation.

DEVOTIONAL THOUGHTS

- **(For children)**: Whatever we do should be done for the Lord and not merely to be seen of men *(Ephesians 6:6; Colossians 3:23)*. The Lord was not pleased with those who did such things *(Matthew 6:2, 5)*.
- **(For everyone)**: Christians should always consider why they do the things they do. What about you? Do you do certain things because you love the Lord or because you want men to praise you for being "spiritual"?
- Can you think of people who do right for the wrong reasons? What is your opinion of those people? Do you respect them and seek to pattern your life after them?

PRAYER THOUGHTS

- Ask the Lord to help your conversation be sincere.
- Ask God to give you a desire to please Him.

SONG: *DARE TO BE A DANIEL*

Day 55: (Friday)
A Desirable Conversation

Philippians 1:27 Only let your conversation be as it becometh the gospel of Christ: that whether I come and see you, or else be absent, I may hear of your affairs, that ye stand fast in one spirit, with one mind striving together for the faith of the gospel;

INTRODUCTORY THOUGHTS

This world, though it consistently fails to recognize and know the Lord, should consistently recognize Christ's conversation through the life of the believer. Our conversation should always match, or *become*, the gospel of Christ and the new life that we have in Him. Our conversation should be holy because the Lord is holy *(1 Peter 1:15)*. In *2 Peter 3:11*, we learn that the dissolving of this world ought to cause us to walk *"in all holy conversation and godliness."* In other words, our practical Christian life should resemble the change inside of us that took place at salvation. Others should see the Lord Jesus Christ in our actions and in our way of life.

DEVOTIONAL THOUGHTS

- **(For children):** Because of Daniel's good conversation, the king gave Daniel the highest position in the land. Others tried to find some fault in Daniel, but failed in their attempts *(Daniel 6:3-4)*. These men decided to trick the king into making a law which said you could only pray to the king or die. Daniel still prayed three times a day to God.
- **(For everyone):** Does your conversation reflect a life dedicated to Christ? Can others learn about the conversation of the Lord by examining your conversation?
- Does your conversation bring a reproach upon the person and work of the Lord? What do others think of the Lord from what they see from your daily conversation?

PRAYER THOUGHTS

- Ask the Lord to help your conversation match your salvation.
- Ask God to help you become concerned as to the nature of your walk.

SONG: *WHERE HE LEADS I'LL FOLLOW*

Day 56: (Saturday)
An Example to Follow

*1 Timothy 4:12 Let no man despise thy youth; but **be thou an example of the believers**, in word, **in conversation**, in charity, in spirit, in faith, in purity.*

INTRODUCTORY THOUGHTS

Timothy's church leadership position put him in a role to influence the lives of others. Only the proper conversation could avoid adversely affecting other believers. Furthermore, Timothy was a young man and Paul knew that others might despise him for his youth. Therefore, Paul instructed Timothy how to eliminate this problem. He was to be the right type of an example to the believers. Paul gave Timothy several areas in which to be that example. One of these involved Timothy's conversation. Paul knew that it was important for other people to be able to look at Timothy's life and glean an idea of what their conversation should resemble. Just as Paul had been an example to Timothy, Timothy was to be an example for others.

DEVOTIONAL THOUGHTS

- **(For children):** After the death of her husband, Ruth traveled to Bethlehem with her mother-in-law because she wanted to be with people who loved the true God. None of the Jews knew her except Naomi, so the people simply watched her life. The Bible says that Ruth displayed a godly behaviour (conversation) before them *(Ruth 2:11; Ruth 3:11)*.
- **(For everyone):** Most people have others who look to them for some type of leadership. Have you ever considered who is watching your life as an example of how to walk with the Lord? What kind of an example are you providing?
- Who are some people that you look to as an example of how to live the Christian life? What are some of the things that you have learned concerning serving the Lord because of them?

PRAYER THOUGHTS

- Ask the Lord to give you a good example of a godly conversation.
- Ask God to help you to be a godly example.

SONG: *O! TO BE LIKE THEE*

Notes: _____

_____

_____

_____

_____

_____

_____

_____

Notes: _____

_____

_____

_____

_____

_____

Quotes from the next volume

(VOLUME 3, WEEK 8)

Subject: Comfort

The world places a premium on the idea of living comfortably. For instance, people desire comfortable clothes, comfortable beds, comfortable cars, comfortable furniture, etc. There are even foods designated as *"comfort foods."* Yet, with this great emphasis concerning comfort, the world seems to experience so little of it.

The Bible does not reflect that the Lord Jesus was ever addressed as *"the Comforter,"* but He alluded to this title when He told His followers that the coming of the Holy Ghost would be God's means of sending them *"another Comforter" (John 14:16)*. Evidently, the Lord Jesus served as the Comforter and the Holy Ghost would function as another Comforter.

When troubles come, and they do, the believer has living within himself a person of the Godhead that specializes in comforting those afflicted in any way.

Though the Bible does not deal specifically with every modern trouble, the work of God in past believers' lives offers the comfort necessary to face any trouble.

God comforts believers in hopes that they will, in turn, extend that comfort toward others during their times of need.

9

Counsel

Counsel—found 159 times in 151 verses

Variations: counsel, counselled, counsels, counseller

First usage: *Exodus 18:19* (counsel)

Last usage: *Revelation 3:18* (counsel)

Defined: advice or input when used as a noun; giving of that advice or input when used as a verb

Interesting fact: The word *counsel* is closely associated to the thoughts that proceed forth from the heart *(Proverbs 20:5)* and mouth *(Joshua 9:14)* of man or God. *Counseller* is found amongst the glorious names of the Saviour in *Isaiah 9:6.* The Bible also refers to Him as *the Word* in *John 1:1, 14.* This reveals that the Lord Jesus came to this earth as an expression of the heart of the Father *(John 14:6-11).*

Bible study tip: When studying for the purpose of ministering to others, we should not focus solely on Bible *study* but incorporate daily Bible *reading.* God will use His word first to speak to your heart, and then use this God-given message to transform lives. Biblical instruction of any kind should always originate from God and His word.

Sunday, Day 57—Church Day (no devotional)
Monday, Day 58—*What Is Counsel?*
Tuesday, Day 59—*The Wisdom of Wise Counsel*
Wednesday, Day 60—Church Night (no devotional)
Thursday, Day 61—*Counsel from the Lord*
Friday, Day 62—*Heeding the Wrong Counsel*
Saturday, Day 63—*Hireling Counsellers*

Day 57: Church Day

Psalm 16:7 I will bless the LORD, who hath given me counsel*: my reins also instruct me in the night seasons.*

Day 58: (Monday)
What Is Counsel?

Judges 20:7 *Behold, ye are all children of Israel;* ***give here your advice and counsel****.*

INTRODUCTORY THOUGHTS

Men who think they need a simplified version of the Bible to assist in understanding misunderstand God's grace found throughout scripture. For instance, the Lord graciously provides associated words to help understand less familiar words. Even if we did not know what the word *counsel* meant, the Bible provides hints like the one found in ***Judges 20:7***. Judges connects the word *counsel* with the word *advice*. Psalms tells us that *counsel* is gained when people *consult* together ***(Psalm 83:3)***. A *counseller* is one who can give an answer when asked a question ***(Isaiah 41:28)***. Additionally, ***Proverbs 20:5*** points to *counsel* as a well of deep water that the wise seek to draw out of a man. Anytime we go to someone to seek his advice or input in a matter, we are seeking his *counsel*. It is important to note that counsel can be wise and righteous, or it can be ungodly. For this reason, the word of God must be the spiritual gauge.

DEVOTIONAL THOUGHTS

- **(For children):** You receive money for your birthday and ask dad and mom what you can do with the money. That is asking for advice or counsel. You should listen very carefully when they guide you on how to spend the money including saving some and giving to the Lord.

- **(For everyone)**: How often do you seek counsel from others? To whom do you go for counsel? Are they simply your peers or people who love the Lord and His word?
- What do you do when someone gives you godly counsel? Do you listen and follow through with the counsel, or do you listen and generally refuse the godly advice?

PRAYER THOUGHTS

- Ask the Lord to give you some good counsellers.
- Ask God to help you obey wise counsels.

SONG: *THE MORE I KNOW OF THEE*

Day 59: (Tuesday)
The Wisdom of Wise Counsel

Proverbs 1:5 A wise man *will hear, and will increase learning; and a* **man of understanding shall attain unto wise counsels:**

INTRODUCTORY THOUGHTS

Though not all counsel received will be wise counsel, it is still wise to receive counsel. A foolish man neglects to consider the need for counsel. He believes his own understanding sufficient *(Proverbs 12:15)*. A wise man, however, not only seeks counsel, but hearkens to the wisdom found in such. The Bible says that the absence of counsel causes people to fall *(Proverbs 11:14)* and purposes to be disappointed *(Proverbs 15:22; Proverbs 20:18)*, and that only a fool would go to war without it *(Proverbs 24:6)*. Not only does counsel help to develop godly plans, but also ensures that our motives are pure. Counsel provides safety on a variety of levels *(Proverbs 11:14; Proverbs 24:6)*.

DEVOTIONAL THOUGHTS

- **(For children)**: God sent a prophet to tell Amaziah not to worship idols. Amaziah told the prophet to leave him alone or he would have him killed. The prophet then told Amaziah of his destruction *(2 Chronicles 25:14-16)*. Amaziah should have listened to good counsel.

- **(For everyone):** Do you have important decisions to make? Have you considered seeking counsel from someone who loves the Lord and knows His word?
- Do you find yourself seeking counsel only from people who would agree with your plans? Why is that so? Is it possible that you seek to justify your actions rather than truly desiring God's will and ways.

PRAYER THOUGHTS

- Ask the Lord to help you see the importance of wise counsel.
- Ask the Lord to give you counsel that checks your motive.

SONG: *LET US RUN THE CHRISTIAN RACE*

Day 60: Church Night

*Psalm 33:11 **The counsel of the LORD standeth for ever**, the thoughts of his heart to all generations.*

Day 61: (Thursday)
Counsel from the Lord

*Joshua 9:14 And **the men** took of their victuals, and **asked not counsel** at the mouth of the LORD.*

INTRODUCTORY THOUGHTS

The devotions on the subject of counsel have thus far dealt specifically with counsel received from another person. Yet counsel received from the Lord is the greatest counsel. In *Joshua 9:14*, the people refused to seek counsel from the Lord and made decisions that caused them trouble for many years. Though God does not speak to us audibly, we are not left to our own devices. We find a more sure word of consultation through His written word. This is why each decision should be carefully checked against the word of God. The Bible is able to discern our thoughts and intentions *(Hebrews 4:12)* and can determine if we are making the right choices. No better counsel can be received than that which you will find in God's word.

DEVOTIONAL THOUGHTS

- **(For children):** If you have a question, the Bible is the best place to get good advice *(Psalm 119:24)*. God speaks to us through His word which has just the right properties. *Psalm 19:7-8* says that His word is perfect, sure (you can trust it), right, and pure. Once you get that advice, you need to follow through on it.
- **(For everyone):** Do you seek counsel from the Bible before making decisions? What are some important decisions that you need to make right now? What does the Bible have to say about those issues?
- Even the best of people can offer faulty counsel. Is the same thing true of the word of God? How trustworthy is the counsel you receive from God's word?

PRAYER THOUGHTS

- Ask God to show you verses pertaining to your current needs.
- Ask the Lord to help you seek Him over the words of men.

SONG: *ALL THE WAY MY SAVIOUR LEADS ME*

Day 62: (Friday)
Heeding the Wrong Counsel

Psalm 1:1 Blessed is the man that walketh not in the counsel of the ungodly, *nor standeth in the way of sinners, nor sitteth in the seat of the scornful.*

INTRODUCTORY THOUGHTS

The scripture offers many examples of those who suffered the consequences of choosing to follow ungodly counsel. As children of God, it is imperative that we do not walk in the counsel of the ungodly. Following the wrong counsel results in severe consequences. For example, Rehoboam in 1 Kings chapter 12 sought counsel from both the older men who had served his father and the younger men who were his peers. However, he chose to follow the counsel of his peers while refusing the counsel and wisdom of the older men. The unwise counsel resulted in splitting the kingdom with the vast majority following Jeroboam as their new king. Jereboam unfortunately led many of the Israelites into pagan worship *(1 Kings 12:25-30)*.

DEVOTIONAL THOUGHTS

- **(For children):** You and your friends are hungry and walk by a neighbour's yard where there is an apple tree. Tom says, *"Let's go get an apple. They can't use all of them and they won't mind."* Joe says, *"But they aren't ours. That's stealing! We should ask first."* Whose advice should you follow? Why?
- **(For everyone):** Can you think of some ungodly counsel that you received? What would have happened if you had followed that advice? What things would be different in your life now?
- How can we determine if counsel is godly or not? What should we do when we receive counsel that does not align with the word of God?

PRAYER THOUGHTS

- Ask the Lord to protect you from ungodly counsel.
- Ask God to give you wisdom to help you follow wise counsel.

SONG: *CLOSE TO THEE*

Day 63: (Saturday)
Hireling Counsellors

Ezra 4:1 *Now when the adversaries of Judah and Benjamin heard that the children of the captivity builded the temple unto the LORD God of Israel;*

2 Then they came to Zerubbabel, and to the chief of the fathers, and said unto them, Let us build with you: for we seek your God, as ye do; and we do sacrifice unto him since the days of Esarhaddon king of Assur, which brought us up hither.

3 But Zerubbabel, and Jeshua, and the rest of the chief of the fathers of Israel, said unto them, Ye have nothing to do with us to build an house unto our God; but we ourselves together will build unto the LORD God of Israel, as king Cyrus the king of Persia hath commanded us.

*4 **Then the people of the land weakened the hands of the people of Judah, and troubled them in building,***

*5 **And hired counsellers against them, to frustrate their purpose,** all the days of Cyrus king of Persia, even until the reign of Darius king of Persia.*

INTRODUCTORY THOUGHTS

The book of Ezra provides the details concerning the time when the Israelites returned to their land to rebuild the temple. As they began to build, adversaries within the land became jealous. They did not want the people of God regaining their strength and restoring their true form of worship. The adversaries hired counsellers against the people of God in order to stop the work. Unfortunately, some things never change. Our work may not involve rebuilding a temple, but God's work always has a purpose that the enemy will seek to undermine. Christians should not be surprised when the Devil sends people into our lives who offer counsel contrary to God's will. God's enemies may even seek to hire counsellers to deter us from what we should be doing.

DEVOTIONAL THOUGHTS

- **(For children):** The Devil knew it was God's plan for Adam and Eve to walk with God. They were instructed to care for the garden in which God had placed them. The Devil was the first one in the Bible to offer bad advice. He told Eve she wouldn't die and that she would be wise if she ate of the tree of which God told her not to eat. We should make sure that the advice we listen to agrees with God's desires.
- **(For everyone):** Have you ever had someone offer advice contrary to the obvious will of God in your life? Why do you think that counsel was given?
- Just as the Lord wants us to receive godly counsel, the Devil wants us to receive ungodly counsel. How can we differentiate between God's counsel and the counsel of the adversary?

PRAYER THOUGHTS

- Ask God to give you wisdom to recognize ungodly counsel.
Ask the Lord to put a hedge about you in His service.

SONG: *WHY SHOULD I FEAR THE TEMPTER?*

Notes: _____

_____

_____

_____

Notes: _____

_____

_____

_____

_____

_____

_____

_____

_____

_____

_____

_____

_____

Quotes from the next volume

(VOLUME 3, WEEK 9)

Subject: Confusion

Confusion does not always result directly from personal sin, but sin surely causes a great deal of confusion.

Sin takes an otherwise clear and indisputable reality and blurs it with corruption and inaccuracies.

The Bible plainly points out that God is not the author of confusion in the life of any believer.

The Christian home should be a place of clarity that serves to protect from the confusion perpetrated by the world, the flesh, and the Devil.

10

Contending

Contending—found twenty-five times in twenty-four verses

Variations: contend, contended, contendest, contendeth, contending

First usage: *Deuteronomy 2:9* (contend)

Last usage: *Jude 9* (contending)

Defined: to fight, debate, or strive

Interesting fact: Throughout church history, those who espoused the Judeo-Christian faith have been deemed by those in power as unworthy to live. The world pays little attention to the men and women who have died for the faith. For instance, the Bible mentions Antipas, God's *"faithful martyr" (Revelation 2:13)*. But what else do we know about him and others? Those who suffered horrific torture, imprisonment, and martyrdom for their faith remain unnamed *(Hebrews 11:36-37)*. And yet, the Bible says that it is the world who is not worthy of such men *(Hebrews 11:38)*. Thankfully, the scripture declares that *"God is not unrighteous to forget your work and labour of love" (Hebrews 6:10)*. The world may have a short attention span, but God does not!

Bible study tip: The Bible contains many absolutes. For instance, sin is wicked and God is righteous. Yet, there are many matters mentioned in scripture that remain neutral unless one considers the context of the issue or the motive behind an action. Be careful not to generalize the nature of any subject without first considering its context.

Sunday, Day 64—Church Day (no devotional)
Monday, Day 65—*Earnestly Contending for the Faith*
Tuesday, Day 66—*Contending with God's People*
Wednesday, Day 67—Church Night (no devotional)
Thursday, Day 68—*Valiant for Truth*
Friday, Day 69—*Contending with the Wicked*
Saturday, Day 70—*Contending till Death*

Day 64: Church Day

*1 Timothy 6:12 **Fight the good fight of faith**, lay hold on eternal life, whereunto thou art also called, and hast professed a good profession before many witnesses.*

Day 65: (Monday)
Earnestly Contending for the Faith

Jude 3 *Beloved, when I gave all diligence to write unto you of the common salvation, it was needful for me to write unto you, and exhort you that **ye should earnestly contend for the faith which was once delivered unto the saints.***

Introductory Thoughts

There are very few matters in this life for which we ought to earnestly contend. Yet *"the faith which was once delivered unto the saints"* stands as one of those things. *"The faith"* in this context refers specifically to the body of doctrine delivered to us. As believers, we should always be ready and willing to take a stand for the truths of God's holy word. This contending does not suggest becoming violent toward those who oppose truth. However, it does mean that we should unwaveringly stand forth proclaiming the truth of God's word despite man's disapproval. The Lord delivered these truths to us and for us and we should not allow the world to attack them unopposed. We must determine to take a bold stand! We must contend! No matter the repercussions, our allegiance to the One who graciously delivered such truths should shine forth as a light in a dark world.

DEVOTIONAL THOUGHTS

- **(For children):** Peter and John were threatened to cease preaching about Jesus. Yet, they stood brave and told the rulers they had to speak the truth *(Acts 4:18-20)*. Instead of wavering, they prayed for God to give them more courage to speak His word and God answered their prayer *(Acts 4:29, 31)*.
- **(For everyone):** When was the last time you boldly took a stand for the Lord and His words? Did you insure that your stand would bring glory solely to the Lord?
- Do people around you degrade the words of God? What do you do when this happens? Do you sit quietly while the One who gave Himself for you is mocked?

PRAYER THOUGHTS

- Ask the Lord to give you boldness to stand for Him no matter the obstacles.
- Ask God to give you wisdom to glorify Him in your stand.

SONG: *TRUMP OF WAR! AWAKE THE SOLDIER!*

Day 66: (Tuesday)
Contending with God's People

*Nehemiah 13:11 Then contended I with the rulers, and said, Why is the house of God forsaken? And I gathered them together, **and set them in their place.***

INTRODUCTORY THOUGHTS

We should not assume that our contentions for the truth will always be directed toward those who know not the Lord. Unfortunately, our stand for truth will often be opposed by the very ones who claim to know the Lord as Saviour. Nehemiah serves as a great example of someone who stood for the Lord against severe opposition from his brethren. In the thirteenth chapter of the book that bears his name, the Bible records his stand against those who were set apart by the Lord. He contended with them for the house of the Lord *(Nehemiah 13:11)*, the law of the Lord *(Nehemiah 13:15-22)*, and the purity of their homes *(Nehemiah 13:23-26)*. Just as Nehemiah contended with those who knew the Lord, God may call upon us to do the very same thing.

DEVOTIONAL THOUGHTS

- **(For children):** Peter gladly fellowshipped with his friends who loved God and knew the truth. Yet, when some of his other friends (who also loved God) came to visit, he treated his newer friends with contempt. He was afraid his visiting friends would not like these friends. Paul told Peter before them all that he was wrong and responsible for the hurt and confusion that he caused *(Galatians 2:11-14)*.
- **(For everyone):** Sometimes, those of us who know and love the Lord grow weary and depart from the Lord's will for our lives. It is during these times when those who truly love us will contend with us and not spare for fear of offending us.
- When is the last time you took a righteous stand against someone who claimed to know the Lord as Saviour? It often seems much more difficult to contend with the saved than with the lost.

PRAYER THOUGHTS

- Ask the Lord to give you wisdom as you contend for the truth.
- Ask God to give you a burden for those who turn from the truth.

SONG: *FELLOW SOLDIER, WHERE'S THINE ARMOUR?*

Day 67: Church Night

*Ephesians 6:10 Finally, my brethren, **be strong in the Lord, and in the power of his might.***

Day 68: (Thursday)
Valiant for Truth

Jeremiah 9:1 Oh that my head were waters, and mine eyes a fountain of tears, that I might weep day and night for the slain of the daughter of my people!

2 Oh that I had in the wilderness a lodging place of wayfaring men; that I might leave my people, and go from them! for they be all adulterers, an assembly of treacherous men.

*3 And they bend their tongues like their bow for lies: but **they are not valiant for the truth upon the earth**; for they proceed from evil to evil, and they know not me, saith the LORD.*

Introductory Thoughts

In Jeremiah's day, the Israelites had grown spiritually cold concerning the truth. The Bible says that they were proceeding from evil to evil and were no longer valiant for the truth. Nobody could be trusted to tell the truth. The outcome was sure to be the judgment of God *(Jeremiah 9:9)*. Jeremiah had a tremendous burden for his people's condition *(Jeremiah 9:1)*. He determined to stand against the opposition so that his people might turn from their wickedness. Times may have changed since Jeremiah's day but not near as much as we might think. Far too many Christians have turned a blind eye toward evil and lost any desire to be valiant for the truth. The church and the rest of the world desperately need faithful Christians similar to the prophet Jeremiah who contended for the truth with a heart burdened for the work and the people.

Devotional thoughts

- **(For children):** The Lord sent the prophet Samuel to tell King Saul to destroy all the Amalekites. When Samuel learned that Saul disobeyed God's directives, he was upset and cried out to the Lord all night for Saul. We too should display the same type of concern for those who disobey God.
- **(For everyone):** Are you valiant for the truth? What about your family? What about your friends? What about your church? What can you do to encourage others in the fight?
- How burdened are we for our nation, our family, our friends, and our church? Do we ever weep because of the believers around us who seem so complacent?

Prayer Thoughts

- Ask the Lord for help in being valiant for the truth.
- Ask God to burden you for those who proceed from evil to evil.

SONG: *THY TESTIMONY'S MY DELIGHT*

Day 69: (Friday)
Contending with the Wicked

*Proverbs 28:4 They that forsake the law praise the wicked: but **such as keep the law contend with them.***

INTRODUCTORY THOUGHTS

Our love for the words of God seems directly proportional to our willingness to contend for the truth. Those who love the law of God do not praise the wicked but instead contend with them. Contending against those who oppose God will not always be easy and will sometimes develop fearfulness from within. Yet, a believer who loves the Lord and His word will not idly sit by in the presence of wickedness without proclaiming the righteousness of God. Unfortunately, Christians are becoming increasingly fearful of speaking up in morally corrupt societies. Sometimes believers have allowed and even facilitated the wicked to spew forth their vile agenda and thoughts. However, those who truly love the Lord should be like the prophet Jeremiah who could not keep silent as he sensed the words of God like a fire shut up in his bones *(Jeremiah 20:9)*.

DEVOTIONAL THOUGHTS

- **(For children):** John the Baptist did not fear to tell wicked King Herod of *"all the evils"* which the king had done. Because John was so outspoken, the king threw him into prison *(Luke 3:19-20)*. We too should not allow our fears to hinder us from proclaiming that God's way is best.
- **(For everyone):** Have you ever been in the presence of wickedness and felt a strong desire to take a stand for righteousness? What did you do? Did you boldly contend for the faith or anxiously keep silent?
- Do you get fearful when you think of contending with the wicked? From whence do you think this fear originates? Since it is not from the Lord, how should we handle it?

PRAYER THOUGHTS

- Ask the Lord to dispel your fears of contending for the faith.
- Ask the Lord to give you a special love for His word that enables you to stand bold.

SONG: *THE KING'S BUSINESS*

Day 70: (Saturday)
Contending till Death

*Acts 7:59 And **they stoned Stephen**, calling upon God, and saying, Lord Jesus, receive my spirit.*

*60 And **he kneeled down, and cried with a loud voice, Lord, lay not this sin to their charge. And when he had said this, he fell asleep**.*

INTRODUCTORY THOUGHTS

Throughout the years, faithful saints have been willing to lay down their lives for the truth. In Acts chapter 7, we read the account of Stephen's final message to the nation of Israel. His message infuriated the people so much that they ran upon him and threw stones at him until they crushed the life out of his body. Stephen was martyred because he cared more for the truth's propagation than even his own life and welfare. Though most Christians are not living amongst such severe persecution, our willingness to contend should remain just as fervent. We should pray that God would give us some modern believers who, like Paul, would say, *"that in nothing I shall be ashamed, but that with all boldness, as always, so now also Christ shall be magnified in my body, **whether it be by life, or by death" (Philippians 1:20)**!*

DEVOTIONAL THOUGHTS

- **(For children):** Shadrach, Meshach, and Abednego knew what would happen if they refused to bow down to King Nebuchadnezzar's golden image. Yet, they were willing to stand for God even if it meant losing their lives *(Daniel 3:14-18)*. Let's ask God to give us such courage.
- **(For everyone):** Would you be willing to give your life in defense of the truth? If not, why not? Is it possible that we do not love the Lord as much as we think we do?
- Stephen's courage made a difference in the life of Paul *(Acts 7:58)*. In what ways could the Lord use the testimony of a martyr to convert the lost in our day?

PRAYER THOUGHTS

- Ask the Lord to give us boldness like Stephen.
- Ask God to give us a willingness to die for the truth.

SONG: *THE SON OF GOD GOES FORTH TO WAR*

Notes: _____

_____

_____

_____

_____

_____

_____

_____

_____

_____

_____

_____

_____

_____

_____

_____

_____

_____

Quotes from the next volume

(VOLUME 3, WEEK 10)

Subject: Contention

Without pride, contention ceases.

There are times when strife remains unavoidable, but no believer should ever strive with others without a just cause and purpose.

Before two people decide to take part in strife, they would be wise to consider the effect their contention will have on the innocent people around them.

11

Edification

Edification—found twenty times in nineteen verses

Variations: edification, edified, edifieth, edify, edifying

First usage: *Acts 9:31* (edified)

Last usage: *1 Timothy 1:4* (edifying)

Defined: related to the word *edifice* and means to build up or construct

Interesting fact: Seven of the twenty appearances of edification are found in 1 Corinthians chapter 14. The emphasis of this chapter upon edifying proves the church's preeminent responsibility. Believers and churches that fail to display charity and refuse to edify others fall short of God's explicit directives.

Bible study tip: It has been said that *repetition* is the key to learning, but repetition serves several purposes. The Bible uses repetition to slow the reader down so that he might concentrate on each part of a verse or passage. For instance, *Acts 1:8* serves as an example of how the Lord repeats the word *and* four times. Look it up and take note of the pattern.

Sunday, Day 71—Church Day (no devotional)
Monday, Day 72—*What Is Edification?*
Tuesday, Day 73—*Not Everything Edifies*
Wednesday, Day 74—Church Night (no devotional)
Thursday, Day 75—*Charity Edifieth*
Friday, Day 76—*Communication Should Always Edify Others*
Saturday, Day 77—*Everything We Do Should Be Edifying*

Day 71: Church Day

***Romans 14:19 Let us therefore follow after** the things which make for peace, and **things wherewith one may edify another**.*

Day 72: (Monday)
What Is Edification?

***2 Corinthians 13:10** Therefore I write these things being absent, lest being present I should use sharpness, according to the power which the Lord hath given me **to edification, and not to destruction**.*

INTRODUCTORY THOUGHTS

The Bible's built-in dictionary defines *edification* by contrasting it with *destruction*. *Destruction* gives the sense of tearing down something; therefore, it makes sense that *edification* refers to the opposite of tearing down. Consider a related word: an *edifice* is a building. This further confirms that edification means to build up something. As saints of God, we should be building ourselves and others on our most holy faith *(Jude 20)*. In fact, everything we do should be judged by whether or not it works to build up or to strengthen us or other believers. Christians should focus on consciously building others in the faith. Consistently edifying others takes thorough planning and direction; whereas, destructive behaviour frequently takes place haphazardly.

DEVOTIONAL THOUGHTS

• **(For children):** Did you ever work hard at building a tower with blocks only to have someone walk by and knock it down? How did you feel? This example demonstrates how much easier it is to destroy than it is to build. Our words function the same way. Satan finds pleasure from those who use their words to hurt and tear down others.

- **(For everyone):** Do you build up other believers or tear them down? Are they spiritually stronger for knowing you? What are some things that you could do to edify others today?
- Why is it important that we edify other believers? In what ways could this please the Lord? How could it be displeasing to the Lord if we destroy others?

PRAYER THOUGHTS

- Ask the Lord to show you the importance of edifying others.
- Ask the Lord to give you a desire to edify those around you.

SONG: *BLEST BE THE TIE THAT BINDS*

Day 73: (Tuesday)
Not Everything Edifies

*1 Corinthians 10:23 All things are lawful for me, but all things are not expedient: all things are lawful for me, but **all things edify not**.*

INTRODUCTORY THOUGHTS

The Christian life usually contains some very difficult decisions. Life's choices do not always involve choosing between good and evil; sometimes our choices involve choosing between something good and something better or best. For instance, a choice may involve something not necessarily wicked, but equally not edifying. This choice may not involve sin, but also fails to build others in the Lord. Believers who truly love the Lord may, at times, have to choose to forsake some things in life because they do not edify. Our passage confirms these truths as it says that all things do not edify. Paul emphasized this when he stated, *"if meat make my brother to offend, I will eat no flesh while the world standeth" (1 Corinthians 8:13)*. Clearly, edification serves a much greater purpose than simple convenience or liberty.

DEVOTIONAL THOUGHTS

- **(For children):** Some people use cards and dice for things condemned in scripture. We may have games that contain these items and play with them because we don't use them wickedly. However, if a Christian friend has a strong conviction about these things, we should show him respect and not play the games around him *(Romans 14:21).*

- **(For everyone):** What are some areas that might not be sinful but would be equally unable to edify others? Would you be willing to give those things up for the glory of God?
- Are there some things in your life that might not be considered sinful but could be used of the Devil to destroy or weaken others around you?

PRAYER THOUGHTS

- Ask the Lord to help you make choices that edify yourself and others.
- Ask the Lord to show you things that destroy.

SONG: *ABOVE THE TREASURES OF THIS WORLD*

Day 74: Church Night

Ephesians 4:11 And he gave some, apostles; and some, prophets; and some, evangelists; and some, pastors and teachers;

*12 For the perfecting of the saints, for the work of the ministry, **for the edifying of the body of Christ:***

13 Till we all come in the unity of the faith, and of the knowledge of the Son of God, unto a perfect man, unto the measure of the stature of the fulness of Christ:

14 That we henceforth be no more children, tossed to and fro, and carried about with every wind of doctrine, by the sleight of men, and cunning craftiness, whereby they lie in wait to deceive;

15 But speaking the truth in love, may grow up into him in all things, which is the head, even Christ:

*16 **From whom the whole body fitly joined together and compacted** by that which every joint supplieth, according to the effectual working in the measure of every part, **maketh increase of the body unto the edifying of itself in love.***

Day 75: (Thursday)
Charity Edifieth

*1 Corinthians 8:1 Now as touching things offered unto idols, we know that **we all have knowledge**. Knowledge puffeth up, but **charity edifieth**.*

Introductory Thoughts

The knowledge of something wrong helps a spiritual person avoid such activity. On the surface, one might fail to distinguish much of a difference between the fruit of knowledge and charity in today's passage. Both evidently build up the believer. Yet, a closer look reveals the major difference. The Bible says that knowledge *"puffeth up."* The idea is that knowledge makes one feel superior and can offer a false strength. Knowledge seems to do the same work as charity, but knowledge without the charity serves as a façade. Charity, however, offers real growth and stability. Unlike knowledge, charity edifieth. Charity not only builds up the believer but also those who associate with that believer. The only way to be edified and the only way to edify others involves seeking the Lord for pure, unadulterated charity.

Devotional thoughts

- **(For children):** Before Paul came to Jesus on the road to Damascus, he knew many things about God. Yet, he never thought he was better than others. He later wrote that to know the love of Christ was better than knowledge *(Ephesians 3:19)*. He shared what he knew with others and wanted them to pass it on *(2 Timothy 2:2)*.
- **(For everyone):** Knowledge often leads to pride and *"pride goeth before destruction"* *(Proverbs 16:18)*. In what ways is charity better than knowledge? How can knowledge destroy you and others?
- What are some ways in which the Lord could use charity through your life to edify other believers? When is the last time you used charity to strengthen a brother or sister in Christ?

Prayer Thoughts

- Ask the Lord to protect you from being destroyed.
- Ask God to give you a pure heart of charity.

SONG: *JESUS, CEMENT OUR HEARTS AS ONE*

Day 76: (Friday)
Communication Should Always Edify Others

*Ephesians 4:29 Let no corrupt communication proceed out of your mouth, but **that which is good to the use of edifying**, that it may minister grace unto the hearers.*

INTRODUCTORY THOUGHTS

Our words should never be used by the Devil as weapons to destroy or discourage others. Any problem with our words reveals a problem with our heart: *"out of the abundance of the heart the mouth speaketh" (Matthew 12:34)*. The mouth can exhibit good or bad and our actions reveal the heart of the problem when the Bible says, *"out of the heart proceed evil thoughts, murders, adulteries, fornications, thefts, false witness, blasphemies" (Matthew 15:19)*. This is why our words are not always profitable to those who hear them. Yet, God admonishes us to *"let no corrupt communication proceed out of"* our mouth. Believers are instead encouraged to make sure their words are *"good to the use of edifying."* The saint of God should speak words that God can use to build up other saints in the faith.

DEVOTIONAL THOUGHTS

- **(For children):** The children of Israel were fighting the Philistines and were greatly outnumbered. Jonathan encouraged his armourbearer to have faith in God *(1 Samuel 14:6-7)*. He and his armourbearer started the attack and God gave a great victory. Our words should be like Jonathan's, helping others to live for God.
- **(For everyone):** Do you remember a time when you spoke words that unnecessarily hurt another believer? Did you repent of that sin and seek the forgiveness of that individual?
- Do your words obey God by ministering to others? Are your words weapons that Satan can use to destroy or tools by which the Lord can build others?

PRAYER THOUGHTS

- Ask the Lord to help you think before you speak.
- Ask God to give you words of edification for others.

SONG: *LITTLE IS MUCH WHEN GOD IS IN IT*

Day 77: (Saturday)
Everything We Do Should Be Edifying

1 Corinthians 14:26 How is it then, brethren? when ye come together, every one of you hath a psalm, hath a doctrine, hath a tongue, hath a revelation, hath an interpretation. **Let all things be done unto edifying***.*

INTRODUCTORY THOUGHTS

The Bible reveals that carnality infected and infested the first century Corinthian church. Divisions were commonplace as the believers were polluted by strife and envy. When the believers gathered together, every man did that which was self-pleasing. Every believer desired to be the center of attention rather than giving others first place. Every one of them had a psalm, or a doctrine, or a tongue, or a revelation, or an interpretation; but nobody sought to use those things for edification. Each of these things could have been used for good, but Paul said that the church being edified was most needed *(1 Corinthians 14:5)*. As believers, every aspect of our service to God should seek to edify others. This most especially includes the times when we gather together.

DEVOTIONAL THOUGHTS

- **(For children):** Sometimes building up others can be with or without words. David said, *"I will behave myself wisely in a perfect way" (Psalm 101:2a)*. At church, do you sing out during the song service, listen during preaching time, and obey the rules? Do you ignore some children while speaking only to those you consider your friends?
- **(For everyone):** Do you take part in the worship services? Could the things that you do be used of God to edify others? Are you self-centered in your "service" to God?
- Does your choice of songs edify the saints or feed the flesh? Does the preaching and teaching edify or weaken the saints? What steps can you take to insure that the saints are edified?

PRAYER THOUGHTS

- Ask the Lord to help you be selfless in your service toward Him.
- Ask God to show you that worshipping Him is not about you.

SONG: *WHO IS ON THE LORD'S SIDE?*

Notes: _____

_____

_____

_____

_____

_____

_____

_____

_____

_____

_____

_____

_____

_____

_____

_____

Quotes from the next volume

(VOLUME 3, WEEK 11)

Subject: Contention (con't)

Strife is birthed from pride and yields foolish behaviour.

The Bible likens strife to the bars of a castle *(Proverbs 18:19)*, creating a prison for some and an impossible barrier for others.

A contentious man notices when the fires of strife begin to be extinguished and seeks to rekindle the flame.

12

Fasting

Fasting—found seventy-seven times in sixty-five verses

Variations: fast, fasted, fastest, fasting, fastings

First usage: *Judges 20:26* (fasted)

Last usage: *2 Corinthians 11:27* (fastings)

Defined: abstaining from all food or food and drink along with other self-pleasing activities

Interesting fact: *Judges 20:26* records the first direct mention of fasting. Yet, the command to the Israelites to *"afflict your souls"* in *Leviticus 16:29* most likely refers to a time of fasting. *Isaiah 58:3* confirms this fact as it directly associates fasting to the afflicting of one's soul: *"**Wherefore have we fasted**, say they, and thou seest not? **wherefore have we afflicted our soul**, and thou takest no knowledge? Behold, in the day of your fast ye find pleasure, and exact all your labours."* Furthermore, the Bible rebukes them for taking pleasure in the day of their fast, rather than abstaining from these things.

Bible study tip: Study the Bible dispensationally by considering it in sections (i.e., the Law, the Gospels, the Epistles, etc.).

Some practices found in scripture are applicable to a single dispensation or several of them, while others cross all dispensational lines. Look for statements suggesting whether or not your study is tied to one dispensation or if it is transdispensational. For example, praying that one's flight not be on the Sabbath *(Matthew 24:20)* would not be applicable to the Church Age when there is no Sabbath today *(Colossians 2:16-17)*.

Sunday, Day 78—Church Day (no devotional)
Monday, Day 79—*What Is Fasting?*
Tuesday, Day 80—*Fasting Not Optional*
Wednesday, Day 81—Church Night (no devotional)
Thursday, Day 82—*Fastings' Proper Motive*
Friday, Day 83—*The Times for Fasting*
Saturday, Day 84—*Fasting Afflicts the Soul*

Day 78: Church Day

*Matthew 9:15 And Jesus said unto them, Can the children of the bridechamber mourn, as long as the bridegroom is with them? but **the days will come, when the bridegroom shall be taken from them, and then shall they fast**.*

Day 79: (Monday)
What Is Fasting?

*Acts 27:33 And while the day was coming on, Paul besought them all to **take meat**, saying, This day is the fourteenth day that **ye have tarried and continued fasting, having taken nothing**.*

INTRODUCTORY THOUGHTS

Modern Christianity has been redefining Bible terminology and fasting is no exception. Perhaps this is because Christians want to look spiritual without the necessary dedication. Some claim to be fasting from certain things like caffeine or sugar intake. The Bible does not offer anyone this type of latitude. True biblical fasting involves much more than refraining from some handpicked pleasure. According to our passage, Paul entreated the people to take *meat* because they had been fasting for two weeks. **Esther 4:16** reveals that fasting consists of taking no food or drink. Although some Bible teachers have suggested that fasting means to simply refrain from earthly joys, fasting in the Bible always includes refraining from food or from both food and drink. Even the results of fasting identify that it is associated with depriving the body of food. In **Psalm 109:24**, David said, *"My knees are weak through fasting; and my flesh faileth of fatness."* Foregoing earthly pleasures is a byproduct of fasting, not the sole object.

Devotional Thoughts

- **(For children):** Read **Matthew 15:32**. Jesus called going without food *fasting*. Fasting can also mean going without food and water **(Exodus 34:28)**.
- **(For everyone):** When is the last time you purposely refused to eat or drink anything for the purpose of bringing glory to God? What was the reason for which you fasted?
- Have you ever fasted? If not, why? Do you think the Lord mentions fasting without purpose or do you think He truly desires for His people to fast?

Prayer Thoughts

- Ask the Lord to give you the courage to fast for Him.
- Ask God to teach you the benefits of fasting.

SONG: *FROM EVERY EARTHLY PLEASURE*

Day 80: (Tuesday)
Fasting Not Optional

*Matthew 6:16 Moreover **when ye fast**, be not, as the hypocrites, of a sad countenance: for they disfigure their faces, that they may appear unto men to fast. Verily I say unto you, They have their reward.*

Introductory Thoughts

Fasting should play a prominent role in the life of a Christian. Just as believers ought to pray, witness, study, and give, we should also fast. In fact, the Lord's words assumed the Christian would fast when He said, *"when ye fast" (Matthew 6:16)*, not IF ye fast. The question was never to be whether or not we would fast, but how we would do so *"when"* we fast. Fasting was not prominent among the disciples, but the Lord explained that His departure would signify an elevated need for fasting *(Mark 2:20)*. The life of the apostle Paul confirmed this as he said he was *"in fastings often" (2 Corinthians 11:27)*. It was a common practice of Paul's devotion to the Lord to deprive his flesh of food, drink, and physical pleasures. The Lord not only desired for the early believers to fast, but His people ought to have times of fasting until He returns.

DEVOTIONAL THOUGHTS

- **(For children):** Many people throughout the Bible fasted: Jesus, Moses, Elijah (40 days); Daniel (21 days); Paul, prisoners, Roman troops (14 days); David (7 days); and Esther, Saul (3 days). The Bible offers no set number of days to fast. You as a child might start by giving up a snack. Never fast without your parents' approval and guidance.
- **(For everyone):** Some of the most difficult facets of the Christian life are those that oppose the desires of the flesh directly. In what ways does fasting resist the desires of the flesh?
- What would be your opinion of a Christian who wouldn't pray, read the Bible, or give? What should be our opinion of a Christian who wouldn't fast?

PRAYER THOUGHTS

- Ask the Lord to help you deny your flesh.
- Ask the Lord to help you obey Him in the matter of fasting.

SONG: *TRUST AND OBEY*

Day 81: Church Night

Psalm 35:13 But as for me, when they were sick, my clothing was sackcloth: I humbled my soul with fasting; and my prayer returned into mine own bosom.

Day 82: (Thursday)
Fastings' Proper Motive

Zechariah 7:5 Speak unto all the people of the land, and to the priests, saying, **When ye fasted** *and mourned in the fifth and seventh* month, *even those seventy years,* **did ye at all fast unto me,** **even** **to** **me?**

INTRODUCTORY THOUGHTS

As recorded in Zechariah, the people of God came to the Lord desiring to know if they should continue weeping and fasting as they had done for many years. In response, the Lord asked the people if they ever really fasted UNTO Him. In other words, were they fasting for simply prideful reasons, to be seen of men, or really fasting unto the Lord? The motive of fasting is also addressed in Matthew chapter 6. Christians should never fast in order to please men or to draw praise and attention to themselves. Fasting should be a private matter between the believer and the Lord. The benefits gained by fasting are lost when the motives are improper or impure. Those behaving hypocritically will ensure that people know they are fasting, desiring the praise of men; whereas, the truly humble seek only to please the Lord.

DEVOTIONAL THOUGHTS

- **(For children):** Biblical fasting is a decision by a person to go without food and physical pleasures for a set period of time. It lets God know that the person wants to draw closer to Him and is concerned enough to take this important step. The person should talk to God often during the time of the fast.
- **(For everyone):** Why do you fast? When you fast, do you hope that others will find out and praise you for your devotion to the Lord? Why do you think this is so?
- What is the proper motive for fasting? What are some reasons why we might fast? How can we ensure that we fast for the right reasons? Remember, it is not wrong for people to find out that you are fasting; it is wrong for you to use the fast as a means for serving your flesh in any way.

PRAYER THOUGHTS

- Ask the Lord to help your motives to be pure.
- Ask the Lord to help you avoid the actions of a hypocrite.

SONG: *MY JESUS, I LOVE THEE*

Day 83: (Friday)
The Times for Fasting

*Ecclesiastes 3:1 To every thing **there is** a season, and **a time to every purpose under the heaven:***

INTRODUCTORY THOUGHTS

Fasting, similar to other actions in life, has specific purposes and appointed times. The Bible offers various reasons why people might fast: an immediate need in prayer *(2 Samuel 12:16)*, a need to loosen the bands of wickedness or undo heavy burdens *(Isaiah 58:6)*, during times of elevated conflict or duty in service *(Matthew 17:21; Acts 13:3)*, as a symbol of mourning *(2 Samuel 1:12)*, and as an outward manifestation of true repentance *(Jonah 3:5)*. This list is not exhaustive, but simply demonstrates that God's people have many good reasons for fasting. Even if none of these circumstances surfaces in our lives, we should fast because we know that the Lord expects us to do so.

DEVOTIONAL THOUGHTS

- **(For children)**: Notice these many examples of real people who fasted for certain reasons. Hannah prayed and fasted for God to give her a son. (Note the wording in *1 Samuel 1:8-10, 18*.) Jehoshaphat and all Judah fasted and prayed when afraid of a powerful enemy *(2 Chronicles 20:1-4)*. David fasted for sick people *(Psalm 35:13)*.
- **(For everyone)**: What are some reasons why you might fast? Do you have some particular sin that constantly troubles you? Do you have an immediate need in prayer? If so, are you willing to fast?
- Fasting is a very real way to deny our flesh and show the Lord how serious we are about Him and His word. In what ways could fasting increase our strength for service?

PRAYER THOUGHTS

- Ask God to show you reasons why you should fast.
- Ask the Lord to give you the strength to obey Him.

SONG: *TAKE TIME TO BE HOLY*

Day 84: (Saturday)
Fasting Afflicts the Soul

Ezra 8:21 Then I proclaimed a fast there, at the river of Ahava, that we might afflict ourselves before our God, to seek of him a right way for us, and for our little ones, and for all our substance.

INTRODUCTORY THOUGHTS

Most Christians would consider biblical fasting a very unpleasant undertaking. Considering the complexities of the affliction offered by fasting might better help to understand its value. In our passage, the people of God determined to fast so that they might afflict themselves before the Lord. Several other passages discuss this affliction in even more detail. *Isaiah 58:3* and *5* describes the affliction as not merely an affliction of the flesh, but also an affliction of the soul. Additionally, we learn that fasting *humbles (Psalm 35:13)* and *chastens (Psalm 69:10)* the soul. Fasting involves much more than merely opposition to one's flesh. Fasting directly *afflicts, chastens,* and *humbles* the soul. Perhaps this is why it is so difficult to fast and so beneficial to do so.

DEVOTIONAL THOUGHTS

- **(For children):** The Devil tested Jesus most when He was in the middle of a long fast. Afterward, Jesus was hungry and the Devil tried three more times to get Him to do wrong *(Luke 4:1-2)*. Fasting is not pleasant, and the Devil does not want us to fast because it brings us closer to God.
- **(For everyone):** If fasting is so important, why do so few Christians fast? Is it possible that the Devil and our flesh oppose it because of its worth and value in the work of God?
- With all of the evidence presented, do you still find yourself offering "reasons" as to why you cannot fast? What do you think is the real root of the problem?

PRAYER THOUGHTS
- Ask the Lord to show you the spiritual benefits of fasting.
- Ask God to give you the necessary faith to obey Him in fasting.

SONG: *IF THOU BUT SUFFER GOD TO GUIDE THEE*

Notes: _____

_____

_____

_____

_____

_____

_____

_____

_____

_____

_____

Quotes from the next volume

(VOLUME 3, WEEK 12)

Subject: Contention (con't)

In a world filled with competition and pride, it seems as though the peacemaker is such because he cannot handle the fight. Once again, it becomes painfully obvious that God and man are complete opposites.

In the Christian warfare, there are times where strife is both necessary and right. There are things for which preachers, teachers, moms and dads, and young people need to take a stand even if taking a stand brings about conflict.

13

Fear

Fear—found 524 times in 501 verses

Variations: fear, feared, fearest, feareth, fearful, fearfully, fearfulness, fearing, fears

First usage: *Genesis 9:2* (fear)

Last usage: *Revelation 21:8* (fearful)

Defined: being afraid or uneasiness brought on by possible danger

Interesting fact: The phrase *fear not* appears sixty-two times in scripture. The first occurrence is when *"the word of the LORD came unto Abram in a vision, saying, **Fear not,** Abram: I am thy shield, and thy exceeding great reward" (**Genesis 15:1**)*. The last occurrence of *fear not* occurs when John, the beloved, saw Jesus Christ and *"fell at his feet as dead."* Christ *"laid his right hand upon"* John, and said unto him, *"**Fear not;** I am the first and the last: I am he that liveth, and was dead; and, behold, I am alive for evermore, Amen; and have the keys of hell and of death" (**Revelation 1:17-18**)*. With the word of God and Jesus Christ, the Christian has nothing to fear.

Bible study tip: The Bible contains no contradictions. When two verses or concepts seem contradictory, the Bible student must consider the varying contexts which account for the supposed contradiction. For instance, **Proverbs 26:4-5** says, *"**Answer not** a fool according to his folly, lest thou also be like unto him. **Answer** a fool according to his folly, lest he be wise in his own conceit."* Obviously, there are times to answer a fool and other times to refuse to answer a fool.

Sunday, Day 85—Church Day (no devotional)
Monday, Day 86—*What Is Fear?*
Tuesday, Day 87—*Do Not Fear What the World Fears*
Wednesday, Day 88—Church Night (no devotional)
Thursday, Day 89—*The Whole Duty of Man*
Friday, Day 90—*The Relationship of Fear and Faith*
Saturday, Day 91—*Godly Fear Yields Service*

Day 85: Church Day

*Psalm 27:1 The LORD is my light and my salvation; **whom shall I fear?** the LORD is the strength of my life; **of whom shall I be afraid?***

Day 86: (Monday)
What Is Fear?

*Psalm 119:120 My flesh trembleth **for fear of thee**; and **I am afraid** of thy judgments.*

INTRODUCTORY THOUGHTS

The Bible refers to both a godly and ungodly fear. The two fears will not and cannot coexist. *Godly* fear pertains to the healthy fear involving fearing the Lord *(Isaiah 8:13)*; however, *ungodly* fear pertains to fearing the things of this world *(Isaiah 8:12)*. Ungodly fear opposes faith and can grievously effect a person *(Job 4:14; Job 22:10; Psalm 48:6; 1 John 4:18)*, but the fear of the Lord is founded upon faith and provides confidence and assurance. The fear of this world brings torment upon its victims, yet the fear of the Lord prolongs life *(Proverbs 10:27)*. Not surprisingly, the world thrives on triggering ungodly fears, especially its entertainment and news programs. God's people should avoid the worldly and major on the fear of the Lord.

DEVOTIONAL THOUGHTS

- **(For children):** To fear something is to be afraid of it. Memorize **Psalm 56:3** and quote it when you are afraid. Also, try singing songs like *"Jesus Loves Me."* Always remember that we are weak but *"He is strong."*
- **(For everyone):** What causes you to fear? Are you afraid of the dark, of people, of death, or of possible troubles? How does this fear generally affect you? Do your fears cause you to draw closer to the Lord?
- What are some differences between the fear of God and ungodly fears? How does each fear change your life? Which one is pleasing to the Lord and why is it pleasing to Him?

PRAYER THOUGHTS

- Ask the Lord to give you the faith to overcome the fears of this world.
- Ask God to give you a holy fear of Himself.

SONG: *ABLE TO DELIVER*

Day 87: (Tuesday)
Do Not Fear What the World Fears

*Isaiah 8:12 Say ye not, A confederacy, to all them to whom this people shall say, A confederacy; **neither fear ye their fear**, nor be afraid.*

13 Sanctify the LORD of hosts himself; and let him be your fear, and let him be your dread.

INTRODUCTORY THOUGHTS

Fear introduced is faith attacked. As such, we should not be partakers of the world's fears. Instead, we should *"sanctify the LORD of hosts himself; and let him be"* our fear *(Isaiah 8:13)*. Throughout scripture, the Lord admonished His people not to fear the world. Why? The answer is twofold: (1) the Lord was with them *(Genesis 26:24)* and (2) fear of the world yields bondage *(Proverbs 29:25)*. This worldly bondage never originates with the Lord *(Romans 8:15)* for He has given Christians a sound mind *(2 Timothy 1:7)*. We need not fear those who can destroy the body *(Matthew 10:28)*; rather, we ought to say the Lord is our helper, and we will not fear what men will do unto us *(Hebrews 13:6)*.

DEVOTIONAL THOUGHTS

- **(For children):** Read *1 Samuel 17:11, 24, 32, 37*. King Saul and all Israel were afraid of Goliath the giant. Only David trusted God. He remembered how God had helped him before when he was keeping sheep.
- **(For everyone):** What are some things that the world fears? Are those fears based upon faith? Do you share in any of those fears? If so, do you think that your fear pleases or displeases the Lord?
- Do your fears keep you from serving the Lord? Fears that keep you from serving the Lord cannot come from Him.

PRAYER THOUGHTS

- Ask God to give you boldness to serve Him.
- Ask the Lord to help you choose the right fears.

SONG: *NEVER BE AFRAID*

Day 88: Church Night

Isaiah 41:10 Fear thou not; for I am with thee: be not dismayed; for I am thy God: I will strengthen thee; yea, I will help thee; yea, I will uphold thee with the right hand of my righteousness.

Day 89: (Thursday)
The Whole Duty of Man

Ecclesiastes 12:13 Let us hear the conclusion of the whole matter: Fear God, and keep his commandments: for this is the whole duty of man.

INTRODUCTORY THOUGHTS

Learning to fear the Lord yields great results in our daily walk with Him. Some facets of man's relationship with the Lord change over time and through the seasons. Yet, one thing that has remained constant from the very beginning concerns God's call upon His people to fear Him. How vital is the fear of God? The Bible refers to it as *"the whole duty of man."* Some Bible teachers have tried to lessen the severity of this truth by saying that this fear merely refers to reverencing God, yet **Hebrews 12:28** presents the fear of God and reverence as two separate and distinct actions. God's people are to fear the Lord as the Creator of all things and the One who will one day bring all things into judgment. As saints of God, we will never please the Lord until we first learn to fear Him *(Deuteronomy 4:10)*.

DEVOTIONAL THOUGHTS

- **(For children):** When Adam and Eve broke God's rule, they were afraid *(Genesis 3:8-11)*. God forgave them, but they had to leave their beautiful garden and life became very difficult. We should fear God and keep His rules because He knows what is best for us.
- **(For everyone):** Why should we fear the Lord? How could the fear of the Lord affect our walk with Him? How could it change the decisions that we make on a daily basis?
- Why does God desire for us to fear Him? Why is He worthy of our fear? How could fear of God keep us from trouble? How could it lead us into righteousness?

PRAYER THOUGHTS

- Ask the Lord to teach you how to fear Him.
- Ask the Lord to use godly fear to shield you from troubles.

SONG: *LORD OF OUR LIFE, GOD WHOM WE FEAR*

Day 90: (Friday)
The Relationship of Fear and Faith

Exodus 20:20 And Moses said unto the people, **Fear not:** *for God is come to prove you, and* **that his fear may be before your faces,** *that ye sin not.*

INTRODUCTORY THOUGHTS

A cursory read of today's passage might lead someone to believe that it contains a glaring contradiction. Yet, the passage simply makes a distinction between the two main kinds of fear, the fear of man and the fear of God. God instructs His people not to fear the things of the world so that they might know the fear of the Lord. Each of these fears reflects the level of faith. A fear of the world reflects an absence of faith. It further reveals a lack of trust in God to provide or take care of the believer. The Lord warned His people to overcome the fears of this world based upon His own presence *(Genesis 15:1)*. Yet, the fear of the Lord is founded strictly upon faith. Those who fear the Lord trust in Him *(Psalm 115:11)*.

DEVOTIONAL THOUGHTS

- **(For children)**: Abraham had great faith in God. God asked him to do a hard thing—to give up his only son when God promised to make a great nation from him. Abraham still believed God *(Hebrews 11:19)*, and God knew Abraham feared Him above all things *(Genesis 22:12)*.
- **(For everyone)**: In what ways would faith cause us to fear the Lord? How could faith be connected to fearing the Lord? What are some things in the Bible that ought to cause us to fear Him?
- What promises has the Lord given us about His watch care? How would faith in these promises keep us from fearing the world and its fears?

PRAYER THOUGHTS

- Ask the Lord to give you the faith to fear Him.
- Ask Him to strengthen your faith to overcome fear of the world.

SONG: *FEAR NOT*

Day 91: (Saturday)
Godly Fear Yields Service

*Joshua 24:14 Now therefore **fear the LORD, and serve him in sincerity and in truth**: and put away the gods which your fathers served on the other side of the flood, and in Egypt; and serve ye the LORD.*

INTRODUCTORY THOUGHTS

The connection of fear and service cannot be missed. Worldly fear brings bondage and hinders Christian service; yet godly fear encourages the believer to serve the Lord in righteousness. In our passage, fear is yoked together with truthful and sincere service. Three different verses in 1 Samuel chapter 12 make the same connection *(1 Samuel 12:14, 20, 24)*. In **Psalm 2:11**, we are admonished to *"serve the Lord with fear, and rejoice with trembling."* According to **Hebrews 12:28**, we should *"serve God acceptably with reverence and godly fear."* The fear of the Lord points forward to a time of judgment and reward. A man who refuses to fear God will never serve God with a sincere heart and pure motives.

DEVOTIONAL THOUGHTS

- **(For children)**: Even though Noah had never seen rain, he feared the judgment of God that was coming upon a wicked world through a great flood. He obeyed God and built an ark to save himself and his family *(Hebrews 11:7)*.
- **(For everyone)**: Why would someone who does not fear the Lord be hindered in his service to the Lord? How is fear a good motivator in our service for God?
- Do you serve the Lord out of a pure and sincere heart? If not, could it be because you do not fear the Lord as you ought to fear Him?

PRAYER THOUGHTS

- Ask the Lord to remind you of the judgment to come.
Ask God to help you to serve Him with fear.

SONG: *ANYWHERE WITH JESUS*

Notes: _____

_____

_____

_____

_____

_____

_____

_____

_____

_____

Notes: _____

_____

_____

_____

_____

_____

_____

_____

_____

_____

_____

_____

_____

_____

_____

_____

_____

Quotes from the next volume

(VOLUME 3, WEEK 13)

Subject: Envy

If a man spends his time envying the wicked, he will eventually travel the direction that he once envied.

Long before an individual outwardly turns from righteousness to worldliness, he does so in his mind without restraint.

Those who refuse to repent of envy will ultimately lead themselves into a spiritual death.

14

Fellowship

Fellowship—found seventeen times in sixteen verses

Variations: fellowship

First usage: *Leviticus 6:2*

Last usage: *1 John 1:7*

Defined: two or more people uniting to accomplish a task

Interesting fact: The Bible incorporates many compound words utilizing the word *fellow*. Fellow is compounded into new words such as *fellowservant(s)* *(Matthew 18:28-29)*, *fellowsdisciples* *(John 11:16)*, *fellowprisoners* *(Romans 16:7)*, *workfellow* *(Romans 16:21)*, *fellowhelper(s)* *(2 Corinthians 8:23; 3 John 8)*, *fellowcitizens* *(Ephesians 2:19)*, *fellowheirs* *(Ephesians 3:6)*, *fellowsoldier* *(Philippians 2:25)*, *fellowlabourer(s)* *(Philippians 4:3; 1 Thessalonians 3:2)*, *fellowworkers* *(Colossians 4:11)*, and even *yokefellow* *(Philippians 4:3)*.

Bible study tip: When seeking a Bible definition for a word, consider other words within a verse that shed light on your word. For instance, to help define the word *fellowship*, the phrase *yoked together* and the word *communion* are combined in a single verse. *"Be ye not unequally **yoked together** with unbelievers: for what **fellowship** hath righteousness with unrighteousness? and what **communion** hath light with darkness?" (2 Corinthians 6:14).* Fellowship entails being *yoked together* and being in *communion* with someone.

Sunday, Day 92—Church Day (no devotional)
Monday, Day 93—*What Is Fellowship?*
Tuesday, Day 94—*Continuing in Fellowship*
Wednesday, Day 95—Church Night (no devotional)
Thursday, Day 96—*Offering the Right Hand of Fellowship*
Friday, Day 97—*No Fellowship with Darkness*
Saturday, Day 98—*Fellowship with the Lord*

Day 92: Church Day

*1 Corinthians 1:9 God is faithful, by whom **ye were called unto the fellowship of his Son** Jesus Christ our Lord.*

Day 93: (Monday)
What Is Fellowship?

*Leviticus 6:2 If a soul sin, and commit a trespass against the LORD, and lie unto his neighbour in that which was delivered him to keep, **or in fellowship**, or in a thing taken away by violence, or hath deceived his neighbour;*

INTRODUCTORY THOUGHTS

The modern description of *fellowship* has been weakened extensively from its original intent. Earlier usage of *fellowship* always inferred a partnership. The word *fellow* was used to signify a coworker in *Exodus 2:13* and each of the various combinations designated something that people did together (i.e., *fellowservants, fellowhelpers, fellowlabours,* etc.). Therefore, it is important to realize that *fellowship* is not merely two people or a group of people coming together in the name of fun. Fellowship involves two or more people uniting together to accomplish a task. *Fellowship* always suggests a foundational unity of purpose and motive *(Amos 3:3)*. This is why, as we will learn, it is so important that we have the proper biblical fellowship with like-minded believers.

DEVOTIONAL THOUGHTS

- **(For children):** Christian fellowship involves working together with those who love the Lord to accomplish the work of God. Some examples include a work day at church, visiting the sick, making cards, delivering a meal, telling others about the Lord, praying, etc. Children can do these things with other believers.
- **(For everyone):** With what type of people do you find yourself in closest fellowship? Do their motives for Christian service align with the Bible? What goals do you have in common? What does your fellowship express concerning your spiritual condition?
- What are some reasons that our fellowship is important? What are some things we ought to consider when yoking together with other people in fellowship?

PRAYER THOUGHTS

- Ask the Lord to help you see the importance of godly fellowship.
- Ask the Lord to teach you the true meaning of fellowship.

SONG: WE'LL WORK TILL JESUS COMES

Day 94: (Tuesday)
Continuing in Fellowship

*Acts 2:42 And **they continued stedfastly in the apostles' doctrine and fellowship**, and in breaking of bread, and in prayers.*

INTRODUCTORY THOUGHTS

It is much easier to serve God together with others rather than alone. There is great wisdom attained through the right kind of fellowship with other like-minded believers. When one believer wavers during times of temptation, his *"fellow"* believers will encourage him to stay faithful to the Lord's work. When one of the saints struggles in times of uncertainty, his fellow believers can remind him of God's faithfulness. The Bible shows us that the early church thrived in the Lord's work. Those early Christians served the Lord with a great zeal. The secret to their success most definitely included their continuation in fellowship and incorporating some basic principles. For instance, the Lord Jesus sent out His disciples by twos *(Mark 6:7)* and the early church followed suit *(Acts 13:2)*. God has given us a great insight into the importance of fellowship by emphasizing it so frequently.

DEVOTIONAL THOUGHTS

- **(For children)**: The walls around the city of Jerusalem had been broken down and the gates burned. Nehemiah worked with a group of people to rebuild those walls and repair the gates. Even with many enemies trying to discourage the work, the walls were finished in fifty-two days. When we work together, much more work can be accomplished.
- **(For everyone)**: What are some of the dangers of seeking to serve the Lord alone? In what ways can it be helpful to serve God with other believers? How can our results be multiplied by serving with others?
- With whom are you fellowshipping most? Do they make you a better servant of the Lord? How do you encourage them to be better servants?

PRAYER THOUGHTS

- Ask God to give you some good people with whom to fellowship.
- Ask the Lord to help you continue in the right fellowship.

SONG: *MY CHRISTIAN FRIENDS IN BONDS OF LOVE*

Day 95: Church Night

*Philippians 3:10 **That I may know him**, and the power of his resurrection, **and the fellowship of his sufferings**, being made conformable unto his death;*

Day 96: (Thursday)
Offering the Right Hand of Fellowship

*Galatians 2:9 And when James, Cephas, and John, who seemed to be pillars, perceived the grace that was given unto me, **they gave** to me and Barnabas **the right hands of fellowship**; that we should go unto the heathen, and they unto the circumcision.*

INTRODUCTORY THOUGHTS

Most churchgoers are familiar with what it means to extend the *"the right hand of fellowship"*; however, the actual biblical meaning is not so well known. Our passage shows James, Cephas (Peter), and John offering *"the right hands of fellowship"* to Paul and Barnabas. What was the significance of this act? By giving the right hands of fellowship, these believers were agreeing to serve God together. James, Cephas, and John would focus on reaching the Jewish people (the circumcision), while Paul and Barnabas would focus on reaching the Gentiles (the uncircumcision). When we offer someone the right hand of fellowship, we are agreeing to serve God with that believer.

DEVOTIONAL THOUGHTS

- **(For children):** *1 Timothy 5:1-2* tells us that our church is a family. When people join the church, we are to love them as family *(1 John 4:21)*. As family, we should pray for them, encourage them, warn them, help them, and work together with them to serve God.
- **(For everyone):** When people join the church, members are invited to come forward and offer the new members the right hand of fellowship. What does this suggest? What are you agreeing to when you give the right hand of fellowship?
- What are some times that would be appropriate to extend the right hand of fellowship? How can this be encouraging to both parties in their service to the Lord?

PRAYER THOUGHTS

- Ask God to show you the importance of serving God with others.
- Ask the Lord to give you godly people with whom to serve.

SONG: *THE UNITY OF THE SPIRIT*

Day 97: (Friday)
No Fellowship with Darkness

*Ephesians 5:11 And **have no fellowship with the unfruitful works of darkness**, but rather reprove them.*

INTRODUCTORY THOUGHTS

The importance of fellowship cannot be underestimated, but neither can the importance of refusing to fellowship. It is important to fellowship with the right people, but also equally important that we *"have no fellowship with the unfruitful works of darkness."* The people of God have no business yoking together with the world in any work of God no matter how beneficial the help might seem. Fellowship suggests an agreement amongst the involved parties. Yet, **2 Corinthians 6:14** drives home the point when it says, *"Be ye not unequally yoked together with unbelievers: for what fellowship hath righteousness with unrighteousness? and what communion hath light with darkness?"* When we fellowship with carnal believers or the unsaved, we accept their motives and objectives as our own.

DEVOTIONAL THOUGHTS

- **(For children):** God wants us to choose good friends with whom to serve Him *(Psalm 119:63)*. He knows we need their help. We have a part of us that loves to do wrong, and choosing the wrong friends will cause us to do the very things of which God disapproves *(Proverbs 28:7b)*. Remember Solomon's failings *(1 Kings 11:4, 9)*.
- **(For everyone):** What are some areas where fellowship with carnal believers or the unsaved could be harmful? Do you have fellowship with those people in these areas? What should you do?
- Why is it important that we have no fellowship with the unfruitful works of darkness? What should we do to separate ourselves from ungodly works?

PRAYER THOUGHTS

- Ask the Lord to give you wisdom in fellowship.
- Ask God to yoke you together with the right people.

SONG: *NOTHING BETWEEN*

Day 98: (Saturday)
Fellowship with the Lord

*1 John 1:3 That which we have seen and heard declare we unto you, that ye also may have fellowship with us: and **truly our fellowship is with the Father, and with his Son Jesus Christ**.*

INTRODUCTORY THOUGHTS

A yoke was an instrument used to help two animals work together when plowing. The Lord Jesus said that believers should take His yoke upon them *(Matthew 11:29)*. In other words, the Lord was saying that we should serve with Him in our service to Him. In *1 Corinthians 3:9*, we learn that *"we are labourers together with God."* Fellowshipping with the Lord means walking with Him *(1 John 1:6-7)*, and walking with Him means being in agreement with Him *(Amos 3:3)*. Just as God desired to fellowship with Adam *(Genesis 3:8)* and Enoch *(Genesis 5:22)*, He desires to have fellowship with us today. It is very important that we have fellowship with other like-minded believers, but even more important that we fellowship with the Lord.

DEVOTIONAL THOUGHTS

- **(For children)**: The Lord made everything *(Nehemiah 9:6)* simply by speaking things into existence *(Hebrews 11:3)*. He knows all about us, even to the number of hairs on our head. The Lord said men ought *"always to pray,"* and Paul said to *"pray without ceasing."* It's wonderful that the Lord wants us to talk to Him *(1 Peter 3:12)*.
- **(For everyone)**: Why would God desire to fellowship with His creation? Is fellowship more beneficial to the Lord or to us? What does this say about the personality of the Lord?
- What areas of our lives should be based upon fellowship with the Lord? What are some areas in which we can know Him better by fellowship (hint: see *Philippians 3:10*)?

PRAYER THOUGHTS

- Ask the Lord to help you walk with Him.
- Ask God to show you the importance of fellowshipping with Him.

SONG: *DRAW ME NEARER*

Notes: _____

_____

_____

_____

_____

_____

_____

Notes: _____

_____

_____

_____

_____

_____

_____

_____

_____

_____

_____

_____

_____

_____

Quotes from the next volume

(VOLUME 3, WEEK 14)

Subject: Envy (con't)

Merciful moments might be displayed during times of anger and wrath, but envy will continue to relentlessly pursue its victim without mercy.

As the fame of Paul's message increased, so did the opposition from the religious leaders of his day. Because of the success of the gospel, many of the Jews were filled with envy and began contradicting and blaspheming Paul's message.

The Bible often speaks of sin as a thing of the past as it pertains to believers. This is not because believers never sin, but the goal of every believer should be to depart from and avoid the sins which controlled his life prior to salvation.

15

Flattery

Flattery—found twenty-one times in twenty-one verses

Variations: flatter, flattereth, flatteries, flattering, flattery

First usage: *Job 17:5* (flattery)

Last usage: *1 Thessalonians 2:5* (flattering)

Defined: dishonest praise, or accurate praise with an impure motive

Interesting fact: The word *flattery* (in its various forms) appears more often in Daniel chapter 11 than in any other chapter *(Daniel 11:21, 32, 34)*. This method of dishonest praise will be the means by which the Antichrist will obtain his kingdom during the tribulation *(Daniel 11:21, 32)*. It is not surprising that the New Testament says his coming is *"after the working of Satan with all power and signs and **lying wonders" (2 Thessalonians 2:9)*.

Bible study tip: The Bible was not written to merely provide knowledge, even if the knowledge is doctrinal in nature. Genuine Bible study leads to the practical application of the learned truths. Study the Bible with the intention of becoming more conformed to its scriptural admonitions.

The more one conforms to scripture, the more this yields additional Bible knowledge because the Lord manifests Himself to you. *"He that hath my commandments, and keepeth them, he it is that loveth me: and he that loveth me shall be loved of my Father, and **I will love him, and will manifest myself to him**" (John 14:21).*

Sunday, Day 99—Church Day (no devotional)
Monday, Day 100—*What Is Flattery?*
Tuesday, Day 101—*Flattering Lips Shall Be Cut Off*
Wednesday, Day 102—Church Night (no devotional)
Thursday, Day 103—*A Flattering Tongue Causes Ruin*
Friday, Day 104—*Rebuke Better than Flattery*
Saturday, Day 105—*Flattering Titles*

Day 99: Church Day

*Proverbs 7:4 Say unto **wisdom**, Thou art my sister; **and** call **understanding** thy kinswoman:*

*5 That they may **keep thee** from the strange woman, **from the stranger which flattereth with her words**.*

Day 100: (Monday)
What Is Flattery?

*Psalm 5:9 For there is no faithfulness in their mouth; their inward part is very wickedness; their throat is an open sepulchre; **they flatter with their tongue**.*

INTRODUCTORY THOUGHTS

The New Testament frequently incorporates minor word variations when quoting Old Testament passages. Some Bible critics have pointed to these variations suggesting that the Bible contains contradictions. However, Bible-believing students know that these variations actually provide additional light and understanding of God's word. For example, **Romans 3:13** quotes **Psalm 5:9** with the variation in wording shedding light on the meaning of the word *flattery*. The phrase from Psalms reads *"they flatter with their tongue" (Psalm 5:9).* Romans modifies this Old Testament quotation by stating that *"with their tongues they have used deceit" (Romans 3:13).* This indicates that *flattery* involves the use of deceitful words; and according to **1 Thessalonians 2:5**, the motive is often connected to covetousness.

DEVOTIONAL THOUGHTS

- **(For children):** It is good to praise someone with the right intention. However, flattery involves saying something nice to someone when your heart feels otherwise *(Psalm 55:21)*. For example, Judas greeted Jesus with a friendly greeting along with a kiss, but his intentions were deceitful *(Matthew 26:47-49)*.
- **(For everyone):** Sometimes people say things that they don't mean to other people in order to get something from them. At other times, people will stretch the truth hoping to receive some personal benefit. What are some examples of this?
- What are some subtle ways in which we might use flattery to get what we want? How can these subtle beginnings lead to much more serious situations?

PRAYER THOUGHTS

- Ask the Lord to teach you the dangers of flattery.
- Ask God to show you when you are using flattery.

SONG: *I SURRENDER ALL*

Day 101: (Tuesday)
Flattering Lips Shall Be Cut Off

Psalm 12:1 Help, LORD; for the godly man ceaseth; for the faithful fail from among the children of men.

*2 They speak vanity every one with his neighbour: **with flattering lips and with a double heart do they speak.***

*3 **The LORD shall cut off all flattering lips**, and the tongue that speaketh proud things:*

4 Who have said, With our tongue will we prevail; our lips are our own: who is lord over us?

INTRODUCTORY THOUGHTS

If you have trusted the Lord Jesus Christ as your Saviour, you are no longer appointed to God's wrath *(1 Thessalonians 5:9)*; however, it helps to fully understand God's hatred for sin. By understanding sin from God's viewpoint, we can seek to emulate His love for righteousness while never abandoning His abhorrence of wickedness. In the days of king David, the Bible tells us that every man spoke vanity with his neighbour *(Psalm 12:2)*. Men spoke with a double heart and with flattering lips *(Psalm 12:2)*. They claimed that their lips were their own and that they possessed freedom to spew forth anything they chose to say *(Psalm 12:4)*. God promised to rise up in judgment and *"cut off all flattering lips" (Psalm 12:3)*.

DEVOTIONAL THOUGHTS

- **(For children):** Absalom stole the hearts of the men of Israel by telling them that if he were king, he would help them with their problems. In his heart, Absalom knew he was only trying to win their love so that they would help him steal the throne from David, his father. God stopped him from doing this evil *(2 Samuel 18:9)*.
- **(For everyone):** Why do you suppose that we so often love to do the things that God hates? How can we learn to love what God loves and hate what He hates? Why is this so very important?
- Do you ever find the pride of *Psalm 12:4* rising up within your own heart? Do you think that God has no right to tell you what you can or cannot say? Do not forget that judgment is inevitable and will soon come!

PRAYER THOUGHTS

- Ask God to show you His hatred for flattering tongues.
- Ask the Lord to show you the pride of flattery.

SONG: STOP, POOR SINNER! STOP AND THINK

Day 102: Church Night

*1 Thessalonians 2:5 For **neither at any time used we flattering words**, as ye know, nor a cloke of covetousness; God is witness:*

Day 103: (Thursday)
A Flattering Tongue Causes Ruin

Proverbs 26:28 *A lying tongue hateth* those that are *afflicted by it;* and *a flattering mouth worketh ruin.*

INTRODUCTORY THOUGHTS

Biblical terminology is very important. For example, ignorance of Bible vocabulary has led people to believe that flattery is considerate if it makes others feel good. Yet, the picture presented by scripture is contrary to this line of thinking. Flattery harms both the giver and the recipient. According to scripture, *"A lying tongue hateth those that are afflicted by it; and a flattering mouth worketh ruin"* **(Proverbs 26:28)**. While we have been led to believe flattery edifies, in reality, it destroys. This truth is confirmed in **Proverbs 29:5** where the Bible says, *"A man that flattereth his neighbour spreadeth a net for his feet."* Even the flatterer is harmed by his flattery: *"He that speaketh flattery to his friends, even the eyes of his children shall fail"* **(Job 17:5)**. Without a doubt, flattery harms all those involved.

DEVOTIONAL THOUGHTS

- **(For children):** The presidents and princes in Daniel's day directed flattering words to king Darius that convinced him to sign a law that couldn't be changed *(Daniel 6:3-9)*. This flattery hurt the king when he had to have Daniel cast into a den of lions. Fortunately, God saved Daniel, and the evil men were cast to the lions.
- **(For everyone):** What are some ways in which a person could be harmed by being flattered? How could flattery set that person up for pride and false confidence?
- How does flattery work to destroy when it appears to build a person up? What are some examples of how this works?

PRAYER THOUGHTS

- Ask the Lord to show you how harmful flattery can be.
- Ask God to protect you from both sides of flattery.

SONG: *HIDE THOU ME!*

Day 104: (Friday)
Rebuke Better than Flattery

*Proverbs 28:23 He that **rebuketh a man** afterwards shall find **more favour than** he that flattereth with the tongue.*

INTRODUCTORY THOUGHTS

Today's passage proves the Bible truth that our thoughts are not God's thoughts, neither our ways His ways *(Isaiah 55:8-9)*. God's thoughts are always unimaginably loftier than ours. Unlike God, our thoughts are bound by our limited knowledge. Contrary to the Lord's, our knowledge is easily corrupted through various influences. This is why scripture reading and preaching often conflicts with our natural thought process. For instance, our natural mind considers rebuke something harmful, negatively affecting the person receiving it. We also naturally consider flattery as something beneficial and uplifting to the recipient. Yet, we have already seen how flattery can be harmful, but have you ever considered the superiority of a rebuke? The Bible says rebuke is better because of what it yields *"afterwards."* In the long run, rebuke is far superior to flattery.

DEVOTIONAL THOUGHTS

- **(For children):** The prophet Nathan did not enjoy telling king David that he had sinned *(2 Samuel 12:7)*. Yet, David had been miserable hiding his sin and felt better once he had confessed it to God *(Psalm 32:1-5)*. Though Nathan rebuked David, David continued to love Nathan *(Psalm 141:5)*.
- **(For everyone):** How do you feel when you have to rebuke someone? How do you feel when you use your tongue to flatter someone? What does this teach us concerning our feelings and their connection to right and wrong?
- A godly rebuke presents the reality of our condition. Flattery, on the other hand, presents a deceitful view of our condition. Knowing this, how can a rebuke be so superior in the long run?

PRAYER THOUGHTS

- Ask the Lord to help you consider what is best over the long term.
- Ask God to give you wisdom to choose rebuke over flattery.

SONG: *SINCE YE ARE NOT YOUR OWN*

Day 105: (Saturday)
Flattering Titles

Job 32:21 *Let me not, I pray you, accept any man's person, **neither let me give flattering titles unto man.***

*22 For **I know not to give flattering titles**; in so doing my maker would soon take me away.*

INTRODUCTORY THOUGHTS

The Book of Job primarily focuses on the conversations between Job and his three friends. The content of many of their speeches seems to lack the expected wisdom until a younger man named Elihu takes the opportunity to speak. His words were packed with wisdom. One of the areas he addressed concerned giving flattering titles to men. Elihu declared that it was sinful to give men flattering titles and that he knew better than to do so. Keep in mind that flattery is based upon deceit and is never favourable. By refusing to give flattering titles to men, Elihu chose not to say anything concerning others simply to gain an advantage for himself. Elihu knew that God would bring this type of flattery into judgment.

DEVOTIONAL THOUGHTS

- **(For children):** The people at Lystra called Paul and Barnabas "gods" because Paul had healed a crippled man. Read how Paul and Barnabas reacted to that flattery in *Acts 14:14-15*. On the other hand, read how wicked king Herod allowed the people to call him a god. What happened to him *(Acts 12:21-23)*?
- **(For everyone):** What are some flattering titles that men bestow upon others? Additionally, what are some flattering titles given by men to men in religious circles, i.e., reverend *(Psalm 111:9)* and father *(Matthew 23:9)*?
- Why should we refuse to use flattering titles to address men? What are some of the things that can happen by refusing to express this type of flattery? How are others harmed by recognizing them with such flattering titles?

PRAYER THOUGHTS
- Ask the Lord to show you the danger of flattering titles.
- Ask God to give you wisdom to avoid flattery.

SONG: *FOOLS MAKE A MOCK AT SIN*

Notes: _____

_____

_____

_____

_____

_____

_____

_____

_____

Quotes from the next volume

(VOLUME 3, WEEK 15)

Subject: Heresy

The world is chock full of ideas, theories, and teachings, yet each of us must diligently separate the truth from error.

The more time an individual spends in his Bible, the more grounded in truth he becomes.

False doctrines may be presented by men, but the ultimate plan of deception is crafted by the Devil himself.

As the world, the flesh, and the Devil war against the truth and those who propagate the truth, believers must determine to hold fast.

16

Flattery (con't)

Flattery—found twenty times in the Old Testament and only once in the New Testament

Variations: flatter, flattereth, flatteries, flattering, flattery

Last usage in the Old Testament: *Daniel 11:34* (flatteries)

Interesting fact: Flatteries come from many different people with many different motives. Some people might believe the flattery of a friend *(Job 17:5)*, others might believe the flattery of a neighbour *(Psalm 12:2; Proverbs 29:5)*, but the Bible points out that only a fool would believe the flattery of a stranger *(Proverbs 2:16; Proverbs 6:24)*.

Bible study tip: Though not all scripture is written directly to you, give equal respect unto all of God's commandments *(Psalm 119:6)*. This will protect you from the shameful practices of the religious leaders of Christ's day who omitted the weightier matters of the law *(Matthew 23:23)*.

Sunday, Day 106—Church Day (no devotional)
Monday, Day 107—*Don't Flatter Yourself*
Tuesday, Day 108—*Meddle Not with a Flatterer*
Wednesday, Day 109—Church Night (no devotional)
Thursday, Day 110—*The Flattery of the Strange Woman*

Friday, Day 111—*The Flattery of the Antichrist*
Saturday, Day 112—*Men of God Should Not Flatter*

Day 106: Church Day

*Isaiah 30:9 That **this** is **a rebellious people**, lying children, children* that *will not hear the law of the LORD:*

*10 **Which say** to the seers, See not; and to the prophets, Prophesy not unto us right things, **speak unto us smooth things**, prophesy deceits:*

Day 107: (Monday)
Don't Flatter Yourself

Psalm 36:1 The transgression of the wicked saith within my heart, that there is no fear of God before his eyes.

*2 For **he flattereth himself in his own eyes**, until his iniquity be found to be hateful.*

Introductory Thoughts

The Devil is both very subtle and sly. He knows that being patient in his attacks against the truth can result in his ultimate victory as he wears down the saints. One of his primary objectives involves a close alliance between the self-help theology crowd and the use of flattery. Those caught up in this type of theology overemphasize the need to develop self-confidence rather than developing a God-confidence. These power of positive thinking proponents teach their followers to think positively of themselves even if those thoughts are unwarranted. Yet, the Bible offers a completely different perspective. According to scripture, the wicked *"flattereth himself in his own eyes" (Psalm 36:2)* and this self-flattery is *"transgression" (Psalm 36:1)*. On the other hand, the faithful Christian realizes that *"at his very best state he is altogether vanity" (Psalm 39:5)*. Christians need their self-confidence replaced with a greater confidence and trust in the Lord.

Devotional Thoughts

- **(For children):** Peter was very sure that he would stay true to the Lord even unto death. But Jesus knew Peter's heart *(Matthew 26:33-35)* and that he would miserably fail *(Galatians 6:3)*. We need to always depend upon the Lord for help even when we might think we can do something on our own.

- **(For everyone):** What are some areas where the world encourages us to flatter ourselves? What godly benefit do we gain from following their instructions?
- How can self-flattery be used as *"a cloke of covetousness"* (*1 Thessalonians 2:5)*? How can flattery ultimately be connected back to the sin of pride?

PRAYER THOUGHTS

- Ask the Lord to build your confidence in Him.
- Ask God to help you see the reality of who and what you are.

SONG: *OFT HAVE I TURNED MY EYES WITHIN*

Day 108: (Tuesday)
Meddle Not with a Flatterer

Proverbs 20:19 He that goeth about as a talebearer revealeth secrets: therefore meddle not with him that flattereth with his lips.

INTRODUCTORY THOUGHTS

Nobody likes to spend time around those who act in a rude or insulting manner. Most people would rather spend people-time with those who focus on saying nice things. However, the truth is that one is just as spiritually dangerous to one's well-being as the other. This is why the Bible warns us to *"meddle not with him that flattereth with his lips."* Flattery is directly connected to deceit and covetousness; therefore, God intends for His warning to help Christians avoid people who say nice things deceitfully. These people intend to take advantage of their target. Far too many people have been mistreated and lied to by others whom they thought to be dear friends. It is best to avoid those with flattering lips.

DEVOTIONAL THOUGHTS

- **(For children):** Everyone who says something nice about you is not necessarily your friend. Read *Luke 20:19-21*. These men acted like they were Jesus' friends but were secretly trying to find something wrong with what He said so they could have Him arrested.

- **(For everyone):** What are some things that we ought to consider when making new friends? What are some of their qualities that might be helpful in determining whether you should allow a friendship to develop?
- What are some ways in which it could be dangerous to be around people who flatter with their lips? How does this change with age (youth, teens, young adults, adults, seniors)?

PRAYER THOUGHTS

- Ask God to keep you from being deceived by flattery.
- Ask the Lord to give you discernment in your relationships.

SONG: *YIELD NOT TO TEMPTATION*

Day 109: Church Night

*Psalm 78:36 Nevertheless **they did flatter him with their mouth, and they lied unto him with their tongues.***

Day 110: (Thursday)
The Flattery of the Strange Woman

Proverbs 6:20 My son, keep thy father's commandment, and forsake not the law of thy mother:

21 Bind them continually upon thine heart, and tie them about thy neck.

22 When thou goest, it shall lead thee; when thou sleepest, it shall keep thee; and when thou awakest, it shall talk with thee.

*23 For **the commandment is a lamp**; and **the law is light**; and **reproofs of instruction are the way of life**:*

*24 **To keep thee** from the evil woman, **from the flattery of the tongue of a strange woman**.*

INTRODUCTORY THOUGHTS

It is difficult for new and sometimes older Christians to fully comprehend sin's effects. From God's perspective, every facet of sin involves a vile act. However, from man's viewpoint, though sin can be extremely harmful, the temporary pleasures *(Hebrews 11:25)* distract from sin's injurious nature. For instance, ***Proverbs 6:24*** warns about the *"evil woman."* We might think this to mean that we should stay away from women who say bad things, yet the evil woman does not always speak negatively. In fact, this woman is said to speak with flattery; she says nice things but with impure motives. This warning is so important that it was given on multiple occasions ***(Proverbs 2:16; Proverbs 6:24; Proverbs 7:5, 21)***. The warning here is given specifically about a strange woman (a woman other than the man's wife), but it applies to men and women alike. We ought to always be on guard about those who flatter us with their words.

Devotional thoughts

- **(For children):** Delilah acted like she was interested in why Samson was so strong. Her words would make Samson feel especially important. She sounded convincing but Delilah was really getting paid by Samson's enemies to find out his secret so that they could take him captive.
- **(For everyone):** Why is the warning concerning flattery so important for young people? What are some dangers that our young people face when it comes to flattering words from the opposite sex?
- In what ways could this warning save marriages? What are some things that married men and women ought to be on the lookout for in their dealings with others?

Prayer Thoughts

- Ask the Lord to protect your home from flattering lips.
- Ask God for wisdom and discernment when dealing with flattery.

SONG: *MY HEART, MY LIFE, MY ALL I BRING*

Day 111: (Friday)
The Flattery of the Antichrist

***Daniel 11:21** And in his estate shall stand up a vile person, to whom they shall not give the honour of the kingdom: but **he shall come in peaceably**, and **obtain the kingdom by flatteries**.*

INTRODUCTORY THOUGHTS

Today's verse deals with a period of time prophesied to shortly come to pass called the time of Jacob's trouble. Fortunately, if you are born again by the grace of God, you will **not** be here during any part of this period *(1 Thessalonians 4:17; 1 Thessalonians 5:9)* when the Antichrist will have his way on this earth. Although Christians will be absent, we still remain responsible to study the word of God concerning this future time. In doing so, we learn from Daniel chapter 11 that the Antichrist will use flattery to obtain his kingdom. As a *"vile"* leader, he will come in peaceably and say nice things to other leaders in order to get them to agree to associate with him. Ultimately, he plans to take full control. Since we are told that the Antichrist of the future will use these methods, we should consider that the Devil likewise devours believers today using the same modus operandi.

DEVOTIONAL THOUGHTS

- **(For children):** One of the key ways that Satan uses flattery involves telling man what he wants to hear. He furthers his lie by convincing people to go against what God says. He offers really convincing arguments that sound so good and plausible. For instance, Eve wanted to eat the forbidden fruit so badly that she believed his lie *(Genesis 3:4)*. Ultimately, we end up miserable as we go against God's word.
- **(For everyone):** Flattery serves as one of the Devil's most effective tools. What are some ways he can use flattery to rob believers of their joy and peace? What are some ways that he uses flattery to ruin a person's testimony?
- What should we think about leaders who use flattery to gather a following? From what we have just learned, whose tactics are they implementing? How should we pray in these situations?

PRAYER THOUGHTS

- Ask the Lord to give us godly leaders who do not use flattery.
- Ask God to show us the Devil's tactics at work in our lives.

SONG: *YE SONS OF GOD, THE TEMPTER FLY*

Day 112: (Saturday)
Men of God Should Not Flatter

1 Thessalonians 2:3 For our exhortation was not of deceit, nor of uncleanness, nor in guile:

4 But as we were allowed of God to be put in trust with the gospel, even so we speak; not as pleasing men, but God, which trieth our hearts.

*5 For **neither at any time used we flattering words**, as ye know, nor a cloke of covetousness; God is witness:*

6 Nor of men sought we glory, neither of you, nor yet of others, when we might have been burdensome, as the apostles of Christ.

INTRODUCTORY THOUGHTS

The Devil works through flattery, but God works through truth. For this reason, the apostle Paul clearly articulated that he did not use words of flattery or operate with a motive of covetousness. God's men were not assigned the task of pleasing others, rather they were assigned the task of preaching the unadulterated truth of God. Today, men of God are not called to say things that please men, but those things that please the Master who called them into the ministry. Using the pulpit to express flattery cheapens the authority of the preaching and clouds the minds of the hearers. In a day when seminary students are more schooled on the finer arts of secular humanism than biblical doctrines, the church desperately needs a remnant of men standing in the pulpits unapologetically preaching the truth.

DEVOTIONAL THOUGHTS

- **(For children):** Four hundred false prophets told king Ahab what he wanted to hear – that the Lord would help him win an upcoming battle. However, Micaiah, a true man of God, was urged by all to agree with them. Even though Micaiah knew Ahab hated him, he spoke the truth. He told them that Ahab would die in battle and his army would be defeated.
- **(For everyone):** Have you ever heard a preacher seek to flatter his audience? How does this harm those who hear his preaching? Do you think people seek preachers who will flatter them? How does this harm the preacher and the hearers?

- Why is it so important that our pulpits be filled with preaching of the truth? When was the last time you prayed that God would give your preacher boldness?

PRAYER THOUGHTS
- Pray for boldness for the men of God.
- Ask God to help you despise flattery from the pulpit.

SONG: *THE PREACHER'S LIFE*

Notes: _____

_____

_____

_____

_____

Quotes from the next volume
(VOLUME 3, WEEK 16)
Subject: Heresy (con't)

The sorry state of affairs in the world today clearly reflects the fact that far too many people think too highly of their level of discernment.

The Devil has his minions who do his bidding. These people are planted in churches all over the world for the sole purpose of leading believers astray.

The enemies of God and His people have always sought to conquer those weak in the faith and destroy the faith of those serving the Lord.

It is always painful to see someone who once walked with the Lord walk away from the truth.

The best defense against departing from truth is feasting upon the truth.

17

Forgiveness

Forgiveness—found 123 times in 105 verses

Variations: forgave, forgavest, forgive, forgiven, forgiveness, forgivenesses, forgiveth, forgiving

First usage: *Genesis 50:17* (forgive)

Last usage: *1 John 2:12* (forgiven)

Defined: releasing an individual from the responsibility of an action

Interesting fact: *Genesis 50:17* contains the first usage of any form of the word *forgiveness*. It involves the request made by Joseph's brethren to forgive their trespass against him. Interestingly, this request is directed toward the man considered the greatest type and foreshadow of Jesus Christ. *1 John 2:12* holds the last occurrence of forgiveness reflecting the fact that our sins are forgiven for His [Jesus Christ, the righteous – *1 John 2:1*] name's sake.

Bible study tip: Pay close attention to the occurrence of your study as it appears in various sections of scripture. For instance, forgiveness appears most frequently in the Law as it pertains to the Old Testament and within the Gospels as it pertains to the New Testament. This indicates that the details in these sections provide specific information concerning forgiveness.

Sunday, Day 113—Church Day (no devotional)
Monday, Day 114—*What Is the Forgiveness of Sins?*
Tuesday, Day 115—*God's Readiness to Forgive*
Wednesday, Day 116—Church Night (no devotional)
Thursday, Day 117—*Forgiven, Yet in Need of Forgiveness*
Friday, Day 118—*Forgiven and Forgotten*
Saturday, Day 119—*God's Forgiveness Demands Action*

Day 113: Church Day

*Psalm 85:2 **Thou hast forgiven the iniquity of thy people,** thou hast **covered all their sin.** Selah.*

Day 114: (Monday)
What Is the Forgiveness of Sins?

*Psalm 32:1 Blessed is he whose **transgression is forgiven, whose sin is covered.***

INTRODUCTORY THOUGHTS

Prior to salvation, every individual comes to understand the need for forgiveness of sins. Forgiveness is directly associated to the nature of man's relationship with God. Yet, apart from the need for initial forgiveness, most Christians have a very shallow concept of how the Bible defines forgiveness in general. According to scripture, forgiveness is directly connected to the covering of sin *(Psalm 32:1)*. Psalm 32 does not stand alone as ***Psalm 85:2*** exhibits the same association: *"Thou hast **forgiven** the iniquity of thy people, thou hast **covered** all their sin. Selah."* It is important to understand the Bible correlation of something being *forgiven* and *covered*. Interestingly, the Bible connects being *forgiven* and *covered* with financial expressions. For example, the Bible uses forgiveness as a financial term in ***Matthew 6:12***. The term *forgiveness* suggests a removal of responsibility, while the term *covered* suggests that the debt was settled by another.

DEVOTIONAL THOUGHTS

- **(For children):** We all sin and our sin separates us from God. We either pay the price (take the punishment for our own sins) or let Christ do it for us. Because Christ died for our sins, we can be forgiven *(Colossians 1:14)*. His blood covers our sins *(Romans 5:11)*. God doesn't see them anymore. This forgiveness can be ours for the asking *(Romans 10:13)*.
- **(For everyone):** Do you know and understand the blessedness of the forgiveness of which David spoke? What does it mean to you to know that the guilt and responsibility of your sin can be removed?
- What does it mean to think that our sins are covered? Who settled the debt for us? What do we owe to the One who settled that debt?

PRAYER THOUGHTS

- Ask the Lord to help you see the blessedness of forgiven sins.
- Ask God to remind you of His work in forgiving men of their sins.

SONG: *GREAT IS HIS LOVE, AND LARGE HIS GRACE*

Day 115: (Tuesday)
God's Readiness to Forgive

Psalm 86:5 *For thou, Lord, art good, and **ready to forgive**; and plenteous in mercy unto all them that call upon thee.*

INTRODUCTORY THOUGHTS

God cannot allow man to simply sin with impunity because of His holy and righteous character that demands a righteous judgment. Yet, the Bible proclaims that the Lord is *"good, and ready to forgive; and plenteous in mercy unto all them that call upon"* Him *(Psalm 86:5)*. It is important to realize that the Lord's ultimate desire involves His desire to forgive a man's sins. Therefore, the key to a relationship with the Creator involves trusting wholly in God's provision. This is what the Bible means by, *"The Lord is . . . not willing that any should perish, but that all should come to repentance"* *(2 Peter 3:9)*. Punishment for sin is death and man's singular hope rests in God's mercy. Based upon this readiness to forgive, the Father sent His only begotten Son to shed His blood for the sins of the world. Salvation is not the end all for forgiveness. Even after salvation, the Lord desires for man to remain in close fellowship with Him, but sin separates. The Bible again holds the key when it says that the Lord *"is faithful and just to forgive us our sins, and to cleanse us from all unrighteousness" (1 John 1:9).* We are clean at salvation but must look to God for an ongoing cleansing.

DEVOTIONAL THOUGHTS

- **(For children):** Read *Luke 23:39-43*. One of the two thieves crucified with Jesus mocked Him. The other thief on the cross recognized that he himself had sinned and confessed that Jesus was Lord and had done nothing wrong. Jesus was dying for the sins of the world, including those of these two men. When the thief asked for the Lord to remember him, Jesus was ready to forgive and did so.
- **(For everyone):** How could the Lord be a God of justice and forgive a sinner at the same time when the sinner is undeserving? How does the word *covered* bring justice and forgiveness into agreement?
- If God is ready to forgive man when he sins against the Lord, how should we be when forgiving others? Why do we find it so hard to forgive others when they wrong us?

PRAYER THOUGHTS

- Ask the Lord to help you to be ready to forgive.
- Ask God to show you His mercy in forgiveness.

SONG: *PRAISE, MY SOUL, THE KING OF HEAVEN*

Day 116: Church Night

Psalm 130:3 If thou, LORD, shouldest mark iniquities, O Lord, who shall stand?

*4 But there is **forgiveness with thee**, that thou mayest be feared.*

Day 117: (Thursday)
Forgiven, Yet in Need of Forgiveness

*Colossians 2:13 And you, being dead in your sins and the uncircumcision of your flesh, hath he **quickened together with him, having forgiven you all trespasses;***

INTRODUCTORY THOUGHTS

The believer's relationship with God is twofold consisting of a positional relationship and one of practice. Positionally, the believer enjoys Christ's imputed righteousness *(Romans 4:6-8)*. In this position, the believer has been forgiven of all trespasses (past, present, and future) *(Colossians 2:13)*. John confirmed this truth as he wrote to believers saying that their sins were already forgiven *(1 John 2:12)*. Because of God's complete forgiveness, sins can never and will never affect a man's position in Christ. However, man must also consider his practice (his daily walk before the Lord). The sins that cannot harm a man's position in Christ can adversely hinder his fellowship with the Lord. Though all our sins are forgiven, we still should daily confess our sins to the Lord in order to keep our fellowship right *(1 John 1:9)*.

DEVOTIONAL THOUGHTS

- **(For children):** How do you feel when you disobey your dad and mom? No matter how you act, you remain their child. David knew he was a child of God, yet when he did wrong, his joy departed *(Psalm 51:12)*. What did David need to do? He needed to confess his failures *(Psalm 51:3)* and sincerely mean it *(Psalm 38:17-18)* to regain that closeness.
- **(For everyone):** When did you last confess your sins to the Lord and seek His forgiveness for those sins? Why is this so very important?
- Have you trusted Christ as your Saviour? Have you sought His forgiveness for your sins? What does this do for your position in Christ? How have you also worked to insure that your practice matches your position?

PRAYER THOUGHTS

- Thank the Lord for His wonderful forgiveness.
- Confess your daily sins to the Lord to insure good fellowship.

SONG: *I STAND, BUT NOT AS ONCE I DID*

Day 118: (Friday)
Forgiven and Forgotten

*Jeremiah 31:34 And they shall teach no more every man his neighbour, and every man his brother, saying, Know the LORD: for they shall all know me, from the least of them unto the greatest of them, saith the LORD: for **I will forgive their iniquity, and** I will **remember their sin no more**.*

INTRODUCTORY THOUGHTS

Most people are familiar with the phrase *forgive and forget,* yet likely not that familiar that its origin is the Bible. *Jeremiah 31:34* refers to a condition yet to be enjoyed by the Jewish people in the kingdom established on this earth following the second coming. Some of these benefits are already enjoyed by the born-again child of God. In this verse, the Lord says that He *"will forgive their iniquity, and . . . will remember their sin no more."* Notice that God said He will not only forgive but also forget. What a day that will be! True forgiveness also forgets the transgression. To claim that someone is forgiven and still remains accountable for a wrongdoing suggests that he was never actually forgiven. It is important to note that God's forgiveness and forgetfulness is not based upon what a person deserves, but an act of God's mercy *(Hebrews 8:11-12).*

DEVOTIONAL THOUGHTS

- **(For children):** Joseph's brothers cruelly treated him. When they asked for forgiveness, he was willing to forgive them and treated them kindly *(Genesis 50:17, 21)*. Because of Joseph's close relationship with God, Joseph forgave them even before they asked. Notice what Joseph named his firstborn son and what the name means *(Genesis 41:51)*.
- **(For everyone):** How is forgiveness tied to forgetting? Can something truly be forgiven if it is not also forgotten? Can we truly forgive others if we will not forget the wrong that they did to us?
- If you are saved, what does the fact that God has forgiven and forgotten your sins mean to you? Can those sins ever be brought up again if God has chosen to forget them?

PRAYER THOUGHTS

- Thank the Lord that He forgives and forgets.
- Ask the Lord to help you learn to forgive and forget.

SONG: *ARE YOU WASHED IN THE BLOOD?*

Day 119: (Saturday)
God's Forgiveness Demands Action

Ephesians 4:32 And be ye kind one to another, tenderhearted, forgiving one another, even as God for Christ's sake hath forgiven you.

INTRODUCTORY THOUGHTS

Why should we forgive others? At first glance, we might think we should do so out of the goodness of our heart. Yet, there must be a deeper and more foundational reason for our forgiveness. Fundamentally, our forgiveness should be centered upon the Lord and His forgiveness toward us. Read *Ephesians 4:32* above again. What should motivate our complete forgiveness of others? Is it not because we have been completely forgiven by the Lord? Look closely and you will see that God forgave us *"for Christ's sake."* If God forgave you for the sake of His Son, should this not also be the basis of our forgiveness of others? John confirmed this foundational truth of God's forgiveness in his first epistle when he said, ". . . *your sins are forgiven you for his name's sake"* *(1 John 2:12)*. When we forgive others, we do so *"for Christ's sake."* Forgiving others because you have been forgiven illustrates God's mercy to others.

DEVOTIONAL THOUGHTS

- **(For children):** Jesus told a story about a servant who owed money to someone but was completely forgiven of that debt. However, he did not treat others in the same fashion. When someone owed this servant money, he did not forgive them the debt but demanded the money owed to him. That was not right (see *Matthew 18:32-33* and *Colossians 3:13*).

- **(For everyone):** How can we tell others about God's mercy concerning His forgiveness if we will not forgive them for the times they have done us wrong? What kind of testimony does this present?
- What does it mean to forgive *"for Christ's sake"*? Should we forgive because we feel like forgiving someone? What will happen if we do not feel like forgiving someone today?

PRAYER THOUGHTS

- Thank God for His forgiveness.
- Ask the Lord to help you forgive *"for Christ's sake."*

SONG: *JESUS MY SAVIOUR, LET ME BE*

Notes: _____

_____

_____

_____

Quotes from the next volume

(VOLUME 3, WEEK 17)

Subject: Hypocrisy

A hypocrite is a person who presents himself one way, when in reality, he is altogether something different.

The hypocrite lives for the present. He seeks the reward of man's praise *(Matthew 6:2)* and finds his greatest joy only when that praise is received.

While the Pharisee was hypocritically thanking the Lord that he was not wicked like the publican, the publican was busy confessing to God how wicked he was.

Hypocrisy requires more effort than most people realize. In fact, the level of effort expended frequently exceeds what would be necessary to simply do right.

18

Frugal

Frugal—The word "frugal" is not found in the scripture though the principle is found throughout.

Defined: economical or thrifty; the opposite of wastefulness

Interesting fact: Frugal living requires character. It does not matter whether someone has great wealth or very little, he can live frugally. Men often claim that if they simply had more possessions, they could and would live frugally; however, the failure to live frugally will often lead to a loss of one's present possessions *(Luke 19:26)*.

Bible study tip: Bible study generally begins with questions and should be focused on allowing the word of God to provide the biblical answers. It is important to ask the right questions in order to yield the right answers. Take time before the onset of study to write out any questions you may have. Even as your study progresses, record new questions generated. Never force an answer, but always allow the Bible to answer the questions you have. It is imperative that you not allow your answers to exceed what the Bible specifically dictates. It is sometimes the wisest move to end a Bible study as you began – with the answer remaining as, "I do not know."

Sunday, Day 120—Church Day (no devotional)
Monday, Day 121—*The Sin of Wasteful Living*
Tuesday, Day 122—*The Steward's Accountability*
Wednesday, Day 123—Church Night (no devotional)
Thursday, Day 124—*A Foolish Man Spends His Treasures*
Friday, Day 125—*Strong Men Retain Their Riches*
Saturday, Day 126—*Precious Is the Substance of a Diligent Man*

Day 120: Church Day

*John 6:12 When they were filled, he said unto his disciples, **Gather up the fragments that remain, that nothing be lost.***

Day 121: (Monday)
The Sin of Wasteful Living

*Luke 15:13 And not many days after the younger son gathered all together, and took his journey into a far country, and **there wasted his substance** with riotous living.*

14 And when he had spent all, there arose a mighty famine in that land; and he began to be in want.

INTRODUCTORY THOUGHTS

Before leaving home, the prodigal son asked his father for all of his inheritance. He left town with everything that would have been his upon his father's death. Certainly his father had hoped that he would make wise decisions in the use of this money. Yet, the Bible says that the prodigal *"wasted his substance with riotous living" (Luke 15:13)*. The next verse further confirms the extent of his waste by saying that *"he . . . spent all" (Luke 15:14)*. The prodigal son asked for his inheritance and then compounded his problem by refusing to wisely spend that inheritance. No doubt when he found himself in that pigpen, he reflected on the fact that he could not offer an accounting for his loss. The substance his father had tirelessly laboured to obtain was squandered because of a foolish son's lust for living unruly.

Devotional Thoughts

- **(For children):** Consider the story of the good Samaritan. We are not told how he acquired his wealth, but we do know he didn't spend it all. He was not selfish but used it to help others. The story tells us that he helped a wounded man by paying for his medicine, transportation, and a place for the man to stay. He also paid for a caretaker.
- **(For everyone):** Think back to the last time you received money (paycheck or otherwise). What happened to that money? Do you have anything of substance or importance to show for that money now?
- What profitable things could be done with your money if you did not frivolously waste it? How much more could you give to the Lord with a little frugality?

Prayer Thoughts

- Ask the Lord to keep you from the sin of waste.
- Ask the Lord to give you wisdom in spending your substance.

SONG: *MY SOUL, DEAR LORD, TO THEE ASCENDS*

Day 122: (Tuesday)
The Steward's Accountability

*Luke 16:1 And he said also unto his disciples, There was a certain rich man, which had a steward; and **the same was accused** unto him **that he had wasted his goods**.*

Introductory Thoughts

A steward is someone responsible to care for the goods of another. He is accountable to his master for the way that he handles the responsibility. In this parable, a steward was accused of wasting the rich man's goods. This was such a serious charge that the rich man called for the steward to give an accounting of his stewardship. The Lord expressed a similar truth in another parable found in *Luke 19:11-27*. In this parable, several servants invested their goods and accrued interest, but one servant simply hid his pound which resulted in no gain. The lord of that servant was so upset with this slothful servant that he took the pound away from him and gave it to one of the others. Remember that it is not up to the steward to choose how to spend that which belongs to the master.

DEVOTIONAL THOUGHTS

- **(For children)**: Potiphar, an officer in Pharoah's army, put Joseph in charge of everything inside his house and on his property. Joseph feared God and could be trusted as a good steward. In fact, Joseph was so trusted that Potiphar never had to question how Joseph spent Potiphar's money *(Genesis 39:5-6)*.
- **(For everyone)**: To whom do your money and your possessions ultimately belong? If they do not belong to you, what does this mean about your level of accountability?
- How are you accountable to God for the money that you have? How are you accountable to Him for the way in which you use your substance?

PRAYER THOUGHTS

- Ask the Lord to show you that nothing truly belongs to you.
- Ask God to help you not waste that which He has entrusted to you.

SONG: *TRUST, TRY, AND PROVE ME*

Day 123: Church Night

*Proverbs 18:9 He also that is slothful in his work is brother **to him that is a great waster**.*

Day 124: (Thursday)
A Foolish Man Spends His Treasures

*Proverbs 21:20 There is treasure to be desired and oil in the dwelling of the wise; but **a foolish man spendeth it up**.*

INTRODUCTORY THOUGHTS

Proverbs 21 contrasts the substance of a wise man versus the substance of a fool. In the home of the wise man, one can find oil and desired treasures. Whenever a need arises, he is prepared to take care of it himself. This is not true of the fool. He cannot take care of himself. We do not know if the fool at some point had treasures and oil as well, but because of his wasteful spending habits, he no longer has those things. In addition to the fool no longer having his substance, he also cannot likely account for how he used those things. Maybe the fool, like far too many Christians, wasted his substance on pleasurable living *(Proverbs 21:17)*.

For whatever reason, the fool cannot hold onto the goods entrusted to him by the Lord. Society today has grown accustomed to living on borrowed money, thus spending the future today.

DEVOTIONAL THOUGHTS

- **(For children):** Because Joseph knew hard times were coming, he saved up much corn. Unlike those who were unable or unwilling to store up for the future, Joseph did no not have to beg when famine came. He had enough food for himself and others.
- **(For everyone):** Do you have goods set aside for times of need? If not, why not? Can you reflect back and see that you could have had more if you had not been so wasteful?
- What percentage of your money do you spend on pleasure-seeking things *(Proverbs 21:17)*? Do you think that that expense was eternally profitable?

PRAYER THOUGHTS

- Ask God to give you wisdom on how to spend what He gives you.
- Ask God to show you what constitutes wise purchases.

SONG: *SOFTLY AND TENDERLY*

Day 125: (Friday)
Strong Men Retain Their Riches

Proverbs 11:16 A gracious woman retaineth honour: and strong men retain riches.

INTRODUCTORY THOUGHTS

When one thinks of strength, he often thinks only in the physical realm. He might focus on the ability to lift weights, endure a great amount of pain, or compete in a strenuous sport. Yet, the Bible points to true strength that has nothing to do with one's physical prowess. The Bible says that the ability to retain riches reflects one of the greatest emblems of strength. Proverbs also warns that *"riches . . . make themselves wings; they fly away as an eagle toward heaven" (Proverbs 23:5)*. This means that a fool simply watches as his substance departs with no benefits to show for the loss. Yet, a strong man sets aside money and wisely preserves what the Lord has entrusted to him. Perhaps our heroes should not be those in sports but those who refrain from spending money to satisfy the lusts of the flesh.

Devotional thoughts

- **(For children):** Many leaders foolishly spent their substance upon unnecessary things. Yet, king David provides an example of someone who had a heart for God. He laid up for Solomon, his son, gold and silver in order to build God a house. Because of David's example, the people also willingly gave to this worthy cause. Do we spend our substance upon ourselves leaving us very little for the work of God?
- **(For everyone):** What is your biggest area of waste when it comes to money? In light of this, what do you think about the phrase *"strong men retain riches"*?
- Does money burn a hole in your pocket? Do you find it difficult to retain riches? What steps could you follow in order to insure that you wisely spend money?

Prayer Thoughts

- Ask the Lord to give you strength to retain riches.
- Ask God to help you use wisdom in spending money.

SONG: *TAKE MY LIFE, AND LET IT BE*

Day 126: (Saturday)
Precious Is the Substance of a Diligent Man

*Proverbs 12:27 The slothful man roasteth not that which he took in hunting: but **the substance of a diligent man is precious**.*

Introductory Thoughts

A slothful man hunts and even makes a kill but considers it too much work to prepare and roast that which he killed. He would rather see the meat go to waste than to put forth the effort necessary to preserve the food. However, a diligent man considers his substance to be precious. He has no desire to see something go to waste. Interestingly enough, the Lord Jesus made a point along these lines at the feeding of the five thousand. After He fed the multitude, the Lord Jesus told the disciples to *"Gather up the fragments that remain[ed], that nothing be lost" **(John 6:12)**.* It was important to the Lord that His followers made full use of the substance given to them of the Father. Nothing was to go to waste. A diligent man considers every part to be precious, even those things the world would allow to spoil.

DEVOTIONAL THOUGHTS

- **(For children):** Jesus fed another large group of people (4,000) and once again the leftovers were taken up *(Mark 8:8)*. The Lord does not approve of wasting food. When getting your food, only take as much as you can eat. When mom serves leftovers on another night, don't complain. You should be willing to thank God for the food He has provided, even if only leftovers.
- **(For everyone):** How much food do you waste? How much money do you spend with no real benefit? How important is it to you to wisely use everything that God gives you?
- Why do we waste? Why have we lost the appreciation for *"the fragments that remain"*? What are some ways we can better use what God provides?

PRAYER THOUGHTS

- Ask God to help you to be diligent.
- Ask the Lord for a distaste for being wasteful.

SONG: *THANKS TO GOD*

Notes: _____

_____

_____

_____

_____

_____

_____

_____

_____

Notes: _____

_____

_____

_____

_____

_____

_____

_____

_____

_____

_____

_____

_____

_____

Quotes from the next volume

(VOLUME 3, WEEK 18)

Subject: Hypocrisy (con't)

Satan has no problem when a man finds fault in others so long as that man finds no fault within himself.

If believers simply worked as hard to lead others to Christ and teach sound Bible doctrine as they do finding fault in others, churches would be full of converts growing in the grace and knowledge of Jesus Christ.

A hypocrite often becomes overzealous in his obedience in one area of life while failing to recognize his rebellion in other important areas.

19

Giving

Giving—found 2,046 times in 1,856 verses. This study will concentrate specifically on giving financially to the Lord.

Variations: gave, gavest, give, given, giver, givest, giveth, giving

Defined: To give indicates the transfer of some possession to another.

Interesting fact: The early church was distinguished in its sacrificial giving. Some sold houses and lands and laid the money at the apostles' feet for the distribution to the saints *(Acts 4:34-35)*. Some, though in *"deep poverty," "gave their own selves to the Lord" (2 Corinthians 8:1-5)*. Of the Galatians Paul said, *"if it had been possible, ye would have plucked out your own eyes, and have given them to me" (Galatians 4:15)*. Every Christian should consider their level of sacrifice!

Bible study tip: The Bible points to biblical revelation as a gradual process. Therefore, it is both unscriptural and unwise to assume that Old Testament saints understood truths later revealed to the New Testament writers. It is equally unwise to assume that everything God intended under the Law remains binding today. Always test the Old

Testament practices against the New Testament teachings before suggesting their continuance.

Sunday, Day 127—Church Day (no devotional)
Monday, Day 128—*The Importance of Giving*
Tuesday, Day 129—*Giving's Bottom Line*
Wednesday, Day 130—Church Night (no devotional)
Thursday, Day 131—*Giving the Firstfruits*
Friday, Day 132—*The Blessings of Giving*
Saturday, Day 133—*Giving Beyond Sufficiency*

Day 127: Church Day

*1 Corinthians 16:2 Upon the first day of the week **let every one of you lay by him in store, as God hath prospered him**, that there be no gatherings when I come.*

Day 128: (Monday)
The Importance of Giving

Numbers 7:1 And it came to pass on the day that Moses had fully set up the tabernacle, and had anointed it, and sanctified it, and all the instruments thereof, both the altar and all the vessels thereof, and had anointed them, and sanctified them;

*2 That the princes of Israel, heads of the house of their fathers, who were the princes of the tribes, and were over them that were numbered, **offered:***

*3 And **they brought their offering before the LORD,** six covered wagons, and twelve oxen; a wagon for two of the princes, and for each one an ox: and they brought them before the tabernacle.*

4 And the LORD spake unto Moses, saying,

*5 **Take it of them, that they may be to do the service of the tabernacle of the congregation**; and thou shalt give them unto the Levites, to every man according to his service.*

INTRODUCTORY THOUGHTS

Psalm 119 is the longest verse-count passage (psalm or chapter) in God's word. Interestingly, that particular psalm focuses upon one of

God's greatest gifts ever provided for mankind, His precious word. The second longest verse-count passage is Numbers chapter 7. Interestingly, God's word focuses this chapter upon mankind giving gifts back to God. The passage could have been dramatically shortened had God chosen to give fewer of the details. However, the Lord chose to specifically delineate each of the gifts received from each tribe. Why? Maybe God wanted to emphasize the importance of every gift from every individual given to Him. No gift represented a lesser degree of importance to God Almighty. God does not need anything from man *(Psalm 50:7-15)* yet finds great pleasure in receiving gifts from those whom He loves.

DEVOTIONAL THOUGHTS

- **(For children):** The greatest commandment is to love the Lord with all our heart, soul, and mind. Love obeys *(John 14:15)* and love gives *(John 3:16)*. God wants us to give back to Him out of love and He takes particular notice of that giving. Read *Mark 12:41-44*.
- **(For everyone):** Why would our gifts to the Lord be so important to Him if He has no need of the things which we have to offer to Him? What do our gifts to the Lord demonstrate about the condition of our hearts?
- What are some possible reasons that the Lord dedicated so much space to delineating the offerings presented to Him by each tribe? What does this teach us about His care for our gifts?

PRAYER THOUGHTS

- Ask the Lord to give you a heart that desires to give to Him.
- Ask God to give you the ability to give Him more.

SONG: JESUS, I MY CROSS HAVE TAKEN

Day 129: (Tuesday)
Giving's Bottom Line

Malachi 3:7 Even from the days of your fathers ye are gone away from mine ordinances, and have not kept them. Return unto me, and I will return unto you, saith the LORD of hosts. But ye said, Wherein shall we return?

₈ *Will a man rob God? Yet ye have robbed me.* But ye say, Wherein *have we robbed thee? In tithes and offerings.*

₉ *Ye are cursed with a curse: for ye have robbed me, even this whole nation.*

₁₀ *Bring ye all the tithes into the storehouse, that there may be meat in mine house, and* **prove me now herewith,** *saith the LORD of hosts, if I will not open you the windows of heaven, and pour you out a blessing, that there shall not be room enough to receive it.*

INTRODUCTORY THOUGHTS

Most people never experience the joy of willingly and cheerfully giving to the Lord and His work. The Old Testament set precedence for how much man would give to the Lord. This standard was not the maximum offering but simply the minimum. The Bible repeatedly identifies the amount in scripture as a tithe, which means a tenth *(Leviticus 27:32)*. Failure to give the tithe to the Lord was deemed robbery by God *(Malachi 3:8)*. Simply put, the tithe belonged to God. The tithe, however, was not to be considered the peak of what man gave back to God. It never was intended to be so, nor ever should it be. Those who truly love the Lord will not use the tithe as a maximum amount to give. Instead, they realize that this portion already belongs to the Lord and it serves as the bare minimum of what they should give to Him. Those who pride themselves on tithing, pride themselves on giving God the least.

DEVOTIONAL THOUGHTS

- **(For children):** Count out ten pennies. Pick up one of them. Every time you gain ten pennies, at least one of these belongs to God. That is called a tenth or a tithe. If you decide to give God extra out of the other nine pennies that remain, that is an offering above the tithe.
- **(For everyone):** How much is too much for the Lord to ask of His people? What does complaining about giving to the Lord reveal about your heart?
- Why do we choose to pay others what we owe them and fail to pay God what we owe Him for all that He has done for us? Do we not owe the Lord so much more than we owe any man?

PRAYER THOUGHTS

- Ask God to help you see tithing as a start rather than an end.
- Ask God to work in your heart so that you enjoy giving to Him.

SONG: *TRUST, TRY, AND PROVE ME*

Day 130: Church Night

*2 Corinthians 9:7 Every man according as he purposeth in his heart, so let him **give; not grudgingly, or of necessity: for God loveth a cheerful giver.***

Day 131: (Thursday)
Giving the Firstfruits

*Proverbs 3:9 **Honour the LORD** with thy substance, and **with the firstfruits of all thine increase:***

INTRODUCTORY THOUGHTS

Giving by faith requires giving God the firstfruits of one's increase. The Lord not only wants us to bring our gifts to Him but also wants us to give to Him first. According to **Proverbs 3:9**, we should honour the Lord with the firstfruits of our increase. We are not to pay all our bills only to give God the leftovers. God is to take first place each and every time. This makes giving to Him an act of faith. After all, *"without faith it is impossible to please him" (Hebrews 11:6)*. This includes the area of giving where so many seem to struggle so much. Is God honoured when we decide to simply give Him the leftovers? Certainly not! Yet, when we give God the first of our increase, we signify to Him that we trust that He will meet the remaining needs we may have.

DEVOTIONAL THOUGHTS

- **(For children):** Lay out ten one dollar bills (real or play money will work). How many of those bills belong to God? Count how many remain after you separate God's portion. What happens if you want a toy that costs the whole $10? You should give to God first and learn to wait until you get some more money to buy the toy.

- **(For everyone):** What does it mean to give God the *"firstfruits of all thine increase"*? What might be considered increase? Are there some areas of increase where you might not give God the increase?
- In *1 Kings 17:13*, Elijah told the widow of Zarephath to first provide for him and then to provide for her and her son. What happened when she was obedient? What can we learn from her example of firstfruits?

PRAYER THOUGHTS

- Ask the Lord to help you give by faith.
- Ask the Lord to show you the importance of putting Him first.

SONG: *OUR BEST*

Day 132: (Friday)
The Blessings of Giving

*Luke 6:38 Give, and it shall be given unto you; good measure, pressed down, and shaken together, and running over, shall men give into your bosom. **For with the same measure that ye mete withal it shall be measured to you again**.*

INTRODUCTORY THOUGHTS

Some have misapplied today's verse to suggest that God is bound to financially give to those who financially give to Him. Some false teachers have used verses like *Luke 6:38* to suggest that a man who gives to God will have his gift restored sevenfold. This seems to be the ploy of most televangelists. Giving to God's work is not a magical formula guaranteeing personal enrichment. In fact, a Christian who sacrificially gives to the Lord may lose his job. He may give to the Lord only to incur some major unexpected expense. Yet, the Christian can be sure that he will never give to the Lord without receiving a resultant blessing from God. Far too many times, we seem to blame God for any bad that may follow but fail to recognize the delayed blessings that are sure to follow obedience. The Lord promises that we will never give to Him without Him giving back to us. Rest assured that you cannot and will not ever out give God.

DEVOTIONAL THOUGHTS

- **(For children):** The lad with the five loaves and two small fishes gave what he had to the Lord. What did the boy receive? He not only was blessed to eat but also had the joy of knowing what he gave to the Lord helped many other people. Did you ever wonder if he was allowed to take home all the leftovers that were gathered?
- **(For everyone):** Think of some blessings that God has given to you since you began giving to Him. Has there ever been a time that you were without the basic necessities (food and raiment) while giving to Him?
- What do you believe are some of the greatest kinds of blessings that you can get from the Lord? What would you be willing to give God in order to receive those blessings?

PRAYER THOUGHTS

- Ask the Lord to meet your needs as you give to Him.
- Ask God to bless you with spiritual blessings as you obey Him.

SONG: *IS THY CRUSE OF COMFORT WASTING?*

Day 133: (Saturday)
Giving Beyond Sufficiency

***Exodus 36:2** And Moses called Bezaleel and Aholiab, and every wise hearted man, in whose heart the LORD had put wisdom, even every one whose heart stirred him up to come unto the work to do it:*

*3 And **they received of Moses all the offering, which the children of Israel had brought for the work of the service of the sanctuary**, to make it withal. And they brought yet unto him free offerings every morning.*

4 And all the wise men, that wrought all the work of the sanctuary, came every man from his work which they made;

*5 And they spake unto Moses, saying, **The people bring much more than enough for the service of the work**, which the LORD commanded to make.*

6 And Moses gave commandment, and they caused it to be proclaimed throughout the camp, saying, Let neither man nor woman make any more work for the offering of the sanctuary. So the people were restrained from bringing.

*7 For **the stuff they had was sufficient for all the work to make it, and too much**.*

Introductory Thoughts

What a scene! The need was great. The people of God had been challenged to bring gifts so that the tabernacle of God could be built. They began to offer as the Lord had worked in their hearts. Yet, there was seemingly no end to their gifts. Every morning the people brought more offerings unto Moses for the work *(Exodus 36:3)*. The offerings were so much that Bezaleel, Aholiab, and the other wise hearted men came to Moses and requested that the people stop bringing offerings. God so moved on the hearts of the people that they had brought *"too much" (Exodus 36:7)*. Fast-forward to the present day. The work of the ministry requires sufficient money to fund its processes. Could you imagine the astonished look if ever the man of God told the congregation that "We have given too much"?

Devotional thoughts

- **(For children)**: *2 Corinthians 9:7* says, *"God loveth a cheerful giver."* When we think of how much the Lord loves us *(2 Corinthians 8:9)*, we can't help but love Him back. One way is through giving. *1 Chronicles 29:9* is a good example of how we should give.
- **(For everyone):** When is the last time you recall God's people coming together to give toward God's work in such a way that too much was given? Why do you think that you have never remembered such a time as this?
- Why do you think the people gave so willingly in Moses' day? What kind of message did they send to God through their willingness to give? How could this abundant offering build faith in God's people?

Prayer Thoughts

- Ask the Lord to give you such a desire to give bountifully.
- Ask God to help His people come together to give toward His work.

SONG: *PRAISE THE SAVIOUR, YE WHO KNOW HIM*

Notes: _____

Notes: _____

_____

_____

_____

_____

_____

_____

_____

_____

_____

_____

_____

_____

_____

_____

_____

_____

Quotes from the next volume

(VOLUME 3, WEEK 19)

Subject: Liberality

When a man, from a sincere heart, is liberal in his care for the Lord and the His people, the Lord will return his liberality to him.

God exhibits the perfect standard of righteousness through His character and work. Any person who desires to know the right way to do something need not look any further than the Lord for his example.

20

Giving (con't)

Giving—found 1,491 times in 1,350 verses in the Old Testament and found 555 times in 506 verses. This study will concentrate specifically on giving financially to the Lord.

Variations: gave, gavest, give, given, giver, givest, giveth, giving

Interesting fact: The scripture presents a strong connection between communication and giving. This will not surprise any diligent Bible student. Communication has to do with taking that which is personal and making it common with another. This is the type of communication referred to by the apostle Paul in *Galatians 6:6*, *Philippians 4:14-15*, and *1 Timothy 6:18*.

Bible study tip: Bible study is not relegated to the study of words per say. Take time to study other elements, like the people of the Bible. Start with a somewhat familiar Bible character. Chronicle the details of that person's life and the relative importance of each event. Then seek the practical strengths and weaknesses of this person and how his or her example might benefit you or others. Do not overlook the less prominent Bible characters who will offer some of the most often missed salient points.

Sunday, Day 134—Church Day (no devotional)
Monday, Day 135—*Purposeful Giving*
Tuesday, Day 136—*Always Give According to Your Ability*
Wednesday, Day 137—Church Night (no devotional)
Thursday, Day 138—Always *Give with Simplicity*
Friday, Day 139—*Always Give with a Willing Heart*
Saturday, Day 140—*Affectionate Giving*

Day 134: Church Day

1 Timothy 6:17 Charge them that are rich in this world, *that they be not highminded, nor trust in uncertain riches, but in the living God, who giveth us richly all things to enjoy;*

18 That they do good, **that they be rich in good works, ready to distribute, willing to communicate;**

19 Laying up in store for themselves a good foundation against the time to come, that they may lay hold on eternal life.

Day 135: (Monday)
Purposeful Giving

2 Corinthians 9:7 *Every man* **according as he purposeth in his heart, so let him give;** *not grudgingly, or of necessity: for God loveth a cheerful giver.*

INTRODUCTORY THOUGHTS

Giving must be purposeful and does not happen by accident. Before giving to the Lord, the Christian must first purpose in his heart to willingly give. Not only must he purpose in his heart to give, but he must also purpose *what* and *when* to give. Furthermore, he must purpose to give according to his ability and to give faithfully. These are important elements that each believer should constantly address. Failure to consider these important aspects breeds confusion and allows the Devil to deter that man from obedience. Each believer or family unit should sit down and purpose with God's leading what and when to give. Then each believer should faithfully give as the Lord leads and as that individual or family has purposed in heart.

DEVOTIONAL THOUGHTS

- **(For children):** Read **Genesis 28:22b.** Jacob made a decision in his heart and promised to give God back a tenth of all that God gave to him. Like Jacob, we should have a heart that desires to give back to God because everything belongs to Him anyway.
- **(For everyone):** How does it help to first purpose in your heart? How does that make it more likely that you will give according to God's will for your life?
- Do you generally purpose in your heart what and when to give? What have you purposed to give? Is your plan in line with God's plan? Are you faithfully fulfilling God's will in this area of your life?

PRAYER THOUGHTS

- Ask the Lord to help you purpose to give.
- Ask God to help you to be faithful to give as you have purposed.

SONG: *LORD, THOU LOVEST THE CHEERFUL GIVER*

Day 136: (Tuesday)
Always Give According to Your Ability

Deuteronomy 16:17 Every man shall give as he is able, according to the blessing of the LORD thy God which he hath given thee.

INTRODUCTORY THOUGHTS

Every person cannot give the same amount, but every person can give. According to our passage, *"Every man shall give as he is able."* Because some people might use this as an excuse not to give, the Lord further states that giving should be *"according to the blessing of the LORD thy God which he hath given thee."* The New Testament repeats this same principle in **1 Corinthians 16:2.** Every man is to give *"as God hath prospered him."* The book of Acts gives a practical example. In **Acts 11:29**, the disciples sent relief to their brethren and every man did so *"according to his ability."* Each believer should give to the Lord corresponding to how the Lord has prospered him.

Devotional Thoughts

- **(For children):** If you earn ten pennies, you set aside one penny for the Lord. If a friend earns twenty pennies, he owes the Lord two pennies. Read *2 Corinthians 8:12*. In God's eyes you both gave equally. You both gave from what the Lord allowed you to earn.
- **(For everyone):** Has God prospered you? What is your ability to give? Could you give more than you are currently giving? Do you think it would please the Lord for you to increase your giving?
- Do you give to the work of the Lord? If not, can you honestly say that God has not given you the ability to give? Is it possible that your priorities could be off balance?

Prayer Thoughts

- Ask the Lord to enable you to give more.
- Ask God to show you if He is pleased with how you are giving.

SONG: *LIVING FOR JESUS*

Day 137: Church Night

*1 Corinthians 13:3 And **though I bestow all my goods to feed** the **poor**, and though I give my body to be burned, **and have not charity, it profiteth me nothing.***

Day 138: (Thursday)
Always Give with Simplicity

Romans 12:6 Having then gifts differing according to the grace that is given to us, whether prophecy, let us prophesy according to the proportion of faith;

7 Or ministry, let us wait on our ministering: or he that teacheth, on teaching;

*8 Or he that exhorteth, on exhortation: **he that giveth, let him do it with simplicity**; he that ruleth, with diligence; he that sheweth mercy, with cheerfulness.*

Introductory Thoughts

What does it mean to give financially to the Lord's work? Does it mean that we give to the Lord only to try and manipulate the spending of every dime? Does it mean that we give without concern whatsoever on how the money will be spent? In our passage, we find that believers should give with simplicity. Before we give, we should pray and insure that our giving is acceptable to the Lord. Is the church receiving the gift doing the Lord's work? Is the money being used to reach the lost and edify the saints? Once certain that the Lord approves of our giving, we should strive to always give with simplicity. The money is the Lord's and we must insure before giving that we are parting with control. To do otherwise means that we are not giving with simplicity.

DEVOTIONAL THOUGHTS

- **(For children)**: Jesus foretold of His death, burial, and resurrection several times. Mary seemed to be the only individual who understood and graciously gave Jesus a costly present. Her gift displayed her grateful spirit looking forward to the sacrifice He was going to do. The disciples said the gift should have been sold with the funds used to help the poor. Yet, they failed to realize that Jesus is God and it is always right to put Him first.
- **(For everyone)**: When you give to the Lord's work, do you mentally hold onto the purse strings as though you never really released control of how the funds are spent? Release control if the money is being spent to please the Lord and further His work.
- To whom does your money really belong? When we give to the Lord, we are really returning money to Him that already belongs to Him. If this is true, can you trust the Lord with your gifts?

PRAYER THOUGHTS

- Ask the Lord to confirm to you if you are giving in an acceptable fashion.
- Ask God to help you give with simplicity.

SONG: *'TIS SO SWEET TO TRUST IN JESUS*

Day 139: (Friday)
Always Give with a Willing Heart

1 Chronicles 29:9 Then the people rejoiced, for that they offered willingly, because with perfect heart they offered willingly to the LORD: and David the king also rejoiced with great joy.

INTRODUCTORY THOUGHTS

For some people, giving to the Lord is the equivalent of going to the dentist to have teeth pulled. They would rather do anything than to dip into their finances for the Lord. Yet, there are others who rejoice in giving to the work of the Lord. What is the difference between these two groups of people? One group gives from a willing heart. The other group, if they give at all, does so grudgingly *(2 Corinthians 9:7)*. While giving instructions to Moses concerning an offering, the Lord said, *"of every man that giveth it willingly with his heart ye shall take my offering"* *(Exodus 25:2)*. The Lord commands His people to give, but He desires that the giving be willing. The right heart in giving will rejoice that he gets to give and never considers that he has to give *(1 Chronicles 29:9)*.

DEVOTIONAL THOUGHTS

- **(For children):** What gives you pleasure or joy? The churches of Macedonia first gave their own selves to the Lord. Because of this, they had joy and pleasure in giving and willingly gave when they themselves had very little *(2 Corinthians 8:1-5; Romans 15:26)*.
- **(For everyone):** Do you find joy in giving to the Lord or do you give grudgingly? Is it hard for you to let go of the funds that you have deposited into the offering plate? What could this suggest about your inordinate love for money?
- What has the Lord done for you? Has He done these things grudgingly or out of a willing heart? How much is too much for Him to ask of you?

PRAYER THOUGHTS

- Ask the Lord to give you a willing heart to give back to Him and His work.
- Thank the Lord for what He has done for you.

SONG: *READY*

Day 140: (Saturday)
Always Give with an Affectionate Heart

*1 Chronicles 29:3 Moreover, **because I have set my affection to the house of my God, I have of mine own proper good, of gold and silver, which I have given to the house of my God**, over and above all that I have prepared for the holy house,*

INTRODUCTORY THOUGHTS

Many historians and certainly the Jews praised Solomon's temple as the most glorious structure ever built. Yet, most people fail to realize that the love of Solomon's father for the Lord supplied much of the material to make the temple a reality. The Bible says that David set his affection on the house of God and gave of his *"own proper good, of gold and silver."* When we love someone, we have no trouble giving to that person. When we love a cause, we have no trouble giving to that cause. Perhaps one reason why some people fail to give to the Lord and His work stems from the fact that they really only love the Lord with lip service. Or possibly the reason why people fail to give to the work of the Lord is because they have no concern for the work of the Lord to continue. David gave because he set his affection on the house of God. Which example applies to you?

DEVOTIONAL THOUGHTS

- **(For children):** The church has a building in which the people meet to worship God, help one another, and carry out plans to bring others to the Lord. A full-time pastor has more time to study God's word and pray and help the ministry to grow. It takes money to keep on the lights, heating, water, and air conditioning. None of this would be possible if not for the people who love God giving to His work.
- **(For everyone):** Is it hard for you to give to the Lord? If so, what does this suggest about your love for Him? What did His love for us cause Him to give? What should our love for Him cause us to give?
- Are you thankful for the work of God that is being done in your local church and around the world? What are you doing to insure that the work does not cease and that it continues unhindered?

PRAYER THOUGHTS

- Ask the Lord to perfect your love for Him.
- Ask the Lord to help you give toward His work.

SONG: *ALL THAT THRILLS MY SOUL*

Notes: _____

_____

_____

_____

_____

_____

_____

_____

_____

Quotes from the next volume

(VOLUME 3, WEEK 20)

Subject: Loyalty

God does not expect blind loyalty from man, but He certainly deserves it from everyone. He first earned man's loyalty by being his Creator. Yet His ultimate claim to loyalty stems from His offering to redeem fallen man.

Throughout man's 6,000 year history, God's people have always had their loyalty to the Lord tested. If loyalty came naturally, everyone would be loyal rather than simply the few.

Loyalty often comes at a steep price! For some, the cost may seem minimal, but for others it has cost them deeply and dearly.

21

Hate

Hate—found 208 times (164 times in the Old Testament and forty-four times in the New Testament) in 194 verses

Variations: hate, hated, hateful, hatefully, haters, hatest, hateth, hatred

First usage: *Genesis 24:60* (hate)

Last usage: *Revelation 18:2* (hateful)

Defined: to feel intense dislike for someone or something; can also mean to love less in comparison *(Genesis 29:30-31)*

Interesting fact: Some have suggested that the ultimate solution to our sin problem involves merely learning to hate sin more. However, the apostle Paul pointed to an inner struggle as he warred against doing that which he hated *(Romans 7:15)*.

Bible study tip: Preconceived ideas and simple unbelief are two of the greatest enemies against sound Bible study. For instance, it is important to keep in check the preconceived ideas concerning hatred as you study the Bible. As always, allow the context to determine the word's meaning in each case. Also, be sure to allow the connotation of the passage to demonstrate whether hatred is an act of righteousness or an act of sin.

Sunday, Day 141—Church Day (no devotional)
Monday, Day 142—*God Hates*
Tuesday, Day 143—*Loving Those Who Hate the Lord*
Wednesday, Day 144—Church Night (no devotional)
Thursday, Day 145—*Those Who Love the LORD, Hate Evil*
Friday, Day 146—*Hated by the World for Doing Right*
Saturday, Day 147—*God's Favour for the Hated*

Day 141: Church Day

*Psalm 45:7 Thou lovest righteousness, and **hatest wickedness**: therefore God, thy God, hath anointed thee with the oil of gladness above thy fellows.*

Day 142: (Monday)
God Hates

*Psalm 5:5 The foolish shall not stand in thy sight: **thou hatest all workers of iniquity**.*

Introductory Thoughts

God hates! For those enamored by the teachers who strictly emphasize the love of God, this fact may be difficult to appreciate. Yet, it is both true and scriptural. In fact, the truth becomes even more peculiar when considering that God's hatred is founded within His love. According to *1 John 4:8*, *"God is love."* He never ceases to be love, and if He did, He would cease to be God. Yet, the Bible specifically points out that God also hates! Let the Bible speak for itself and it will clear up any preconceived ideas. God hates because He loves. God loves the righteous; therefore, He hates *"all workers of iniquity"* **(Psalm 5:5)**. The Bible also points out that He hates the wicked and those who love violence **(Psalm 11:5)**. These truths are frequently contrary to the common teaching by men who fail to consider the whole of scripture and the depth of God. The old saying, *"God hates the sin, but loves the sinner"* apparently fails when considering the whole matter. God does, in fact, hate the wicked!

Additionally, God hates wicked deeds and wicked doctrines *(Revelation 2:6, 15)*. Each of us must insure that we declare all the counsel of God and not conveniently limit our understanding to only the most positive aspects *(Acts 20:27)*.

DEVOTIONAL THOUGHTS

- **(For children):** To hate something is to have an extreme dislike for it. The Bible points to some specific things that God hates in *Proverbs 6:16-19* and *Zechariah 8:17*.
- **(For everyone):** Why does God hate the wicked? Why does He hate false doctrine and wicked deeds? Is it possible that this hatred is founded within His love? Can you explain how God hating wickedness helps to display His all-consuming love?
- How should the knowledge of God's hatred change the life of a believer? Should believers hate anything? Where should the believer learn what to love and what to hate?

PRAYER THOUGHTS

- Ask the Lord to help you grasp the truth that He hates.
- Ask the Lord to help you hate what He hates.

SONG: TREMBLE, YE SINNERS

Day 143: (Tuesday)
Loving Those Who Hate the Lord

*2 Chronicles 19:2 And Jehu the son of Hanani the seer went out to meet him, and said to king Jehoshaphat, **Shouldest thou help the ungodly, and love them that hate the LORD?** therefore is wrath upon thee from before the LORD.*

INTRODUCTORY THOUGHTS

This passage poses an important question to those who are drawn too close to those who live as God's enemies. *"Shouldest thou help the ungodly, and love them that hate the LORD?"* Furthermore, the Bible also says, *"that the friendship of the world is enmity with God."* Immediately, our flesh rebels against what this could mean for our worldly relationships. We might conclude: "But shouldn't we love the lost?" Your mind might be directed toward those loved ones who are yet unsaved. These truths are not meant to convey that we should no longer be concerned with the eternal destination of those that we know. The Bible does, however, teach that we should not develop close associations with those who live ungodly. God drives this truth home by saying, *"Be ye not unequally yoked together with unbelievers"* **(2 Corinthians 6:14)**.

DEVOTIONAL THOUGHTS

- **(For children):** We should tell lost people about the Lord but they should not be our best friends *(Ephesians 5:11, Proverbs 24:1)*. If our closest associations are those who do not love the Lord, we are in danger of becoming like them and learning their ways *(Psalm 106:35-36)*.
- **(For everyone):** How can we insure that we are balanced on this truth? Should we *"help the ungodly"*? Should we *"love them that hate the LORD"*?
- Read **Galatians 6:14**. What does this verse say and mean? How does it apply to the subject of this study? How should the cross impact and change our fellowship with the world?

PRAYER THOUGHTS

- Ask the Lord to soften your heart to the truth of scripture.
- Ask God to help you love what He loves and hate what He hates.

SONG: *LET THOUGHTLESS THOUSANDS CHOOSE THE ROAD*

Day 144: Church Night

Ecclesiastes 3:1 To every thing there is a season, and a time to every purpose under the heaven:

8 A time to love, and a time to hate; a time of war, and a time of peace.

Day 145: (Thursday)
Those Who Love the LORD, Hate Evil

Psalm 97:10 Ye that love the LORD, hate evil: he preserveth the souls of his saints; he delivereth them out of the hand of the wicked.

INTRODUCTORY THOUGHTS

The Lord is a jealous God *(Exodus 34:14)*. He calls upon His people to follow Him with an undivided heart. One facet of our calling involves hating evil. Our love for the Lord will naturally breed a hatred for the things of this world. Throughout the psalms, we find statements of hatred from the people of God. They hated *"the congregation of evil doers"* *(Psalm 26:5)*, *"them that regard lying vanities"* *(Psalm 31:6)*, *"the work of them that turn aside"* *(Psalm 101:3)*, *"every false way"* *(Psalm 119:104, 128)*, *"vain thoughts"* *(Psalm 119:113)*, and *"covetousness"* *(Proverbs 28:16)*. God never intended for these truths to be limited to His children in Old Testament times. Just as the Bible commands that we should love the Lord and the brethren, it also commands that we should hate things contrary to the Lord.

DEVOTIONAL THOUGHTS

- **(For children):** We are supposed to hate evil and should have *"perfect hatred"* as king David describes in **Psalm 139:21-22**. We must love God and stay away from evildoers *(Psalm 119:115)*.
- **(For everyone):** Why did the people of God hate evil, vain thoughts, and covetousness? How do these things affect our fellowship with the Lord?
- Do you hate evil? Do you hate every false way? Do you hate vain thoughts? If not, what is the root of the problem? Is it possible that you do not love the Lord the way that He demands?

PRAYER THOUGHTS

- Ask the Lord to increase your love for Him.
- Ask Him to increase your hatred for this world.

SONG: *JESUS, THOU JOY OF LOVING HEARTS!*

Day 146: (Friday)
Hated by the World for Doing Right

*2 Chronicles 18:7 And the king of Israel said unto Jehoshaphat, There is yet one man, by whom we may inquire of the LORD: but **I hate him; for he never prophesied good unto me**, but always evil: the same is Micaiah the son of Imla. And Jehoshaphat said, Let not the king say so.*

INTRODUCTORY THOUGHTS

The truths of God's word naturally divide believers from those in the world. The preaching of God's word and His truths has often been the source of much of the world's disdain for God's people. The king of Israel hated and despised Micaiah because *"he never prophesied good . . . but always evil."* Any believer who consistently stands upon the truth of God's word will be hated by those who love the world. John the Baptist serves as another prime example. He was despised and ultimately killed because of his love for righteousness. Amos sheds light on why people hate those who speak and do right things. *"They hate him that rebuketh in the gate, and they abhor him that speaketh uprightly"* *(Amos 5:10)*. The Bible confirms these truths repeatedly. For instance, John warned believers not to marvel if the world hated them *(1 John 3:13)* because it first hated the Lord Jesus *(John 15:18)*. Seek not to be loved or admired by the world and you will not be disappointed when they despise you.

DEVOTIONAL THOUGHTS

- **(For children):** *Ephesians 4:15* says we must speak the truth in love. Stephen did just that in Acts chapter 7. After hearing Stephen's preaching, the men stopped their ears, took him outside the city, and killed him. Read what Jesus told His younger brothers (who did not believe in Him) in *John 7:7*. He told them why the world hated Him.
- **(For everyone):** Do you find that the world is too friendly with you? Do you find that you are too friendly with the world? How does this relationship reflect upon your presentation of the truth?
- Does knowing that the world will hate you give you a free pass to being unkind toward others? The truth you proclaim may offend the world, but the way in which you deliver the truth should not be the cause of the offense.

PRAYER THOUGHTS

- Ask the Lord to give you boldness to proclaim His truths.
- Ask God to give you wisdom in how to deliver the message.

SONG: *BE THOU OUR SURE DEFENCE*

Day 147: (Saturday)
God's Favour for the Hated

*Genesis 29:31 And **when the LORD saw that Leah was hated, he opened her womb***: *but Rachel was barren.*

*32 And Leah conceived, and bare a son, and she called his name Reuben: for she said, **Surely the LORD hath looked upon my affliction**; now therefore my husband will love me.*

*33 And she conceived again, and bare a son; and said, **Because the LORD hath heard that I was hated**, he hath therefore given me this son also: and she called his name Simeon.*

34 And she conceived again, and bare a son; and said, Now this time will my husband be joined unto me, because I have born him three sons: therefore was his name called Levi.

35 And she conceived again, and bare a son: and she said, Now will I praise the LORD: therefore she called his name Judah; and left bearing.,

INTRODUCTORY THOUGHTS

This passage demonstrates the kindness of our God. The story is not simply narrative involving God miraculously opening Leah's womb, but also provides insight as to why He did. Because Leah was hated, God came to her aid, not once, not twice, not three times, but four times. It is common in scripture to find the Lord coming to the aid of His own. God will look even more favourably upon His children as the world refuses, rejects, and abuses them. Though disdained by the heathen and mocked of men for the Lord's sake, God will never allow those forsaken by the world to be isolated from His blessings. Moses, hated by Egypt, found the Lord faithful in the wilderness. Jeremiah, hated because of his prophecies, found the Lord faithful in the dungeon. John, exiled to Patmos, heard the Lord speak to him and supernaturally received and wrote the final book of our Bible. God was faithful to His people then and remains so today.

DEVOTIONAL THOUGHTS

- **(For children):** Haman hated Mordecai because he would not bow down to him. Haman wanted to get rid of all of God's people and even built a gallows on which to hang Mordecai. God would not allow

Haman to fulfill his wicked plan and agenda. Haman was hanged on his own gallows and Mordecai was promoted to Haman's position.

- **(For everyone):** Have you found yourself in times where you were despised by the world? Did you find the Lord faithful during those times? What did you learn about the Lord in those trying times?
- If we are hated for righteousness' sake, the Lord will be faithful to bestow favour upon us. Does the same always hold true when we are hated because of some failure brought about by our own devices?

PRAYER THOUGHTS

- Ask the Lord to grant you favour in times of isolation.
- Ask the Lord to help you faithfully serve Him till death.

SONG: *HIDING IN THEE*

Notes: _____

_____

_____

_____

_____

_____

_____

_____

Quotes from the next volume

(VOLUME 3, WEEK 21)

Subject: Loyalty (con't)

Loyalty is a godly trait, and like most godly traits, difficulties can accompany it.

David was loyal and his loyalty was contagious. Throughout his life, he had those who would attempt great feats in order to assist, protect, or be a blessing to him.

22

Hospitality

Hospitality—found four times in four verses, all in the New Testament

Variations: hospitality

First usage: *Romans 12:13*

Last usage: *1 Peter 4:9*

Defined: genuine demonstration of kindness to others

Interesting fact: Two of the four mentions of hospitality specifically involve and point to the qualifications of a bishop *(1 Timothy 3:2; Titus 1:8)*. The Bible says that he is to be *"given to hospitality" (1 Timothy 3:2)* and *"a lover of hospitality" (Titus 1:8)*. Apparently, hospitality serves as a vital aspect of any church or ministry.

Bible study tip: Bible study involves so much more than simply looking up Bible words in a concordance or computer software. Oftentimes, a principle can be found in a passage without mentioning the corresponding Bible word. For example, though the qualifications of the widow do not mention hospitality by name, the widow certainly demonstrated such when she *"lodged strangers," "washed the saints' feet,"* and *"relieved the afflicted" (1 Timothy 5:10).*

Sunday, Day 148—Church Day (no devotional)
Monday, Day 149—*What Is Hospitality?*
Tuesday, Day 150—*The Believer's Responsibility*
Wednesday, Day 151—Church Night (no devotional)
Thursday, Day 152—*A Hospitable Widow*
Friday, Day 153—*The Barbarians Who Understood Hospitality*
Saturday, Day 154—*The Good Samaritan: A Hospitable Man*

Day 148: Church Day

1 Timothy 3:2 A bishop then must be blameless, the husband of one wife, vigilant, sober, of good behaviour, given to hospitality, apt to teach;

Day 149: (Monday)
What Is Hospitality?

1 Peter 4:9 Use hospitality one to another without grudging.

INTRODUCTORY THOUGHTS

On the surface, today's passage does not offer a specific definition for the word *hospitality*, yet we are not left without clues. First of all, *hospitality* is something that is done *"one to another."* This means that it is an action that should be done to other believers. It should also be done *"without grudging."* Additional insight can be gleaned by considering hospitality's root word, *hospital*. A basic definition for the word *hospital* involves a shelter for the needy or a place where the sick can recover. Thus, *hospitality* involves taking others in, even for a short time, to strengthen them in some area of need. Hospitality can be as simple as sharing a meal together or it may require more effort and time.

DEVOTIONAL THOUGHTS

(For children): God has always wanted His people to be kind and help others who have needs whether our own family, church family, or even those who are strangers *(Leviticus 19:33-34)*. Read how Job helped others *(Job 29:15-16b, Job 31:32)*. Can you think of some ways to help people?

- **(For everyone):** What are some ways in which you can show hospitality to your brothers and sisters in Christ? How can the Lord use you in order to strengthen others in areas of need or areas of weakness?
- How does hospitality present a strong testimony for Christianity? How could your hospitality lead others to desire to know more about Christ?

PRAYER THOUGHTS

- Ask the Lord to give you a desire to be hospitable toward others.
- Ask the Lord to help you see those in need of your hospitality.

SONG: JESUS, CEMENT OUR HEARTS AS ONE

Day 150: (Tuesday)
The Believer's Responsibility

Romans 12:10 Be *kindly affectioned one to another with brotherly love; in honour preferring one another;*

11 Not slothful in business; fervent in spirit; serving the Lord;

12 Rejoicing in hope; patient in tribulation; continuing instant in prayer;

13 Distributing to the necessity of saints; **given to hospitality***.*

INTRODUCTORY THOUGHTS

All good motives for Christian service should be rooted in love. As believers, we have a God-given responsibility in the area of hospitality. Twice the Bible refers to being *"given to hospitality"* *(Romans 12:13; 1 Timothy 3:2)*. The First Timothy passage specifically speaks of the qualifications of a bishop. However, God never intended for hospitality to be limited to church leadership. In fact, the passage in Romans identifies hospitality as a responsibility for all believers. To be *"given to hospitality"* means to be led by or under the control of hospitality. In other words, everything we do involving others should be motivated by the desire to be hospitable. *Titus 1:8* takes hospitality a step further by declaring that a bishop must be *"a lover of hospitality."* Christians should purpose to find joy spending time with others, sincerely desiring to strengthen and encourage them in some area of need.

DEVOTIONAL THOUGHTS

- **(For children):** Elisha passed through Shunem often and was urged by a godly woman to eat with her and her husband as he passed through. She also saw the need for Elisha to have a place to stay so they made him a room of his own in their home *(2 Kings 4:8-10)*.
- **(For everyone):** What does it mean to be *"given to hospitality"*? How can understanding hospitality effect your daily walk with the Lord and your dealings with other people?
- Why is it important for a pastor or a bishop to be *"given to"* and *"a lover of hospitality"*? How would it also be helpful for other believers within a congregation to exhibit a hospitable spirit?

PRAYER THOUGHTS

- Ask the Lord to show you the importance of hospitality.
- Ask God to help you to become more hospitable.

SONG: *BLEST BE THE TIE THAT BINDS*

Day 151: Church Night

*Hebrews 13:2 **Be not forgetful to entertain strangers**: for thereby some have entertained angels unawares.*

Day 152: (Thursday)
A Hospitable Widow

1 Timothy 5:9 Let not a widow be taken into the number under threescore years old, having been the wife of one man,

*10 Well reported of for good works; if she have brought up children, **if she have lodged strangers**, **if she have washed the saints' feet**, **if she have relieved the afflicted**, if she have diligently followed every good work.*

INTRODUCTORY THOUGHTS

Today's passage provides the qualifications for a widow before considering her for financial support by the church. Interestingly, several qualifications are strongly connected to her efforts involving hospitality. Did she lodge strangers? Did she wash the saints' feet? Did she relieve the afflicted? These questions basically sum up whether or not the lady was *"given to hospitality" (Romans 12:13)*. A woman who had given her life to others was counted worthy of receiving help from others once she was no longer able to support herself. She was to be held in high esteem if she had taken others in when they had no place to go, or washed the feet of other saints when they entered into her home, or relieved those around her who were afflicted.

DEVOTIONAL THOUGHTS

- **(For children):** Jesus *"went about doing good" (Acts 10:38)*. All of us should look for opportunities to help other people. The Philippian jailer shows the change of a person who gets saved. He immediately fed Paul and Silas and washed their wounds. Another great example is Dorcas who was full of good works and made coats and garments for widow women.
- **(For everyone):** What can every Christian learn from the qualifications for a widow? How can these qualities teach us to be more personally hospitable? How could we implement some of these things into our own lives?
- What are some different examples of ways you could exemplify hospitality? When is the last time you did something for others that would qualify as hospitality?

PRAYER THOUGHTS

- Ask God to help you find ways to be hospitable to others.
- Ask the Lord to set others before you who will be good examples.

SONG: *BE FIRM AND BE FAITHFUL*

Day 153: (Friday)
The Barbarians Who Understood Hospitality

*Acts 28:2 And **the barbarous people shewed us no little kindness**: for they kindled a fire, and received us every one, because of the present rain, and because of the cold.*

INTRODUCTORY THOUGHTS

A shipwreck landed Paul and others on an island called Melita *(Acts 28:1)*. The Bible says that those people of that land were barbarians. When a viper latched onto Paul's arm, these barbarians assumed that this was judgment because of some crime he had committed *(Acts 28:3-4)*. When Paul simply shook off the viper into the fire and remained unharmed, the people claimed that Paul must have been a god *(Acts 28:6)*. Although these people were superstitious and ignorant concerning the truth, it appears that they had an understanding of hospitality. Because of the rain and cold, the native people kindled a fire and received Paul and those with him. In addition to this, a man named Publius received Paul and lodged him three days. The world should never consistently display more hospitality than Christians.

DEVOTIONAL THOUGHTS

- **(For children):** When Pharaoh's daughter saw baby Moses in the ark, she knew he was helpless and hired his own mother to care for him. When Moses was old enough, he moved to the palace and was brought up as the son of Pharaoh's daughter *(Exodus 2:2-10)*. How did Pharaoh's daughter demonstrate hospitality?
- **(For everyone):** How did these barbarians understand the concept of hospitality? How is it that other people who have never trusted Christ as their Saviour often exemplify hospitality?
- If barbarians understood hospitality, how much more should we understand and implement hospitality toward others? What can we learn from the example of these barbarians?

PRAYER THOUGHTS

- Ask God to show you how and when to demonstrate hospitality.
- Ask the Lord to show you when others need your help.

SONG: *OUR BEST*

Day 154: (Saturday)
The Good Samaritan: A Hospitable Man

Luke 10:30 And Jesus answering said, A certain man went down from Jerusalem to Jericho, and fell among thieves, which stripped him of his raiment, and wounded him, and departed, leaving him half dead.

33 But a certain Samaritan, as he journeyed, came where he was: and when he saw him, he had compassion on him,

34 And went to him, and bound up his wounds, pouring in oil and wine, and set him on his own beast, and brought him to an inn, and took care of him.

35 And on the morrow when he departed, he took out two pence, and gave them to the host, and said unto him, Take care of him; and whatsoever thou spendest more, when I come again, I will repay thee.

INTRODUCTORY THOUGHTS

The story of the good Samaritan is a wonderful illustration of hospitality. The Lord Jesus told of a man who began a trip to Jericho. While on his way, he *"fell among thieves" (Luke 10:30)* who robbed him, stripped him of his clothes, and wounded him. When they were finished, they left this man for dead. The Lord then told of some men who passed by but were unwilling to help the dying man. Finally, a Samaritan, a people not generally known for their friendship with the Jews, stopped to help. He saw the wounded, dying man and had compassion on him. The Samaritan took the man, *"bound up his wounds . . . brought him to an inn, and took care of him" (Luke 10:34)*. Even when the Samaritan left, he provided additional monies to the inn keeper to insure that the injured man would be cared for as he finished his recovery. The good Samaritan man also assured the innkeeper that he would cover any additional funds necessary.

DEVOTIONAL THOUGHTS

- **(For children):** David's men found an Egyptian in a field. He was sick and David gave him food and water before he knew anything about him. He was a slave to David's enemies. Because of David's care, the slave gave David valuable information *(1 Samuel 30:11-15)*.

- **(For everyone):** Samaritans and Jews were not necessarily friendly toward one another, yet the Samaritan helped the wounded man although he knew that he was a Jew. What does this teach us about hospitality?
- What are some ways in which you can show hospitality to others in your church? What are ways you can show hospitality to those in your family or your community?

PRAYER THOUGHTS

- Thank the Lord for those who have been hospitable toward you.
- Ask the Lord to help you help others when they have need.

SONG: *MAKE US KIND AND TENDER-HEARTED*

Notes: _____

_____

_____

_____

_____

_____

_____

_____

_____

Quotes from the next volume

(VOLUME 3, WEEK 22)

Subject: Loyalty (con't)

Loyalty is a beautiful trait. It leads men to do significant things for others for what could be considered insignificant reasons.

Loyalty may seem to go unnoticed but will eventually yield great rewards.

23

Laughter

Laughter—found forty times in thirty-eight verses

Variations: laugh, laughed, laugheth, laughing, laughter

First usage: *Genesis 17:17* (laughed)

Last usage: *James 4:9* (laughter)

Defined: an audible sound demonstrating an instinctive expression of amusement or, at times, of derision

Interesting fact: The first seven uses of the word *laugh* (in its various forms) describe the faithless reaction of Abraham and Sarah to God concerning a promised seed.

Bible study tip: Words associated with your Bible word study can offer great assistance. For instance, *laughter* is associated with the word *scorn* a little over 25 percent of the time in the Bible. Understanding and defining the associated words often sheds light upon your original study.

Sunday, Day 155—Church Day (no devotional)
Monday, Day 156—*What Are You Laughing At?*
Tuesday, Day 157—*A Mouth Filled with Laughter*
Wednesday, Day 158—Church Night (no devotional)

Thursday, Day 159—*Sorrow Is Better than Laughter*
Friday, Day 160—*Jesus: A Man of Sorrows*
Saturday, Day 161—*The Last Laugh*

Day 155: Church Day

Ecclesiastes 2:2 I said of laughter, It is mad: and of mirth, What doeth it?

Day 156: (Monday)
What Are You Laughing At?

Genesis 18:9 And they said unto him, Where is Sarah thy wife? And he said, Behold, in the tent.

10 And he said, I will certainly return unto thee according to the time of life; and, lo, Sarah thy wife shall have a son. And Sarah heard it in the tent door, which was behind him.

11 Now Abraham and Sarah were old and well stricken in age; and it ceased to be with Sarah after the manner of women.

*12 Therefore **Sarah laughed within herself**, saying, After I am waxed old shall I have pleasure, my lord being old also?*

*13 And **the LORD said** unto Abraham, **Wherefore did Sarah laugh**, saying, Shall I of a surety bear a child, which am old?*

*14 **Is any thing too hard for the LORD?** At the time appointed I will return unto thee, according to the time of life, and Sarah shall have a son.*

15 Then Sarah denied, saying, I laughed not; for she was afraid. And he said, Nay; but thou didst laugh.

INTRODUCTORY THOUGHTS

We tend to think of laughter in a positive light, generally envisioning emotions like happiness or joyfulness. Yet, far too much laughter results from things opposed to God and His will. The Bible provides this same assessment. A careful study of the word *laughter* in the Bible demonstrates that the connotation is overwhelmingly bad. Today's passage shows Sarah laughing in disbelief of the promises of God. ***Genesis 17:17*** shows that Abraham did the same when he heard the news. These were two godly people; yet, much of the laughter found in the Bible occurred when the ungodly mocked God's people and God's promises *(Nehemiah 2:19)*. Our Saviour too was *"laughed . . . to scorn"* when He declared that the daughter of Jairus was not dead *(Mark 5:40)*. Laughter, in and of itself, is not wicked, but the cause of one's laughter reveals its true makeup.

DEVOTIONAL THOUGHTS

- **(For children):** Read *Psalm 22:7-8*. People laughed and made fun of Jesus while He was dying on the cross for the sins of mankind. They did not believe He was the Son of God though we know that He is and that they were wrong. Be very careful what you laugh at and why.
- **(For everyone):** In *Ephesians 5:4*, believers are warned about taking part in inconvenient jesting. What are some examples of inconvenient jesting? Why is it important that we do not laugh at foolish jesting?
- What makes you laugh? Are the things at which you laugh wholesome and godly? Do you laugh at things that bring hurt to others? Do you laugh at God's people or with God's people?

PRAYER THOUGHTS

- Ask the Lord to help you to laugh and rejoice in Him.
- Ask God to help you avoid jesting which is not convenient.

SONG: *WITH CHRIST, I SMILE AT THE STORM*

Day 157: (Tuesday)
A Mouth Filled with Laughter

Psalm 126:1 When the LORD turned again the captivity of Zion, we were like them that dream.

*2 **Then was our mouth filled with laughter**, and our tongue with singing: then said they among the heathen, **The LORD hath done great things for them**.*

3 The LORD hath done great things for us; whereof we are glad.

INTRODUCTORY THOUGHTS

The Old Testament shows that God's people (the Jews) repeatedly turned from the Lord and worshipped idols. Because of their sinful ways, they spent a considerable amount of time in captivity. Each time they turned back to God, He was faithful to bring them out of their times of captivity. Today's passage details one of those times when the people found joy in God's deliverance. The Bible testifies that their mouths were filled with laughter and their tongues with singing. The heathen took note and said, *"The LORD hath done great things for them."* When God did something special for His people, the overflowing emotions turned to laughter. They were grateful to God for His unmerited goodness to them and it was manifested in that their mouths were filled with laughter. Christians should likewise be glad when God pours out His manifold blessings by delivering from physical or spiritual captivity.

DEVOTIONAL THOUGHTS

- **(For children):** *Psalm 107:22b* tells us *"to declare his works with rejoicing."* Jesus gave His disciples power over many things and they rejoiced in that power. It was good to rejoice over this power, but Jesus told them the best thing to rejoice over was the fact that their names were written in heaven *(Luke 10:20b)*.
- **(For everyone):** When is the last time you were so grateful for the goodness of God in your life that you rejoiced, perhaps with laughter? How could this effect the world around you?
- Do you at times laugh over things that would displease the Lord and additionally fail to rejoice when God gives you some special blessing? If so, what does this say about your walk with the Lord?

PRAYER THOUGHTS

- Ask the Lord to help you find laughter in the right things.
- Ask God to give you a joy in knowing Him.

SONG: *HEAVENLY SUNLIGHT*

Day 158: Church Night

*Luke 6:21 Blessed are ye that hunger now: for ye shall be filled. **Blessed are ye that weep now: for ye shall laugh.***

*25 Woe unto you that are full! for ye shall hunger. **Woe unto you that laugh now! for ye shall mourn and weep.***

Day 159: (Thursday)
Sorrow Is Better than Laughter

Ecclesiastes 7:3 Sorrow is better than laughter: for by the sadness of the countenance the heart is made better.

INTRODUCTORY THOUGHTS

Most people would readily admit that they would rather laugh than cry. Yet, these are not God's thoughts concerning the matter *(Isaiah 55:8-9)*. According to the Bible, *"Sorrow is better than laughter: for by the sadness of the countenance the heart is made better" (Ecclesiastes 7:3)*. Laughter seems much more enjoyable than sorrow, yet life's lessons are learned much faster from sorrow than they are from amusement. Sorrow teaches us and molds us into better servants for the Lord. This does not mean that laughter is evil or harmful. It simply means that from God's perspective, sorrow is a much better teacher. Solomon bluntly spoke of what he knew concerning laughter in *Ecclesiastes 2:1-2*. The Bible says that Solomon gave himself to mirth and pleasure. In the end, he found this mirth and pleasure to be vain.

DEVOTIONAL THOUGHTS

- **(For children):** Even though we don't necessarily like sorrow, it brings us closer to God. When the psalmist found troubles and sorrow, he prayed *(Psalm 116:3-4)*. His ongoing troubles also caused him to turn to God's word and learn it *(Psalm 119:71)*.
- **(For everyone):** Laughter is enjoyable but often ends in heaviness *(Proverbs 14:13)*. In what ways does laughter offer a temporary escape from the cares of the world?
- How is sorrow a better teacher than laughter? What are some times of sorrow in your life where you learned the most? What are some times of laughter where you learned?

PRAYER THOUGHTS

- Ask the Lord to help you see things from His perspective.
- Ask the Lord to give you laughter and sorrow in His time.

SONG: *MORE LOVE TO THEE*

Day 160: (Friday)
Jesus: A Man of Sorrows

*Isaiah 53:1 Who hath believed our report? and to whom is **the arm of the LORD** revealed?*

2 For he shall grow up before him as a tender plant, and as a root out of a dry ground: he hath no form nor comeliness; and when we shall see him, there is no beauty that we should desire him.

*3 **He is** despised and rejected of men; **a man of sorrows**, and acquainted with grief: and we hid as it were our faces from him; he was despised, and we esteemed him not.*

INTRODUCTORY THOUGHTS

Most of us would assume that the Lord laughed at some point during His earthly ministry, yet the scripture never focuses on this point. Rather, the scripture seems to focus on the fact that He was *"a man of sorrows, and acquainted with grief"* **(Isaiah 53:3)**. We know very little of any laughter, yet we do know that He wept at the tomb of Lazarus **(John 11:35)**. He further lamented over Jerusalem because of their rebellion **(Luke 13:34)**. We also know that He sighed at the healing of the deaf man who had a speech impediment **(Mark 7:34)**. Heaven affords the Lord great rejoicing, yet His earthly ministry was consumed by heartache rather than mirth. This most likely was a result of dealing with the consequences of man's sin.

DEVOTIONAL THOUGHTS

- **(For children)**: Jesus knew He would take our sins on Him at the cross. That was troubling since He had no sin of His own **(John 12:27; 2 Corinthians 5:21)**. Yet, He endured the cross and completed what He came to do. We should constantly be mindful to thank Him and be willing to go through sorrows for the glory of God **(2 Timothy 4:7)**.
- **(For everyone)**: What can we learn from the emphasis on the Lord's sorrow in His earthly ministry? What might be the overriding theme for those who serve the Lord with their lives?
- Why was the Lord's earthly ministry filled with sorrows? Do the same conditions exist today? Would you be willing to be called a person of sorrows if that meant you walked closer to the Lord because of those sorrows?

PRAYER THOUGHTS

- Ask God to remind you that His sorrows brought us great joy.
- Thank the Lord for bearing your sin and burdens.

SONG: *HALLELUJAH, WHAT A SAVIOUR!*

Day 161: (Saturday)
The Last Laugh

Psalm 2:4 He that sitteth in the heavens shall laugh: the Lord shall have them in derision.

INTRODUCTORY THOUGHTS

Sorrows and tears fill the life of many people, yet one day all that will gloriously change for the child of God. Today, this world may laugh, mock, and ridicule the Lord and His people, but one day soon, the tide will turn. The Bible has some shocking truths. In fact, several passages attest to the fact that God will laugh at the wicked *(Psalm 2:4; Psalm 37:13; Psalm 59:8)*. This may seem harsh, but God is gracious, merciful, and longsuffering. The Lord will never laugh at the difficulties of any to whom He has not first offered refuge and deliverance. In like manner, wisdom personified in the Bible warns her rejecters that she too will laugh at their calamity and mock when their fear cometh *(Proverbs 1:26)*. On the other hand, the Bible assures a glorious future time of laughter for the people of God *(Luke 6:21)*.

DEVOTIONAL THOUGHTS

- **(For children):** Would you be happy if you unexpectedly stumbled across a great treasure? Read *Psalm 119:162*. We can rejoice now in God's promises *(Revelation 21:4)* even if others say He doesn't exist or isn't coming back *(2 Peter 3:3-4)*.
- **(For everyone):** Our laughter here is often interrupted by sorrows. In heaven, there will be no sorrows to interrupt our laughter. What does this mean about the abundance of our future joy?
- What is the source of God's laughter in heaven? What will be the source of our laughter and joy in heaven? What should be the source of these things now?

PRAYER THOUGHTS

- Thank God that He will one day wipe away all tears.
- Thank the Lord that your sorrows will be replaced with laughter.

SONG: *WHEN THE RANSOMED GET HOME*

Notes: _____

_____

_____

_____

_____

_____

_____

_____

_____

_____

Quotes from the next volume

(VOLUME 3, WEEK 23)

Subject: Meddling

Unfortunately, it has been a common practice in the history of nations to provoke others to battle when war was unnecessary and often contrary to God's will.

Meddling in the problems of others is a dangerous practice with unanticipated results.

The world contradicts the truths of God. For instance, it has convinced mankind that it is manly to start a fight and cowardly to cease from strife. As is almost always the case, the world's natural way of thinking is completely opposite to the scriptural teachings.

24

Judging

Judging—found 758 times in 674 verses

Variations: judge, judged, judges, judgest, judgeth, judging, judgment, judgments

First usage: *Genesis 15:14* (judge)

Last usage: *Revelation 20:13* (judged)

Defined: can be a position of authority but as a verb it means to make a decision or to form an opinion on a matter

Interesting fact: According to scripture, judging is one of the distinct responsibilities relegated to the Son of God by the Father *(John 5:22-23; Acts 10:34-42; Acts 17:31; Romans 2:16; 2 Timothy 4:1)*. In like manner, it is an important responsibility for God's children to judge, both now *(1 Corinthians 2:15)* and in the future *(1 Corinthians 6:3)*.

Bible study tip: In any Bible study, attention to even the smallest of details is of utmost importance. Sometimes adding or subtracting even a letter from a single word can form an altogether different word and convey a completely different meaning. Additionally, the Bible also sometimes utilizes capitalization to express variations in the meaning of a word. For instance, *"The Word of God" (Revelation*

19:13) is not synonymous with *"the word of God" (1 Peter 1:23)* though the two are closely associated. The Bible uses the capital "W" in *Word* to refer to the incarnate Son of God, whereas the lower case *word* refers to the written word of God.

Sunday, Day 162—Church Day (no devotional)
Monday, Day 163—*Judge Not?*
Tuesday, Day 164—*Judge Righteous Judgment!*
Wednesday, Day 165—Church Night (no devotional)
Thursday, Day 166—*The Spiritual Person Judges All Things*
Friday, Day 167—*Judge Yourself or Be Judged*
Saturday, Day 168—*Judging Responsibly*

Day 162: Church Day

Romans 2:1 *Therefore thou art inexcusable, O man,* **whosoever thou art that judgest**: *for wherein thou judgest another,* **thou condemnest thyself; for thou that judgest doest the same things**.

2 But we are sure that **the judgment of God is according to truth** *against them which commit such things.*

3 And **thinkest thou this, O man, that judgest them which do such things, and doest the same, that thou shalt escape the judgment of God?**

Day 163: (Monday)
Judge Not?

Matthew 7:1 Judge not, *that ye be not judged.*

INTRODUCTORY THOUGHTS

This verse, apart from **John 3:16**, may be the most recognized and certainly the most quoted verse by those who have little concern for God or the things of God. **Matthew 7:1** also happens to be one of the most misinterpreted and misapplied verses in all of scripture. This verse is abused by non-Christians as well as those living a carnal lifestyle. Non-Christians do not want to be held to any biblical standard while carnal Christians attempt to use the verse to avoid having judgment passed upon them and their questionable actions. The spiritual Christian knows that the context of the verse simply discourages judging hypocritically. God never intended for His children to not judge. This passage, along with many others, simply points out the inexcusability of passing judgment upon matters where those judging are likewise guilty of the same actions. The point is not to avoid judgment altogether but to avoid hypocrisy while judging. This truth was taught during the Lord's ministry but also reiterated by the apostle Paul in **Romans 2:1**.

DEVOTIONAL THOUGHTS

(For children): Before trying to help others by telling them the things they need to do better for God, we need to be insured we are not guilty of doing the same things *(Romans 2:21)*. Start by reading what *Lamentations 3:40* says to do.

- **(For everyone):** Why is it important that we first remove the beam from our own eye before casting the mote out of our brother's eye *(Matthew 7:3-5)*?
- The judgment men pass upon others will in turn be passed upon them. What should we do before we judge others? How careful should we be in passing judgment in areas where we too are struggling? Why?

PRAYER THOUGHTS

- Ask the Lord to give you the proper balance on judgment.
- Ask God to give you wisdom and patience in judging others.

SONG: *NOTHING BETWEEN*

Day 164: (Tuesday)
Judge Righteous Judgment!

*John 7:24 Judge not according to the appearance, but **judge righteous judgment**.*

INTRODUCTORY THOUGHTS

Carnal Christians and those who do not know the Lord consider judging others as the greatest of sins. The opposite actually holds true. Believers fail when they refuse to judge *"righteous judgment."* So often, men judge people and situations simply by what is seen or through an emotional response. Yet, this is completely contrary to the scriptural admonition to judge. Instead, we are to *"judge righteous judgment."* How can this be consistently done? First and foremost, we need a righteous standard by which to compare all things. In **John 12:48**, we learn of that righteous standard when the Lord Jesus said that His words would judge men. The Bible is a perfect Book containing perfect laws and offers a perfect standard for making judgments. Therefore, all judgment should be based upon the infallible standards provided by God within His glorious word. We will never go wrong with judging according to God's perfect standard.

DEVOTIONAL THOUGHTS

- **(For children):** The Lord judges not by what He sees or hears but by the truth *(Isaiah 11:3b; Psalm 96:13b)*. His word is truth *(John 17:17b)*. Consider a few examples. Did Asa judge his grandmother correctly *(1 Kings 15:13)*? Did the barbarous people judge Paul correctly *(Acts 28:3-4)*?
- **(For everyone):** Upon what basis do you judge people or circumstances? Is it possible that your judgment is inaccurate and unfair? What can you do to insure that you *"judge righteous judgment"* according to the Bible standard?
- How can a believer use the Bible to aid in executing proper judgment? How can failure to use the Bible in judgment leave the believer in danger of flawed judgment?

PRAYER THOUGHTS

- Ask the Lord to help your judgments to be based upon scripture.
- Ask God to help you judge righteously.

SONG: *STEPPING IN THE LIGHT*

Day 165: Church Night

John 8:14 Jesus answered and said unto them, Though I bear record of myself, yet my record is true: for I know whence I came, and whither I go; but ye cannot tell whence I come, and whither I go.

15 Ye judge after the flesh; I judge no man.

16 And yet if I judge, my judgment is true: for I am not alone, but I and the Father that sent me.

Day 166: (Thursday)
The Spiritual Person Judges All Things

*1 Corinthians 2:15 But **he that is spiritual judgeth all things**, yet he himself is judged of no man.*

INTRODUCTORY THOUGHTS

The last few studies have sought to dispel the notion that the Bible condemns judging. Today's verse is no exception. Notice that the verse begins with a coordinating conjunction. The word *but* indicates that our verse serves a continuation of the thought that preceded it. The previous verse refers to the *natural man* which is someone who does not know the Lord as Saviour. Because he is not saved, he cannot discern the things of God. Today's passage states that the *"spiritual* [man] *judgeth all things."* A *spiritual man* is not only a saved man but one who enjoys the peace of God and daily fellowship with God. The other scriptural designation for man (in addition to the *natural man* [unsaved], and *spiritual man* [saved and in good fellowship]) is the *carnal man* [saved, but not in good fellowship]. Since the carnal man lacks the proper fellowship with the Lord *(1 Corinthians 3:1)*, he may discern but fails in the proper execution of that discernment. Those claiming that believers should not judge are simply foolish. In fact, a *spiritual man* will judge all things but do so only based upon righteous judgment *(John 7:24)*.

DEVOTIONAL THOUGHTS

- **(For children):** Solomon prayed that the Lord would show him who was right or wrong as he judged *(1 Kings 3:9)*. Read how he discovered which mother was the true mother of the child *(1 Kings 3:24-27)*.
- **(For everyone):** Do you judge others? Upon what do you base your judgment? Are you able to discern between right and wrong, truth and error? If not, why do you think that you struggle?
- Have you trusted the Lord as your Saviour? If so, would you consider yourself a carnal believer or a spiritual believer? Upon what do you base your thoughts?

PRAYER THOUGHTS

- Ask the Lord to help you be spiritual in all matters.
- Ask the Lord to teach you proper judgment.

SONG: *O WORD OF GOD INCARNATE*

Day 167: (Friday)
Judge Yourself or Be Judged

*1 Corinthians 11:31 For **if we would judge ourselves, we should not be judged**.*

INTRODUCTORY THOUGHTS

Far too many Christians fear being judged by others more than they fear being judged by Almighty God. Christians should have a healthy respect and fear concerning the coming judgment seat of Christ. Yet, very few actually understand the biblical admonition concerning how to reduce this judgment. In today's passage, we learn that *"if we would judge ourselves, we should not be judged."* Christians should devote their time and strength to comparing themselves against the precepts of God's word to help correct their shortcomings. In doing so, the time of judgment at Christ's judgment seat would lose much of its dread. In like manner, Christians should learn to become their own honest critic making it harder for others to find legitimate fault with us. The importance of this self-evaluation of judging ourselves would equate in a better testimony to the world.

DEVOTIONAL THOUGHTS

- (**For children**): The people of Samaria faced starvation from being surrounded by the Syrians. God caused the Syrians to flee *(2 Kings 7:6-7)*, but no one in the city knew that they fled the city. Four lepers who lived outside the city were the only ones who knew. Read what they did *(2 Kings 7:5, 8)*. They examined themselves and knew they should share the information *(2 Kings 7:9-10)*.
- (**For everyone**): Do you judge yourself? Do you find it easier to find fault in others while missing the same faults within your own life? What efforts can you take to become a more honest critic of yourself?
- How could it help at the judgment seat of Christ to judge yourself on a daily basis? How could this conform you more to the Lord?

PRAYER THOUGHTS

- Ask the Lord to help you judge yourself.
- Ask the Lord to make you more like His Son each day.

SONG: *WHOLLY THINE*

Day 168: (Saturday)
Judging Responsibly

1 Corinthians 6:1 Dare any of you, having a matter against another, go to law before the unjust, and not before the saints?

*2 Do ye not know that **the saints shall judge the world?** and if the world shall be judged by you, are ye unworthy to judge the smallest matters?*

*3 Know ye not that **we shall judge angels? how much more things that pertain to this life?***

4 If then ye have judgments of things pertaining to this life, set them to judge who are least esteemed in the church.

5 I speak to your shame. Is it so, that there is not a wise man among you? no, not one that shall be able to judge between his brethren?

6 But brother goeth to law with brother, and that before the unbelievers.

7 Now therefore there is utterly a fault among you, because ye go to law one with another. Why do ye not rather take wrong? why do ye not rather suffer yourselves to *be defrauded?*

8 Nay, ye do wrong, and defraud, and that your *brethren.*

INTRODUCTORY THOUGHTS

The scriptural form of church judgment was fashioned according to the practice that will take place in the future. However, the role of judgment in the early church seems to be much more involved than generally practiced in churches today. The spiritual believers took their disputes with other believers to be judged by the church. Those believers who failed to follow this guideline were considered to be the carnal believers at Corinth. They were unwisely taking their disputes before unsaved judges. Paul rebuked these believers and explained in context their future role of judgment: believers would take part in judging the world *(1 Corinthians 6:2)*. Additionally, believers will have a lofty responsibility of judging angels *(1 Corinthians 6:3)*.

DEVOTIONAL THOUGHTS

- **(For children):** If you and a sibling had an argument, would you go to a next door neighbour whom you did not know to settle the matter?

Of course not, you would go to dad or mom. The same is true with our church family. God wants us to settle any problems we have with someone at church within our church family, not by those outside the church.

- **(For everyone):** How could our judgment within a local body of believers actually work to preserve the testimony of our Lord Jesus Christ? How could it insure biblical solutions to our disputes?
- In our day, people love to sue others over the smallest matters. What kind of impression does it give the world when believers take part in this type of behaviour?

PRAYER THOUGHTS

- Ask God to help you learn to judge now.
- Ask the Lord to help you obey Him in all matters of life.

SONG: *WHAT THEN, SHALL CHRISTIANS SIN*

Notes: _____

_____

_____

_____

Quotes from the next volume

(VOLUME 3, WEEK 24)

Subject: The Home

As the world seeks to further dilute the distinction between men and women, it becomes ever more important to stand firm upon God's principles. God has a defined order in the home and the world's opinions do not alter God's precepts.

A godly home follows the scripture even when it contradicts the generally accepted teachings of the day.

A man that will not pray for the family God has given him is really no man at all. A godly man will always intercede between his home and impending danger.

25

Leading

Leading—found 145 times in 141 verses

Variations: lead, leader, leaders, leadest, leadeth, led, leddest

First usage: *Genesis 24:27* (led)

Last usage: *Revelation 13:10* (leadeth)

Defined: to guide

Interesting fact: The Lord Jesus was *"led up of the Spirit into the wilderness to be tempted of the devil" (Matthew 4:1)*, *"led . . . unto the brow of the hill . . . that they might cast him down headlong" (Luke 4:29)*, *"led . . . away to Caiaphas" (Matthew 26:57)*, *"led . . . away . . . to Pontius Pilate" (Matthew 27:2)*, and *"led . . . away"* to be crucified *(Matthew 27:31)*. Through it all, *"He was led as a sheep to the slaughter" (Acts 8:32)*. Because of this, He will one day *lead* His own *"unto living fountains of waters: and God shall wipe away all tears from their eyes" (Revelation 7:17)*.

Bible study tip: Learn how to identify the parts of speech and understand their various purposes and uses. In this particular study, it will be helpful to understand how prepositions and prepositional phrases serve in a sentence.

God's choice of prepositions will help to unveil the intended meanings of the passage.

Sunday, Day 169—Church Day (no devotional)
Monday, Day 170—*Learn to Follow Your Leader*
Tuesday, Day 171—*Leaders Can Influence Followers Unexpectedly*
Wednesday, Day 172—Church Night (no devotional)
Thursday, Day 173— *With Leadership Comes Responsibility*
Friday, Day 174—*The Best Leaders Are Also the Best Followers*
Saturday, Day 175—*Softly Leading*

Day 169: Church Day

Matthew 15:14 *Let them alone: they be **blind leaders of the blind**. And **if the blind lead the blind, both shall fall into the ditch**.*

Day 170: (Monday)
Learn to Follow Your Leader

1 Corinthians 11:3 *But I would have you know, that **the head of every man is Christ**; and **the head of the woman is the man**; and **the head of Christ is God**.*

INTRODUCTORY THOUGHTS

People, especially the young or those new in the Lord, have many misconceptions. Leadership serves as a prime example because of a failure to grasp how it truly works. Many people dream of a future time when they will no longer have to submit to any authority. However, everyone has a leader to which he must submit and follow. God designed the home to have a specified order of authority: the children submit to the parents *(Ephesians 6:1)*; the wife submits to her husband *(Colossians 3:18)*; and the husband submits to the Lord *(1 Corinthians 11:3)*. In the country, the citizens are to submit to the government *(1 Peter 2:13-14)* as the government submits to the Lord *(1 Peter 3:22)*. Everyone is under some authority. Saved people are commanded to follow their Lord *(John 8:42)*; whereas lost people follow their father, the Devil *(John 8:44)*. Everyone answers to someone whether or not they acknowledge that submission.

DEVOTIONAL THOUGHTS

- **(For children):** King Saul's son Jonathan held command over one thousand soldiers. He was in line to become the next king of Israel, but God chose David instead. Jonathan did not fight against the will of God but graciously submitted *(1 Samuel 23:15-17)*. He even helped and encouraged David many times. What might have happened if Jonathan wanted to be the king regardless of God's plan?
- **(For everyone):** Rebellion is often mislabeled as being independent. Everyone must be led by someone else. Who is your leader? Whom are you leading? Are you leading and following in a way that pleases the Lord?
- Under whose authority do you operate? Who lives under your authority? Why is it important that a leader submits to his God-given authority?

PRAYER THOUGHTS

- Ask the Lord to build you into a godly leader.
- Thank the Lord for the godly leaders in your life.

SONG: *I SURRENDER ALL*

Day 171: (Tuesday)
Leaders Can Influence Followers Unexpectedly

John 21:1 After these things Jesus shewed himself again to the disciples at the sea of Tiberias; and on this wise shewed he himself.

2 There were together Simon Peter, and Thomas called Didymus, and Nathanael of Cana in Galilee, and the sons of Zebedee, and two other of his disciples.

*3 **Simon Peter saith** unto them, **I go a fishing. They say unto him, We also go with thee.** They went forth, and entered into a ship immediately; and that night they caught nothing.*

INTRODUCTORY THOUGHTS

A leader who has no followers is no leader. The disciples were given some explicit instructions from the Lord. Like each of us, they had a responsibility to do God's work, yet Simon Peter chose instead to go fishing. His decision influenced others to move in the same direction away from the will of God. The disciples blindly followed his lead. The Lord had admonished Peter to strengthen his brethren *(Luke 22:32)*, but under Peter's leadership, the disciples became weak through disobedience. Perhaps Peter never desired to be a leader. He may have been satisfied to simply follow others, but God knew what was best for Peter and the other apostles. When Peter made the wrong decisions, he had others that he negatively affected. Every leader must consider that the direction he chooses will lead others in his footsteps.

Devotional Thoughts

- **(For children)**: God made Jeroboam king over the ten tribes of Israel. Instead of leading the people to worship the true God, he chose to set up two calves of gold and told the people that these were the gods which brought them out of Egypt. His decision caused those people to eventually be taken captive out of their land, never to return.
- **(For everyone)**: Who is following in your footsteps? What kind of influence are you having in the lives of others? Does it please the Lord when others choose to follow your path?
- Have you made wrong decisions only to find that your decisions influence others to likewise make the same unwise decisions? How can you encourage them to go in a different direction?

Prayer Thoughts

- Ask the Lord to help you lead others the right way.
- Ask the Lord to help your leadership strengthen other believers.

SONG: *HOLY LORD GOD! I LOVE THY TRUTH*

Day 172: Church Night

*Proverbs 16:29 A **violent man** enticeth his neighbour, and **leadeth** him **into the way that is not good.***

Day 173: (Thursday)
With Leadership Comes Responsibility

*James 3:1 My brethren, **be not many masters**, knowing that **we shall receive the greater condemnation.***

INTRODUCTORY THOUGHTS

Far too many people allow themselves to accept unbalanced viewpoints. For instance, people focus on the glory of leadership while failing to realize the tremendous responsibility that comes with leadership. A student, for example, is only responsible for his own studies, while a teacher takes on the added responsibility for how he leads each of his students. A pastor who can't rule well his own home has no business taking on the added responsibility of caring for the church of God *(1 Timothy 3:4-5)*. An employee within a company is responsible to God for his own work. Yet, a company owner takes upon himself the responsibility for leading and caring for every individual affected by the company. With these truths in mind, we again focus upon today's passage. James suggests that believers consider the responsibility that accompanies leadership before taking on a position of leadership.

DEVOTIONAL THOUGHTS

- **(For children):** Being a leader is not easy. David's men were upset with him when the Amalekites burned their city and stole their goods and took their families. David was not at fault, but as a leader, the responsibility fell to him. He first prayed to God for direction and then led the men to victory and the recovery of all that was taken.
- **(For everyone):** What is the level of responsibility that you currently bear? Whom are you responsible for leading? Are you leading those people in the right direction? If not, what might be the consequences?
- How should leadership responsibility bring about a sobriety within your life? How should it effect the decisions that you make and the way that you make those decisions?

PRAYER THOUGHTS

- Ask the Lord to show you the responsibility of leadership.
- Ask God to give you wisdom in leading others.

SONG: *WHO IS ON THE LORD'S SIDE?*

Day 174: (Friday)
The Best Leaders Are Also the Best Followers

Joshua 1:1 Now after the death of Moses the servant of the LORD it came to pass, that **the LORD spake unto Joshua** *the son of Nun,* **Moses' minister, saying,**

2 Moses my servant is dead; now therefore **arise, go over this Jordan, thou, and all this people,** *unto the land which I do give to them, even to the children of Israel.*

INTRODUCTORY THOUGHTS

Before a man will ever learn how to be a great leader, he must first learn how to be a dependable follower. If he cannot serve without receiving recognition, he will never know how to handle the recognition once he takes on a leadership role. If a man will not follow instructions, he will never be equipped to give instructions that others should follow. Long before Joshua led the children of Israel into the land of promise, he faithfully served as the minister of Moses. Before Joshua became known as the leader of a nation, he faithfully gave himself to the previous leader of Israel. Likewise, before David became the king of Israel, he submitted himself as a servant to Saul. And lastly, before Elisha ever became a great prophet of God, he faithfully served under Elijah's tutelage.

DEVOTIONAL THOUGHTS

- **(For children):** Samuel was a great example of a judge, prophet, and priest for God's people. However, like most other leaders, he had humble beginnings. As a child, he started receiving instructions from Eli on how to serve the Lord in the tabernacle. Read *1 Samuel 2:26*. Samuel was a good follower who did not cause problems for those whom he served.
- **(For everyone):** To whom have you ministered taking on a role as a student, servant, or assistant? Do others consider you to be a good follower, or are you difficult to lead?
- What kind of a leader would you desire to be? How can you set a good example now as someone who follows in a godly manner? How are you going to feel if God gives you followers just like yourself?

PRAYER THOUGHTS

- Ask the Lord to help you first learn how to follow.

- Ask the Lord to show you if your manner of following is godly or ungodly.

SONG: *BELOVED OF THE LORD*

Day 175: (Saturday)
Softly Leading

Genesis 33:14 *Let my lord, I pray thee, pass over before his servant: and **I will lead on softly**, according as the cattle that goeth before me and the children be able to endure, until I come unto my lord unto Seir.*

INTRODUCTORY THOUGHTS

Godly leadership shows itself as fair, flexible, and just. Many different things are taken into consideration before directing those under authority. Does the individual's personality demand a strong hand of leadership or patience and gentleness? Although leadership presents varying challenges, the astute leader considers these challenges as opportunities for excellence. In turn, the effective leader always develops within himself the ability to discern how to lead and motivate the different people types. For instance, today's passage shows Jacob explaining to Esau the need to lead on *softly* because the children could not endure a demanding journey. The same leadership methods simply will not work for every individual. A godly leader seeks out the Lord for help in determining what will best accomplish the will of God by strengthening his followers.

DEVOTIONAL THOUGHTS

- **(For children):** In Sunday School class, when some children are nicely asked to stop talking or to sit down, they do so immediately. Others have to be told more than once. The teacher may speak more firmly to them and set them in their chairs because the teacher loves them and wants them to learn to do right.
- **(For everyone):** Do you have children or people that you lead? Does each one require the same method of leadership, or do you have to implement different styles of leadership?

- Why is it important that we lead in a way that our followers can endure? How can we know the right way to lead each person for whom we are responsible?

PRAYER THOUGHTS

- Ask God for wisdom as you lead.
- Ask the Lord to show you how to lead each person.

SONG: *JESUS, I MY CROSS HAVE TAKEN*

Notes: _____

_____

_____

_____

_____

_____

_____

_____

_____

_____

Quotes from the next volume

(VOLUME 3, WEEK 25)

Subject: The Home (con't)

A good wife and mother exemplifies selflessness like no one else on earth.

God made the heart of the woman tender, but this tender heart can be unfortunately hardened by sin.

With all the difficult challenges that a woman faces within the home, it should not be surprising that the Lord repeatedly gave warnings against a woman with a contentious spirit.

26

Love

Love—found 668 times in 568 verses

Variations: beloved, beloved's, love, loved, lovedst, lovely, lover, lovers, loves, lovest, loveth, loving, lovingkindness, lovingkindnesses

First usage: *Genesis 22:2* (lovest)

Last usage: *Revelation 22:15* (loveth)

Defined: to cherish, delight in, or to approve

Interesting fact: In both the Old and New Testaments, the first usage of the word *love* declares the love of a father for his son. In the Old Testament, Abraham is told, *"Take now thy son, thine only son Isaac, whom thou **lovest**, and get thee into the land of Moriah"* *(Genesis 22:2)*. In the New Testament, God the Father says of God the Son, *"This is my **beloved** Son, in whom I am well pleased"* *(Matthew 3:17)*. This is no accident but providentially designed by a God that never wastes words or lacks purpose.

Bible study tip: *Matthew 12:18* is a quote originating from *Isaiah 42:1*. As is often the case, this scenario offers a great opportunity to glean understanding on the Bible definitions of several words. It takes a little work, but is well worth the effort. Note the interchanging of the words *chosen (**Matthew 12:18**)* for *uphold (**Isaiah 42:1**), beloved (**Matthew 12:18**)* for *elect (**Isaiah 42:1**), well pleased (**Matthew 12:18**)* for *delighteth (**Isaiah 42:1**),* and *shew (**Matthew 12:18**)* for *bring forth (**Isaiah 42:1**).* God purposed that we glean a greater understanding with these interchangeable words within their context. The connection of *beloved* and *elect* is especially insightful.

Sunday, Day 176—Church Day (no devotional)
Monday, Day 177—*What Is Love?*
Tuesday, Day 178—*The Love of the Father for the Son*
Wednesday, Day 179—Church Night (no devotional)
Thursday, Day 180—*Giving: The Truest Fruit of Love*
Friday, Day 181—*Expressions of Love*
Saturday, Day 182—*Ungodly Love*

Day 176: Church Day

*1 John 4:7 Beloved, let us love one another: for **love is of God**; and **every one that loveth is born of God**, and knoweth God.*

Day 177: (Monday)
What Is Love?

*Deuteronomy 6:5 And **thou shalt love the LORD thy God** with all thine heart, and with all thy soul, and with all thy might.*

Introductory Thoughts

The common misconception concerning love is that it simply involves an emotion felt for those for whom we care. Although love is associated with our emotions, love is, in reality, much deeper than an emotion. It is first and foremost a choice that we consciously make. When God commanded His people to love Him, He was not asking them to feel an emotion, but rather, to choose to care for Him. In like manner, when the Lord commanded husbands to love their wives *(**Ephesians 5:25**),*

He was not asking merely for an emotional attachment, but something much deeper and far greater. In fact, love is something that can be taught and learned. In *Titus 2:4*, the older women are to teach the younger women to love their husbands and children. Therefore, when God asks us to love, He is asking us to make a choice to love others regardless of our swinging moods or wavering feelings. Love is a choice to make and a decision to do what God has directed His children to do.

DEVOTIONAL THOUGHTS

- **(For children)**: Read *Luke 5:1-6*. Peter fished all night and caught nothing. He was tired and didn't want to fish anymore. When Jesus told him to go out again, read Peter's answer *(Luke 5:5)*. Peter chose to obey though he really did not desire to do it. This is true love *(John 14:15)*.
- **(For everyone):** If love is a choice, what does that suggest about the phrase "falling in love"? How does this also show the error of statements such as, "we just don't love each other anymore"? People *choose* either to love or withhold love, but rest assured, it is a *choice*.
- How does the fact that love is a choice change our concept of loving the Lord? How does that same fact demonstrate the greatness of God's love for man?

PRAYER THOUGHTS

- Ask the Lord to teach you how to love Him.
- Ask God to help you gain a deeper understanding of biblical love.

SONG: *MY JESUS, I LOVE THEE*

Day 178: (Tuesday)
The Love of the Father for the Son

Genesis 22:2 And he said, ***Take now thy son****, thine only son Isaac,* ***whom thou lovest****, and get thee into the land of Moriah; and offer him there for a burnt offering upon one of the mountains which I will tell thee of.*

INTRODUCTORY THOUGHTS

Sometimes the Bible's first usage of a word offers the greatest insights into the overall usage of the word throughout the scriptures.

For instance, today's verse affords a glimpse into the first use of a form of the word *love*. This first occurrence is by divine design representing the greatest of truths. This first mention of love reflects the love of a father for his beloved son. Of even greater significance is the fact that despite this father's love for his son, he was willing to sacrifice him in obedience to his heavenly Father. Bible students have always considered this father and son duo as a wonderful picture of the relationship of our heavenly Father (God the Father) to God the Son. The first mention of the word *love* is a father's love for his son and the first love ever was the love of God the Father for God the Son *(John 15:9; John 17:23, 26)*. Only the Lord could orchestrate such wonderful and profound truths.

Devotional thoughts

- **(For children):** God the Father loves God the Son. When we receive Jesus as our Saviour, God the Father accepts us as part of His family and we are called the sons of God *(John 1:12)*. What wonderful love He has for us.
- **(For everyone):** God is love *(1 John 4:8)*. Before God ever loved man, God the Father and God the Son shared a love in eternity past. What does this mean for believers (see *John 17:23*)?
- If God is love, and He is, the moment He ceases to be love, He would cease to be God. What does this suggest about God's motive in all of His works throughout eternity (past and future)?

Prayer Thoughts

- Thank the Lord for His love.
- Ask God to teach you how to love as He loves.

SONG: *THIS IS MY FATHER'S WORLD*

Day 179: Church Night

*1 John 4:11 Beloved, **if God so loved us, we ought also to love one another**.*

Day 180: (Thursday)
Giving: The Truest Fruit of Love

John 3:16 *For **God so loved** the world, **that he gave** his only begotten Son, that whosoever believeth in him should not perish, but have everlasting life.*

INTRODUCTORY THOUGHTS

Today's verse is by far the most well-known and beloved verse in all of scripture. Yet, it contains a concept that is most often misunderstood and misconstrued by Christians and non-Christians alike. Although society flippantly uses this word *love*, real biblical love sacrifices. Christ's love for us demonstrates this truth ***(Galatians 2:20; Ephesians 5:25)***. True love costs the person who chooses to love. When an individual loves someone else, his love is best demonstrated by the sacrifices he makes. This holds true concerning God's demonstrated love for the world. God gave His only begotten Son to die for the sins of the world. God loved so God gave! In like manner, any person who truly loves the Lord will gladly sacrifice in order to manifest that love.

DEVOTIONAL THOUGHTS

- **(For children):** While David was hiding from Saul in a cave, he longed for a drink of water from a well in Bethlehem. The Philistines had control of the well. Because of their love for David, three mighty men risked their lives to get David a drink.
- **(For everyone):** What sacrifices has the Lord made to demonstrate His love for you in salvation? What has the Lord done to manifest His love for you after salvation?
- What do you give to those you love? What have you given for the Lord in order to demonstrate that you truly love Him? What would you be willing to give to Him?

PRAYER THOUGHTS

- Ask the Lord to help you show the fruit of biblical love.
- Thank God for His sacrifice for you in salvation and afterwards.

SONG: *HERE IS LOVE*

Day 181: (Friday)
Expressions of Love

*Proverbs 3:12 For **whom the LORD loveth he correcteth**; even as a father the son* in whom *he delighteth.*

INTRODUCTORY THOUGHTS

Worldly misconceptions have caused many believers to struggle with the biblical concept of love. Love can originate from what is generally considered a negative expression. Our passage shows that the Lord corrects those whom He loves. Love does not express itself for the satisfaction of the one who loves, but for the benefit of the one that is the object of one's love. When we think of how to express our love for someone, a hug or kind words generally come to mind. These expressions are often used to send a message of love; however, the Bible presents additional insights often not directly associated to loving someone. This is why the Bible points out that chastening can be used to express love toward the recipient. Furthermore, *Proverbs 13:24* shows that a father who loves his son chastens that son because of his love for that child. We are led to believe that expressing love for others is best expressed by bailing them out every time they are in trouble. Yet, the Lord declares that love does what is best for the recipients of that love, even if that includes correction.

DEVOTIONAL THOUGHTS

- **(For children):** God expects your dad and mom to correct you because He wants you to learn to do right *(Proverbs 19:18)*. Eli's sons did wickedly and Eli spoke to them, yet they continued in their evil ways *(1 Samuel 2:23-24)*. He should have taken more serious action *(1 Samuel 3:13)* but did not, and his two sons were killed in battle as a result of their wicked living.
- **(For everyone):** Why does God allow bad things to happen to good people? Is it possible that God allows things to happen to us, good or bad, for our benefit?
- When God corrects or chastens His people out of love, He does so not for His own enjoyment, but for the benefit of those He loves. What can we learn from His example?

PRAYER THOUGHTS

- Thank the Lord for loving you enough to chasten you.
- Ask the Lord to help you manifest love in His way.

SONG: *AFFLICTIONS, THOUGH THEY SEEM SEVERE*

Day 182: (Saturday)
Ungodly Love

1 John 2:15 Love not the world, neither the things that are in the world. If any man love the world, the love of the Father is not in him.

INTRODUCTORY THOUGHTS

God is love, but that does not mean that everything that people love is of God. Today's verse warns believers not to love the world or the things that are in the world. God's people are repeatedly admonished about this because believers are prone to love things and people contrary to the will of God. The Christian's heroes are generally no different than the world's heroes. We have many Bible examples of men who loved those of whom God disapproved. Samson exemplified this in his love for Delilah *(Judges 16:4)*. Amnon had an unrighteous love for his sister Tamar *(2 Samuel 13:1)*. Solomon failed in this area by loving *"many strange women" (1 Kings 11:1)*. Demas left the ministry because he *"loved this present world" (2 Timothy 4:10)*. Unfortunately, the heart of a believer can be drawn to love things and people displeasing to the Lord. It is always important to consider the object of our love and refuse to make excuses when we know better.

DEVOTIONAL THOUGHTS

- **(For children):** Ananias and Sapphira loved money. They sold some land and told Peter they gave all of the money received for the land to God. They kept back a portion for themselves and then lied about it. They purposely covered up their love for money with the lie. This greatly displeased the Lord and God judged them.
- **(For everyone):** What or whom do you love? Are those loves pleasing or displeasing to the Lord? Do those loves strengthen your fellowship with the Lord, or do they hinder your Christian walk?

- Why are Christians becoming increasingly prone to loving the things of this world? Why are we so easily drawn away from fellowship with the Lord by Satan's temptations?

PRAYER THOUGHTS
- Ask the Lord to guard your love for Him.
- Ask the Lord to show you what and whom to love.

SONG: *JESUS IS MINE*

Notes: _____

_____

_____

_____

_____

_____

_____

Quotes from the next volume
(VOLUME 3, WEEK 26)
Subject: The Home (con't)

The Lord Jesus is the King of kings, Lord of lords, and the Creator of the universe. However, in His earthly ministry, He made it obvious that He cared for the *"little ones"* **(Matthew 18:6, 10, 14)**.

One should begin early in life to learn the most important lessons of life. As a child, one should learn *"the fear of the LORD"* **(Psalm 34:11)**, to *"praise the name of the LORD"* **(Psalm 148:12-13; Matthew 21:15)**, and to *"remember"* his Creator **(Ecclesiastes 12:1)**.

Much of a young person's character or lack thereof is demonstrated in his behaviour toward adults.

27

Love (con't)

Love—found 344 times in the Old Testament and 324 times in the New Testament

Variations: beloved, beloved's, love, loved, lovedst, lovely, lover, lovers, loves, lovest, loveth, loving, lovingkindness, lovingkindnesses

First usage in the New Testament: *Matthew 3:17* (beloved)

Last usage in the Old Testament: *Malachi 2:11* (loved)

Interesting fact: The apostle John never named himself in his gospel or his epistles. Instead, he was identified as *"the disciple whom Jesus loved" (John 21:20)*. It should, therefore, come as no surprise that John's gospel contained more verses on love (39 verses) than the other three gospels combined (35 verses). Likewise, his first epistle (First John) contained more verses on love (29 verses) than any other epistle.

Bible study tip: Look for chapters that focus the most upon your particular subject of study. For instance, Numbers chapter 30 is considered the *"vow* chapter" because of the magnitude of its mention, while Psalm 119 is considered the *"word of God* chapter" due to its emphasis upon God's word in most every verse. Many people throughout the years have identified 1 Corinthians chapter 13 as the "*love* chapter," but this distinction clearly goes to 1 John chapter 4 where *love*, in all its various forms, is mentioned thirty times.

Sunday, Day 183—Church Day (no devotional)
Monday, Day 184—*Why Should We Love?*
Tuesday, Day 185—*Grounds for Love*
Wednesday, Day 186—Church Night (no devotional)
Thursday, Day 187—*What Should We Love?*
Friday, Day 188—*When Should We Love?*
Saturday, Day 189—*What Should Happen When We Love?*

Day 183: Church Day

*Proverbs 10:12 Hatred stirreth up strifes: but **love covereth all sins**.*

Day 184: (Monday)
Why Should We Love?

*1 John 4:19 **We love** him, **because he first loved** us.*

INTRODUCTORY THOUGHTS

A careful survey of the Bible concerning *the object of our scriptural love* demonstrates that each object has a connection to the Lord Jesus Christ. In fact, these loves stem from a love for the Lord. For instance, we love the *brethren* because the Lord loves them and we love Him *(1 John 3:17)*. We love *righteousness* because it is what God loves *(Psalm 11:7)*. We love the *words of the Bible* because they are God's words and therefore, they are pure *(Psalm 119:140)*. There would be nothing worth loving and no reason to love if it were not for the Lord's love. People might provide various reasons when asked why they love the Lord, but in reality there is only one reason why we love Him or anything else for that matter. *"We love him, because he first loved us."* The fact of the matter is that we love and should love because God loved us and loves us.

DEVOTIONAL THOUGHTS

(For children): God is love. Because He loves us, He expects us to love one another *(1 John 4:7)*. Jesus told His disciples that others would know that they were His followers if they had love one to another *(John 13:34-35)*. Are we showing this love to a world that so desperately needs to see it?

- **(For everyone):** Lost people cannot truly know love. Knowing this, who taught us to love *(1 Thessalonians 4:9)*? If knowing the Lord is the only way we can know the truth concerning love, how should this affect what objects to which we devote our love?
- Perhaps one of the saddest experiences takes place when a person loves someone but that love is not reciprocated or returned. How often do you think this happens to the Lord? Do you ever fail to return His love?

PRAYER THOUGHTS

- Ask the Lord to give you a stronger love for Him.
- Thank the Lord for first loving you.

SONG: *OH, HOW I LOVE JESUS*

Day 185: (Tuesday)
Grounds for Love

*Deuteronomy 10:19 Love ye therefore **the stranger**: for ye were strangers in the land of Egypt.*

INTRODUCTORY THOUGHTS

It is easier to love those with whom we feel a common bond and share a special relationship. In fact, the Lord suggests as much in the scripture. When the Lord encouraged His people to love strangers, He did so by reminding them that they too had been strangers in the land of Egypt. By recalling their past associations, the Israelites would know how to better deal with those who were strangers to them. It would be good for them to recall some of the trials they faced when they were strangers in a strange land. With this in mind, they would know how to care for and minister to the strangers. Though Christians are not under the law and most are not Israelites, much can be learned from these truths. It becomes easier to love those to whom we can closely relate.

DEVOTIONAL THOUGHTS

- **(For children):** We cannot know everyone but we can have a love for all people because all of us are alike in this way: we all have sinned *(Romans 3:23)* and Christ died for us *(Romans 5:8)*. We should be willing to share this message with everyone, even those whom we consider different from us.
- **(For everyone):** As the Lord's coming draws nigh, people are becoming increasingly wicked. As such, it should be more difficult for the Christian to relate to them. What common ground might help you to show your love toward them?
- If finding common ground helps us love others, how could the Lord better use us to minister to others? How could it help us to be more effective if we endured more trials and difficulties?

PRAYER THOUGHTS

- Ask the Lord to help you see yourself in others.
- Ask the Lord to give you a love for others around you.

SONG: *RESCUE THE PERISHING*

Day 186: Church Night

Proverbs 15:17 Better is *a dinner of herbs* **where love is,** *than a stalled ox and hatred therewith.*

Day 187: (Thursday)
What Should We Love?

John 3:16 For **God so loved** *the world,* **that he gave** *his only begotten Son, that whosoever believeth in him should not perish, but have everlasting life.*

INTRODUCTORY THOUGHTS

When you truly love someone, you find yourself developing a love for the things that he or she loves. It should be no different concerning our relationship with the Lord. The more love we have for the Lord, the more love we display for the things dearest to Him. This means that the closer we draw to Him, the more we will love things that He loves, like judgment *(Isaiah 61:8)* and righteousness *(Psalm 11:7)*, the lost *(John*

3:16) and the saved *(1 John 4:21)*, peace and truth *(Zechariah 8:19)*. We will also have a greater love for the Jewish people *(Zechariah 2:8)*. Perhaps a more accurate gauge by which to judge your love for the Lord is to gauge your love for the things which He loves.

DEVOTIONAL THOUGHTS

- **(For children):** *Ephesians 5:25* says that Christ *"loved the church and gave himself for it."* Do you love the church (God's people) and love to meet with them in God's house? God does *(Matthew 18:20)*.
- **(For everyone):** What are some other things we can find in the Bible that the Lord loves? How should we feel about those things? How do you feel about those things?
- Why is it important for God's people to love what God loves? How does our love grow as we draw closer to the Lord? Have you ever found that your love for the things of God grows colder as your love for the Lord grows more distant?

PRAYER THOUGHTS

- Ask God to help you love the things and people that He loves.
- Ask the Lord to help you draw closer to Him.

SONG: *DO NOT I LOVE THEE, O MY LORD?*

Day 188: (Friday)
When Should We Love?

Proverbs 17:17 A friend loveth at all times, and a brother is born for adversity.

INTRODUCTORY THOUGHTS

In a day when the world uses the word *love* rather flippantly, the people of God need to revisit the concept of biblical love. The Bible says, *"A friend loveth at all times."* This infers that the concept of falling in and out of love is unscriptural. Biblically defined love is not a fleeting emotion controlled by one's feelings. It remains a choice based on the truths of scripture and falls outside the whims of one's emotional passions. The world declares its love for something and in the same breath declares its love lost for the latest passing fad. Just as God's love for us remains permanent, so ought our love for others. Unfortunately, this fickleness has crept into the lives of the believers. We could learn much by considering the example of the Lord's love for His enemies even after they had so cruelly nailed Him to the tree *(Luke 23:34)*. Biblical love forgives and continues to unconditionally forgive regardless of any objectionable response to one's love *(Proverbs 10:12)*.

Devotional thoughts

- **(For children)**: Read *Hebrews 13:1*. *"Let brotherly love continue."* To *continue* indicates that we should keep loving whether we feel like it or not and whether the person deserves it or not. The disciples forsook Jesus and fled when they could have remained faithful. The Lord expressed His continued love for them anyway *(Mark 16:7; John 13:1b)*.
- **(For everyone)**: Why did Stephen say, *"Lord, lay not this sin to their charge"*? What were the people doing to him when he said this? What can we learn from this?
- How easy is it for you to get upset with others and stop loving them? What kind of friend does that make you? What are you going to do to repent of this sin?

Prayer Thoughts

- Ask the Lord to make you a better friend to others.
- Thank the Lord for His unending love for you.

SONG: *HOLD FAST TILL I COME*

Day 189: (Saturday)
What Should Happen When We Love?

*Genesis 29:20 And **Jacob served seven years** for Rachel; and **they seemed unto him but a few days, for the love he had to her**.*

Introductory Thoughts

Jacob made an agreement with Laban to serve him in exchange for Rachel's hand in marriage. His tenure of service was filled with great difficulties. Not only was the service itself hard work, but his service was marked with change and troubles. No doubt Jacob could have bemoaned these difficulties, but instead the Bible says that the seven years of service *"seemed unto him but a few days."* How could Jacob give such testimony when we know that those were seven arduous years of labour? The Bible explains that he made it through those difficult days *"for the love he had to her."* Our love for the Saviour ought to parallel and even exceed Jacob's love for Rachel. Similar to Jacob's determination to serve, we too have a purpose. At times, our service for the Lord may seem filled with great difficulties, but a deep and genuine love for the Saviour will make one's service seem *"but a few days."*

DEVOTIONAL THOUGHTS

- **(For children):** Paul suffered many things because of his service to God *(2 Corinthians 11:23-27)*. His love for God caused him to look on his suffering as a *"light affliction, which is but for a moment"* *(2 Corinthians 4:17)*. Oh, that we had a similar kind of love for the Lord *(Acts 21:13)*!
- **(For everyone):** Are God's commandments grievous to you? Sometimes our service may be difficult, but our love for the Lord should keep His commandments from being grievous *(1 John 5:3)*.
- Do you often feel like your service to God is difficult? Do you find yourself complaining about the sacrifices you have made for the Lord? Why do you think this is?

PRAYER THOUGHTS

- Ask the Lord to help you serve Him by love.
- Ask Him to give you a love for others.

SONG: *WE'LL WORK TILL JESUS COMES*

Notes: _____

_____

_____

_____

_____

_____

_____

_____

Notes: _____

_____

_____

_____

_____

_____

_____

_____

_____

_____

_____

_____

_____

Quotes from the next volume

(VOLUME 3, WEEK 27)

Subject: Resolution

Problems, trials, and tribulations occur because of the presence of sin, and as long as sin is in this world, men will be faced with these difficulties.

The Devil would have man believe that hiding from problems solves them. This is a lie!

God knows what man has need of before it is ever brought to Him in prayer *(Matthew 6:8)*, but He still desires for man to come to Him for help.

28
Meditation

Meditation—found twenty-one times in twenty-one verses, eighteen of which are in the Old Testament

Variations: meditate, meditation, premeditate

First usage: *Genesis 24:63* (meditate)

Last usage: *1 Timothy 4:15* (meditate)

Defined: to ponder or to contemplate

Interesting fact: With all the talk about success and prosperity, one would think that *Joshua 1:8* would be the focus of many of these discussions. That verse gives the ordered process by which we can obtain success and prosperity: (1) *meditation* leads to *observance*, (2) *observance* yields spiritual *prosperity*, and (3) spiritual *prosperity* yields *success*.

Bible study tip: Be careful not to allow preconceived notions to taint your view of scriptural admonitions. The world's practice of *meditation* is unscriptural, but we are still called to learn and implement scriptural meditation. Approach the Bible with an open mind, refusing to apply the unscriptural philosophy implemented by the world.

Sunday, Day 190—Church Day (no devotional)
Monday, Day 191—*What Is Meditation?*
Tuesday, Day 192—*An Acceptable Meditation*
Wednesday, Day 193—Church Night (no devotional)
Thursday, Day 194—*Meditating in God's Word*
Friday, Day 195—*Meditation Becomes Conversation*
Saturday, Day 196—*Give Thyself Wholly to Them*

Day 190: Church Day

*Joshua 1:8 This book of the law shall not depart out of thy mouth; but **thou shalt meditate therein day and night**, that thou mayest observe to do according to all that is written therein: for then thou shalt make thy way prosperous, and then thou shalt have good success.*

Day 191: (Monday)
What Is Meditation?

*Mark 13:11 But when they shall lead you, and deliver you up, **take no thought beforehand** what ye shall speak, neither do ye **premeditate**: but whatsoever shall be given you in that hour, that speak ye: for it is not ye that speak, but the Holy Ghost.*

Introductory Thoughts

The Bible's built-in dictionary defines *meditation* as taking thought. The world most often thinks of *meditation* in its own man-made context which is pagan in origin and practice. However, Bible-believing Christians should not allow this to discourage them from practicing scriptural meditation. Notice the phrase in today's verse: *"take no thought beforehand"* followed by the word *premeditate*. The prefix *pre* means beforehand, while the word *meditate* means *"to take thought."* Thus, a person who takes thought on something, perhaps a Bible verse or some particular truth in a sermon or a hymn of the faith, is said to be meditating. Unfortunately, far too many of our busy lives have choked out the quiet moments of meditating upon the things of God.

DEVOTIONAL THOUGHTS

(For children): Read *John 1:3a: "All things were made by him."* Think of some precious things made by God. When we take time to read a verse of scripture but also stop and think about it, that is true meditation.

- **(For everyone):** Upon what do you spend your time and strength thinking? Do you find that your thought life draws you closer to the Lord or does it drive you further away from Him?
- What are some of the things upon which believers ought to meditate? How could quality time of meditating upon those things help believers to love the Lord more and serve Him even better?

PRAYER THOUGHTS

- Ask the Lord to teach you to enjoy biblical meditation.
- Ask God to give you some good things upon which to meditate.

SONG: *TIS SOMETIMES SWEET TO BE ALONE*

Day 192: (Tuesday)
An Acceptable Meditation

Psalm 19:14 Let *the words of my mouth, and* **the meditation of my heart, be acceptable in thy sight, O LORD,** *my strength, and my redeemer.*

INTRODUCTORY THOUGHTS

Meditation can be a godly practice, but can also express the exact opposite connotation. Nonbelievers go to great lengths to push their concept of meditation upon the world, but their meditation remains ungodly in every aspect. Rather than asking whether or not we should meditate, we should ask upon what we should meditate. Perhaps the Christian's most important question in this matter should be, *"Is my meditation pleasing to the Lord?"* Interestingly, David, a man after God's own heart *(Acts 13:22)*, prayed, *"Let the words of my mouth, and the meditation of my heart, be acceptable in thy sight, O LORD" (Psalm 19:14)*. David wanted to insure that his meditation was acceptable to the Lord.

DEVOTIONAL THOUGHTS

- **(For children):** *Philippians 4:8* tells us to think about good and pleasant things. Thinking about God in the right way will always please Him. Read *Psalm 104:34*. How is thinking about God sweet? What has He done for us?
- **(For everyone):** Is your meditation acceptable to the Lord? Are the subjects of your thoughts things that would please the Lord or displease Him? How could you fix this problem?
- What are some things upon which we could meditate that would prove to be acceptable in the eyes of the Lord? How often do you meditate upon those things?

PRAYER THOUGHTS

- Ask the Lord to help your meditation to be acceptable to Him.
- Ask the Lord to change your thought life if need be.

SONG: *TAKE MY LIFE, AND LET IT BE*

Day 193: Church Night

*Psalm 143:5 I remember the days of old; **I meditate on all thy works**; I muse on the work of thy hands.*

Day 194: (Thursday)
Meditating in God's Word

*Psalm 119:15 **I will meditate in thy precepts**, and have respect unto thy ways.*

INTRODUCTORY THOUGHTS

Psalm 119 is filled with statements promoting the necessity of the word of God. Seven times in this psalm we find a statement declaring the writer's desire to meditate upon the words of God. Three of these times he states emphatically that he will meditate in God's statutes or His precepts *(Psalm 119:15, 48, 78)*. Not only was meditating upon God's words something that the psalmist desired to do in the future, but he had formed this habit long ago *(Psalm 119:23, 99)*. The writer of this psalm, like other successful believers in the past, made it common practice to meditate in the words of God both day and night *(Psalm 119:97; Psalm 1:2; Joshua 1:8)*.

DEVOTIONAL THOUGHTS

- **(For children):** God's word is very important to Him *(Psalm 138:2)*. As a child, Timothy knew the Holy Scriptures. God wants you as a child to learn them too. When? Read *Deuteronomy 11:19* to find the answer.
- **(For everyone):** How often do you read your Bible in the morning and meditate upon it throughout the day? How often do you go to sleep at night with the words of God in your mind?
- What are some benefits that you could enjoy by meditating upon the words of God? How could this help you draw closer to the Lord?

PRAYER THOUGHTS

- Ask God to give you verses upon which to meditate.
- Ask the Lord to help you to be faithful reading His word.

SONG: *THE BIBLE STANDS*

Day 195: (Friday)
Meditation Becomes Conversation

Psalm 77:12 I will meditate also of all thy work, and talk of thy doings.

INTRODUCTORY THOUGHTS

When a believer meditates upon the things of God, those truths become more firmly planted in the heart. Eventually, the contents of the heart become evident from the words that escape the mouth *(Luke 6:45)*. Therefore, the meditations of our heart will eventually be the words of our conversations. This is exactly the truth conveyed by Asaph in our passage from Psalm 77. He understood that meditation upon the work of God would eventually cause him to talk of God's doings. It is right for God's people to speak truth, especially when it concerns testifying to the truth of God's holy words. Yet, this is not possible unless a believer first hides the words of God in his heart *(Psalm 119:11)*, and one way to do so is through meditation.

DEVOTIONAL THOUGHTS

- **(For children)**: In *Psalm 143:5,* David said he meditated on all of God's works. The result of this meditation is found in *Psalm 145:4-6.* Why should this be important to us?
- **(For everyone)**: Knowing the truths covered in this study, why is it so important that we meditate upon the right things? What happens when we spend our time meditating upon worldly things?
- What subjects offer you the most joy when talking with others? Why do you enjoy speaking on those subjects? Are these things the source of your meditation? Does this please the Lord?

PRAYER THOUGHTS

- Ask the Lord to help you please Him in your meditation.
- Ask the Lord to help you see the outcome of your meditation.

SONG: *JESUS! THE VERY THOUGHT OF THEE*

Day 196: (Saturday)
Give Thyself Wholly to Them

1 Timothy 4:12 Let no man despise thy youth; but be thou an example of the believers, in word, in conversation, in charity, in spirit, in faith, in purity.

13 Till I come, give attendance to reading, to exhortation, to doctrine.

14 Neglect not the gift that is in thee, which was given thee by prophecy, with the laying on of the hands of the presbytery.

*15 **Meditate upon these things; give thyself wholly to them**; that thy profiting may appear to all.*

INTRODUCTORY THOUGHTS

Worldly meditation primarily focuses upon clearing the mind and making it devoid of thought. The Bible reveals the opposite process. Today's passage comes from a more extensive letter that Paul sent to his son in the faith, Timothy. In this letter, Paul encouraged Timothy to be an example to those around him. As a young man, Timothy was instructed not to allow his youth to hinder his service to the Lord. In Paul's absence, Timothy was to major upon three things: reading, exhortation, and doctrine *(1 Timothy 4:13)*. Paul told Timothy to *"meditate upon these things" (1 Timothy 4:15)*, or give himself wholly to them. In doing so, Timothy's profiting would appear to all.

DEVOTIONAL THOUGHTS

- **(For children):** We should think on our ways *(Psalm 119:59)*. If we're not doing what God says, then we should start doing it. If we haven't obeyed dad and mom *(Colossians 3:20)*, then we should start doing this very thing. Other children may notice our example and follow.
- **(For everyone):** How would Timothy's meditation lead to others being able to see his profit? How is this connected to Joshua's meditation leading to success?
- Do you give yourself to reading, exhortation, and doctrine? Do you meditate upon these things? Do you find that others profit from your meditation?

PRAYER THOUGHTS

- Ask the Lord to help you give yourself to His word.
- Ask God to use your time of meditation for the benefit of others.

SONG: *TEACH ME THE MEASURE OF MY DAYS*

Notes: _____

_____

_____

_____

_____

_____

_____

_____

_____

_____

_____

Notes: _____

_____

_____

_____

_____

_____

_____

_____

_____

_____

_____

_____

_____

_____

_____

_____

_____

Quotes from the next volume

(VOLUME 3, WEEK 28)

Subject: Resolution (con't)

When a problem presents itself, man should take the time to seek the cause of the problem. He should do so by willingly taking personal responsibility.

Oftentimes the right solutions do not resolve the problem overnight. Patience is a necessity!

A man who demands a hasty solution to his problems often fails to find God's solution.

29
Ministry

Ministry—found 196 times in 181 verses

Variations: minister, ministered, ministereth, ministering, ministers, ministry

First usage: *Exodus 24:13* (minister)

Last usage: *2 Peter 1:11* (ministered)

Defined: to serve the needs of others

Interesting fact: The Lord chose and still chooses ministers to go forth as *"ministers of the word" (Luke 1:2)*. Because Satan is the epitome of a counterfeiter, he also calls and sends forth his ministers *(2 Corinthians 11:13-15)*. The unfortunate truth is that it can be extremely difficult to always distinguish between the two groups because Satan's ministers are transformed to look, act, and sound like the Lord's ministers. Those determined to deceive are the hardest to discern.

Bible study tip: *Daniel 7:10* gives the Old Testament prophecy concerning the judgment of *Revelation 20:11-15*. In Daniel's account, we are told of *"thousand thousands"* who minister unto Christ. *Revelation 22:3* identifies those ministers as *"his servants"* that *"serve him."* The Lord repeated the phrase *"and the books were opened"* in order to draw our attention to the association of **Daniel 7:10** and **Revelation 20:12.** God wants the diligent Bible student to draw upon these sometime inconspicuous associations in order to clearly expound upon God's truths.

Sunday, Day 197—Church Day (no devotional)
Monday, Day 198—*What Is Ministry?*
Tuesday, Day 199—*The Ministry of the Word*
Wednesday, Day 200—Church Night (no devotional)
Thursday, Day 201—*The Ministry of Reconciliation*
Friday, Day 202—*The Ministry of the Saints*
Saturday, Day 203—*The Ministry to the Lord*

Day 197: Church Day

*Matthew 20:26 But it shall not be so among you: but **whosoever will be great among you, let him be your minister;***

*27 And **whosoever will be chief among you, let him be your servant:***

*28 Even as **the Son of man came not to be ministered unto, but to minister**, and to give his life a ransom for many.*

Day 198: (Monday)
What Is Ministry?

*2 Kings 3:11 But Jehoshaphat said, Is there not here a prophet of the LORD, that we may inquire of the LORD by him? And one of the king of Israel's servants answered and said, Here is Elisha the son of Shaphat, which **poured water on the hands of Elijah**.*

INTRODUCTORY THOUGHTS

Sometimes we forget that the first four letters of the word *ministry* spell out the word *"mini."* Ministry is never about becoming popular or famous or lording over others. Ministry involves decreasing while allowing others to increase. Two of the greatest men of the Bible (Joshua and Elisha) got their start as ministers to their predecessors. Before

Joshua led the Israelites into Canaan, he was the minister of Moses *(Joshua 1:1)*. His ministry entailed submitting himself to the needs of the man of God. Elisha, another great leader, did not begin as the great prophet of God that performed miracles. He, instead, began as Elijah's minister *(1 Kings 19:19-21)*. His ministry included the "lofty task" of pouring water on the hands of Elijah. Far too many young men graduate Bible college with the intention of making a name for themselves rather than humbly serving a God who humbled Himself *(Philippians 2:8)*.

DEVOTIONAL THOUGHTS

- **(For children):** All of us should have an intense desire to do *great things* for the Lord. Interestingly, the Lord defined *greatness* as serving others *(Matthew 20:26-28)*. Think about how much God humbled Himself when He came to earth. He was God manifest in the flesh and could have demanded that everyone serve Him. Instead, He served others *(Philippians 2:5-8)*.
- **(For everyone):** What are some things you can think of that might qualify as ministry? If there is a need to fill, are you busy doing those things? Are you doing those things to gain advantage, or are you doing them for the glory of God?
- Who is more well known, Moses or Joshua? Who is more well known, Elijah or Elisha? What does this teach us about the sacrifices of ministry? Are you willing to make those sacrifices to insure that God's will is done no matter who gets the credit?

PRAYER THOUGHTS

- Ask the Lord to give you the humility to be a minister.
- Ask God to teach you how to minister to others.

SONG: *WHERE HE LEADS I'LL FOLLOW*

Day 199: (Tuesday)
The Ministry of the Word

Acts 6:4 But we will give ourselves continually to prayer, and to the ministry of the word.

INTRODUCTORY THOUGHTS

As is common with church growth, problems arose very early in the church at Jerusalem. Acts chapter 6 tells us of the Grecians who began to murmur against the Hebrews because their widows were being neglected *(Acts 6:1)*. The apostles chose *not* to ignore the problem but to tackle it head on. Yet, they understood their primary responsibilities of not leaving their study of the word of God in order to focus on handling the strife. The apostles instructed the disciples in the church to choose seven men to deal with this particular issue and similar issues that might arise later *(Acts 6:3)*. The Bible also points out that the apostles determined to give themselves *"continually to prayer, and to the ministry of the word"* *(Acts 6:4)*. They understood that their study and distribution of the word of God was to take the preeminence in their ministry.

DEVOTIONAL THOUGHTS

- **(For children):** The Ethiopian eunuch in Acts chapter 8 was reading the book of Isaiah but did not understand what he read. Because Philip had studied the scriptures, he was able to explain to the eunuch what he was reading *(Acts 8:30-35)*. Ezra is another example of someone who studied *(Ezra 7:10)* and helped others learn God's word *(Nehemiah 8:8)*. God wants us to learn His word so we too can help others.
- **(For everyone):** According to *2 Timothy 2:2*, it seems as though everyone has some responsibility to teach others the word of God. What are some ways in which you could fulfil this ministry in the life of others?
- Who has the primary responsibility for teaching your family the word of God? Who is responsible for teaching new believers or those who might be weak in the faith? Are you willing to devote your time and strength to minister to them?

PRAYER THOUGHTS

- Ask the Lord to give you a burden to minister God's word to others.
- Ask God to help you to be diligent in studying His word.

SONG: *YE SERVANTS OF GOD, YOUR MASTER PROCLAIM*

Day 200: Church Night

*Acts 20:24 But none of these things move me, neither count I my life dear unto myself, so **that I might finish** my course with joy, and **the ministry, which I have received of the Lord Jesus,** to testify the gospel of the grace of God.*

Day 201: (Thursday)
The Ministry of Reconciliation

*2 Corinthians 5:18 And all things are of **God, who hath reconciled us** to himself by Jesus Christ, **and hath given to us the ministry of reconciliation;***

INTRODUCTORY THOUGHTS

The Bible points to the unsaved man as an enemy of God *(Romans 5:10)*. Fortunately, those who have trusted Christ as Saviour have been *reconciled* to God through the blood of Jesus Christ *(Romans 5:10; 2 Corinthians 5:18)*. This reconciliation transforms the enemies of God into His ambassadors *(2 Corinthians 5:20)*. What a wonderful salvation! But there is more! The Lord Jesus has given the ministry of reconciliation to all those who have been reconciled. As such, we are to submit ourselves to the work of telling others how they too can be reconciled to God. Paul understood this and declared that he was a *"debtor both to the Greeks, and to the Barbarians; both to the wise, and to the unwise"* *(Romans 1:14)*.

DEVOTIONAL THOUGHTS

- **(For children):** God wants us to tell others what He did for them so they too can go to heaven. Andrew told Peter *(John 1:41-42a)*. Many Christians look for ways to witness; sometimes you can reach people for the Lord by inviting them to church, giving them a gospel tract or a Bible, and by giving to your church and to missions.
- **(For everyone):** A person that is a debtor to someone is, in a sense, his servant. What does it mean to be a debtor to others for the gospel's sake? To whom are you a debtor? What are you doing about this debt that you owe to others?
- How can witnessing to others be considered ministry? What kind of sacrifices can you make to help others come to a saving knowledge of Christ? Are you making those sacrifices?

PRAYER THOUGHTS

- Ask the Lord to give you a burden for those who are lost.
- Ask the Lord to show you the necessity of this ministry.

SONG: *TELL ME THE OLD, OLD STORY*

Day 202: (Friday)
The Ministry of the Saints

*1 Corinthians 16:15 I beseech you, brethren, (ye know **the house of Stephanas,** that it is the firstfruits of Achaia, and that they **have addicted themselves to the ministry of the saints,**)*

INTRODUCTORY THOUGHTS

God designed and willed for the Christian home and the local body of believers to function as two of the closest experiences to heaven on this side of eternity. As believers, we ought to love one another *(John 13:34-35)* and serve one another by that love *(Galatians 5:13)*. Rather than backbiting and devouring each other *(Galatians 5:15)*, believers ought to give themselves to ministering to each other. In Paul's epistle to the Corinthian believers, God led Paul to mention a family addicted to the ministry. At some point, this family decided to sacrifice their own gain for the sake of ministering to others. Because of this commitment, the Bible says that Stephanas refreshed the spirit of other believers.

DEVOTIONAL THOUGHTS

- **(For children):** God wants us to help our church family *(Galatians 6:10)*. Read how Onesiphorus was a friend to the apostle Paul *(2 Timothy 1:16-18)*. The Lord gives us other ideas how to help too *(Matthew 25:35-36)*. He will remember your kindness *(Hebrews 6:10)*.
- **(For everyone):** Do you know of any brothers or sisters in Christ who are spiritually going through difficult times? What could you do to minister to them? Are you willing to do what you can?
- What are some sacrifices that you might have to make in order to minister to others? Which is more important in eternity: the things you sacrificed or the ministering that you have done for others?

PRAYER THOUGHTS

- Ask God to give you a heart for ministering to others.
- Ask the Lord to give you a servant's heart.

SONG: *IS THY CRUSE OF COMFORT WASTING?*

Day 203: (Saturday)
The Ministry to the Lord

*Acts 13:2 As **they ministered to the Lord**, and fasted, the Holy Ghost said, Separate me Barnabas and Saul for the work whereunto I have called them.*

INTRODUCTORY THOUGHTS

The Christian's relationship at times is unfathomable. For this reason, it may be difficult to conceive that believers can actually minister to the Lord. Yet, the pages of God's word declare that it is not only possible but a big part of being saved. Ministering to the Lord is done by fulfilling the ministry of the word, the ministry of reconciliation, and the ministry of the saints. Additionally, you can visualize it by considering that ministering to the Lord is accomplished when believers do anything that offers God the praise and honour due Him. In Acts chapter 13, the believers *"ministered unto the Lord"* and though the passage does not offer specifics on what this entailed, an understanding of the previously mentioned ministries sheds light on their efforts.

DEVOTIONAL THOUGHTS

- **(For children):** One way we can minister to the Lord is to thank Him often *(Hebrews 13:15)* for what He is: He is powerful *(Psalm 62:11)*, holy *(Psalm 99:9)*, great *(Psalm 104:1)*, good *(Psalm 107:1)*, the only God *(Isaiah 45:5a)*, and true *(John 3:33)*.
- **(For everyone):** What are some ways in which you can minister to the Lord? What are some things that would indicate God's worth to you? How could prayer, giving, and praise be considered ministry?
- Do you want the Lord to use you to do greater things for Him? What are you doing to minister to Him right now? What happened when the believers ministered to Him in Acts chapter 13?

PRAYER THOUGHTS

- Ask the Lord to teach you how to minister to Him.
- Ask God to help you submit to His will for your life.

SONG: *COME THOU FOUNT OF EVERY BLESSING*

Notes: _____

_____

_____

_____

_____

_____

_____

_____

_____

Quotes from the next volume

(VOLUME 3, WEEK 29)

Subject: Communication

The Bible tells us that words or thoughts originate in the heart *(Matthew 12:34)*; therefore, communication is the searching and revealing of the heart.

Man communicates with God in prayer. This can be accomplished simply in the heart or verbally but is only accomplished when a man conveys his thoughts or concerns to the Lord using words.

Due mostly to man's ever increasing dependence upon technology, Christians have lost their effectiveness in communicating with others. This may seem insignificant, until one considers how it has weakened our ability to communicate our faith.

30

Modesty

Modesty—specifically mentioned only once in scripture although the concept is alluded to with much greater frequency

Variations: modest

First and only usage: *1 Timothy 2:9*

Defined: appropriate or within moderation; this study approaches the subject as it relates to clothing

Interesting fact: Beginning with the garden in Eden, reconciliation to God has always modified a person's apparel *(Genesis 3:21)*. It was no different during the Lord's earthly ministry *(Luke 8:35)*. It should be no different today.

Bible study tip: The best way to study and teach the scripture is to do so line upon line or in an expository manner. Word-by-word, verse-by-verse, and chapter-by-chapter is the safest and most effective way to insure that one declares *"all the counsel of God" (Acts 20:27)*. Sometimes, a topical study helps to develop a particular subject in greater depth and detail. However, we must be very careful in a topical study not to make the scripture say what we want it to say by ignoring the greater context merely to fit our preconceived ideas concerning a topic.

Sunday, Day 204—Church Day (no devotional)
Monday, Day 205—*Nakedness and Shame*
Tuesday, Day 206—*What Is Nakedness?*
Wednesday, Day 207—Church Night (no devotional)
Thursday, Day 208—*The Attire of an Harlot*
Friday, Day 209—*Adorned in Modest Apparel*
Saturday, Day 210—*Why Hast Thou Made Me Thus?*

Day 204: Church Day

*Zechariah 3:4 And he answered and spake unto those that stood before him, saying, **Take away the filthy garments from him**. And unto him he said, Behold, I have caused thine iniquity to pass from thee, and **I will clothe thee with change of raiment**.*

Day 205: (Monday)
Nakedness and Shame

Genesis 2:21 And the LORD God caused a deep sleep to fall upon Adam, and he slept: and he took one of his ribs, and closed up the flesh instead thereof;

22 And the rib, which the LORD God had taken from man, made he a woman, and brought her unto the man.

23 And Adam said, This is now bone of my bones, and flesh of my flesh: she shall be called Woman, because she was taken out of Man.

24 Therefore shall a man leave his father and his mother, and shall cleave unto his wife: and they shall be one flesh.

*25 And **they were both naked**, the man and his wife, **and were not ashamed**.*

INTRODUCTORY THOUGHTS

Adam and Eve, before the fall of man, were naked and rightfully unashamed *(Genesis 2:25)*. The Bible indicates that the first notable difference following the fall came when the couple felt shame over their nakedness *(Genesis 3:10)*. This shame led them to cover themselves with aprons sewn from fig leaves *(Genesis 3:7)*. From that day forward, nakedness and shame have been inseparable. In *Exodus 32*, Aaron led the people of God in idolatrous worship which included dancing and nakedness. In that passage, the Bible says, *"Aaron had made them naked unto their shame" (Exodus 32:25)*. The Lord reiterates this affiliation in a warning to the Laodiceans by saying that they should be clothed lest the shame of their nakedness appear *(Revelation 3:18)*.

DEVOTIONAL THOUGHTS

- **(For children):** David sent servants to comfort Hanun when his father died, but Hanun thought the men were spies. Read what he did in *1 Chronicles 19:4-5*. The men were not properly clothed and felt ashamed. The lesson we should learn would be to dress properly.
- **(For everyone):** Adam and Eve, in their innocence, had no concept of any shame associated with nakedness. When they lost their innocence, they understood immediately that nakedness was to be covered.
- How can Adam and Eve's innocence be like that of small children? How can parents protect their children as they grow older and lose that initial innocence?

PRAYER THOUGHTS

- Ask the Lord to teach you what nakedness is.
- Ask the Lord to help you please Him in every aspect of your life.

SONG: ASHAMED, BUT NOT OF JESUS

Day 206: (Tuesday)
What Is Nakedness?

*2 Corinthians 5:3 If so be that being **clothed** we shall **not** be found **naked**.*

INTRODUCTORY THOUGHTS

At first glance, this passage appears to be less expressive than many others which cover a wider range of study. After all, a single reading of our passage proves that nakedness is the opposite of being clothed or covered. This truth is confirmed by other similar passages as well *(Leviticus 18:6; Job 24:7; Isaiah 58:7)*. However, this subject is much more complicated than merely whether someone is covered or not. It is important to understand the full context. For example, is nakedness the failure to cover every part of the body or are there parts of the body considered secret or private *(Isaiah 3:17)*? Though there are certainly other secret or private parts, the Lord plainly declared that uncovering the legs and thighs was nakedness *(Isaiah 47:1-3)*. For this reason, the priests were told to wear breeches to cover these parts under their priestly attire *(Exodus 28:42)*.

Devotional thoughts

- **(For children):** A baby is born wearing nothing *(Job 1:21a)*. The Bible calls this nakedness. Wearing clothing looking like undergarments in front of others is also nakedness. Read what Peter did when he was fishing and knew the Lord was on the shore *(John 21:7)*.
- **(For everyone):** If failure to cover certain parts of our body is considered nakedness, what should we do? Should we be ashamed if we fail to cover those parts?
- The Lord should have the ultimate say in what we wear and what we cover. Does He have authority in this area of your life? Could He convict you about what you wear?

Prayer Thoughts

- Ask the Lord to give you a willing heart to conform to His will.
- Ask God to teach you how to dress in a way that pleases Him.

SONG: *I AM RESOLVED*

Day 207: Church Night

*Deuteronomy 22:5 **The woman shall not wear that which pertaineth unto a man, neither shall a man put on a woman's garment**: for **all that do so** are **abomination** unto the LORD thy God.*

Day 208: (Thursday)
The Attire of an Harlot

*Proverbs 7:10 And, behold, there met him **a woman with the attire of an harlot**, and subtil of heart.*

INTRODUCTORY THOUGHTS

God's people should conscientiously cover themselves so that the shame of their nakedness does not appear to others. Yet, it is also important that their choice of covering be acceptable in the sight of the Lord. Some people have wrongfully assumed that the Lord does not give any thought to the attire of His people. God's word emphasizing the inward man does not reflect a lack of concern for the outward adornments. The assumption that it does is sometimes based upon a misapplication of *1 Samuel 16:7* where the Bible says, *"for man looketh on the outward appearance, but the LORD looketh on the heart."* Truly, man is generally limited to looking upon the outward appearance, but God sees both the outward appearance and the inward man. In fact, *Proverbs 7:10* testifies to the validity of this truth. In that passage, the Holy Ghost plainly indicated that a woman's clothing was representative of a harlot's attire. Apparently, the Holy Ghost was keenly aware of what was seen on the outside.

DEVOTIONAL THOUGHTS

- **(For children):** God wants us to properly cover our bodies. Missionaries tell stories of tribes who wear no clothing, but when many of them respond to the gospel for salvation, they "instinctively" cover up their nakedness. Luke tells the story of a man who *"ware no clothes."* After he met the Lord, the Bible says he put on clothes *(Luke 8:27, 35)*. People who love God ought to learn and know how to dress accordingly.
- **(For everyone):** Does your outward apparel suggest a certain godliness or ungodliness about you? Would you be pleased if the Lord came and found you wearing what you are wearing right now?
- Do you desire to please the Lord in your choice of clothing? Would you be willing to prayerfully go through your closets and get rid of anything that would displease the Lord?

PRAYER THOUGHTS

- Ask God to show you what constitutes godly clothing.
- Ask the Lord to soften your heart to His will for your life.

SONG: *YIELD NOT TO TEMPTATION*

Day 209: (Friday)
Adorned in Modest Apparel

*1 Timothy 2:9 In like manner also, that **women adorn themselves in modest apparel**, with shamefacedness and sobriety; not with broided hair, or gold, or pearls, or costly array;*

INTRODUCTORY THOUGHTS

Many Bible words have been subjected to loose interpretations and the word *modest* is one such word. Generally, today's passage is used to teach that a lady's apparel ought to be loose fitting and flowing. Though this is certainly true, that is not the primary interpretation and application. Something that is *modest* is something that is not extravagant. In fact, the Lord placed an explanation within the passage. The lady was not to adorn herself with such items as *"gold, or pearls, or costly array."* In other words, a person should not dress in a way that would purposely draw the attention of others to the attire itself (see *1 Peter 3:3-5*). This includes insuring that clothes are not form fitting, but the application has a much broader context.

DEVOTIONAL THOUGHTS

- **(For children):** We should not want to draw attention to ourselves through our clothing or our jewelry. As a beautiful queen, Vashti had expensive clothes and jewels, yet she refused her wicked husband's command to show off in front of his friends *(Esther 1:10-12)*.
- **(For everyone):** Do your clothes suggest that you are wealthy? Do they draw the attention of others? Do you wear things that suggest that you are haughty *(Isaiah 3:16)*?
- Do your clothes inappropriately draw the attention of those of the opposite gender? Do you wear things for the purpose of pleasing the Lord or appealing to the eyes of man?

PRAYER THOUGHTS

- Ask the Lord to give you a humility in your attire.
- Ask the Lord to work in your heart concerning your clothes.

SONG: *TEMPLES OF THE HOLY GHOST*

Day 210: (Saturday)
Why Hast Thou Made Me Thus?

Romans 9:20 Nay but, O man, who art thou that repliest against God? **Shall the thing formed say to him that formed it, Why hast thou made me thus?**

INTRODUCTORY THOUGHTS

God made you! He either made you a male or a female *(Genesis 1:27; Matthew 19:4)*. As such, He expects each of us to act, look, and live like what He made us in every way. Ever more frequently, the world and the Devil have blurred the lines of distinction between male and female. One of the most grievous outcomes of the blurring of distinctions between male and female has resulted in the public's acceptance of the sin which led to the destruction of Sodom and Gomorrah. God condemned it then and condemns it no less today. The Lord wants men and women to be distinct and look differently in every possible way. As such, He created the genders with obvious physical differences. He even admonished each gender to bear clear and distinct differences in length of hair *(1 Corinthians 11:14-15)* and commanded them to maintain obvious distinctions in apparel *(Deuteronomy 22:5)*. In other words, focus upon looking like what God created you to be.

DEVOTIONAL THOUGHTS

- **(For children):** Doing the opposite of what God says is rebellion and pride. It will always harm us and cause us to miss out on God's intended blessings. Absalom was proud of his long hair. It eventually cost him his life *(2 Samuel 18:9, 14-15)*. Mary used her long hair to show honour to Jesus. Could she have done this if her hair was the length of a man's *(John 12:3)*?
- **(For everyone):** Why would the Lord create male and female distinctly and then be satisfied for them losing their distinctions? What are some of these distinctions that have been lost that need to be restored to societies?
- What does the word *abomination* mean? What kind of clothes might pertain to a man? What kind of clothes might be considered a woman's garment?

PRAYER THOUGHTS

- Ask God to help you to distinguish yourself as a male or female.
- Ask God to help you refrain from questioning how He made you.

SONG: *SUBMISSIVELY, O LORD, WE'D BOW*

Notes: _____

_____

_____

_____

_____

_____

_____

_____

_____

_____

Quotes from the next volume

(VOLUME 3, WEEK 30)

Subject: Chastening or Punishment

A Bible-believer trusts that God chose His words very carefully in order to accomplish His purpose in any given passage.

Though it may be seen as harsh by those who receive it, punishment is a calculated response to wrongdoing.

God chastens His people, not for the sake of justice, but for the sake of strengthening and correcting them.

Chastening is not merely a means of judgment implemented by the Lord for wrongdoing, but is a proof of sonship.

31

Murmuring

Murmuring—found forty times in thirty-three verses

Variations: murmur, murmured, murmurers, murmuring, murmurings

First usage: *Exodus 15:24* (murmured)

Last usage: *Jude 16* (murmurers)

Defined: a vocal expression of discontentment

Interesting fact: Of the forty times the Bible uses a form of the word *murmur*, twenty-four reference the time between Israel's departure from Egypt and Israel's arrival in the land of promise. Herein lies a great biblical truth, the wilderness wanderings of our lives often unveil the murmurings of our hearts.

Bible study tip: Pay close attention to the word immediately following your word of study. This word will often yield great insight to the meaning and connotation of your Bible word. For instance, the word *against* follows the word *murmuring* eighteen times in the scriptures. Immediately, one learns that murmuring is an act of conflict and puts two parties at odds.

Sunday, Day 211—Church Day (no devotional)
Monday, Day 212—*What Is Murmuring?*
Tuesday, Day 213—*Murmur Not Among Yourselves*
Wednesday, Day 214—Church Night (no devotional)
Thursday, Day 215—*Murmuring Hinders Education*
Friday, Day 216—*The Source of Our Murmurings*
Saturday, Day 217—*Murmuring Breeds Lies*

Day 211: Church Day

Philippians 2:14 Do all things without murmurings and disputings:

Day 212: (Monday)
What Is Murmuring?

*Exodus 15:24 And **the people murmured** against Moses, **saying**, What shall we drink?*

INTRODUCTORY THOUGHTS

Murmuring is a grievous sin harmful to everyone involved or impacted. When God's people murmur, they do so because their heart is not sufficiently focused upon the Lord. Various forms of the word *murmur* occur forty times in the word of God. Interestingly, the number forty throughout scripture is frequently connected to a time of testing or trial. The vast majority of these occurrences reflect people who were displeased with something the Lord was responsible for doing. Their displeasure with the Lord caused them to voice their frustrations to others. Murmuring generally manifests itself outwardly, but at its root is a heart problem *(Matthew 12:34; Matthew 15:19)*. It comes as no surprise that the medical community uses the term *murmur* to describe a heart problem.

DEVOTIONAL THOUGHTS

- **(For children):** Your parents tell you to put away your toys and get ready for bed. You complain to yourself or to a younger sibling that you don't see why you have to do this since you are not finished playing. That is murmuring! You are also complaining to the Lord because He gave dad and mom authority over you.

- **(For everyone):** What causes you to murmur? How easily do you become frustrated and disgruntled with the events of your life? To whom do you normally murmur?
- How does murmuring manifest problems within your heart? With whom are you ultimately frustrated when you murmur? Why are you frustrated?

PRAYER THOUGHTS

- Ask the Lord to cleanse you of the sin of murmuring.
- Ask God to work in your heart so that you cease to murmur.

SONG: *HAPPY THE MEN WHOSE BLISS SUPREME*

Day 213: (Tuesday)
Murmur Not Among Yourselves

*John 6:43 Jesus therefore answered and said unto them, **Murmur not among yourselves**.*

INTRODUCTORY THOUGHTS

The Lord detests murmuring. He hates it so much that He sent fire among the Israelites because of their murmurings *(Numbers 11:1)*. In the New Testament, He warned believers to avoid falling prey to the same sin as the Israelites *(1 Corinthians 10:1-14)*. Additionally, New Testament believers are admonished to do all things without murmurings *(Philippians 2:14-16)*. People murmur as they focus on events within their lives rather than upon the Lord and His word. Yet, the Christian's life events are ultimately brought to pass, either directly or indirectly, by a loving and caring God. The Lord abhors murmuring because it directly insults His working and provision in our lives.

DEVOTIONAL THOUGHTS

- **(For children):** God promised His people a new land. Yet they chose to believe that they could not overcome the walled cities and giants. They murmured in their tents *(Numbers 14:1-2)*. God despised their murmuring and allowed those who did not believe to die in the wilderness.

- **(For everyone):** Do you murmur? Do you murmur before others? What kind of a testimony do you think this gives to a world that needs Jesus? Does your murmuring please or greatly displease the Lord?
- What events have ever come into your life without the Lord allowing them to take place? Who are you ultimately complaining against when you murmur?

PRAYER THOUGHTS

- Ask God to show you the serious nature of your murmurings.
- Ask the Lord to help you understand His hatred for murmuring.

SONG: *AFFLICTIONS SHALL A BLESSING PROVE*

Day 214: Church Night

1 Corinthians 10:10 Neither murmur ye, as some of them also murmured, and were destroyed of the destroyer.

Day 215: (Thursday)
Murmuring Hinders Education

*Isaiah 29:24 They also that erred in spirit shall come to understanding, and **they that murmured shall learn doctrine**.*

INTRODUCTORY THOUGHTS

Life's trials and difficulties are intended to draw people into a deeper knowledge of the Lord. However, murmuring hinders the lessons that result from the trials. The Lord uses trials to draw the unsaved to an understanding of their need to trust Jesus Christ as Saviour. At the same time, the Lord uses trials to teach saved people that they need to fully rely on Him and Him alone. These trials are meant to better the individual afflicted. However, the benefits of trials can be minimized when those enduring the trials begin to murmur and complain about the very thing intended to teach them. Murmuring hinders the education offered by trials. It puts the focus on the apparent wrong of the trial rather than upon what lesson the Lord might hope to come from the trial.

DEVOTIONAL THOUGHTS

- **(For children):** God's people were on a long, hard journey. They forgot how God had delivered them from Egypt *(Psalm 106:21-22)* and started complaining of having no water. God provided *(Exodus 15:22-25, 27)*. Because of their complaining, they faced this same trial twice more *(Exodus 17:1-6; Numbers 20:2, 8)*.
- **(For everyone):** What trials have you gone through of late? What lesson or lessons could the Lord have possibly desired to teach you through the trial? Did you fail the test by murmuring?
- Do you enjoy enduring the same trials multiple times? Do you ever wonder why you continue to endure the same trials? Is it possible that murmuring hindered your education and you are having to repeat the lesson multiple times?

PRAYER THOUGHTS

- Ask the Lord to help you learn His intended lesson in trials.
- Ask God to remind you not to murmur in times of difficulty.

SONG: *MORE ABOUT JESUS*

Day 216: (Friday)
The Source of Our Murmurings

*Jude 16 These are **murmurers**, complainers, **walking after their own lusts**; and their mouth speaketh great swelling words, having men's persons in admiration because of advantage.*

INTRODUCTORY THOUGHTS

Why do people murmur? What causes them to get so frustrated to the point where they would publicly discuss their disappointment with their circumstances? The Bible provides several reasons. In *Jude 16*, the Bible says that people complain or murmur because they are *"walking after their own lusts."* In John chapter 6, the Lord Jesus indicated another reason why an individual might complain. When the Lord knew that His disciples murmured within themselves, He asked them if they were offended *(John 6:61)*. In other words, people murmur when things turn out differently than they had hoped. It is not so much the trial that bothers them but the offense to their self-will.

DEVOTIONAL THOUGHTS

- **(For children):** Korah was not happy with his God-given job of serving in the tabernacle. He wanted to have the priestly duties like Aaron. He went against the Lord, Moses, and Aaron and murmured against Aaron *(Numbers 16:1-3, 11)*. Read what happened to Korah and his followers in **Numbers 16:32-33**.
- **(For everyone):** When is the last time you murmured? Why did you murmur? What transpired that led you to do so? Why did the trial frustrate you so much? Did you fail to learn the Lord's lessons?
- What happens when you do not get what you want? Do you become frustrated? Do you murmur or complain? What does this say about you? Does this reflect a selfishness?

PRAYER THOUGHTS

- Ask the Lord to help you submit your will to His will.
- Ask the Lord to deliver you from murmuring.

SONG: *MY HEART'S THE SEAT OF WAR*

Day 217: (Saturday)
Murmuring Breeds Lies

Deuteronomy 1:27 And ye murmured in your tents, and said, Because the LORD hated us, he hath brought us forth out of the land of Egypt, to deliver us into the hand of the Amorites, to destroy us.

INTRODUCTORY THOUGHTS

In **Deuteronomy 7:7-8**, the Lord expressed His great love for the nation of Israel. In the midst of this declaration, the Lord provided reasons why He placed His love upon this particular nation. In **Deuteronomy 1:27**, the people began to murmur and their murmurings bred lies. They stated that the Lord brought them out of Egypt to destroy them because of His great hatred for them. Their statements were completely false. This is true in most circumstances when people turn to murmuring. The problem gets exaggerated and the truth corrupted. Fabricating lies helps the one murmuring to feel better about voicing the complaint. Interestingly, the truth is usually not worth murmuring about.

DEVOTIONAL THOUGHTS

- **(For children):** Read *Numbers 21:5*. The people spoke against God and Moses by complaining there was no bread. They lied because in the very same verse they showed their wicked hearts, for God had given them bread. They simply hated God's provision. The Lord was very displeased with their murmuring *(Numbers 21:6)*.
- **(For everyone):** Have you ever heard someone say, *"We don't have anything to eat"*? Was that really true? Most people who complain like that have plenty to eat. Why did the person speak a lie rather than speaking the truth?
- Do you lie when you murmur? Does the Lord approve of this lying? Does the Lord approve of your murmuring? Are you willing to repent?

PRAYER THOUGHTS

- Ask the Lord to forgive you for murmuring.
- Ask the Lord to convict you the next time you begin to murmur.

SONG: *HOW TEDIOUS AND TASTELESS THE HOURS*

Notes: _____

_____

_____

_____

_____

_____

_____

_____

_____

_____

_____

_____

_____

Notes: _____

_____

_____

_____

_____

_____

_____

_____

_____

_____

_____

_____

_____

_____

_____

_____

_____

_____

_____

Quotes from the next volume

(VOLUME 3, WEEK 31)

Subject: Chastening or Punishment (con't)

One who has little understanding of chastening might suggest that it is an act born of hatred, but it actually represents an overflowing from a heart of love.

The only proper response to chastening is given in *Revelation 3:19: "be zealous therefore, and repent."*

Far too many times what is done in the home under the guise of chastening is far from God's scriptural pattern.

32

Praise

Praise—found 314 times in 269 verses

Variations: praise, praised, praises, praiseth, praising

First usage: *Genesis 29:35* (praise)

Last usage: *Revelation 19:5* (Praise)

Defined: to laud or to testify of someone's or something's worth

Interesting fact: It would take approximately thirty minutes to read all the Bible verses using a form of the word *praise*. On the contrary, the heavens can only refrain from declaring Christ's praises for *"about the space of half an hour" (Revelation 8:1).*

Bible study tip: Culture and history should never dictate our methods of praise. Instead, our praise should follow the precepts of sound Bible study. Take time to write out the things specifically identified in scripture as manifestations of praise. If your idea of praise falls outside the identified practices of scripture, you might want to reconsider your understanding of praise. If your Bible study fails to correct your daily practice, your time of study is vain.

Sunday, Day 218—Church Day (no devotional)
Monday, Day 219—*What Is Praise?*
Tuesday, Day 220—*The Praise of Others*
Wednesday, Day 221—Church Night (no devotional)
Thursday, Day 222—*The Foundation of Praise*
Friday, Day 223—*The Time of Our Praise*
Saturday, Day 224—*The Failure of Praise*

Day 218: Church Day

*Psalm 148:1 Praise ye the LORD. Praise ye the LORD from the heavens: **praise him** in the heights.*
*2 **Praise ye him**, all his angels: **praise ye him**, all his hosts.*
*3 **Praise ye him**, sun and moon: **praise him**, all ye stars of light.*
*4 **Praise him**, ye heavens of heavens, and ye waters that be above the heavens.*
*5 Let them **praise the name of the LORD**: for he commanded, and they were created.*
6 He hath also stablished them for ever and ever: he hath made a decree which shall not pass.
*7 **Praise the LORD** from the earth, ye dragons, and all deeps:*
8 Fire, and hail; snow, and vapour; stormy wind fulfilling his word:
9 Mountains, and all hills; fruitful trees, and all cedars:
10 Beasts, and all cattle; creeping things, and flying fowl:
11 Kings of the earth, and all people; princes, and all judges of the earth:
12 Both young men, and maidens; old men, and children:
*13 Let them **praise the name of the LORD**: for his name alone is excellent; his glory is above the earth and heaven.*
*14 He also exalteth the horn of his people, the praise of all his saints; even of the children of Israel, a people near unto him. **Praise ye the LORD**.*

Day 219: (Monday)
What Is Praise?

*2 Samuel 22:4 I will call on the LORD, who is **worthy to be praised**: so shall I be saved from mine enemies.*

INTRODUCTORY THOUGHTS

Most Christians have an incorrect concept of the meaning of the word *praise*. Perhaps one reason for this is the fact that some believers have labeled many charismatic tendencies as praise in order to justify their behaviour. Historically, the word was understood to have a connection to value or worth. Even today, people understand this connection when considering the word *appraisal*. In fact, many verses that deal with praise also include some statement of the Lord's worth. *2 Samuel 22:4* says, *"I will call on the LORD, who is worthy to be praised."* One must declare the worth of the object of praise in order to praise someone or something. If an action fails to declare the personal value of a person or thing, it cannot rightly be considered praise.

DEVOTIONAL THOUGHTS

- **(For children):** Praising God is expressing to Him that we know He is perfect, holy, good, great, etc. It is also thanking Him for something He's done. Some examples are Moses *(Exodus 15:1, 6, 11)*; Hannah *(1 Samuel 2:1-3)*; Solomon *(1 Kings 8:22-24)*.
- **(For everyone):** What are some actions that could be considered praise unto the Lord? How do those things declare the Lord's worth or value to you personally?
- What does it say about your appreciation for the Lord if you fail to praise Him? Why should He be of great worth to you? When is the last time you praised Him?

PRAYER THOUGHTS

- Take some time to praise the Lord in prayer.
- Ask God to help you to be more aware of your praise for Him.

SONG: *JOYFUL, JOYFUL, WE ADORE THEE*

Day 220: (Tuesday)
The Praise of Others

Proverbs 31:28 Her children arise up, and call her blessed; her husband also, and he praiseth her.

29 Many daughters have done virtuously, but thou excellest them all.

30 Favour is *deceitful, and beauty* is *vain:* but *a woman* that *feareth the LORD,* **she shall be praised.**

31 Give her of the fruit of her hands; and let **her own works praise her** *in the gates.*

INTRODUCTORY THOUGHTS

Initially, one might think that praising others or receiving the praise of others might be a wicked act, but the Bible does not reflect this. In Acts chapter 12, Herod was smitten by the Lord when he received praise from the people. The problem was not so much the praise he received, but his failure to, in turn, give glory to God *(Acts 12:22-23)*. Contrary to what most Christians think, the Lord allows for the praise of others. In our passage, the Lord suggests that a virtuous woman will receive praise from her husband. In *Proverbs 27:2*, the Lord declares that one requirement in this matter is that a man only receive praise from the lips of another. When a man begins to praise himself, he does so in direct rebellion to the words and direction of God.

DEVOTIONAL THOUGHTS

- **(For children):** Name some things dad and mom do for you every day. Have you ever told them that you are thankful for what they do? How would your praise of their actions make them feel?
- **(For everyone):** When is the last time you told someone else of his or her worth to you? When is the last time someone told you that you were of great worth to them? How did you handle the praise that was directed toward you?
- Read *John 12:43*, *Romans 2:29*. Is it possible that men can receive praise from God? How could this be possible? What reasons would lead you to your conclusion?

PRAYER THOUGHTS

- Ask God to help you encourage others.
- Ask the Lord to help you receive praise by giving Him the glory.

SONG: *TAKE MY LIFE, AND LET IT BE*

Day 221: Church Night

*Psalm 150:1 **Praise ye the LORD**. **Praise God** in his sanctuary: **praise him** in the firmament of his power.*
*2 **Praise him** for his mighty acts: **praise him** according to his excellent greatness.*
*3 **Praise him** with the sound of the trumpet: **praise him** with the psaltery and harp.*
*4 **Praise him** with the timbrel and dance: **praise him** with stringed instruments and organs.*
*5 **Praise him** upon the loud cymbals: **praise him** upon the high sounding cymbals.*
*6 **Let every thing that hath breath praise the LORD**. Praise ye the LORD.*

Day 222: (Thursday)
The Foundation of Praise

*Psalm 22:3 **But thou art holy**, O **thou that inhabitest the praises of Israel**.*

Introductory Thoughts

Praise is the natural overflowing of affection that occurs when one individual views some positive quality in another. Men praise God because they find His attributes and actions worthy of worship. They may praise Him for His overall greatness *(1 Chronicles 16:25)* or for His mercy *(2 Chronicles 5:13)*. They may praise Him because of His great name *(Psalm 7:17)* or because of His power *(Psalm 21:13)*. They may praise Him because of something He has done for them personally *(Psalm 28:7)*. The foundation may vary, but men praise the Lord because they have reason to do so. In other words, the Lord has given His people ample reason to speak of His worth.

Devotional thoughts

- **(For children):** Children should praise God *(Psalm 148:12-13)*. He made you so wonderful and you can enjoy many things *(Psalm 139:14)*. What can you do with your eyes, ears, hands, feet, mouth? Thank God that He created you and everything in this world.

- **(For everyone):** For which of God's attributes do you generally praise Him? What attributes of the Lord specifically speak to your heart at this point in your life? Have you praised God for those things?
- Has the Lord recently done something special in your life? Did His favour move you to praise Him? If not, why? What does this suggest about the condition of your heart?

PRAYER THOUGHTS

- Take time to praise the Lord for who He is and what He does.
- Ask God to give you a heart overflowing with praise for Him.

SONG: *HOLY, HOLY, HOLY*

Day 223: (Friday)
The Time of Our Praise

*Psalm 115:17 **The dead praise not the LORD,** neither any that go down into silence.*

*18 But **we will bless the LORD from this time forth and for evermore. Praise the LORD.***

INTRODUCTORY THOUGHTS

The Bible repeatedly states that the Lord will receive praise and worship throughout eternity *(Psalm 45:17; Psalm 145:2)*; yet, at the same time, there appears to be a shift in the praise at death *(Psalm 30:9)*. Perhaps a man's praise for the Lord while on earth is distinctly different from his praise for God in eternity. This would make sense in that man can choose to offer the sacrifice of praise *(Psalm 54:6; Hebrews 13:15)* from the overflow of his carnal heart now. While in eternity, he will praise the Lord from a soul sealed in righteousness. Therefore, a man ought to praise the Lord morning and evening *(1 Chronicles 23:30)*, all the day long *(Psalm 35:28)*, and continually *(Psalm 34:1)*.

DEVOTIONAL THOUGHTS

- **(For children):** We can praise God by singing *(Psalm 69:30a)*. As soon as children can learn a song and even into old age, we should be singing to the Lord *(Psalm 104:33a)*. Honour the Lord right now by singing *"Jesus Loves Me"* to Him.

- **(For everyone):** How much time do you think will be spent in eternity praising the Lord? How much time do you spend on this earth in praise toward the Lord? Are you satisfied with your time of praise?
- Why does the Bible describe praise as a sacrifice that is to be offered? Will praise still be a sacrifice in eternity? What kind of an offering of praise are you presenting to the Lord?

PRAYER THOUGHTS

- Take a moment to give God a sacrifice of praise.
- Ask God to help you spend the remnant of your days in praise.

SONG: *COME YE SAINTS! AND RAISE AN ANTHEM*

Day 224: (Saturday)
The Failure of Praise

*Nehemiah 9:5 Then the Levites, Jeshua, and Kadmiel, Bani, Hashabniah, Sherebiah, Hodijah, Shebaniah, and Pethahiah, said, Stand up and bless **the LORD** your God for ever and ever: and blessed be thy glorious name, **which is exalted above all blessing and praise**.*

INTRODUCTORY THOUGHTS

Men should praise the Lord, and they ought to praise Him often. They should praise Him in scriptural manners and for scriptural reasons. Yet, no matter how lofty the praise may be that man offers to the Lord, it still falls short of declaring the greatness of God. In **Nehemiah 9:5**, the Levites admonished the people to *"stand up and bless the LORD,"* while at the same time expressing that the name of God far surpassed all their praises. Some might suggest that the failures of men's praise should altogether exclude the praise, but the Levites emphasized that men still ought to offer their praise. Though the praise of men can never reach to the height of God's worth, God still chose to inhabit the praises of His people *(Psalm 22:3)*.

DEVOTIONAL THOUGHTS

- **(For children):** There is so much for which to praise God. The psalmist did it at least seven times a day *(Psalm 119:164)*. God wants us to praise Him *(Psalm 150:6)*. Read what Jesus said would happen if no one praised Him *(Luke 19:40)*.

- **(For everyone):** Why does the praise of men fall short of declaring the worth or value of the Lord? Should this reality move men to praise the Lord less or more and more *(Psalm 71:14)*?
- What does the failure of praise suggest about the splendour and greatness of God? How does it demonstrate God's humility when He accepts the praise of men?

PRAYER THOUGHTS

- Praise God for accepting your praise.
- Ask the Lord to help your praises glorify Him.

SONG: *O WORSHIP THE KING!*

Notes: _____

_____

_____

_____

_____

Quotes from the next volume

(VOLUME 3, WEEK 32)

Subject: Rebellion

Rebellion thrives on self-will.

A man with a wicked heart and a wrong spirit cannot enjoy sweet fellowship with the Lord.

The Devil works subtly because he knows how to gradually lead men astray by keeping them from noticing any abrupt changes within their hearts and outward deeds.

In order for a rebel to remain in his rebellion, he must keep his distance from the truth.

33

Prayer

Prayer—found 545 times in 511 verses

Variations: pray, prayed, prayer, prayers, prayest, prayeth, praying

First usage: *Genesis 12:13* (pray)

Last usage: *Revelation 8:4* (prayers)

Defined: to ask or request; however, doctrinally, it suggests simply speaking to God

Interesting fact: *Genesis 4:26* does not use the word *prayer*; however, it does teach an important truth concerning prayer. The scripture uses texts, chapters, and sometimes even books of the Bible to transition from one spiritual facet to another. Genesis chapter 4 reveals when men began the transition from speaking to God face-to-face to calling upon Him in prayer *(Genesis 4:26)*. Prayer has certainly served a special purpose and great blessing to God's people, yet God's people should anxiously anticipate the future return to face-to-face communication.

Bible study tip: Be careful not to allow preconceived ideas to narrow your understanding of a Bible word. Some well-meaning teachers have taught that prayer is merely asking and receiving. However, the Bible contains prayers void of questions or requests. Read *1 Samuel 2:1-10* as an example.

Sunday, Day 225—Church Day (no devotional)
Monday, Day 226—*What Is Prayer?*
Tuesday, Day 227—*When Did Prayer Begin?*
Wednesday, Day 228—Church Night (no devotional)
Thursday, Day 229—*The Godhead at Work in Prayer*
Friday, Day 230—*Praying in Jesus' Name*
Saturday, Day 231—*The Form of Prayer*

Day 225: Church Day

*1 Samuel 12:23 Moreover as for me, **God forbid that I should sin against the LORD in ceasing to pray for you**: but I will teach you the good and the right way:*

Day 226: (Monday)
What Is Prayer?

*Philippians 1:4 Always **in every prayer** of mine for you all **making request** with joy,*

Introductory Thoughts

Simply stated, prayer is talking to God. Most Christians think of prayer as simply *asking* and *receiving* from God, but the Bible points out that prayer also involves the making of *requests*. Both **Philippians 1:4** and **Philippians 4:6** mention making requests. Yet, considering the whole counsel of God indicates that prayer is not merely asking and receiving nor is it simply limited to making requests. This is why the Lord taught that prayer should include a time of praise. When asked by His disciples how they should pray, the Lord began by speaking of the greatness of the Father's name *(Matthew 6:9)*. Prayer often includes a time when requests are made and praise occurs. Yet, the overall purpose of prayer involves portraying the greatness of God while testifying to man's inherent frailties.

DEVOTIONAL THOUGHTS

- **(For children):** When we come to God in prayer, we are letting Him know that we depend upon Him for all things, whether we need forgiveness for wrongdoing, help in time of trouble, healing when we or others are sick, etc. Our prayer should include praise for Him for He alone has every answer and the ability to answer every prayer *(Psalm 86:7-8, 10)*.
- **(For everyone):** Why is it dangerous for a believer to think of prayer as merely a time of asking or making of requests? Would you find joy in others who selfishly asked for something every time you saw them?
- Why should we insure a time of praising God during our prayer time? What can we do to insure that our praise of the Lord is without dissimulation *(Romans 12:9)*?

PRAYER THOUGHTS

- Ask God to help your times of prayer to be acceptable to Him.
- Ask the Lord to teach you more about prayer.

SONG: *DID YOU THINK TO PRAY?*

Day 227: (Tuesday)
When Did Prayer Begin?

*Genesis 4:26 And to Seth, to him also there was born a son; and he called his name Enos: **then began men to call upon the name of the LORD**.*

INTRODUCTORY THOUGHTS

One might think that prayer has always existed in the exact manner in which it presently exists, but such is not the case. It appears that the first major shift in prayer took place in *Genesis 4:26*. We know that Adam and Eve freely spoke with the Lord face-to-face in the garden *(Genesis 3:8)*. However, it seems that the fall of man caused men to have to begin *"to call upon the name of the LORD."* Even then, prayer was not as it is today. The very fact that prayer has not always existed parallels a time in the future when prayer as we know it will not exist. When man had full access to the Lord, there was no need for prayer. In eternity, the same will be true. For now, the Lord has given us access to Him through prayer *(Hebrews 4:16)*.

DEVOTIONAL THOUGHTS

- **(For children):** When you want to talk to someone, dad and mom may be busy and your friends may not be home. God says we are His friends *(John 15:15b)*. He is always near *(Psalm 145:18)* and invites us to talk to Him *(Jeremiah 33:3)*. Have you talked to Him today?
- **(For everyone):** Why does God desire for His people to be able to have access to Him? How does prayer fill the void caused by the fall in the garden. Are you excited that that access to the Lord will be restored in eternity?
- If God made prayer available in order to allow access to Him, what does it suggest when we do not take advantage of prayer? He wants to hear from us, do we want to talk to Him?

PRAYER THOUGHTS

- Ask God to help you see the blessing of being able to pray.
- Ask God to help you take advantage of the access you have.

SONG: *NEAR TO THE HEART OF GOD*

Day 228: Church Night

*1 Chronicles 17:25 For thou, O my God, hast told thy servant that thou wilt build him an house: therefore **thy servant hath found** in his heart **to pray before thee**.*

Day 229: (Thursday)
The Godhead at Work in Prayer

*John 16:23 And in that day ye shall ask me nothing. Verily, verily, I say unto you, Whatsoever **ye shall ask the Father in my name**, he will give it you.*

INTRODUCTORY THOUGHTS

The 2,000-year history of the church reveals that there have been teachers and whole religions who have rejected the biblical teaching of the coexistence of a Father, Son, and Holy Ghost. Others have accepted their existence but rejected the fact that these three are one with each being fully God *(1 John 5:7)*. Some have simply been unable to comprehend or unwilling to accept that God could exist as one God in three persons.

Regardless of man's intellectual inadequacies, the Bible reveals that each member of the Godhead works together on our behalf in prayer. The Lord told us that every believer should pray to God the Father in the name of the Lord Jesus *(John 15:16)*. The prayers are directed toward the Father with the Son acting as the mediator *(Hebrews 7:25)*. The book of Romans further reveals that the Spirit of God makes intercession for us in our prayers *(Romans 8:26)*.

DEVOTIONAL THOUGHTS

- **(For children)**: God's people need assistance in praying to God the Father. When we sin, God the Son presents us faultless (as if we had never sinned) to the Father because He paid the penalty for that sin *(1 John 2:1-2; Jude 24)*. God the Holy Ghost intercedes on our behalf by taking our words and making them acceptable for the Father to hear.
- **(For everyone)**: Why is it so important for God's people to pray according to the manner in which the scriptures prescribe? What will happen if we are disobedient in our prayer life?
- Why do we need the Spirit to make intercession for us? Why do we need the Son to act as our mediator? What does this teach us about our frailty and the grace of God?

PRAYER THOUGHTS

- Thank the Lord for His help in your prayer life.
- Thank God for the access He has provided through His Son.

SONG: *FROM EVERY STORMY WIND THAT BLOWS*

Day 230: (Friday)
Praying in Jesus' Name

*John 14:13 And whatsoever **ye shall ask in my name**, that will I do, that the Father may be glorified in the Son.*

*14 **If ye shall ask any thing in my name**, I will do it.*

INTRODUCTORY THOUGHTS

Many believers have made it a practice to end their prayers with the phrase *"in Jesus' name."* They do so because of the Saviour's command to pray in His name. However, the command carries a far deeper relevance than simply a formula habitually added at the end of a prayer. This phrase added at the end of the prayer serves as a reminder that we are performing the action in the name of another. It is also taking place at the request of and under the authority of another person. By coming to the Father in the name of the Son, believers are approaching the Father under the Son's authority and at His request. Because of Christ's request and authority, believers can approach the throne with boldness *(Hebrews 4:16)*. Without Christ's request and authority, our boldness would be turned into presumptuousness.

DEVOTIONAL THOUGHTS

- **(For children):** When you end a prayer by saying, *"In Jesus' name, Amen!"* you are not simply telling God that you are finished praying. You are acknowledging that Jesus is why you came to God in prayer. Sin separates us from God *(Isaiah 59:2)*, but Jesus died for our sins and that is the only way the Father accepts our prayers *(Ephesians 2:13, 18)*.
- **(For everyone):** Why is it so important to pray in the name of the Lord Jesus Christ? How does this provide access to the Father? Why does this make it more important to pray according to God's will?
- Is it possible to say the words *"in Jesus' name"* without truly praying in Jesus' name? How can you insure that you are praying in the name of Jesus?

PRAYER THOUGHTS

- Thank God that you can come to Him in the name of His Son.
- Ask God to teach you what it is to pray in the name of Jesus.

SONG: *WAIT ON THE LORD, YE SAINTS*

Day 231: (Saturday)
The Form of Prayer

*1 Timothy 2:8 I will therefore that men **pray** every where, **lifting up holy hands**, without wrath and doubting.*

INTRODUCTORY THOUGHTS

Prayer is an important subject that has unfortunately been tainted by men's traditions. Some teach that in order to truly pray, you must bow your head and close your eyes. Others have added that you must also kneel in order to pray properly. The problem with both of these practices is that the Bible does not demand either. In fact, in Bible times, prayer was often made by the lifting up of one's hands *(Psalm 141:2)*. In other Bible passages, we see that believers might both kneel and lift up their hands *(1 Kings 8:54)*. The Bible also teaches that the bowing of the head was an act of worship *(Genesis 24:26)*. What does all of this mean? The most important aspect of prayer is not the position of the body but the condition of the heart.

DEVOTIONAL THOUGHTS

- **(For children):** God deserves our full attention when we pray. As children, it might be best for us to close our eyes to avoid being distracted by looking around. Another good habit is to avoid having any objects in your hands with which to play. Folding our hands will keep us from touching another child in a group setting when someone is leading in prayer. However, it is very important to realize that the most important thing is to talk to God.
- **(For everyone):** What dangers exist by putting the emphasis of prayer upon the bodily positions implemented? Is it more important to pray with a humble heart or in a humble position?
- Though a bodily position of humility is not necessary, in what ways could it be helpful in prayer? How could closing your eyes and bowing your head be helpful as you pray?

PRAYER THOUGHTS

- Ask God to help you approach Him with a humble heart.
- Ask the Lord to teach you to pray according to the scriptures.

SONG: *I LOVE THE PLACE, FOR GOD IS THERE*

Notes: _____

_____

_____

_____

_____

_____

_____

Notes: _____

_____

_____

_____

_____

_____

_____

_____

_____

_____

_____

_____

_____

_____

_____

_____

_____

_____

_____

_____

_____

Quotes from the next volume

(VOLUME 3, WEEK 33)

Subject: Rebellion (con't)

Man's opinion of sin and God's opinion of the same sin are as different as heaven and earth.

Rebellion is a willing and conscious decision to refuse the instruction of another.

34

Prayer (con't)

Prayer—found 371 times in 346 verses in the Old Testament and 174 times in 165 verses in the New Testament

Variations: pray, prayed, prayer, prayers, prayest, prayeth, praying

Last usage in Old Testament: *Malachi 1:9* (pray)

First usage in the New Testament: *Matthew 5:44* (pray)

Interesting fact: Throughout the years, many well-meaning Christians have identified Matthew chapter 6 as *the Lord's prayer*. In reality, that was the disciples' prayer as the Lord was teaching them how to pray. John chapter 17 records the Lord's prayer.

Bible study tip: Always assess your motive before, during, and after studying the scripture. Far too frequently, our approach to the scripture resembles that of the Athenians who approached life always desiring *"to tell, or to hear some new thing" (Acts 17:21)*. God may graciously give you some new understanding, but do not formulate a teaching that does not exist merely to have *"some new thing"* that others have not *"seen."*

Sunday, Day 232—Church Day (no devotional)
Monday, Day 233—*For Whom Should We Pray?*
Tuesday, Day 234—*When Should We Pray?*
Wednesday, Day 235—Church Night (no devotional)
Thursday, Day 236—*Where Should We Pray?*
Friday, Day 237—*Hindrances to Prayer*
Saturday, Day 238—*Vain Repetitions*

Day 232: Church Day

Proverbs 15:8 *The sacrifice of the wicked* is *an abomination to the LORD: but* **the prayer of the upright** is **his delight**.

Day 233: (Monday)
For Whom Should We Pray?

1 Timothy 2:1 *I* **exhort** *therefore,* **that,** *first of all, supplications,* **prayers**, *intercessions,* and *giving of thanks,* **be made for all men;**

INTRODUCTORY THOUGHTS

We know that believers should pray for others, but should we limit our scope of prayers? The apostle Paul admonished the believers of Thessalonica to pray for him but also wanted those who served the Lord by his side included *(1 Thessalonians 5:25)*. He admonished the believers in Ephesus to pray for all saints *(Ephesians 6:18)*. Then, he instructed Timothy, the young preacher, to pray *"For kings, and for all that are in authority" (1 Timothy 2:2)*. In verse one of the same chapter *(1 Timothy 2:1)*, Paul gave Timothy a much broader scope when he said *"that . . . supplications, prayers, intercessions, and giving of thanks"* should *"be made for all men."* If believers fail to pray for others, who will take up the slack to pray for those in need?

DEVOTIONAL THOUGHTS

• **(For children):** It's easy to pray for those whom we love, but the Bible tells us to pray for those who may not like us or who do not love God. Paul prayed that God's enemies would be saved *(Romans 10:1)*. David prayed for his enemies who were sick *(Psalm 35:13)*. Stephen prayed for those who were stoning him *(Acts 7:60)*.

- **(For everyone):** Why should we pray for the saved who are serving the Lord? Why should we pray for other believers, even if they are not serving the Lord?
- Why should we pray for a government that is opposed to the things of God? Why should we pray for the lost who despise our Saviour?

PRAYER THOUGHTS

- Ask God to work in the hearts of those who serve in government.
- Ask the Lord to give you a heart to pray for others in need.

SONG: I AM PRAYING FOR YOU

Day 234: (Tuesday)
When Should We Pray?

1 Thessalonians 5:17 Pray without ceasing.

INTRODUCTORY THOUGHTS

Some Bible teachers have suggested that there are specific times of the day in which believers ought to go to the Lord in prayer. In *Psalm 5:3*, David vowed to present his prayers before the Lord in the *morning*. In the 88th psalm, the psalmist acknowledged that he prayed to the Lord *day* and *night (Psalm 88:1)*. Of course, many know about the pattern followed by Daniel, even in the face of persecution, when he sought the Lord three *times a day (Daniel 6:10)*. From these passages, one might suggest that there are specific times of prayer, but according to *1 Thessalonians 5:17*, believers are to *pray without ceasing*. In other words, believers ought to always be in a constant state of prayer before the Lord.

DEVOTIONAL THOUGHTS

- **(For children):** Children of God should have a time when they meet daily with the Lord. The rest of the time, we should be *"continuing instant in prayer" (Romans 12:12)*. That means we remain ready to pray immediately for anyone who has a need – day or night.
- **(For everyone):** When is the best time for you personally to regularly set aside some time to pray? What are some problems with only going to the Lord in prayer during that set time?

- How can believers constantly be in prayer? Why is it important that we *"pray without ceasing"*? What keeps us from spending the time in prayer that we ought to spend?

PRAYER THOUGHTS

- Ask the Lord to help you spend more time with Him in prayer.
- Ask God to help you faithfully present your prayers before Him.

SONG: *TELL IT TO JESUS*

Day 235: Church Night

*Psalm 109:4 For my love they are my adversaries: but **I** give myself unto prayer.*

Day 236: (Thursday)
Where Should We Pray?

*1 Timothy 2:8 **I will therefore that men pray every where**, lifting up holy hands, without wrath and doubting.*

INTRODUCTORY THOUGHTS

Should prayer be kept private or can it be done in publick? For various reasons, some believers have grown increasingly concerned about the appropriate places to call upon the Lord. In *Matthew 6:5-6*, the Lord rebuked the *publick* prayers of the hypocrites and suggested that His people should enter into their closets to pray. The Lord Himself followed this pattern by seeking a *"solitary place"* in which to pray *(Mark 1:35)*. Does this mean that the Lord opposed all publick prayer? It is important to consider the whole counsel of God. Obviously the Lord was not displeased with the publick prayer meeting held by believers in the early church – He answered their prayer by freeing Peter *(Acts 12:12)*. Furthermore, the Lord expressed His will – for men to *"pray every where."*

DEVOTIONAL THOUGHTS

- **(For children):** Sometimes Jesus prayed when He was all alone *(Matthew 14:23)*. Sometimes He prayed out loud in front of others. For example, He prayed publickly on the cross *(Luke 23:34)* and before He fed the 5,000 *(John 6:11)*. We should be able to pray alone or aloud when the need arises. Could you pray aloud for a sick friend?

- **(For everyone):** Why did the Lord rebuke the publick prayer of the hypocrites? Why would the Lord disapprove of the publick prayer of those who refuse to pray in private?
- Why is it important that God's people pray in places other than those which are solitary? Why is it important that we pray together? Why is it important that we pray in publick?

PRAYER THOUGHTS

- Ask the Lord to give you a strong private prayer life.
- Ask God to help you not be ashamed to pray in publick.

SONG: *LEAVE IT THERE*

Day 237: (Friday)
Hindrances to Prayer

1 Peter 3:7 Likewise, ye husbands, dwell with them *according to knowledge, giving honour unto the wife, as unto the weaker vessel, and as being heirs together of the grace of life;* **that your prayers be not hindered**.

INTRODUCTORY THOUGHTS

The Bible clearly proclaims that believers have full access to the throne of God through the shed blood of the Lord Jesus Christ. Yet, the Bible also identifies circumstances that can and will hinder a believer's prayer life. According to *James 1:6-7*, a lack of faith hinders the Lord's response to a person's prayer. According to *1 John 3:22*, disobedience can also be a hindrance to prayer. In *1 Peter 3:7*, the Bible declares that the prayers of a troubled home will be hindered. In addition to this, the Lord acknowledges the benefit of praying according to His will *(1 John 5:14)*. It is important to pray but also important to insure that your prayer life is not hindered by your personal walk and ways.

DEVOTIONAL THOUGHTS

- **(For children):** When we have done something wrong, dad and mom want us to talk about it and apologize before we try to talk to them about other things. This holds true for when we talk to the Lord. Read **Psalm 66:18**.

- **(For everyone):** How can praying according to God's will provide a believer with assurance? Why is it important that we pray believing that God can answer our prayers?
- What efforts have you made to ensure your prayers are not hindered? Is there anything in your life right now that you know would hinder your prayers? What will you do to change that?

PRAYER THOUGHTS

- Ask God to help you pray in faith.
- Ask the Lord to teach you to pray according to His will.

SONG: *YE WHO KNOW THE WORTH OF PRAYER*

Day 238: (Saturday)
Vain Repetitions

*Matthew 6:7 But **when ye pray, use not vain repetitions**, as the heathen do: for they think that they shall be heard for their much speaking.*

INTRODUCTORY THOUGHTS

Man always seems to find a way to corrupt that which is good. Prayer was meant to give man a means of communicating with the Creator. It is to originate from the depths of the heart and never to be memorized and repeated. This is why true prayer is speaking to God from the depths of the heart. As such, God never intended for man to script His prayers to the Lord. In fact, the Lord warned His people against using *"vain repetitions"* while talking to Him *(Matthew 6:7)*. Unfortunately, many people find it easier to simply repeat a prayer commonly called the Lord's prayer *(Matthew 6:9-13)* rather than communing with God with heartfelt sincerity. God never intended this example of praying to be repeated. In fact, the Lord clearly made His intentions understood when He said, *"After this manner . . . pray ye."* The Lord provided a manner (or an example) for His disciples to follow, not words for them to inattentively repeat. With this example of prayer, the Lord certainly was not instructing His followers to do the very thing that He warned against a few verses earlier.

DEVOTIONAL THOUGHTS

- **(For children)**: The prophets of Baal called on their god and said, *"O Baal, hear us,"* from morning until noon. Elijah did not say the same thing over and over, but told God what was on his heart *(1 Kings 18:26, 36-37)*. You don't keep saying the same thing when talking to dad or mom and neither do we when speaking to an all-knowing God.
- **(For everyone)**: Do you use vain repetitions in your prayer time? Do you repeat the same things each time? Do you pray scripted prayers? How can these things hinder genuine heartfelt prayer?
- Do you often repeat the Lord's prayer? Have you ever considered that the prayer given was specifically associated with the Jewish disciples to whom the Lord was talking?

PRAYER THOUGHTS

- Ask God to help you pray from the heart.
- Ask the Lord to show you the vanity of repeating prayers.

SONG: *PRAYER IS THE SOUL'S SINCERE DESIRE*

Notes: _____

_____

_____

_____

_____

_____

_____

_____

_____

_____

_____

_____

_____

Notes: _____

_____

_____

_____

_____

_____

_____

_____

_____

_____

_____

_____

Quotes from the next volume

(VOLUME 3, WEEK 34)

Subject: Relationships

Like other callings upon a person's life, God prepares those He leads to marry.

Modern society is increasingly mocking purity, yet God is pleased with those who endeavour to keep themselves pure before marriage.

Increasing temptations combined with the declining standards concerning courting have made purity a rarity rather than the norm. Regardless of this trend, young people with a deep and abiding love for the Lord will continually strive to overcome these obstacles and remain pure. Those who have failed in the past will renew their commitment to the Lord seeking to prevent further regrets.

35

Teaching

Teaching—found 259 times in 245 verses

Variations: taught, teach, teacher, teachers, teachest, teacheth, teaching

First usage: *Exodus 4:12* (teach)

Last usage: *Revelation 2:20* (teach)

Defined: the giving of instruction

Interesting fact: Many well-meaning men today have unfortunately cast doubt upon the scriptural nature and necessity of Bible teaching. In fact, most of the emerging churches emphasize *sharing the word* in a short Sunday homily rather than mentoring and discipling believers beyond a superficial level. However, the overriding emphasis of the ministry of Christ was not focused upon preaching but rather teaching. In fact, most of Christ's earthly titles pointed to His office as teacher. These include *Master (Matthew 10:24-25)*, *Rabbi (John 1:38; John 3:2)*, and *Rabboni (John 20:16)*.

Bible study tip: As languages change, the meanings of words likewise change. This is especially true for works that have existed for several centuries like the Bible. In order to properly understand the Bible words, it is best to consider the biblical usage of the word. The word *scholar* is a prime example. The context most commonly used today refers to someone who has mastered a particular subject. Unfortunately, this usage does not align with the biblical usage. The Bible refers to a scholar as one who is a student *(1 Chronicles 25:8; Malachi 2:12)*. As we learn scriptural truths, we should implement them into our speech. For example, we should never refer to someone who fails to uphold the ultimate authority of the scriptures as a Bible *scholar* simply because he is highly educated or esteemed by the world.

Sunday, Day 239—Church Day (no devotional)
Monday, Day 240—*Be Teachable*
Tuesday, Day 241—*Take In to Give Out*
Wednesday, Day 242—Church Night (no devotional)
Thursday, Day 243—*Teach Others*
Friday, Day 244—*What Shall We Teach?*
Saturday, Day 245—*Live What You Teach*

Day 239: Church Day

Psalm 25:4 Shew me thy ways, O LORD; teach me thy paths.

5 Lead me in thy truth, and teach me: for thou art the God of my salvation; on thee do I wait all the day.

8 Good and upright is the LORD: therefore will he teach sinners in the way.

9 The meek will he guide in judgment: and the meek will he teach his way.

12 What man is he that feareth the LORD? him shall he teach in the way that he shall choose.

Day 240: (Monday)
Be Teachable

Proverbs 5:12** And say, How have **I hated instruction**, and **my heart despised reproof;

13 And have not obeyed the voice of my teachers, nor inclined mine ear to them that instructed me!

INTRODUCTORY THOUGHTS

The book of Proverbs serves as a chronicle of a father's instruction to his son. Those who approach Proverbs with a teachable spirit can gain much practical help in making wise decisions. In chapter five, Solomon warned his son to heed wise instruction. He told his son that failure to do so would lead to regrets later in life when the son would say, *"How have I hated instruction, and my heart despised reproof; and have not obeyed the voice of my teachers, nor inclined mine ear to them that instructed me!"* Chapter one of Proverbs offers the solution to the matter: *"A wise man will hear, and will increase learning"* **(Proverbs 1:5)**. Those who are wise are continually learning. When an individual refuses to have a teachable spirit, he identifies himself as the fool that he is. Everyone has much to learn so be teachable or stay a fool! The choice is yours.

DEVOTIONAL THOUGHTS

- **(For children)**: Your dad and mom are trying to teach you the ways of God. Are you listening and practicing what God says to do **(Proverbs 8:32-33)**? This teaching is for your own good **(Proverbs 13:18)**.
- **(For everyone)**: How do we demonstrate arrogance and pride when we refuse to be taught by others? How will it ultimately hinder our spiritual growth in the Lord?
- Why is it important that, from an early age, children be taught the importance of being teachable? How does this affect us in our homes, jobs, and churches?

PRAYER THOUGHTS

- Ask the Lord to help you receive proper instruction.
- Ask God to remove any pride that would keep you from learning.

SONG: *FOOTPRINTS OF JESUS*

Day 241: (Tuesday)
Take In to Give Out

*Exodus 24:12 And the LORD said unto Moses, Come up to me into the mount, and be there: and **I will give thee tables of stone**, and a law, and commandments which I have written; **that thou mayest teach them.***

Introductory Thoughts

The prevailing philosophy today seems to be that each person should be allowed to do what is right in his own eyes. With this philosophy, anything goes! Unfortunately, even Christians have bought into this wicked mindset as they raise their children and allow them to decide what to believe to be true. This contradicts the very foundation of biblical faith that teaches believers to pass on the truths that they have received. The Lord called Moses to the mount to receive commandments with the end purpose that he would teach the people what he had received. This theme was quite common in the history of the nation of Israel *(Deuteronomy 4:9-10)*. God gave His truth to His people with instructions to give those truths to others. The New Testament follows this same pattern. *"And the things that thou hast heard of me among many witnesses, the same commit thou to faithful men, who shall be able to teach others also" (2 Timothy 2:2).*

Devotional thoughts

- **(For children):** Read *1 Corinthians 4:17*. Timothy was teachable and faithful. Paul taught Timothy what the Lord taught Paul. Paul was then able to send him to the church at Corinth so Timothy could teach them what he had learned from Paul.
- **(For everyone):** We know that it is important that we be teachable. Why is it just as important that we receive the truth with the mindset of passing it on to others?
- Are you thankful that you know the way of salvation through Jesus Christ? How beneficial is this knowledge if you fail to give it out to others?

Prayer Thoughts

- Ask God for opportunities to teach what you have received.
- Ask God to help you see the importance of receiving and giving.

SONG: *JESUS, I MY CROSS HAVE TAKEN*

Day 242: Church Night

*Acts 20:20 And how I kept back nothing that was profitable unto you, but **have shewed you**, and **have taught you publickly, and from house to house**,*

Day 243: (Thursday)
Teach Others

*2 Timothy 2:2 And the things that thou hast heard of me among many witnesses, the same **commit thou to faithful men, who shall be able to teach others also**.*

INTRODUCTORY THOUGHTS

Those with their ear toward the world have many accessible teachers. Unfortunately, far too frequently, that which is being taught contradicts the plain teaching of scripture. In order to combat the propagation of false teaching, the Lord calls upon His people to teach the truth. God placed men within the New Testament church to spread the truth through teaching and preaching *(Acts 13:1)*. He placed older men and women in the church in order to teach the younger men and women *(Titus 2:1-8)*. He placed godly moms and dads in the home to teach the children. Every believer should have a desire to come to a point where he or she can teach others. According to the scriptures, this is the will of God *(Hebrews 5:12)*.

DEVOTIONAL THOUGHTS

- **(For children):** When Aquila (a tentmaker) and his wife Priscilla heard Apollos speak in the synagogue, they realized he needed further instruction and taught him the way of God more perfectly. Apollos was willing to learn and changed his message to align it with the truth that he now knew. God wants us to know His word and be able to teach others *(Acts 18:24-26)*.
- **(For everyone):** What are some sources of education for today's youth? Are those sources generally teaching the truth or mixing some falsehoods with the truth? What are you doing to ensure that young people know the truth?
- Those who do not believe in God or His word understand the importance of education. This is why they have systematically taken

control of the schools and universities. What efforts are you making to teach people the Bible?

PRAYER THOUGHTS

- Ask God to give you people who are hungry to learn the truth.
- Ask the Lord to help you to be biblical in your teaching.

SONG: *IF JESUS GOES WITH ME*

Day 244: (Friday)
What Shall We Teach?

1 Timothy 4:11 These things command and teach.

INTRODUCTORY THOUGHTS

Paul served as Timothy's mentor. In fact, Paul referred to Timothy as his *"son in the faith" (1 Timothy 1:2)*. As Timothy's mentor, Paul gave Timothy truths with the intent that he would pass along those teachings to other believers. Though there are certainly variations of what should be taught, Paul laid out two foundational categories when he mentioned *"words of faith and of good doctrine" (1 Timothy 4:6)*. Though specifics are given in the epistles of First and Second Timothy and Titus, every teaching should reflect the categories set forth by the apostle Paul. Even practical teaching ought to be based upon the words of God, as some teachings are good *(2 Thessalonians 2:15)*, and some are bad *(Matthew 15:9)*. Every teacher should teach with hopes of eventually learning from his students when they too become the teachers.

DEVOTIONAL THOUGHTS

- **(For children):** The prophet Samuel told the children of Israel that he would teach them *"the good and the right way" (1 Samuel 12:23b)*. God wants us to learn and be able to teach His word. His word is pure and true *(Psalm 119:140, 160)*.
- **(For everyone):** Through your words and actions, what are you teaching others? Are you teaching them words of faith and good doctrine? Does your teaching help people to have a better walk with the Lord?

- Why is it so important that we check all our teaching against the word of God? What authority does it give a believer to have a Bible verse to back up his or her teaching?

PRAYER THOUGHTS

- Ask God to help you teach things that become sound doctrine.
- Ask the Lord to help you change when you are wrong.

SONG: *JESUS! AND SHALL IT EVER BE!*

Day 245: (Saturday)
Live What You Teach

Romans 2:21 Thou therefore which teachest another, teachest thou not thyself? ***thou that preachest a man should not steal, dost thou steal?***

INTRODUCTORY THOUGHTS

It is easy to tell others what to do and how to do it, but very unwise to fail to follow one's own instructions and teachings. In fact, man naturally seems to want to place greater burdens upon others than he himself is willing to bear. This was one of the primary issues addressed by those attending the council of Acts chapter 15 in Jerusalem. Peter concluded with the other apostles in agreement that it was not right to ask others to bear a yoke that previous generations were unable to bear *(Acts 15:10)*. This does not mean that believers change their teaching to fit their obedience. Rather, believers ought to obey the truth and teach these truths to others. How many preachers and teachers have spoken about subject matters only to refuse to obey the very truths they have taught to others?

DEVOTIONAL THOUGHTS

- **(For children):** Paul told Timothy not only to teach, but to be a good example *(1 Timothy 4:11-12)*. When we do wrong, we may cause others not to believe in God or to think that they don't have to do what He says. King David's sin gave God's enemies great occasion to speak against the Lord *(2 Samuel 12:14)*.

- **(For everyone):** What truths have you taught to others only to disregard them yourself? How does this harm those to whom you initially taught the truth?
- How many people have been turned away from the truths you taught because of your own disobedience to the truth? What will you do to mend what you have broken?

Prayer Thoughts

- Ask the Lord to help you live what you teach.
- Ask the Lord to make you an example for other believers.

SONG: *SOLDIERS OF CHRIST, IN TRUTH ARRAYED*

Notes: _____

_____

_____

_____

_____

_____

_____

_____

_____

_____

Quotes from the next volume

(VOLUME 3, WEEK 35)

Subject: Relationships (con't)

God instituted marriage and He alone has the right to establish the rightful candidates to join together in this union.

God instituted marriage so that man would not have to be alone, but man should enter into marriage for the purpose of glorifying God.

36
Reading and Studying

Reading and Studying—found eighty-five times in seventy-nine verses

Variations: read, readest, readeth, reading, study

First usage: *Exodus 24:7* (read); *Ecclesiastes 12:12* (study)

Last usage: *Revelation 5:4* (read); *2 Timothy 2:15* (study)

Defined: To read is to take in the sense of words as they appear in their intended structure and to study in this context is to contemplate the meaning and purpose of what is read.

Interesting fact: All scripture is worthy of our time spent in reading and studying, but the book of Revelation promises *"Blessed is he that **readeth**, and they that **hear** the words of this prophecy, and **keep** those things which are written therein: for the time is at hand" (**Revelation 1:3**).*

Bible study tip: Take the Bible literally unless the scripture itself gives cause to do otherwise. In such cases, look for symbolism like that used in *Revelation 1:12-13, 16*. Often in these passages, the literal truth represented will be identified in the context. In this case, the stars and the candlesticks are defined as the angels of the churches and the churches, respectively *(Revelation 1:20)*.

Sunday, Day 246—Church Day (no devotional)
Monday, Day 247—*Seek the Book of the Lord and Read*
Tuesday, Day 248—*He Read All the Words*
Wednesday, Day 249—Church Night (no devotional)
Thursday, Day 250—*Spending Time in the Word*
Friday, Day 251—*Reading with a Purpose*
Saturday, Day 252—*Understanding the Reading*

Day 246: Church Day

Deuteronomy 17:14 When thou art come unto the land which the LORD thy God giveth thee, and shalt possess it, and shalt dwell therein, and shalt say, I will set a king over me, like as all the nations that are about me;

*15 **Thou shalt in any wise set** him **king over thee, whom the LORD thy God shall choose**: one from among thy brethren shalt thou set king over thee: thou mayest not set a stranger over thee, which is not thy brother.*

*18 And it shall be, **when he sitteth upon the throne of his kingdom, that he shall write him a copy of this law in a book out of** that which is **before the priests the Levites**:*

*19 And it shall be with him, and **he shall read therein all the days of his life**: that he may learn to fear the LORD his God, to keep all the words of this law and these statutes, to do them:*

Day 247: (Monday)
Seek the Book of the Lord and Read

*Isaiah 34:16 **Seek ye out of the book of the LORD, and read**: no one of these shall fail, none shall want her mate: for my mouth it hath commanded, and his spirit it hath gathered them.*

INTRODUCTORY THOUGHTS

The Lord laboured to reveal, inspire, and preserve His words for man to read, learn, and study. Did He do so but then insure that no one could possibly understand? No! The Lord gave man His word with the expectation that each believer would read it and heed what it says. In *Isaiah 34:16*, the Lord commanded His people to *"Seek . . . out of the book of the LORD, and read."* In fact, a constant theme of the Lord's rebukes, during His earthly ministry, pertained to man's failure to read the scriptures. In *Matthew 12:3*, the Lord rebuked the Pharisees for their failure to read about the exploits of David. In another place, the Lord rebuked the Sadducees by saying, *"Ye do err, not knowing the scriptures, nor the power of God" (Matthew 22:29)*. The Lord obviously expected His people to know and heed His word.

DEVOTIONAL THOUGHTS

- **(For children)**: Children who have yet to learn how to read can learn the scripture this way. Start with simple verses like *1 John 4:19*. Take their finger and point to each word. You say the word then have them repeat the word. Do the same verse a few days in a row. They will learn to recognize some words and be excited that they are "reading" God's word.
- **(For everyone)**: Do you have the words of God? Do you spend quality time reading those words? What benefits do you find from faithfully reading your Bible?
- If the Lord returned today, would He rebuke you for your failure to spend time in His word? Would you hear statements similar to those expressed to the Pharisees and Sadducees?

PRAYER THOUGHTS

- Ask the Lord to give you a desire to read His word.
- Ask the Lord to convict you when you fail to do so.

SONG: *BREAK THOU THE BREAD OF LIFE*

Day 248: (Tuesday)
He Read All the Words

*Joshua 8:34 And afterward **he read all the words of the law**, the blessings and cursings, according to all that is written in the book of the law.*

35 There was not a word of all that Moses commanded, which Joshua read not before all the congregation of Israel, with the women, and the little ones, and the strangers that were conversant among them.

INTRODUCTORY THOUGHTS

According to *2 Timothy 3:16*, *"All scripture . . . is profitable."* No portion of scripture is irrelevant or unnecessary. This is not to say that some passages are not difficult or even labourious to read. The Bible contains a variety of different subjects and historical events. Some passages read very easily and offer great encouragement while others serve other purposes. Nevertheless, it is expedient that God's people read *"all the words"* of the Bible. When Joshua stood before the people and read the scriptures, the Bible states, *"There was not a word of all that Moses commanded, which Joshua read not before all the congregation of Israel"* *(Joshua 8:35)*. He read *"the blessings and cursings"* *(Joshua 8:34)*. In like manner, it is important for New Testament believers to read all the words of God.

DEVOTIONAL THOUGHTS

- **(For children):** During the reign of some of the wicked kings, the Bible points out that God's word had been forgotten. Fortunately for Israel, Josiah was a godly king. He ordered the temple to be cleansed and repaired. Hilkiah the priest found the book of the law and gave it to king Josiah who read *"all the words"* to the people *(2 Kings 23:1-2)*.
- **(For everyone):** If God took the time to give us every word, what does it say about the condition of our hearts when we refuse to read each of those words?
- What sections of scripture do you find more difficult to read? Do you skip those sections when reading through the Bible? Will you repent of this sin and read *"all the words"*?

PRAYER THOUGHTS

- Ask God to help you long for *"every word of God"* *(Proverbs 30:5)*.
- Take time to thank God for carefully giving us every word.

SONG: *I'LL NOT GIVE UP THE BIBLE*

Day 249: Church Night

1 Timothy 4:13 Till I come, **give attendance to reading,** *to exhortation, to doctrine.*

Day 250: (Thursday)
Spending Time in the Word

Nehemiah 9:3 And **they stood up in their place, and read in the book of the law of the LORD their God one fourth part of the day;** *and another fourth part they confessed, and worshipped the LORD their God.*

INTRODUCTORY THOUGHTS

The world is filled with all sorts of time-saving devices, but mankind seems to have less time for important matters now than ever before. In Nehemiah chapter 9, the children of Israel found themselves in serious need from the Lord. They *"were assembled with fasting, and with sackclothes, and earth upon them" (Nehemiah 9:1).* They *"separated themselves from all strangers, and stood and confessed their sins" (Nehemiah 9:2).* As part of their efforts to get the Lord's attention, the children of Israel *"read in the book of the law of the LORD their God one fourth part of the day" (Nehemiah 9:3).* This would have consisted of a minimum of three hours spent in the reading or hearing of the words of God. Imagine the difference in people's lives and the overall church today if we got that serious about God's word.

DEVOTIONAL THOUGHTS

- **(For children):** To study the Bible means to examine it closely. God wants us to study His word *(2 Timothy 2:15).* Ask questions and have someone read the Bible answers. For example, what does the Bible say about dogs? Why did David use a slingshot to kill Goliath?
- **(For everyone):** Do you spend quality time in your Bible? Do you have a Bible reading plan that causes you to rush through in order to meet a quota? How much profit do you get by rushing through the Bible with little attention?
- When is the last time you spent several hours in your Bible? Do you ever listen to the Bible being read, or have you read the Bible together with family or friends?

- Ask God to give you more time in His word.
- Ask the Lord to help you see the importance of His word.

SONG: *"SEARCH THE SCRIPTURES," SAITH THE LORD*

Day 251: (Friday)
Reading with a Purpose

Deuteronomy 17:19 And it shall be with him, and he shall read therein all the days of his life: **that he may learn to fear the LORD his God, to keep all the words of this law and these statutes, to do them:**

INTRODUCTORY THOUGHTS

The Bible is not meant to be read merely for the sake of reading. God intends for the Bible to be read with a deliberate purpose! Sometimes that purpose may be learning, while at other times it may be for purification. There will be times when one might not know the purpose for reading, but there can be no doubt that the Lord has a purpose. In **Deuteronomy 17:18-19**, the Lord states that His king should spend time in the law of God so that *"he may learn to fear the LORD his God"* and *"keep all the words of"* God's law *"to do them."* In **Ephesians 5:26**, the Lord describes one of these purposes when He speaks of *"the washing of water by the word."* God's purposes may be missed when one indiscriminately hastens through the scriptures.

DEVOTIONAL THOUGHTS

- **(For children):** God gave us the Bible to tell us about Himself, how we can live with Him forever, and how He expects us to behave here on earth. We need to read His word to find out these things *(John 5:39; John 20:31; Psalm 119:11)*.
- **(For everyone):** Have you ever written to someone with a purpose in mind? How would it feel if that person failed to see the purpose of your note? How often do you read God's word without looking for a purpose?
- What does God do in your heart when you read His word? Do you ever feel that He is convicting you? Are there other times when you feel that He is comforting you through His words?

PRAYER THOUGHTS

- Ask the Lord to help you see that there is always a purpose.
- Ask God to work His purpose in your life as you read the Bible.

SONG: *O BLESSED WORD*

Day 252: (Saturday)
Understanding the Reading

Acts 8:30 And Philip ran thither to him, *and heard him read the prophet Esaias, and said,* **Understandest thou what thou readest?**

INTRODUCTORY THOUGHTS

Many people who fail to understand the Bible's contents foolishly judge the Bible as a closed book except to those academically superior. The problem does not rest with God's words but with man's spiritual inabilities. This should be expected as the Bible says, *"the natural man receiveth not the things of the Spirit of God: for they are foolishness unto him: neither can he know them, because they are spiritually discerned" (1 Corinthians 2:14).* Even the saved at times may have difficulty understanding certain Bible passages, but God has given His Spirit to those who are saved to teach them and guide them in their understanding of His words. This truth is confirmed in *John 14:26* when the Bible says, *"the Comforter . . . shall teach you all things."*

DEVOTIONAL THOUGHTS

- **(For children):** God wants you to understand His word. God's Spirit helps us *(Nehemiah 9:20a; Psalm 32:8).* Sometimes when people say they don't understand, it is because they don't want to do what God says *(Isaiah 5:24b).*
- **(For everyone):** Do you ever have difficulty understanding what you read in the Bible? First of all, have you made sure of your salvation? Secondly, have you asked the Lord to help you as you read?
- Why did the Eunuch have trouble understanding what he was reading? Why can the natural man not understand the things of God?

PRAYER THOUGHTS

- Ask the Lord to help you understand as you read.
- Ask God to give you a hunger for His word.

SONG: *OPEN MY EYES, THAT I MAY SEE*

Notes: _____

_____

_____

_____

_____

_____

_____

_____

_____

_____

_____

_____

_____

Quotes from the next volume

(VOLUME 3, WEEK 36)

Subject: Relationships (con't)

Even the best of homes will have times when trouble arises. Unfortunately, there seem to be ever fewer homes possessing the strength to endure the difficulties of life.

Throughout scripture, the Lord promises to minister to and defend those whose homes are broken because of the sting of death.

37
Reading and Studying (con't)

Reading and Studying—found forty-seven times in forty-four verses in the Old Testament and thirty-eight times in thirty-five verses in the New Testament

Variations: read, readest, readeth, reading, study

First usage in the New Testament: *Matthew 12:3* (read); *1 Thessalonians 4:11* (study)

Last usage in the Old Testament: *Habakkuk 2:2* (readeth); *Ecclesiastes 12:12* (study)

Interesting fact: A proper response to God's word will get His attention every time. Isaiah tells us that response: *"but to this man will I look, even to him that is poor and of a contrite spirit, and trembleth at my word (Isaiah 66:2).* Josiah's response to the hearing of God's word *(2 Kings 22:11)* prevented him from personally reaping the consequences set forth by the passage he heard *(2 Kings 22:16-20).*

Bible study tip: Many Bible passages cannot be effectively studied without considering other passages. Specifically, there are some passages that are not fully understood without taking into account their parallel passages. This is especially true concerning details found within the books of First and Second Samuel, First and Second Kings, and First and Second Chronicles within the Old Testament and Matthew, Mark, Luke, and John in the New Testament.

Sunday, Day 253—Church Day (no devotional)
Monday, Day 254—*Reading the Bible in Publick*
Tuesday, Day 255—*The Blessing of Reading and Hearing*
Wednesday, Day 256—Church Night (no devotional)
Thursday, Day 257—*Searching the Scriptures Daily*
Friday, Day 258—*The Command to Study*
Saturday, Day 259—*Much Study Wearies the Flesh*

Day 253: Church Day

*Nehemiah 8:8 So **they read** in the book in the law of God **distinctly**, and **gave the sense**, and **caused them to understand the reading**.*

Day 254: (Monday)
Reading the Bible in Publick

*Luke 4:16 And he came to Nazareth, where he had been brought up: and, **as his custom was**, **he** went into the synagogue on the sabbath day, and **stood up for to read**.*

INTRODUCTORY THOUGHTS

On the sabbath day, the Lord Jesus stood to read the scriptures. This was a common practice in New Testament times as the Jews would read the scriptures every sabbath day *(Acts 13:27; Acts 15:21)*. Publick scripture reading was not uncommon and appears to have also been a practice of the Israelites in the Old Testament *(Exodus 24:7; Deuteronomy 31:11; 2 Kings 23:2; Nehemiah 8:3)*. The Bible also records that publick reading was common in the early church. Unlike today, believers did not own personal copies of the scriptures. Believers learned the scripture from publick reading *(1 Thessalonians 5:27; 1 Timothy 4:13)*. Even now, believers should make an effort to publickly read the scriptures.

DEVOTIONAL THOUGHTS

- **(For children):** Have you ever practiced a Bible verse or sang a scripture song to your mom or whomever you were with while waiting in the doctor's office, on the playground, or waiting in line at a store? The Lord may have someone there who needs to hear His word and your glorifying Him. You could also do this over the phone for a relative or friend.
- **(For everyone):** Why is it important that believers publickly read scripture? What are some of the benefits that can be enjoyed by reading the Bible together as a family or congregation?
- How could believers find opportunities to publickly read the scriptures within their cities or towns? How could this work in the hearts of those who would never enter a church service?

PRAYER THOUGHTS

- Ask God to give you opportunities to read the Bible in publick.
- Ask the Lord to show you the benefits of publick Bible reading.

SONG: *A GLORY GILDS THE SACRED PAGE*

Day 255: (Tuesday)
The Blessing of Reading and Hearing

Revelation 1:3 Blessed is he that readeth, and they that hear the words of this prophecy, and keep those things which are written therein: for the time is at hand.

INTRODUCTORY THOUGHTS

No other book ever written apart from the Bible can offer the spiritual blessings received from reading, hearing, and heeding it. The Bible specifically indicates a special blessing can be received from reading the book of Revelation. However, there can be no doubt that blessings are received any time any of the words of God are read and heard. Perhaps these blessings will not immediately show themselves; but eventually, believers devoting time to the reading and/or hearing of scripture will begin to receive great spiritual benefits. As the word of God enters the eyes and ears, it works its way into the heart and mind. As the word of God moves into these areas, it begins a purification process *(Ephesians 5:26)*.

DEVOTIONAL THOUGHTS

- **(For children):** There is no greater joy or blessing than to know for sure you are going to heaven. You can only know this by reading or hearing the word of God *(Romans 10:17; John 3:16; John 6:37b)*.
- **(For everyone):** People have different methods of learning in which they excel. How do you learn best? Do you implement this method in your study of the scripture?
- What are some blessings that can be received by reading or by hearing the Bible read? Have you ever considered the blessings that you are missing when you fail to read the Bible or hear it read?

PRAYER THOUGHTS

- Ask God to help you to be faithful to read and hear His word.
- Thank the Lord for the blessings you have received from hearing and reading His word.

SONG: *WONDERFUL WORDS OF LIFE*

Day 256: Church Night

*Matthew 19:4 And he answered and said unto them, **Have ye not read**, that he which made them at the beginning made them male and female,*

Day 257: (Thursday)
Searching the Scriptures Daily

*Acts 17:11 These were more noble than those in Thessalonica, in that **they received the word with all readiness of mind, and searched the scriptures daily**, whether those things were so.*

INTRODUCTORY THOUGHTS

Historically, most believers did not have the option of searching the scriptures every day. In fact, local bodies of believers might have had only one copy of the scriptures or a portion of the scriptures that could be read only when the believers came together to worship the Lord. As time progressed, more and more copies of the scriptures began to circulate. In Acts chapter 17, the Bereans were declared to be noble because they searched the scriptures on a daily basis. Perhaps they each had copies, or they met at a place of worship and studied together, but either way, they were commended for their faithfulness to delve into God's word. Now, as the Bible is readily available, believers should be more faithful than any previous generation to daily search of the scriptures.

DEVOTIONAL THOUGHTS

- **(For children):** So that we can grow and be strong and healthy, we eat several times a day. God wants us to feed (read and study) on His word so that we can grow (learn to fear God and do what He says) in our Christian life *(1 Peter 2:2)*. This too should be daily *(Job 23:12b)*.
- **(For everyone):** Would you like to be labeled as noble? Do you search the scriptures on a daily basis? Do you only spend time in the scriptures when you attend your local worship services?
- Why is it important that believers spend time in the word of God each day? What can happen if a believer fails to spend time in the scripture?

PRAYER THOUGHTS

- Ask God to give you something special out of His word each day.
- Ask the Lord to give you a love for His word.

SONG: *THE DEAR OLD BIBLE*

Day 258: (Friday)
The Command to Study

2 Timothy 2:15 Study to shew thyself approved unto God, a workman that needeth not to be ashamed, rightly dividing the word of truth.

INTRODUCTORY THOUGHTS

Every believer ought to faithfully read the word of God, but there is another command that is not to be neglected. According to *2 Timothy 2:15*, believers can show themselves approved unto God by studying the scriptures. One can read through the scriptures on a daily basis without ever truly studying the scriptures. In order to study, one must delve into the words and phrases of the Bible and consider their meaning both historically and doctrinally. Few believers take time to read their Bibles, but even fewer take time to study it. In fact, the modern versions have removed the command to study from *2 Timothy 2:15*. Somebody has tried to hide God's desire for believers to study. No doubt it is the same one who walks about seeking someone to devour *(1 Peter 5:8)*.

DEVOTIONAL THOUGHTS

- **(For children)**: God gave us His word to tell us what's right, what's wrong, how to get right and how to stay right *(2 Timothy 3:16)*. Consider this analogy. A flashlight would be of little value to you in the dark if you never turned it on. God's word will be of more value to you if you study it *(Psalm 119:105)*.
- **(For everyone)**: How often do you take the time to study the definition of a word or phrase as used by the Lord? Do you run straight to the dictionary or do you look it up in the scriptures?
- Reading the Bible gives surface knowledge while study of the scriptures delves into the deeper thoughts. Why is it important that believers delve into individual passages?

PRAYER THOUGHTS

- Ask the Lord to teach you how to study His word.
- Ask the Lord to give you a special blessing as you study.

SONG: *THE OLD BOOK AND THE OLD FAITH*

Day 259: (Saturday)
Much Study Wearies the Flesh

*Ecclesiastes 12:12 And further, by these, my son, be admonished: of making many books there is no end; and **much study is a weariness of the flesh**.*

INTRODUCTORY THOUGHTS

One might think that people who spend a great deal of time studying would not be as weary as one who spends the majority of his time performing physical labour. Perhaps this is true at times, but the Bible indicates that *"much study is a weariness of the flesh" (Ecclesiastes 12:12)*. This is specifically true when it comes to Bible study. Interestingly, man's flesh can sit for hours reading a novel or watching television, but studying the scripture manifests a weariness of the flesh rather quickly. The eyes begin to feel the burden of remaining open and the mouth begins to yawn. Why? Because the flesh is wearied by study and the Devil uses our natural tendencies against us.

DEVOTIONAL THOUGHTS

- **(For children):** Cleaning your room may be hard work, but it is necessary. Don't you love to hear dad and mom say, "Good job"? *2 Timothy 2:15* tells us to study God's word as a *"workman that needeth not to be ashamed."* Would the Lord be pleased with your Bible study?
- **(For everyone):** Why does your flesh not appreciate God's command to study? How does your flesh war against God's Spirit in this endeavour? Do you put your flesh in submission and study?
- What can we learn from the fact that our flesh grows so weary when we try to read and study God's word? What should this drive us to do?

PRAYER THOUGHTS

- Ask the Lord to give you victory over your flesh.
- Ask God to help you faithfully obey His commands.

SONG: *O LORD, 'TIS MATTER OF HIGH PRAISE*

Notes: _____

_____

_____

_____

_____

_____

_____

_____

_____

_____

_____

_____

_____

_____

_____

_____

Notes: _____

_____

_____

_____

_____

_____

_____

_____

_____

_____

_____

_____

_____

_____

_____

_____

_____

_____

_____

Quotes from the next volume

(VOLUME 3, WEEK 37)

Subject: Reputation

A good name is of far greater value to a wise man than accumulating the wealth of the entire world.

The path to favour in the sight of God heads in the same direction as favour in the sight of the right kind of men.

38

Rebuking

Rebuking—found eighty-two times in eighty verses

Variations: rebuke, rebuked, rebuker, rebukes, rebuketh, rebuking, unrebukeable

Defined: a reproof or correction

First usage: *Genesis 31:42* (rebuked)

Last usage: *Revelation 3:19* (rebuke)

Interesting fact: The Lord, through the apostle Paul, admonished young pastors to rebuke *"with all longsuffering and doctrine" (2 Timothy 4:2)* and *"with all authority" (Titus 2:15)*. Pastors should seek God's help in finding the balance between longsuffering and duly constituted scriptural authority.

Bible study tip: Though it may seem quite simplistic, make sure to pray before reading or studying the scripture. The writer of *Psalm 119* prayed, *"Open thou mine eyes, that I may behold wondrous things out of thy law" (Psalm 119:18)*. It certainly makes sense to ask the author of the Bible (the Lord) to allow the teacher of the Bible (the Holy Ghost) to open our understanding *(Luke 24:45)*.

Sunday, Day 260—Church Day (no devotional)
Monday, Day 261—*The Foundation for Rebuking*
Tuesday, Day 262—*The Purpose of Rebuking Others*
Wednesday, Day 263—Church Night (no devotional)
Thursday, Day 264—*Rebuking with Authority*
Friday, Day 265—*A Mixed Reaction to Rebukes*
Saturday, Day 266—*Love and Rebukes*

Day 260: Church Day

Ecclesiastes 7:5 It is better to hear the rebuke of the wise, *than for a man to hear the song of fools.*

Day 261: (Monday)
The Foundation for Rebuking

2 Timothy 4:2 *Preach the word; be instant in season, out of season;* *reprove,* ***rebuke,*** *exhort* ***with all longsuffering and doctrine.***

INTRODUCTORY THOUGHTS

The apostle Paul knew that there would be times when Timothy, as a minister of the gospel, would have to rebuke or correct others. However, Timothy was not to rebuke others on a whim. In fact, Paul specifically laid out two premises which Timothy's rebuke should follow: *"with all longsuffering and doctrine."* Timothy was to rebuke others while *suffering* with them for a *long* time, thus *longsuffering*. He was to exhibit grace by offering others the opportunity to rectify their areas of failure. At the same time, he was to rebuke others with sound doctrine and not simply based upon mere opinion. This was going to be even more necessary as some would begin to depart from sound doctrine and practice *(2 Timothy 4:3-4)*.

DEVOTIONAL THOUGHTS

- **(For children):** You are playing with a friend (or maybe a sibling) when his mother calls him. He just keeps playing. You need to remind him of **Colossians 3:20**. It may happen another time. Remind him again. Keep doing this until he learns to obey quickly.

- **(For everyone):** Why is it important that we rebuke others *"with all longsuffering"*? How will it hinder the working of God in the lives of others when we fail to rebuke with longsuffering?
- Do you rebuke others based upon your opinion or based upon the eternal words of God? What happens when we rebuke without the authority of God's word?

PRAYER THOUGHTS

- Ask God to help you to be gracious when you must rebuke others.
- Ask God to give you a scriptural foundation for your rebukes.

SONG: *LET ME LIVE TO PREACH THE WORD*

Day 262: (Tuesday)
The Purpose of Rebuking Others

Titus 1:12 *One of themselves,* even *a prophet of their own, said, The Cretians* are *alway liars, evil beasts, slow bellies.*

13 *This witness is true. Wherefore* **rebuke them** *sharply,* **that they may be sound in the faith***;*

14 *Not giving heed to Jewish fables, and commandments of men, that turn from the truth.*

INTRODUCTORY THOUGHTS

Believers are to rebuke others in one form or another, but what primary purpose should the rebuking serve? Some rebuke with a prideful heart leaving the person rebuked with feelings of inferiority. Some rebuke because they themselves are guilty of the same glaring fault within their own lives. However, what purpose should rebuking others serve? According to **Titus 1:13**, believers are told to rebuke others *"that they may be sound in the faith."* Scripturally rebuking someone never serves as a self-gratifying act. Rather, it focuses upon helping others grow, improve, and spiritually mature in the Lord. It should never be the desire of a believer to see another person destroyed through a rebuke but always edified. **Galatians 6:1** reiterates this same truth.

Devotional Thoughts

- **(For children):** Samuel rebuked the children of Israel for asking for a king. Then he encouraged them to keep following God and said he would pray for them and teach them the good and right way *(1 Samuel 12:16-25)*. He truly loved and wanted to help God's people.
- **(For everyone):** Do you rebuke others in order to feel superior? Do you rebuke others to cover up for an area of weakness within your own life?
- How can you harm others when you rebuke them out of the wrong spirit? How could this truly grieve the Lord? Have you ever harmed anyone with unscriptural rebukes?

Prayer Thoughts

- Ask God to help you rebuke others with the right purpose.
- Ask the Lord to help you care for others.

SONG: *A CHARGE TO KEEP I HAVE*

Day 263: Church Night

*Hebrews 12:5 And ye have forgotten the exhortation which speaketh unto you as unto children, My son, **despise not thou the chastening of the Lord, nor faint when thou art rebuked of him***:

Day 264: (Thursday)
Rebuking with Authority

*Zechariah 3:2 And **the LORD said** unto Satan, **The LORD rebuke thee**, O Satan; even **the LORD** that hath chosen Jerusalem **rebuke thee**: is not this a brand plucked out of the fire?*

Introductory Thoughts

Too many people have assumed that believers may freely rebuke in their own authority, but there exists no scriptural basis for this. The LORD gave us an excellent example when He said, "*The LORD rebuke thee, O Satan.*" When rebuking the Devil, the LORD emphasized the importance of authority. No believer should ever rebuke except according to the God-given authority of scripture. In *Zechariah 3:2*, the LORD was His own authority, but believers do not have any such authority in themselves apart from the Lord and His word. Paul spoke expressly about this when he charged Titus to *"speak, exhort, and rebuke with all authority" (Titus 2:15).* It is not sufficient to flippantly invoke the Lord's name; one must base any rebuke upon the scripture. Henceforth, it is the Lord that rebukes, never the believer.

DEVOTIONAL THOUGHTS

- **(For children):** Paul said the only way he knew right and wrong was from God's word *(Romans 3:20b).* We need to know God's word *(2 Peter 3:18)* so we can sufficiently warn the unruly *(1 Thessalonians 5:14a)* and warn one another *(Romans 15:14).* The scripture is our authority.
- **(For everyone):** How can we rightfully rebuke others apart from the authority of God's word? How do we know that the actions of another are wrong if we do not have God's word on the matter?
- What is the only source of truth that we have in this world? How can you accurately rebuke others apart from that source of truth? How could you harm others by doing so?

PRAYER THOUGHTS

- Ask the Lord to help you use His authority when rebuking.
- Ask the Lord to show you the importance of authority.

SONG: *THE KING'S BUSINESS*

Day 265: (Friday)
A Mixed Reaction to Rebukes

Proverbs 28:23 He that rebuketh a man afterwards shall find more favour than he that flattereth with the tongue.

INTRODUCTORY THOUGHTS

When someone receives rebuke from another person, it is rarely easy to accept. The person receiving the rebuke may lash out in anger even when the rebuke is scripturally made with longsuffering. The Bible confirms this type of reaction when it says, *"They hate him that rebuketh in the gate, and they abhor him that speaketh uprightly" (Amos 5:10).* This type of reaction is not one of a wise man, nor is it from one who has taken the time to consider the godly rebuke's content and intention. The Bible also says that afterwards the one who rebukes finds *"more favour than he that flattereth with the tongue."* Ultimately, the Lord's reaction is what matters and the scriptural practice of rebuking others within the authority of scripture pleases Him.

DEVOTIONAL THOUGHTS

- **(For children):** When Amaziah was rebuked, he got angry and told the prophet to leave him alone or be killed *(2 Chronicles 25:14-16)*. When David was rebuked, he was sorry for his sin *(2 Samuel 12:9, 13; Psalm 51:3-4a)*. When we are rebuked, we should respond more like David.
- **(For everyone):** How should we expect others to react when we must rebuke them from the scriptures? How can it help us to think upon their reaction before the rebuke is offered?
- How should we react when others become distraught because they have received a rebuke? How can a godly reaction on our end help them to be restored?

PRAYER THOUGHTS

- Ask the Lord to prepare you for various responses to rebukes.
- Thank God for His longsuffering when you respond poorly.

SONG: *WHAT OPPOSITES I FEEL WITHIN!*

Day 266: (Saturday)
Love and Rebukes

Revelation 3:19 As many as I love, I rebuke and chasten: be zealous therefore, and repent.

INTRODUCTORY THOUGHTS

The purpose of rebuking someone has been completely distorted in these days of emphasizing political correctness and personal self-esteem. The world now associates a scriptural rebuke with hatred, anger, and envy. In reality, a godly rebuke demonstrates a supreme act of love. The spiritual mindset helps all of this to make sense; whereas, the carnally minded will reject God's perfect ways. When it is known that an individual is heading in a dangerous direction, hate remains silent; love cries "stop." Many people under the guise of *"secret love"* have allowed friends and family to head off into the ways of the world thinking they were doing those people right. Yet, the Bible plainly says, *"Open rebuke is better than secret love" (Proverbs 27:5).* Once again, the carnal mind struggles to receive this truth, but godly rebukes are based upon love and result from an expression of that love.

DEVOTIONAL THOUGHTS

- **(For children):** Dad and mom warn us when we are not doing what God wants us to do. They hope we will pay attention and do right. If we do not listen and they have to take a harsher action, does this mean that they don't love us *(Proverbs 13:24; Proverbs 29:15)*?
- **(For everyone):** Do you love others enough to offer them a godly rebuke when they are headed in a direction that will harm them spiritually? What would keep you from helping them?
- Why does our mind naturally think the opposite of scripture to be true? What can we do in order to be more spiritually minded? How can this benefit us in our service to the Lord?

PRAYER THOUGHTS

- Thank God for His loving rebukes in your life.
- Ask God to give you that pure love for others.

SONG: *AFFLICTIONS DO NOT COME ALONE*

Notes: _____

_____

_____

_____

_____

_____

_____

_____

_____

_____

_____

Notes: _____

_____

_____

_____

_____

_____

_____

_____

_____

_____

_____

_____

_____

_____

_____

_____

_____

Quotes from the next volume

(VOLUME 3, WEEK 38)

Subject: Reputation (con't)

Paul was converted in Acts chapter 9, but it took years for his reputation to change.

Sometimes people wonder why they are not used more in the Lord's service and work. They fail to realize that their reputation has limited many opportunities. These opportunities will remain hampered until their reputation is repaired.

39

Rebuking (con't)

Rebuking—found forty-nine times in forty-seven verses in the Old Testament and thirty-three times in thirty-three verses in the New Testament

Variations: rebuke, rebuked, rebuker, rebukes, rebuketh, rebuking, unrebukeable

First usage in the New Testament: *Matthew 8:26* (rebuked)

Last usage in the Old Testament: *Malachi 3:11* (rebuke)

Interesting fact: When Jesus *"rebuked the winds and the sea"* and made them *"a great calm" (Matthew 8:26)*, He was declaring Himself to be much more than a man. The scriptures show that the Christ's rebuke carried a much deeper meaning. For example, the rebuke of the LORD created *(2 Samuel 22:16; Psalm 104:5-7)*, and the LORD's rebuke dried up the Red Sea *(Psalm 106:9; Isaiah 50:2; Nahum 1:4)*.

Bible study tip: Pay particular attention to the various punctuation marks used in scripture. Learn how punctuation is used and consider why it is or is not used in one passage of scripture versus another. Consider, for example, that the exclamation point is found 313 times in scripture, but only appears six times in all of Paul's combined epistles. However, in the book of Jeremiah, the exclamation point appears thirty-nine times. Why do you think the Lord would have so many exclamatory statements in this one book?

Sunday, Day 267—Church Day (no devotional)
Monday, Day 268—*Publick Rebuke*
Tuesday, Day 269—*Responses to Rebuke*
Wednesday, Day 270—Church Night (no devotional)
Thursday, Day 271—*Rebuke Not an Elder*
Friday, Day 272—*Rebuking the Lord*
Saturday, Day 273—*Receiving Rebuke*

Day 267: Church Day

Amos 5:10 They hate him that rebuketh in the gate, *and they abhor him that speaketh uprightly.*

Day 268: (Monday)
Publick Rebuke

1 Timothy 5:20 *Them that sin* **rebuke before all**, *that others also may fear.*

Introductory Thoughts

Far too few preachers and teachers have taken the time to consider the context of today's passage. Paul admonished that a rebuke is sometimes unavoidable, but the context reveals that the individual receiving the rebuke is an elder *(1 Timothy 5:17-19)*. It also appears that the rebuke only takes place under specific conditions. Paul informed Timothy that there are times a rebuke must be given in the presence of others. The purpose served to bring fear upon those who witnessed the rebuke so that they too would not repeat the errors of the elder receiving the rebuke. Though a publick rebuke is not a pleasant sight, **Proverbs 27:5** says, "*Open rebuke is better than secret love.*"

DEVOTIONAL THOUGHTS

- **(For children):** Some of God's people would travel great distances to the temple at Jerusalem to give an offering to the Lord. Their money had to be changed into Hebrew money, but the moneychangers were greedy and charged far too much for this service. Jesus publickly rebuked their greed *(Matthew 21:12-13)*.
- **(For everyone):** Why should God's people be careful about hastily rebuking others in publick? What should we take into consideration before rebuking someone publickly?
- Do some sins call for a private rebuke, while others call for a publick rebuke? If so, what would be the distinguishing circumstances for each?

PRAYER THOUGHTS

- Ask the Lord to give you wisdom as to how to rebuke others.
- Ask the Lord to keep you from sins that would demand rebuke.

SONG: *BLEST BE THE TIE THAT BINDS*

Day 269: (Tuesday)
Responses to Rebuke

*Proverbs 9:7 He that reproveth a scorner getteth to himself shame: and **he that rebuketh a wicked man getteth himself a blot.***

*8 Reprove not a scorner, lest he hate thee: **rebuke a wise man, and he will love thee.***

INTRODUCTORY THOUGHTS

The Lord never intended for a believer to consider it his duty in life to rebuke others. As the believer gains additional Bible knowledge, he begins to see the world in a far different light. He gains insights that often remain unavailable to those who ignore the truths of scripture. Sin becomes more noticeable and the individual becomes increasingly offended at the world's corruption. His increased knowledge emboldens him to point out the errors of others. Though in and of itself there is nothing wrong with this, the Bible warns concerning the various responses when someone is rebuked. According to **Proverbs 13:1**, *"a scorner heareth not rebuke."* In fact, a scorner rebuked will return shame and hatred *(Proverbs 9:7-8)*. On the other hand, a believer will find great reward in rebuking the wise *(Proverbs 9:8)*.

DEVOTIONAL THOUGHTS

- **(For children):** To someone who truly loves the Lord, rebuke is an act of kindness and likened to a medicine which cleanses his heart *(Psalm 141:5)*. Those who do not love God will despise rebuke *(Proverbs 23:9; Matthew 7:6)*.
- **(For everyone):** If we purpose to restore through rebuke, what type of people will we rebuke? Are there times when people are not yet ready for rebuke and we may need to show patience?
- How can you be reproached when rebuking a scorner or a wicked man *(Proverbs 9:7)*? What kind of blessings can you receive when you rebuke a wise man *(Proverbs 9:8)*?

PRAYER THOUGHTS

- Ask the Lord to give you discernment in rebuking others.
- Ask God to show you the right time to offer rebuke to others.

SONG: *FOLLOW ON*

Day 270: Church Night

*Psalm 38:1 O LORD, **rebuke me not in thy wrath**: neither chasten me in thy hot displeasure.*

Day 271: (Thursday)
Rebuke Not an Elder

*1 Timothy 5:1 **Rebuke not an elder**, but intreat him as a father; and the younger men as brethren;*

INTRODUCTORY THOUGHTS

Though the Bible refers to the elder in various contexts, today's passage refers to the elder as simply an older gentleman. The elder here is contrasted first with the younger men while the next verse contrasts it with the elder women. The issue at hand is one of respect. It is important to note that the scripture does not imply or teach that believers can never question the actions of an older man. However, it does indicate the method of this questioning. An elder is not to be rebuked but intreated *"as a father."* To *intreat* a person is to plead with or earnestly ask them. Intreating reflects approaching him with respect which is the method by which the Lord demands an elder be approached.

DEVOTIONAL THOUGHTS

- **(For children):** In the book of Job, we are told of Elihu. He respected his elders and would not interrupt what they were saying to Job although he disagreed with them *(Job 32:6, 11-12)*. Especially while living with your parents, you are to obey them *(Ephesians 6:1)*. As you get older, you are to give respectful attention to them *(Proverbs 23:22; Ephesians 6:2)*.
- **(For everyone):** In *Leviticus 19:32*, the Bible says, *"Thou shalt rise up before the hoary head, and honour the face of the old man."* What does this teach us about God's method of approaching older men?
- *Proverbs 16:31* teaches that the hoary head is a crown of glory if it be accompanied by righteousness. What does this suggest about the elderly? Are there times when they will err in the Lord?

PRAYER THOUGHTS

- Ask the Lord to give you the proper respect for the elderly.
- Ask God to give you wisdom in dealing with an elder in error.

SONG: *I AM RESOLVED*

Day 272: (Friday)
Rebuking the Lord

> *Mark 8:32 And he spake that saying openly. And **Peter** took him, and **began to rebuke him.***
>
> *33 But when he had turned about and looked on his disciples, he rebuked Peter, saying, Get thee behind me, Satan: for **thou savourest not the things that be of God, but the things that be of men.***

INTRODUCTORY THOUGHTS

Many have erroneously assumed that the disciples readily accepted Christ's teachings concerning His death, burial, and resurrection. When Simon Peter first heard the Lord teach on the subject, he immediately took the Lord and rebuked Him for what He said. The Lord Jesus responded by rebuking Peter, going so far as calling him Satan. Peter rebuked the Lord because the Lord's teaching did not align with Peter's perception and plans. He had no authority for rebuking the Lord and should have submitted himself to the Lord's teaching. Some things have changed, but some have not. Believers today "rebuke" the Lord when they respond carnally to God's working within their lives. They fail to realize their duty is to submit to the Lord.

DEVOTIONAL THOUGHTS

- **(For children):** Because the disciples were in a storm and were afraid, they asked the Lord if He cared. They should have known better *(Mark 4:37-40)*. Martha asked the Lord the same question *(Luke 10:38-42)*.
- **(For everyone):** What are some ways in which believers can rebuke the Lord? What does it suggest when we complain about something the Lord allows to enter into our lives?
- What does it suggest about the condition of your heart when you begin to rebuke the Lord's teaching and working in your life? How did this fare for Peter? How will it fare for you?

PRAYER THOUGHTS

- Ask the Lord to help you accept His will in your life.
- Ask the Lord to soften your heart to His truth.

SONG: *I SURRENDER ALL*

Day 273: (Saturday)
Receiving Rebuke

*Hebrews 12:5 And ye have forgotten the exhortation which speaketh unto you as unto children, My son, **despise not thou the chastening of the Lord, nor faint when thou art rebuked of him**:*

6 For whom the Lord loveth he chasteneth, and scourgeth every son whom he receiveth.

INTRODUCTORY THOUGHTS

The Bible clearly teaches that no believer is sinless. As such, each believer experiences times when he is rebuked of the Lord. It is a natural part of the Christian life. At the same time, there will be circumstances which will bring about rebuke from other believers *(Ecclesiastes 7:5)*.

These are healthy elements of Christian growth. Yet, the goal of every believer should be one where he lives a life beyond rebuke. Paul's desire for the Philippian believers was that they *"may be blameless and harmless, the sons of God, **without rebuke,** in the midst of a crooked and perverse nation" (Philippians 2:15).* He then admonished Timothy to keep God's commandment *"without spot"* and *"unrebukeable" (1 Timothy 6:14).*

DEVOTIONAL THOUGHTS

- **(For children):** If someone points out to us that we could do better in some areas of our lives, we should be grateful to him or her. The Lord wants us to live so others will know that we love and serve Him *(Matthew 5:16).* Read what He says about those who don't receive rebuke *(Proverbs 10:17b; Proverbs 12:1b).*
- **(For everyone):** How should we respond when rebuked by the Lord? How should we respond when rebuked by someone who loves the Lord and has wisdom?
- What are some measures we could take to insure that we are *"without rebuke"*? How could   *1 Corinthians 11:31* assist us in this endeavour?

PRAYER THOUGHTS

- Thank the Lord for those who love you enough to rebuke you.
- Ask the Lord to help you receive rebuke in a godly manner.

SONG: *AFFLICTIONS, THOUGH THEY SEEM SEVERE*

Notes: _____

_____

_____

_____

_____

_____

_____

_____

_____

_____

Notes: _____

_____

_____

_____

_____

_____

_____

_____

_____

_____

_____

_____

_____

_____

_____

_____

_____

Quotes from the next volume

(VOLUME 3, WEEK 39)

Subject: Sacrifices

In shedding His blood, the Lord Jesus Christ became man's sacrifice, and man need look no further than the shed blood of Christ for the means by which God is satisfied.

Though the scriptures are plain that Christ gave Himself as man's complete and only sacrifice, the New Testament declares that the believer, because of salvation, will offer unto God spiritual sacrifices *(1 Peter 2:5)*.

40

Self-Examination

Self-examination—This concept is found throughout scripture under a variety of words and phrases.

Variations: consider, examine, meditate, remember, think, etc.

Defined: personal reflection or the study of oneself for the sake of improvement

Interesting fact: One of the purposes of man's spirit serves to act as a candle lighting the inner being of man *(Proverbs 20:27)*. It demonstrates to man the true nature of the heart *(Psalm 4:4; Psalm 77:6)*.

Bible study tip: Take the time to consider why the Lord, who is omniscient, ever asks man a question. According to *John 6:5-6*, Jesus asked Philip a question in order to prove Philip for the Lord *"knew what he would do."* With this in mind, consider other passages where the Lord asked man questions including the first man Adam *(Genesis 3:9-13)*. What might be God's purpose in asking questions of man?

Sunday, Day 274—Church Day (no devotional)
Monday, Day 275—*Examine if Ye Be in the Faith*
Tuesday, Day 276—*Consider Thyself*

Wednesday, Day 277—Church Night (no devotional)
Thursday, Day 278—*I Thought on My Ways*
Friday, Day 279—*Take Heed How You Build*
Saturday, Day 280—*Look to Yourselves*

Day 274: Church Day

Revelation 2:5 Remember therefore from whence thou art fallen, and repent, and do the first works; or else I will come unto thee quickly, and will remove thy candlestick out of his place, except thou repent.

Day 275: (Monday)
Examine if Ye Be in the Faith

2 Corinthians 13:5 Examine yourselves, whether ye be in the faith; prove your own selves. Know ye not your own selves, how that Jesus Christ is in you, except ye be reprobates?

INTRODUCTORY THOUGHTS

Self-examination serves as a tool for man to use to find out who and what he is. Though some preachers suggest that believers should never question their own salvation experience, the scripture encourages self-examination. If there are doubts, believers should certainly ask questions concerning the basis for their salvation. Was it based upon one's feelings or solely upon the scriptures? They should ask what they did in order to be saved. Did they join a church, do some penitent work, or did they call upon the name of the Lord Jesus Christ by faith as dictated by the scriptures? They should ask about the effects of their salvation. Have they seen a change of heart, or are they the same that they were before trusting Christ as Saviour?

DEVOTIONAL THOUGHTS

- **(For children):** The Bible is the only book that definitively reveals how to get to heaven *(Acts 16:30-31; Ephesians 2:8-9; 1 Corinthians 15:1-4)*. We must believe what it says, not what we want to believe *(Proverbs 14:12)*.

- **(For everyone):** Why is it important for believers to examine themselves concerning their salvation experience? What benefit can be derived from this examination?
- What could be the danger of teaching others to refuse to call their personal testimony into question? Why did Paul admonish the Corinthian believers to examine themselves?

PRAYER THOUGHTS

- Ask the Lord for wisdom to be able to examine your salvation.
- Ask God to give you a scriptural foundation for your salvation.

SONG: *ARE YOU WASHED IN THE BLOOD?*

Day 276: (Tuesday)
Consider Thyself

Galatians 6:1 Brethren, if a man be overtaken in a fault, ye which are spiritual, restore such an one in the spirit of meekness; ***considering thyself, lest thou also be tempted***.

INTRODUCTORY THOUGHTS

It has always been easier for man to see the problems in the lives of others. In fact, the problems we most easily identify in others are often the sins with which we personally struggle. Oftentimes, believers see these problems and immediately rush to rebuke or admonish those in error without considering their own lives first. According to *Galatians 6:1*, those overtaken in a fault should not be admonished until the restorer has first considered himself. The Bible says, *"lest thou also be tempted."* *1 Corinthians 10:12* contains a similar principle and admonition: *"Wherefore let him that thinketh he standeth take heed lest he fall."* Believers should not be easily deceived by their own conditions and must be willing to call their own standing into question first. Remember that those who have fallen should serve as a warning to every believer.

DEVOTIONAL THOUGHTS

- **(For children):** A child of God can still do wrong and often does according to *1 John 1:8*. However, when we confess, we are forgiven in order to restore our fellowship with the Lord *(1 John 1:9)*. Then, like king David, we will be able to help others *(Psalm 38:18; Psalm 51:13)*.

- **(For everyone):** What should we learn when others fall prey to sin? How should their failings help us to see our own vulnerabilities? What steps should we take to insure that we do not fall as well?
- How do you presently see your condition before the Lord? Upon what do you base your assessment? Is it possible that your heart has deceived you?

PRAYER THOUGHTS

- Ask the Lord to help you take an honest look at your condition.
- Ask the Lord to give you wisdom in helping others.

SONG: *CLOSE TO THEE*

Day 277: Church Night

Deuteronomy 32:29 *O that they were wise, that they understood this, **that they would consider their latter end!***

Day 278: (Thursday)
I Thought on My Ways

Psalm 119:59 ***I thought on my ways,*** *and turned my feet unto thy testimonies.*

INTRODUCTORY THOUGHTS

Life is a journey. Oftentimes, people spend far too much time and strength traveling in the wrong direction. To some degree, this is the psalmist's testimony. In **Psalm 119:59**, he says, *"I thought on my ways, and turned my feet unto thy testimonies."* At some point, the psalmist examined his *"ways."* In doing so, he found that he was heading in a direction contrary to the will of God. Upon his consideration, he determined to turn his feet unto the Lord's testimonies. Had he never taken the time to think upon his ways, he would never have repented and turned in the right direction. This truth is confirmed in **Lamentations 3:40** where the Bible says, *"Let us search and try our ways, and turn again to the LORD."* The Bible frequently warns man not to be deceived.

DEVOTIONAL THOUGHTS

- **(For children):** The Bible says the prodigal son *"came to himself."* That means he thought about what he had chosen to do and where it had led him. He did the right thing by returning to his father who stood ready to receive him *(Luke 15:17-20)*.
- **(For everyone):** When is the last time you paused to consider your ways? Did you find your feet had strayed from the testimonies of the Lord? Did you turn your feet to follow Him?
- How can believers use the Bible in order to think upon their ways? How often should believers be willing to do self-examination?

PRAYER THOUGHTS

- Ask the Lord to help you examine your ways.
- Ask the Lord to guide you to walk in His testimonies.

SONG: *DRAW ME NEARER*

Day 279: (Friday)
Take Heed How You Build

> *1 Corinthians 3:10 According to the grace of God which is given unto me, as a wise masterbuilder, I have laid the foundation, and another buildeth thereon. But **let every man take heed how he buildeth thereupon**.*
>
> *11 For other foundation can no man lay than that is laid, which is Jesus Christ.*

INTRODUCTORY THOUGHTS

The Bible clearly points out that by God's grace the apostle Paul laid the foundation which is Jesus Christ and Him crucified. All those who have come after the apostle Paul have built upon that foundation. It is with this in mind that Paul warned believers to take heed how they built upon the foundation. The foundation has been laid, and no other foundation can be laid, but each believer must carefully examine the means by which he builds upon Christ. Not only should believers take heed to their daily walk, but self-examination is also necessary in their manner of service for the Lord Jesus Christ. Each believer should search the scriptures to ensure that his efforts glorify the Lord. Far too much effort is self-serving and selfish and not God-centric. Self-examination helps define one's motives.

DEVOTIONAL THOUGHTS

- **(For children):** Every saved person should live so that his life encourages others to want to know God. He should depart from evil and do good *(Psalm 34:14a; 2 Timothy 2:19; Ephesians 2:10; Titus 3:8).*
- **(For everyone):** Is your service for the Lord scriptural? Are you careful to consider the importance of the manner in which you serve? Upon what basis do you judge your work and motives?
- What are some reasons why it is so important that believers examine their service for the Lord? How can our service harm others? How can our work for the Lord help others in their labours?

PRAYER THOUGHTS

- Ask God to guide you in building upon the foundation.
- Ask the Lord to help you examine your labour for Him.

SONG: *HIS WAY WITH THEE*

Day 280: (Saturday)
Look to Yourselves

2 John 8 Look to yourselves, that we lose not those things which we have wrought, but that we receive a full reward.

INTRODUCTORY THOUGHTS

In John's epistle to the elect lady and her children *(2 John 1)*, he encouraged them to look to themselves so that he, and those with him, might not lose those things which they had wrought. In order for John to receive a full reward, those to whom he had ministered must take heed to their own service and their walk before the Lord. This line of thinking seems to be less emphasized today in many Bible-believing groups. However, it is a truth set forth by the scriptures. Paul reiterated this truth in *Galatians 4:11* when he said, *"I am afraid of you, lest I have bestowed upon you labour in vain."* In *1 Thessalonians 2:19*, he declared that God's people were his hope, joy, and crown of rejoicing. You might say that Paul concluded the matter when he asked, *"are not ye my work in the Lord?" (1 Corinthians 9:1)*.

Devotional thoughts

- **(For children):** You have many people who love you and want to help you by teaching you from God's word: dad and mom, your pastor, your Sunday School teacher, etc. Do the things you do please these people? Are they pleasing to God *(Proverbs 19:20)*?
- **(For everyone):** How could the walk of those to whom you have ministered cause you to lose some rewards? How could your walk harm those who have ministered to you?
- What are you doing that may cause others to lose rewards? Are you willing to repent and turn to walk in the will of the Lord? How could your repentance encourage other believers?

Prayer Thoughts

- Ask the Lord to help you consider others in your service.
- Thank the Lord for those who have ministered to you.

SONG: *WHEN WE ALL GET TO HEAVEN*

Notes: _____

Notes: _____

_____

_____

_____

_____

_____

_____

_____

_____

_____

_____

_____

_____

_____

_____

_____

Quotes from the next volume

(VOLUME 3, WEEK 40)

Subject: Sacrifices (con't)

The Devil despises all praise toward God. Men who sacrifice unto God demonstrate their valuation of Him. For this reason, the Devil longs to eliminate godly sacrifices.

The Lord loves to receive sacrifices from men. Yet, it is important to recognize that the Lord looks far beyond the sacrifice into the heart of those making the offering. What He sees is far more important to Him than the sacrifice itself.

41

Separation

Separation—found ninety-seven times in eighty-eight verses

Variations: separate, separated, separateth, separating, separation

Defined: As an adjective, it is something that is detached or kept apart; as a verb, it is the act of pulling apart or detaching from.

First usage: *Genesis 13:9* (separate)

Last usage: *Jude 19* (separate)

Interesting fact: Moses expressed that God separated Israel from the other nations *not* because of their outward actions. They were separated because God accompanied them: *"For wherein shall it be known here that I and thy people have found grace in thy sight? **is it not in that thou goest with us? so shall we be separated"** (Exodus 33:16).* The believer understands today that the cross of Christ separates us *"by whom the world is crucified unto me, and I unto the world" (Galatians 6:14).*

Bible study tip: The Bible is a peculiarly one of a kind book. The words contained within scripture are certainly purposeful, but the opposite holds true too. The Lord chooses to omit words just as He chooses to insert particular words. When scripture seems to read somewhat awkwardly or especially when words appear to be missing, consider why the Lord uses this method to emphasize or deemphasize something.

For example, *John 6:11* says, Jesus *"distributed* [the loaves] *to the disciples, and the disciples to them that were set down."* One would think the scripture would say, "and the disciples *distributed* to them that were set down"; however, the omission of the second verb *distributed* in the latter phrase serves a divine purpose. By omitting the second *distributed,* the disciples' role in the matter is deemphasized while the greater emphasis points to the fact that the blessings all came from Jesus. What a wonderful truth! *2 Kings 4:5* offers an additional example as it abruptly ends with *"and she poured out."* Did the woman only pour out the oil or the blessings of God?

Sunday, Day 281—Church Day (no devotional)
Monday, Day 282—*The Command to Separate*
Tuesday, Day 283—*Separation Because of Separation*
Wednesday, Day 284—Church Night (no devotional)
Thursday, Day 285—*The Dual Nature of Separation*
Friday, Day 286—*Grounds for Separation*
Saturday, Day 287—*Have No Fellowship*

Day 281: Church Day

2 Corinthians 6:17 Wherefore **come out from among them, and be ye separate,** *saith the Lord, and touch not the unclean* thing; *and I will receive you,*

Day 282: (Monday)
The Command to Separate

*Genesis 9:1 And God blessed Noah and his sons, and said unto them, Be fruitful, and multiply, and **replenish the earth**.*

INTRODUCTORY THOUGHTS

Twenty-first century believers hold onto many misconceptions concerning the Lord's desire for harmony. Far too many believers desire harmony at any cost. This harmony is commonly promoted on various ecumenical levels as spirituality and truth are sacrificed upon the altar of unity. Though the Lord certainly promotes unity within smaller units, He has never commanded unity in spite of diversity. All the way back to man's earliest days, the Lord established His desire for His people to separate (read Genesis chapter 9). The only way for Noah to *"replenish the earth"* was for him and his seed to multiply and spread out upon the face of the earth. The people refused to divide, so we read the resulting judgment upon the world in Genesis chapter 11. The people stayed together and united to build a tower *(Genesis 11:4)*. The Lord had other plans and divided the people by confounding their languages so that they could no longer communicate and cooperate in their godless endeavours *(Genesis 11:5-8)*.

DEVOTIONAL THOUGHTS

- **(For children):** When the Lord asks us to separate from someone, it is always for a very good reason. Read *Genesis 12:1-3*. The Lord asked Abraham to leave his kinfolk and his country for a new land to make of him a great nation there. God blessed the world by sending His Son from heaven's glory to be born into this great nation of Israel.
- **(For everyone):** In what places did the Lord tell his people to be witnesses in *Acts 1:8*? What happened when the people did not split up as the Lord had commanded (see *Acts 8:1*)? Sometimes people do not understand why persecutions come, but God always has a reason.
- What reasons could the Lord have for wanting people to separate? What has to happen in order for all peoples to come together? What might have to be forsaken for the sake of unity?

PRAYER THOUGHTS

- Ask God to help you have a better understanding of separation.
- Ask God for wisdom in the matter of separation.

SONG: *AND MUST I PART WITH ALL I HAVE?*

Day 283: (Tuesday)
Separation Because of Separation

John 15:19 If ye were of the world, the world would love his own: but because ye are not of the world, but I have chosen you out of the world, therefore the world hateth you.

INTRODUCTORY THOUGHTS

Separation is the outcome of separation! When a nation (i.e., Israel in the Old Testament) or an individual (i.e., a believer in the New Testament) is set apart by the Lord, that nation (or person) has become disassociated with the rest of the world. Moses made this point in *Exodus 33:16* when he said, *"For wherein shall it be known here that I and thy people have found grace in thy sight?* **is it not in that thou goest with us? so shall we be separated,** *I and thy people,* **from all the people that are upon the face of the earth."** Separation is not something accomplished through diligence but occurs naturally after a person comes to know Christ as Saviour. Christians who remain attached to the world find little satisfaction with the things of the world or less appeal for the things of God.

DEVOTIONAL THOUGHTS

- **(For children):** *John 15:19* tells us that when you know the Lord and live for Him, others who don't know Him will hate you. Read one account in *1 John 3:12-13*. Those caught up in worldly endeavours may make fun of you when you go to church faithfully, read your Bible diligently, or dress godly, etc. *(1 Peter 4:4)*.
- **(For everyone):** Have you trusted the Lord as Saviour? How has this wisest of decisions changed your ability to closely associate with those who have not yet trusted the Lord as their Saviour? How has it affected your relationship with those who are saved but love the world *(1 John 2:15)*?

- Who were your closest friends before you were born again? Who are your closest friends now? Are they the same? Why is that? Are they different? Why?

PRAYER THOUGHTS
- Ask the Lord to help you examine your separation from others.
- Thank the Lord for the changes He has brought about in your life.

SONG: *THOU ART MY ALL*

Day 284: Church Night

Romans 16:17 *Now I beseech you, brethren,* **mark them which cause divisions and offences** *contrary to the doctrine which ye have learned; and* **avoid them**.

Day 285: (Thursday)
The Dual Nature of Separation

Numbers 6:1 *And the LORD spake unto Moses, saying,*

2 Speak unto the children of Israel, and say unto them, When either man or woman shall separate themselves to vow a vow of a Nazarite, to **separate** *themselves* **unto the LORD**:

3 He shall **separate** *himself* **from** *wine and strong drink, and shall drink no vinegar of wine, or vinegar of strong drink, neither shall he drink any liquor of grapes, nor eat moist grapes, or dried.*

INTRODUCTORY THOUGHTS

Separation is good and a necessary aspect of the Christian walk. However, when separation becomes based upon personal conviction rather than scriptural principles, it generally leads to a false sense of holiness and hypocrisy. This takes place when Christians fail to consider the multi-faceted nature of scriptural separation. They readily recognize the scriptural command to separate *from* the things of this world but fail to see the first component of scriptural separation which encompasses the need for separation to be *unto* the Lord. The vow of the Nazarite plainly encompasses both aspects of separation. In fact, the primary aspect of biblical separation encompasses separation unto the Lord *(Numbers 6:2)*. Once a person separates himself *unto* the Lord, he will naturally separate *from* those things of this world *(Numbers 6:3)*.

DEVOTIONAL THOUGHTS

- **(For children):** When King Josiah was yet young, he began to seek after God *(2 Chronicles 34:3; 2 Kings 23:25)*. He eliminated idols, repaired the temple, and read God's law to the people. Additionally, he wanted nothing to do with wicked things *(2 Chronicles 34:33)*.
- **(For everyone):** Why is it important to understand both aspects of separation? What could be detrimental about only seeing one aspect or the other?
- Which aspect of separation ought to be foremost? Why? What will happen if the principles of separation are sought in the wrong order of importance?

PRAYER THOUGHTS

- Ask the Lord for balance in your separation.
- Ask God to help you first separate yourself unto Him.

SONG: *NEARER, MY GOD, TO THEE*

Day 286: (Friday)
Grounds for Separation

*2 Thessalonians 3:6 Now we command you, brethren, in the name of our Lord Jesus Christ, that ye **withdraw yourselves from every brother that walketh disorderly, and not after the tradition which he received of us.***

INTRODUCTORY THOUGHTS

Separation is scriptural under a variety of different scenarios. Most commonly, believers understand that they are to separate from unbelievers *(2 Corinthians 6:14)*. This does not imply that believers should not witness to the lost but that there should be no *"fellowship"* between the two. The Bible also indicates that there are times in which one believer should separate from another believer. Most often, this happens because of the propagation of false doctrine *(Romans 16:17-18; 2 Thessalonians 3:6)* or immoral practices *(1 Corinthians 5:11)*. However, there may also be instances when believers separate for the purpose of furthering the work of God *(Galatians 2:6-9)*.

Devotional thoughts

- **(For children):** While Barnabas and Saul, also known as Paul *(Acts13:9a)* were teaching in the church at Antioch, God wanted them to separate (leave) to do the special work of a missionary *(Acts 13:1-3)*. Because of their willingness and the church's, many came to know the Lord.
- **(For everyone):** Are there some people in your life now with whom you should separate? How has your walk with the Lord been hindered by your failure to be obedient to the Lord?
- Why is it so important that believers separate from unbelievers? Why is it important that godly believers separate from those promoting false doctrine or living an immoral lifestyle?

Prayer Thoughts

- Ask God to help you understand the importance of separation.
- Ask God to show you those from whom you need to separate.

SONG: *DARE TO BE A DANIEL*

Day 287: (Saturday)
Have No Fellowship

*Ephesians 5:11 And **have no fellowship with the unfruitful works of darkness**, but rather reprove them.*

Introductory Thoughts

What does the Bible mean when it says to *"have no fellowship with the unfruitful works of darkness"*? Does this mean that believers should never speak to those who do not know Christ as Saviour? The key involves understanding Bible terminology. The word *fellowship* is a two part compound word. A simple Bible study of the root word *fellow* indicates that it involves two people working as one *(John 11:16; 3 John 8)*; therefore fellowship involves two people being closely associated. The command for believers to avoid close association with unbelievers is further confirmed when the Bible says believers and unbelievers should not be *"unequally yoked together"* *(2 Corinthians 6:14)*. When two people are yoked together, they are united in work; but the saved should never unite with the lost in such matters. More importantly, believers must never yoke up with unbelievers in God's work *(Ezra 4:3)*.

Devotional Thoughts

- **(For children):** King Jehoshaphat agreed to help wicked king Ahab fight the Syrians. He received a harsh rebuke from the Lord through the prophet Jehu *(2 Chronicles 19:1-2)*.
- **(For everyone):** What are some areas where fellowship should be severed? Is it scriptural for the saved to accept aid from the world in order to accomplish the work of God *(Genesis 14:21-24; 3 John 7)*?
- Are you yoked up with the world? Are you fighting alongside them with the same goals? Do you need to break away from their yoke and separate yourself unto the Lord?

Prayer Thoughts

- Ask the Lord to help you see when you are yoked with the lost.
- Ask the Lord to continue to teach you biblical separation.

SONG: *THY TESTIMONY'S MY DELIGHT*

Notes: _____

_____

_____

_____

_____

_____

Quotes from the next volume

(VOLUME 3, WEEK 41)

Subject: Salvation

All those born of Adam's seed bear Adam's image *(1 Corinthians 15:47-49)* and the Bible points out that *"in Adam all die" (1 Corinthians 15:22)*.

Man made himself the enemy of God when he chose sin *(Romans 5:10)*, but God had no desire to remain man's enemy so He provided a solution.

42

Singing

Singing—found 161 times in 134 verses

Variations: sang, sing, singeth, singing; Note: The Bible also speaks of songs and singers.

Defined: the making of musical sounds with the voice or in one's heart

First usage: *Exodus 15:1* (sang)

Last usage: *Revelation 15:3* (sing)

Interesting fact: David was forbidden from building the physical structure of the temple for the worship of God because he was *"a man of war"* and had *"shed blood" (1 Chronicles 28:3)*. However, the Lord used David in another very interesting way concerning temple worship. Interestingly, David orchestrated much of the spiritual aspect of the worship that took place in and around that physical structure, especially as it pertained to the musick *(1 Chronicles 23:1-5; 2 Chronicles 5:1; 2 Chronicles 7:5-6)*.

Bible study tip: Typology (the study of types and pictures found within scripture) should never be used independently to teach a doctrinal or literal truth unless the scripture offers a literal text to support it. In fact, the very nature of a type or picture suggests that it falls short in some form or another of the antitype or the literal subject to which it points. For instance, Isaac served as a beautiful type of Christ; however, Isaac needed a substitute sacrifice whereas Christ was the Lamb of God and the supreme sacrifice for sin.

Sunday, Day 288—Church Day (no devotional)
Monday, Day 289—*The Origin of Singing*
Tuesday, Day 290—*To Whom Shall We Sing?*
Wednesday, Day 291—Church Night (no devotional)
Thursday, Day 292—*What Shall We Sing?*
Friday, Day 293—*Why Shall We Sing?*
Saturday, Day 294—*How Shall We Sing?*

Day 288: Church Day

1 Chronicles 16:9 Sing unto him, sing psalms unto him, talk ye of all his wondrous works.

Day 289: (Monday)
The Origin of Singing

Job 38:4 Where wast thou when I laid the foundations of the earth? declare, if thou hast understanding.

5 Who hath laid the measures thereof, if thou knowest? or who hath stretched the line upon it?

6 Whereupon are the foundations thereof fastened? or who laid the corner stone thereof;

7 When the morning stars sang together, and all the sons of God shouted for joy?

INTRODUCTORY THOUGHTS

Rarely does man have the opportunity to participate in heavenly activity while still on earth. Singing is one of those rare events that enables the Christian a glimpse into a heavenly behaviour. Job chapter 38 sheds light on some of the events surrounding creation when it proclaims that *"the morning stars **sang** together, and all the sons of God shouted for joy"* *(Job 38:7)*. These spiritual beings saw the creation of God and could not help themselves but to burst into song. The origin of singing is heavenly, though it has been more often used in unholy ways. Not only is musick's origin heavenly, but long after the world has sung its last song, heaven will continue to enjoy God's gift of musick *(Revelation 5:9)*. For this reason, God's people should never take this for granted but enjoy this heavenly benefit as often as possible.

DEVOTIONAL THOUGHTS

- **(For children):** The heavenly beings rejoiced over God's creation and we too have something to sing about. Salvation is the beginning of our walk with God and there is no end to it *(Psalm 95:1-3; Isaiah 61:10)*.
- **(For everyone):** What are some other heavenly activities that believers can enjoy while on earth? How do these activities offer praise unto the Lord? How often do you participate in these acts of worship?
- In what areas has the world corrupted musick? How has the world specifically corrupted the act of singing? What can God's people do to insure singing is done in a godly manner?

PRAYER THOUGHTS

- Ask the Lord to help you enjoy singing to Him.
- Ask God to help you see the idolatry of singing worldly musick.

SONG: *JOYFUL, JOYFUL, WE ADORE THEE*

Day 290: (Tuesday)
To Whom Shall We Sing?

*Exodus 15:1 Then **sang** Moses and the children of Israel **this song unto the LORD**, and spake, saying, I will **sing unto the LORD**, for he hath triumphed gloriously: the horse and his rider hath he thrown into the sea.*

INTRODUCTORY THOUGHTS

Singing may involve one person, but there are always a minimum of two parties involved in any song: the person singing and the person receiving the song. *Exodus 15:1*, among many other passages, teaches that God's people are to sing *"unto the LORD."* This indicates that a song is much like an offering to the Lord. The person singing offers the song and the offering is received by the Lord. Singing serves as an important act of praise and worship; however, modern Christianity has lost much of its focus. This especially applies to singing. Every week, individuals and groups in churches stand up in worship services and sing unto the people rather than to the Lord. This should not be the case. God's people need refocused to learn that the singing should be *"unto the LORD"* and not man.

DEVOTIONAL THOUGHTS

- **(For children):** *Psalm 47* is speaking to *"all ye people" (Psalm 47:1). Psalm 47:6* tells us to whom we should sing. *Psalm 47:7* tells us why we should sing. In another psalm, the writer said not only will he sing unto the Lord, but he will be singing forever *(Psalm 104:33)*.
- **(For everyone):** Unto whom do you sing? How does this affect the songs that you choose to sing? How can we sing the world's songs unto the Lord? If it is not possible, unto whom are those songs being sung?
- If singing is an act of worship, what kind of worship have you been offering unto the Lord? Have you, at the same time, been offering praise to the Devil by singing his type of musick?

PRAYER THOUGHTS

- Ask the Lord to help you see singing as worship.
- Thank the Lord for giving you a way to praise His name.

SONG: *LET ALL THINGS NOW LIVING*

Day 291: Church Night

*1 Corinthians 14:15 What is it then? I will pray with the spirit, and I will pray with the understanding also: **I will sing with the spirit, and I will sing with the understanding also**.*

Day 292: (Thursday)
What Shall We Sing?

Colossians 3:16 *Let the word of Christ dwell in you richly in all wisdom; teaching and admonishing one another in **psalms and hymns and spiritual songs**, singing with grace in your hearts to the Lord.*

INTRODUCTORY THOUGHTS

God gave us the Bible to serve as our final authority in all matters of faith and practice. This certainly includes the types of songs that should be sung. In fact, the Bible contains an entire book of songs, the Book of Psalms. According to **Colossians 3:16**, the psalms is only one of three categories of songs to be sung by New Testament believers. Basically, *psalms* are scriptures set to musick, *hymns* are doctrinal songs speaking specifically of the Lord, and *spiritual songs* deal with the Christian life and practice. A diligent study of history yields evidence that God's people have been singing songs from each of these categories since the church's inception.

DEVOTIONAL THOUGHTS

- **(For children):** It pleases the Lord when we sing His songs to Him. Sing to the Lord while you play or while you clean your room. Sing with your friends, or your family, or by yourself.
- **(For everyone):** Much of the modern "Christian" musick focuses on self. How is this contrary to the godly categories of musick? Why should God's people return to godly musick?
- How can we use these categories to check our musick? What should we do if our musick does not fit into any of the categories listed in **Colossians 3:16**?

PRAYER THOUGHTS

- Ask the Lord for wisdom in singing the right kind of musick.
- Ask God to help you know when your musick is ungodly.

SONG: *SINGING I GO*

Day 293: (Friday)
Why Shall We Sing?

*Psalm 13:6 I will sing unto the LORD, **because he hath dealt bountifully with me**.*

INTRODUCTORY THOUGHTS

Throughout history, various motives have moved men to sing unto the Lord. Some men sang as a testimony of some specific thing God had done for them *(Exodus 15:1; Psalm 126:1-2)*. Others sang in order to teach truths set forth in the word of God *(Colossians 3:16; Psalm 101:1)*. Some even sang songs that would testify against them in times of disobedience *(Deuteronomy 31:19)*. Though some things have changed throughout history, God's people still should sing songs of personal testimony like *My Jesus, I Love Thee*; songs that teach like *Holy and Reverend Is the Name*; and songs that witness against disobedience like *He Was Not Willing*.

DEVOTIONAL THOUGHTS

- **(For children):** There are many reasons to sing: when we feel good *(James 5:13b)*, during troubles *(Acts 16:25)*, or when we want to praise God *(Psalm 69:30)*. It is also a command *(Psalm 100:2)* and Jesus sang *(Hebrews 2:12)*.
- **(For everyone):** Why do you sing? How often do you take time to consider the message of the songs you sing? Do your songs line up with scriptural reasons for singing?
- Make a list of your favorite songs. What are the purposes or reasons for singing each song? Do these reasons testify as to why these songs would be your favorite?

PRAYER THOUGHTS

- Ask the Lord to help your choice of songs to please Him.
- Ask God to show you reasons to sing unto Him.

SONG: *STAND UP AND BLESS THE LORD*

Day 294: (Saturday)
How Shall We Sing?

*Ephesians 5:19 Speaking to yourselves in psalms and hymns and spiritual songs, **singing and making melody in your heart to the Lord;***

INTRODUCTORY THOUGHTS

Singing has become more of a performance than worship because most churches have lost any concept of biblical singing. Singing was not intended to be something performed by the few to be witnessed by the multitudes. All of God's people ought to sing, but how shall we sing? According to *1 Chronicles 13:8,* God's people should worship the Lord in song *"with all their might."* In agreement with that passage, the Bible suggests that God's people should be singing aloud *(Nehemiah 12:42; Psalm 51:14).* This is further confirmed when the Bible likens singing to a breaking forth *(Isaiah 14:7).* This breaking forth should come from an overflowing heart *(Ephesians 5:19).*

DEVOTIONAL THOUGHTS

- **(For children):** A noise is a sound that is loud. *Psalm 66:1* says to make a *"joyful noise unto God." Psalm 66:2* tells us that noise is singing. *Psalm 81:1* tells us the same thing. God deserves our best singing from the heart.
- **(For everyone):** How much effort do you put into singing unto the Lord? Do you sing from the heart? Do you sing with all the volume you can give?
- Do you prefer being entertained by song or participating in worship of the Lord? Why do churches drop congregational singing? What does that say about the heart condition of most believers?

PRAYER THOUGHTS

- Ask the Lord to help you sing with all your might.
- Ask the Lord to help you sing from the heart.

SONG: *THY TESTIMONY'S MY DELIGHT*

Notes: _____

_____

_____

_____

_____

_____

_____

_____

_____

_____

_____

_____

_____

_____

Quotes from the next volume

(VOLUME 3, WEEK 42)

Subject: Salvation (con't)

Man does not change in order to be saved, but true salvation always brings about change in the life of the new believer.

People spend much time and effort discussing the benefits believers will enjoy after this life, but just as grand are the benefits of salvation that can be enjoyed in this present life.

Similar to the responsibility to tell others about a known cure for a dreaded disease, every Christian has the responsibility to express to others their knowledge of the cure for the coming judgment of God and how to be reconciled.

43

Thoughts

Thoughts—found 223 times in 211 verses

Variations: bethink, think, thinkest, thinketh, thinking, thought, thoughtest, thoughts

Defined: As a verb, the idea involves the giving of consideration to something or someone; as a noun, it is that which is conceived in such consideration.

First usage: *Genesis 6:5* (thoughts)

Last usage: *2 Peter 1:13* (think)

Interesting fact: During the Lord's earthly ministry, He frequently sought to direct the thought life of those under His care into a certain direction. In fact, the Lord focused much attention upon counteracting the inaccurate or improper thinking of His audience *(Matthew 5:17; Matthew 6:25-34; Luke 9:46-48; John 5:39)*.

Bible study tip: At times, God even uses sarcasm within the scripture to prove His point. (Read *Amos 4:4-5*.) Did the Lord truly want the people to *"Come to Bethel, and transgress"*? No! In fact, He stated why He suggested such at the end of verse five when He said, *"for this liketh you,*

O ye children of Israel." Be careful not to take such verses out of context and suggest that the Lord sincerely desired behaviour contrary to His known will and character.

Sunday, Day 295—Church Day (no devotional)
Monday, Day 296—*Think on These Things*
Tuesday, Day 297—*The Origin of Our Thoughts*
Wednesday, Day 298—Church Night (no devotional)
Thursday, Day 299—*God Knows Your Thoughts*
Friday, Day 300—*When Thoughts Hinder Faith*
Saturday, Day 301—*The Thoughts of the Wicked*

Day 295: Church Day

Isaiah 55:8 For my thoughts are **not your thoughts**, *neither* are *your ways my ways*, **saith the LORD.**

9 *For as the heavens are higher than the earth, so are my ways higher than your ways, and* **my thoughts than your thoughts.**

Day 296: (Monday)
Think on These Things

Philippians 4:8 *Finally, brethren, whatsoever things are* **true**, *whatsoever things are* **honest**, *whatsoever things are* **just**, *whatsoever things are* **pure**, *whatsoever things are* **lovely**, *whatsoever things are* **of good report**; *if there be any* **virtue**, *and if there be any* **praise**, **think on these things**.

Introductory Thoughts

Of course, God encourages man to think. This may come as a shocker to many but the Lord does not want man to blindly accept information without first giving it thought. During the Lord's earthly ministry, He often asked men what they thought *(Matthew 17:25; Matthew 18:12; Matthew 21:28)*. His purpose was not because He valued men's opinions; but, rather, to cause men to think. The problem for the Lord is not that man thinks, but that man thinks and focuses upon the wrong things. God has specific things upon which He wants man to ponder. These involve things that are true, honest, just, pure, lovely, of good report, virtue, and praise *(Philippians 4:8)*. As such, believers should focus their attention upon these righteous thoughts rather than those thoughts espoused by the world, the flesh, and the devil.

DEVOTIONAL THOUGHTS

- **(For children):** We are always thinking about something, but the best person to think about is God Himself. This includes His word *(Psalm 1:2)*, His works *(Psalm 143:5)*, and His ways *(Psalm 48:9; Psalm 63:5-7)*.
- **(For everyone):** Why would God want you to think? What dangers exist when men fail to think? What benefits are derived from a healthy thought life (see *Psalm 119:59*)?
- Upon what do you spend your time thinking? Are these things found in the list given in *Philippians 4:8*? If not, should you be thinking about those things if your desire is to live a life pleasing to the Lord?

PRAYER THOUGHTS

- Ask the Lord to strengthen your thought life.
- Ask the Lord to teach you righteous things about which to think.

SONG: *OH LET YOUR THOUGHTS DELIGHT TO SOAR*

Day 297: (Tuesday)
The Origin of Our Thoughts

*Acts 8:22 Repent therefore of this thy wickedness, and pray God, if perhaps **the thought of thine heart** may be forgiven thee.*

INTRODUCTORY THOUGHTS

If asked concerning the origin of thoughts, the average person would swiftly respond with "the mind" or some similar answer. This is not, however, the emphasis of scripture. Overwhelmingly, scripture indicates that thoughts proceed from the heart. This does not mean the beating organ within one's chest since the scriptures use "heart" in a different manner. When God brought judgment in the days of Noah, He saw that the thoughts of man's *"heart was only evil continually" (Genesis 6:5)*. In *Matthew 15:19*, the Bible says, *"For out of the heart proceed evil thoughts."* In *Luke 24:38*, the Lord Jesus asked the disciples, *"why do thoughts arise in your hearts?"* When one's thoughts are not according to God's will, it is a matter of the heart not being right with God.

DEVOTIONAL THOUGHTS

- **(For children):** *Jeremiah 4:14* tells us our thoughts come from within. God wants us to keep our thoughts right with Him because He knows we tend to become that upon which we think. (Read *Proverbs 23:7a* for a clear explanation.)
- **(For everyone):** If thoughts come from the heart, how do they first enter the heart? Why is their origin so very important? What can we do to ensure that our thoughts are righteous thoughts?
- What was David's prayer in *Psalm 139:23*? When would God know David's thoughts? Is this something you would be willing to pray?

PRAYER THOUGHTS

- Ask the Lord to guard your heart from evil thoughts.
- Ask God to search you, try you, and know your thoughts.

SONG: *ALL FOR JESUS*

Day 298: Church Night

2 Corinthians 10:3 For though we walk in the flesh, we do not war after the flesh:

4 (For the weapons of our warfare are not carnal, but mighty through God to the pulling down of strong holds;)

5 Casting down imaginations, and every high thing that exalteth itself against the knowledge of God, and bringing into captivity every thought to the obedience of Christ;

Day 299: (Thursday)
God Knows Your Thoughts

Psalm 94:11 The LORD knoweth the thoughts of man, that they are vanity.

INTRODUCTORY THOUGHTS

Only a foolish man thinks he can hide anything from the Lord. This includes his thought life. The Lord knows all man's thoughts *(1 Chronicles 28:9)* which includes the good *(Malachi 3:16)* and the bad

(Psalm 94:11). David expressed this truth to the Lord when he said, *"Thou knowest . . . my thought afar off. . . . For there is not a word in my tongue, but, lo, O LORD, thou knowest it altogether"* *(Psalm 139:2-4)*. The Lord Jesus Christ often exhibited this capability during His earthly ministry *(Matthew 12:25; Luke 5:22; Luke 6:8; Luke 9:47; Luke 11:17)*. Even the written word of God reveals this ability by being *"a discerner of the thoughts and intents of the heart"* *(Hebrews 4:12)*.

DEVOTIONAL THOUGHTS

- **(For children):** We can hide our inner thoughts from other people but never from God. Read *Job 42:1-2*. Read what Job did when he realized God was not pleased with his way of thinking *(Job 42:6)*. That was his way of telling God he was sorry.
- **(For everyone):** What are you thinking about right now? Are you thinking about some of the bad thoughts you have had, wondering if God knows about them? He does!
- Why is it important that we yield our thought life to the Lord? How can our impure thoughts grieve the Lord? What blessings can come from God's knowledge of our righteous thoughts?

PRAYER THOUGHTS

- Ask the Lord to forgive you for your unclean thoughts.
- Ask God to help you remember that He knows your thoughts.

SONG: *THE LORD BEHOLDS WHAT MORTALS DO*

Day 300: (Friday)
When Thoughts Hinder Faith

*Genesis 20:11 And Abraham said, Because **I thought, Surely the fear of God is not in this place**; and they will slay me for my wife's sake.*

INTRODUCTORY THOUGHTS

Thoughts do not have to be wicked in order to be troublesome. Any thought contrary to faith will eventually cause a man to stumble. In *Genesis 20:11*, Abraham's thoughts hindered his faith. He perceived that the fear of God was not in Gerar and decided to lie about the identity of his wife in order to insure his personal well-being. Rather than trusting

God, he trusted his thoughts. Another example is Naaman. He refused to wash in the Jordan River because he thought that the prophet should have recovered his leprosy by coming out, calling upon the name of the Lord, and striking his hand over the place of leprosy *(2 Kings 5:11)*. When a man trusts in his own thoughts over the words of God, that man shows a complete disregard for truth.

DEVOTIONAL THOUGHTS

- **(For children):** Read *1 Samuel 13:8-14*. Saul failed to trust God's timing. He thought his enemies would come and defeat him prior to Samuel showing up to offer prayers and an offering to God. Because of his thoughts, he unwisely offered the sacrifice just prior to Samuel arriving. Because of this, his sons never got to be kings.
- **(For everyone):** How do your thoughts hinder your faith? How is trusting your own thoughts over the written words of God equivalent to idolatry? How does the Lord feel about idolatry?
- What are some Bible examples of those who have considered their own thoughts more valid than the words of God? What dangers do those people face? Are you ever guilty of the same sinful actions?

PRAYER THOUGHTS

- Ask the Lord to build your faith.
- Ask God to help you have a proper perspective on your thoughts.

SONG: *I WANT THAT MOUNTAIN*

Day 301: (Saturday)
The Thoughts of the Wicked

Psalm 10:4 The wicked, through the pride of his countenance, will not seek after God: **God is not in all his thoughts.**

INTRODUCTORY THOUGHTS

Our passage tells us that God is not in all the thoughts of the wicked *(Psalm 10:4)*. It also points out that the thoughts of the wicked *"are thoughts of iniquity" (Isaiah 59:7)*. Obviously, the wicked despise the Lord in their thoughts, but the Lord also despises the thoughts of the wicked. This is why we are told that *"The thoughts of the wicked are an abomination to the LORD" (Proverbs 15:26)*. King David, whom

God called *"a man after mine own heart" (Acts 13:22)*, added that the thoughts of the wicked were against him for evil *(Psalm 56:5)*. These wicked thoughts are based upon pride *(Psalm 10:4)*. Conversely, a man yielded to the Lord desires to bring *"into captivity every thought to the obedience of Christ" (2 Corinthians 10:5)*.

DEVOTIONAL THOUGHTS

- **(For children):** God was not in the thoughts of the rich young fool. He lived his life the way he wanted to live it and never considered that one day he would face God *(Luke 12:16-20)*.
- **(For everyone):** Do your thoughts match the thoughts of a wicked man or of a righteous one? How frequently are your thoughts toward the Lord? Do you often find yourself entertaining thoughts against God's people when they are trying to do right?
- Do you desire to bring your thoughts into captivity to the obedience of Christ? Do you allow your thoughts to lead you into sin and away from the will of God?

PRAYER THOUGHTS

- Ask the Lord to guide your thought life.
- Ask God to protect you from thinking like the wicked.

SONG: *TO LIVE IS CHRIST; TO DIE IS GAIN*

Notes: _____

_____

_____

_____

_____

_____

_____

_____

_____

_____

_____

Notes: _____

_____

_____

_____

_____

_____

_____

_____

_____

_____

_____

_____

_____

_____

_____

_____

_____

_____

Quotes from the next volume

(VOLUME 3, WEEK 43)

Subject: Sobriety

Sobriety is not a special requirement expected from an elite group of believers, but rather the expectation God has for all who have called upon the name of the Lord.

As time continues, the need for sobriety intensifies. Temptations seem to be escalating from every angle. Even if sin did not have the ability to lure the believer, busyness and hobbies tug at his heart to steal away one's time and strength.

44

Trusting

Trusting—found 191 times in 181 verses

Variations: trust, trusted, trustedst, trustest, trusteth, trusting, trusty

Defined: having confidence in or relying upon

First usage: *Deuteronomy 28:52* (trustedst)

Last usage: *3 John 14* (trust)

Interesting fact: The various forms of the word *trust* appear 156 times in all the Old Testament with seventy-one of them occurring in the Book of Psalms. This frequency numbers more than the entire New Testament combined which only contains a form of the word *trust* thirty-five times. This means that the Book of Psalms focuses much attention upon man's trust.

Bible study tip: When the Bible attributes to God features that relate to man (i.e., eyes, ears, hands, arms, a soul, a heart, etc.), it is important to consider the significance of such an attribution. Is it possible that each one might tend to emphasize a different feature of the person of God?

Sunday, Day 302—Church Day (no devotional)
Monday, Day 303—*A Choice to Trust*
Tuesday, Day 304—*Trusting in Lies*
Wednesday, Day 305—Church Night (no devotional)
Thursday, Day 306—*Trusting in Vanity*
Friday, Day 307—*Trusting in Riches*
Saturday, Day 308—*Trusting in Man*

Day 302: Church Day

> *Ruth 2:12 The LORD recompense thy work, and a full reward be given thee of **the LORD God of Israel, under whose wings thou art come to trust.***

Day 303: (Monday)
A Choice to Trust

> *Psalm 20:7 Some **trust** in chariots, and some in horses: **but we will remember the name of the LORD our God.***

INTRODUCTORY THOUGHTS

To trust in someone or something involves an act of the will. The focus of this trust is something that each individual must personally decide. David expressed as much when he said, *"Some trust in chariots, and some in horses: but we will remember the name of the LORD our God"* **(Psalm 20:7)**. David identified a few of the many things upon which one might trust. The Bible also refers to those who trust in vanity **(Isaiah 59:4)**, others in lies **(Jeremiah 7:8)**, and still others in riches **(1 Timothy 6:17)**. Interestingly, the Lord does not force any individual to trust in Him, nor is anyone ever forced to trust in the things of this world. It is important to point out that one's trust cannot be divided. An individual cannot simultaneously trust in vanity, riches, or lies while trusting in the Lord.

DEVOTIONAL THOUGHTS

- **(For children):** Job chose to trust God when he lost his family, his health, and his wealth **(Job 13:15a)**. The three Hebrew men trusted God when faced with a burning fiery furnace **(Daniel 3:17-18)**. David chose to trust God when he was afraid *(Psalm 56:3-4)*. Now, consider Ruth's choice: *Ruth 1:16; Ruth 2:11-12.*

- **(For everyone):** What are some things upon which you rely? Have any of those things become the recipient of your trust? What will happen when, or if, those things are removed?
- The choice of trust is not a onetime decision. How often do you commit to trusting the Lord, only to find that your trust has veered toward the things of the world?

PRAYER THOUGHTS

- Ask the Lord to help you examine the recipients of your trust.
- Ask the Lord to help you to be conscious of your trust.

SONG: *TRUSTING JESUS*

Day 304: (Tuesday)
Trusting in Lies

Jeremiah 7:3 Thus saith the LORD of hosts, the God of Israel, Amend your ways and your doings, and I will cause you to dwell in this place.

*4 **Trust ye not in lying words**, saying, The temple of the LORD, The temple of the LORD, The temple of the LORD, are these.*

5 For if ye throughly amend your ways and your doings; if ye throughly execute judgment between a man and his neighbour;

6 If ye oppress not the stranger, the fatherless, and the widow, and shed not innocent blood in this place, neither walk after other gods to your hurt:

7 Then will I cause you to dwell in this place, in the land that I gave to your fathers, for ever and ever.

*8 Behold, **ye trust in lying words, that cannot profit**.*

INTRODUCTORY THOUGHTS

Few people would readily admit to trusting in lies; however, any individual placing his trust in something outside of the words of God is in danger of doing so. Through the prophet Jeremiah, the Lord warned His people of this danger on numerous occasions *(Jeremiah 7:4, 8; Jeremiah 13:25; Jeremiah 29:31)*. Even today, people all over the world choose to bow down to idols and images, thinking these creations of wood, stone, or metal can assist them in some way. Other people who would never think to bow to an idol place their trust in education or something similar. Unfortunately, there are going to be multitudes sorely disappointed for they have unwittingly placed their trust in the lies of this world.

DEVOTIONAL THOUGHTS

- **(For children):** The people at Lystra worshipped many gods. When Paul healed a man, they were going to make Paul a god. These men and women were believing lies. Paul quickly told them of the only One who could help them *(Acts 14:11-15; Psalm 115:4-9)*.
- **(For everyone):** What are some things in which the people of this world place their trust? What is the worst thing that could happen for all eternity to those who place their trust in lies?
- What are some ways in which believers can place their trust in lies (i.e., media, politics, science, education)? How can this hinder believers in their fellowship with the Lord?

PRAYER THOUGHTS

- Ask the Lord to guard you from trusting in lies.
- Ask God to show you the lies in which you might be trusting.

SONG: *MY FAITH LOOKS UP TO THEE*

Day 305: Church Night

2 Samuel 22:3 The God of my rock; in him will I trust: he is my shield, and the horn of my salvation, my high tower, and my refuge, my saviour; thou savest me from violence.

Day 306: (Thursday)
Trusting in Vanity

Job 15:31 Let not him that is deceived trust in vanity: for vanity shall be his recompence.

INTRODUCTORY THOUGHTS

When man trusts in nothing, he receives nothing in return. That is the primary point of *Job 15:31*. Yet, that is not the only truth being taught. It is also true that people should not trust in anything of little to no value. This would include beauty *(Ezekiel 16:15; Proverbs 31:30)* and riches *(Psalm 62:10)*. Unfortunately, many in this world have become accustomed to trust in their intellect, beauty, and riches. The end result is borne out in the entertainment and business worlds, but the seeds of this troubling problem usually begin in early childhood. Young people often hear the emphasis placed upon their appearance or education as the primary means of getting the things that these young people want most in life.

DEVOTIONAL THOUGHTS

- **(For children):** In his own heart, Paul thought he was serving God *(Proverbs 28:26)* by trying to do good works and keep God's laws. He was wrong *(Psalm 39:5)*. The law points us to Christ *(Galatians 3:24)*. Paul realized this later when he got saved *(Philippians 3:4-7)*.
- **(For everyone):** Do you, in any way, trust in your beauty to get what you want? Do you do this with family, friends, or at work? What true blessings have you received by trusting in vanity?
- What are some other vain things in which people might trust? How do those things bring false results? How does this hurt us over time?

PRAYER THOUGHTS

- Ask the Lord to help you realize when you are trusting in vanity.
- Ask God to show you that He is the only One worthy of our trust.

SONG: *'TIS SO SWEET TO TRUST IN JESUS*

Day 307: (Friday)
Trusting in Riches

Proverbs 11:28 He that trusteth in his riches shall fall: but the righteous shall flourish as a branch.

INTRODUCTORY THOUGHTS

Most people in the world would not consider themselves rich. For this reason, they might think it impossible to trust in riches. They might point to their meager bank accounts as evidence. Yet, a person does not have to be rich in order to trust in riches. No matter the amount of riches or treasures that one might have, there is a very real danger in trusting in those things. Riches, however, are of little value. According to *Psalm 49:6-8*, riches are of no assistance in man's greatest need, the redemption of his soul. Not only can riches not help, but they are uncertain *(1 Timothy 6:17)*. Those who trust in them will be disappointed and will ultimately fall *(Proverbs 11:28)*. Even if riches increase, man should not set his heart upon them *(Psalm 62:10)*.

DEVOTIONAL THOUGHTS

- **(For children)**: It is hard for those that trust in riches to believe in God *(Mark 10:24-25)*. Most think they earned the money by getting a good education and then obtaining a good job. They do not realize that the Lord gave them the power to get the job or the riches *(Deuteronomy 8:17-18)*.
- **(For everyone)**: Are you trusting in riches? What would happen if you failed to receive a paycheck? Would you immediately begin to panic, or would you patiently trust the Lord to provide?
- How dependent have you become upon your riches, treasures, and possessions? What would happen to your walk with the Lord if these things were removed?

PRAYER THOUGHTS

- Ask the Lord to help you cease from trusting in your riches.
- Ask God to help you fully rely upon Him for all things.

SONG: *HIS EYE IS ON THE SPARROW*

Day 308: (Saturday)
Trusting in Man

Psalm 118:8 It is better to trust in the LORD *than to put confidence in man.*

9 It is better to trust in the LORD *than to put confidence in princes.*

INTRODUCTORY THOUGHTS

Romans 3:4 says, *"let God be true, but every man a liar."* Perhaps this truth serves as the foundational reason why God warned believers not to place their trust in man. Though the primary reason, it is not the only reason. In *Psalm 146:3* the Lord warns, *"Put not your trust in princes, nor in the son of man, in whom there is no help."* The real needs of mankind cannot be satisfied by man, even the best of men. Those who put their trust in man do so in disobedience to the Lord which results in their own personal harm. **Psalm 118:8-9** twice stresses that *"It is better to trust in the LORD."* An improper trust in man is, in many ways, a departure from the Lord *(Jeremiah 17:5)*.

DEVOTIONAL THOUGHTS

- **(For children):** When Jesus came to earth, He could have trusted in Himself since He was God, but He willingly gave us an example that we should trust in our heavenly Father *(Hebrews 2:13)*. No one loves you more or has more power to help you than God *(2 Corinthians 1:9-10)*. Read *Jeremiah 17:5, 7* and *Micah 7:5*.
- **(For everyone):** Though we are certainly to have loved ones in our lives, we are not to put our trust in them in disregard of trusting the Lord. How can we insure that this does not happen?
- In what men should we be careful to put our trust (i.e., politicians, teachers, preachers, media, friends, family)? What could be the dangers in putting our trust in each?

PRAYER THOUGHTS

- Ask the Lord to teach you the dangers of trusting in man.
- Ask the Lord to guide you in fully trusting Him above all others.

SONG: *WE REST ON THEE*

Notes: _____

_____

_____

_____

_____

_____

_____

_____

_____

_____

Notes: _____

_____

_____

_____

_____

_____

_____

_____

_____

_____

_____

_____

_____

_____

_____

_____

Quotes from the next volume

(VOLUME 3, WEEK 44)

Subject: Sobriety (con't)

A man's thoughts are the foundations of his actions. If a man fails to be sober minded, he will likely fail to be sober in his actions.

Sobriety is more than a way of thinking, it is the scriptural approach to Christian living.

Sobriety is a companion with gravity *(1 Timothy 3:11; Titus 2:2)* and causes a believer to perceive himself as he really is.

45

Trusting (con't)

Trusting—found 156 times in 153 verses in the Old Testament and thirty-five times in thirty-five verses in the New Testament

Variations: trust, trusted, trustedst, trustest, trusteth, trusting, trusty

First usage in the New Testament: *Matthew 12:21* (trust)

Last usage in the Old Testament: *Zephaniah 3:12* (trust)

Interesting fact: For the Israelites, Egypt represented the past. It represented the good and bad of life before deliverance. Surprisingly, after all of the wonders and miracles, God had to admonish Israel not to trust in Egypt *(Isaiah 30:1-3; Isaiah 31:1)*. The saint living today faces the same temptation to long for a return to his old life or old ways when looking for something to trust *(Philippians 3:3)*.

Bible study tip: Sometimes Bible pictures are presented in distinct passages and do not make complete sense unless independently collected and pieced together like a puzzle. For example, consider the following truths and piece them together. God *"stretcheth out the heavens as a curtain, and*

spreadeth them out as a tent to dwell in" **(Isaiah 40:22)**. *"The LORD is in his holy temple, the LORD's throne is in heaven"* **(Psalm 11:4)**. *"Thus saith the LORD, The heaven is my throne, and the earth is my footstool"* **(Isaiah 66:1)**. These truths combined depict God's dwelling place as it relates to the earth.

Sunday, Day 309—Church Day (no devotional)
Monday, Day 310—*Trusting in Ourselves*
Tuesday, Day 311—*Trusting in Worldly Safety*
Wednesday, Day 312—Church Night (no devotional)
Thursday, Day 313—*Unconditional Trust*
Friday, Day 314—*The Blessings of Trust*
Saturday, Day 315—*To Know Him Is to Trust Him*

Day 309: Church Day

Psalm 28:7 The LORD is my strength and my shield; ***my heart trusted in him, and I am helped****: therefore my heart greatly rejoiceth; and with my song will I praise him.*

Day 310: (Monday)
Trusting in Ourselves

2 Corinthians 1:9 But we had the sentence of death in ourselves, ***that we should not trust in ourselves****, but in God which raiseth the dead:*

INTRODUCTORY THOUGHTS

The Bible plainly and repeatedly warns believers not to put their trust in men. In addition to this truth, men are not to trust in themselves. As today's passage shows, sometimes God allows circumstances to come into our lives in order to teach us not to trust in ourselves. If any mere mortal could stake a claim to self-trust, it would have been the apostle Paul. He was *"circumcised the eighth day,"* *"an Hebrew of the Hebrews,"* and *"a Pharisee"* **(Philippians 3:5)**. In spite of this, Paul knew these attributes were not sufficient to trust for eternal life. In fact, he counted these things but dung, that he may win Christ **(Philippians 3:8)**. If Paul understood that he could not put his trust in himself or his accomplishments, everyone else should realize that his or her ability or merits are not worthy of trust.

DEVOTIONAL THOUGHTS

- **(For children):** Read *Matthew 26:31-34*. Peter trusted in himself that he would never say he didn't know the Lord. He failed miserably. Cain trusted in himself that he was giving the Lord the correct offering. The Lord refused his offering *(Genesis 4:5)*. We should always trust in the Lord and believe and do what He says *(Proverbs 3:5)*.
- **(For everyone):** What are some areas of life where you might not put your trust in others, but you would quickly put your trust in yourself? How is one just as wicked as the other?
- In whom did the Pharisees trust *(Luke 18:9)*? Why did they begin to trust in themselves? Of what did they lose sight in order to begin trusting in themselves?

PRAYER THOUGHTS

- Ask the Lord to guard you against trusting in yourself.
- Ask the Lord to help you to be conscious of your trust.

SONG: *JESUS, I AM RESTING*

Day 311: (Tuesday)
Trusting in Worldly Safety

Proverbs 21:31 *The horse is prepared against the day of battle: but safety is of the LORD.*

INTRODUCTORY THOUGHTS

Though the means of worldly safety have changed throughout time, people have always put their trust in various things to offer temporary safety. The Bible depicts those who trusted in fenced walls *(Deuteronomy 28:52)*, nations *(Isaiah 30:2-3)*, horses, horsemen and chariots *(Isaiah 31:1)*, weapons *(Psalm 44:6)*, and mountains *(Amos 6:1)*. People today place their trust in weapons, security systems, governments, insurance policies, and even medicines. Though the sources of trust have changed, the Lord remains just as grieved today when men place their trust upon the things of this world rather than upon Him. Ultimately, every source of worldly safety will fail, often in the moment we perceive as our greatest time of need.

DEVOTIONAL THOUGHTS

- **(For children):** When outnumbered by the Philistines, Jonathan trusted God completely and was going to attack a certain camp *(1 Samuel 14:6)*. Elisha told his servant to trust God when surrounded by their enemies *(2 Kings 6:15-17)*. Safety is of the Lord *(Psalm 112:7)*.
- **(For everyone):** In what ways do you trust this world for safety? Who should you trust in times of war, danger, sickness, chaos, or inclement weather? What are the chances of the Lord failing you?
- Why does it displease the Lord when His people put their trust in this world for safety? How many people have had to find out the hard way that this world cannot be trusted?

PRAYER THOUGHTS

- Ask the Lord to help you see that He is faithful.
- Ask God to show you the inability of the world to offer safety.

SONG: *IF, ON A QUIET SEA*

Day 312: Church Night

Psalm 34:8 O taste and see that the LORD is good: **blessed is the man that trusteth in him***.*

Day 313: (Thursday)
Unconditional Trust

Job 13:15 Though he slay me, yet will I trust in him: but I will maintain mine own ways before him.

INTRODUCTORY THOUGHTS

The Lord is faithful at all times. In return, He rightfully desires the trust of His people at all times. With the exception of the Lord, nobody in the history of mankind endured the difficulties that Job encountered. Job ultimately knew that his trials were sent by the Lord though Satan was certainly God's instrument. The test would be whether Job would continue to trust the Lord who had taken his material wealth, his health, and his children. Or would Job, like many believers, turn from the Lord because of the seemingly overwhelming difficulties? The Bible records Job's answer, *"Though he slay me, yet will I trust in him" (Job 13:15).*

Because of Job's determination to trust the Lord unconditionally, he determined that he was not going to be a fair weather follower of the Lord.

DEVOTIONAL THOUGHTS

- **(For children):** God promised Abraham that He would make a great nation from him through his son Isaac. Abraham completely trusted God when asked to do something that seemed to make this impossible *(Hebrews 11:17-19)*.
- **(For everyone):** Job said that he would trust the Lord even if the Lord killed him. Could you say the same thing? What does it take to get you to cease trusting in the Lord?
- What trials have you endured that are greater than those endured by Job? If you cannot honestly claim any, then do you really have any excuse for not trusting in the Lord? Will you renew your trust in the Lord?

PRAYER THOUGHTS

- Ask the Lord to forgive you for wavering in your trust.
- Thank the Lord for being faithful even when you are not.

SONG: *BE STILL, MY SOUL!*

Day 314: (Friday)
The Blessings of Trust

*Psalm 2:12 Kiss the Son, lest he be angry, and ye perish from the way, when his wrath is kindled but a little. **Blessed are all they that put their trust in him**.*

INTRODUCTORY THOUGHTS

Trusting in worldly safety, uncertain riches, vanity, other people, or even oneself always yields certain disappointment and ultimate defeat. However, those that put their trust in the Lord are blessed with far different outcomes. According to *Psalm 2:12*, the people who trust in the Lord are blessed. According to *Psalm 5:11*, trusting saints will *"rejoice"* and *"ever shout for joy."* David testified of this truth when he said his heart would rejoice in God's salvation *(Psalm 13:5)*. In *Psalm 28:7*, David further rejoiced in the help he received because of his trust in God. Furthermore, believers are assured of both mercy *(Psalm 32:10)* and happiness *(Proverbs 16:20)* when trusting God. These examples express only the tip of the iceberg concerning the benefits of trusting God. These benefits far outweigh those gained by trusting in oneself or the world.

Devotional thoughts

- **(For children):** Joseph was sold into slavery and ended up in prison. Through all this, he trusted in God and God blessed him *(Psalm 31:19)*. Joseph became second in command to the king and saved his family from starvation. Joseph was blessed *(Psalm 34:8)*.
- **(For everyone):** What are some of the blessings you have received from trusting God? How is this different from the disappointments you have experienced when failed by the world?
- How do you feel when you fail to consistently place your trust in the Lord? How do you feel when you are trusting the Lord during times of testing? Which feeling is more enjoyable?

Prayer Thoughts

- Ask the Lord to teach you the blessings of trusting Him.
- Ask God to build your faith in His ability.

SONG: *IF THOU BUT SUFFER GOD TO GUIDE THEE*

Day 315: (Saturday)
To Know Him Is to Trust Him

> *Psalm 9:10* **And they that know thy name will put their trust in thee**: *for thou, LORD, hast not forsaken them that seek thee.*

Introductory Thoughts

One does not have to read much Bible before finding that God is completely worthy of man's trust. The Lord preserved Noah and his family from a worldwide flood. God gave Abraham and Sarah a son long after it was thought to be physically possible. The Lord delivered the Israelites from Egypt and led them through a barren wilderness, providing their every need on the way to the land of Canaan. The Lord gave David a great victory when he faced the giant Goliath. God sent His only begotten Son to die on the cross for the sins of the world. He brought His Son out of the grave and now hears that Son as He intercedes on behalf of believers. No wonder David said, *"they that know thy name will put their trust in thee."*

DEVOTIONAL THOUGHTS

- **(For children)**: Paul's desire was to know God *(Philippians 3:10a)*. Read about his trust in God's word even in the midst of a bad storm *(Acts 27:22-25)*. Oh, that we might read God's word, get to know Him better, and believe that *"it shall be"* even as He tells us *(Acts 27:25)*.
- **(For everyone)**: What are some things you have learned about the Lord from reading your Bible? How have these things pushed you to trust in the Lord?
- Do you fail to trust in the Lord even though you know He is the only one capable of helping you in your time of trouble? Why? Is it possible you do not truly believe what you have read in the Bible?

PRAYER THOUGHTS

- Ask the Lord to show you even more reasons to trust Him.
- Thank the Lord for allowing you to know His name.

SONG: *DAY BY DAY*

Notes: _____

_____

_____

_____

_____

_____

_____

_____

_____

_____

_____

Notes: _____

_____

_____

_____

_____

_____

_____

_____

_____

_____

_____

_____

_____

_____

Quotes from the next volume

(VOLUME 3, WEEK 45)

Subject: Stewardship

A steward is a man of great responsibility. He may have a greater or lesser area of oversight, but he always has something placed under his care that is of great importance to the master of the house.

Whether the master of the house is present or absent, the steward is to do as he has been commissioned by the one who owns that for which he is a steward.

Every believer will stand before the Lord Jesus Christ to give an account for his stewardship while on this earth.

46
Unity

Unity—found five times in five verses

Variations: unite, united, unity; Note: The word *one* may also be used to denote the same concept *(John 17:11)* though this study is limited to the actual use of the word *unity* or *unite*.

Defined: the state or property of being one

First usage: *Genesis 49:6* (united)

Last usage: *Ephesians 4:13* (unity)

Interesting fact: Unity was obviously of the utmost importance to Christ. The Lord's prayer is found in John chapter 17. In that prayer, the Lord Jesus placed a great deal of emphasis on the unity of those believers who would be left after His departure. Four times the Saviour asked of His Father that the disciples could know unity like that of the Son and the Father *(John 17:11, 21-23)*. In the same spirit, the Saviour said that all men would know the disciples were His followers by their love one for another *(John 13:35)*.

Bible study tip: Pay attention to details when judgment is suggested or meted out in scripture. Oftentimes, the resulting judgment is specific to the practice that called for the judgment. For example, the Galatian believers were being troubled primarily over the matter of circumcision (a circular cutting). So what was Paul's response to those who were troubling the Galatians? He said, *"I would they were even **cut off** which trouble you" (**Galatians 5:12**)*. The judgment was equated to the practice itself.

Sunday, Day 316—Church Day (no devotional)
Monday, Day 317—*Though Hand Join in Hand*
Tuesday, Day 318—*How Good and How Pleasant*
Wednesday, Day 319—Church Night (no devotional)
Thursday, Day 320—*Endeavouring to Keep the Unity*
Friday, Day 321—*Sowing Discord*
Saturday, Day 322—*The Peace of the Perfect Man*

Day 316: Church Day

Philippians 2:2 *Fulfil ye my joy, that ye **be likeminded**, having the same love, being of one accord, of one mind.*

Day 317: (Monday)
Though Hand Join in Hand

Proverbs 11:21 Though hand join in hand, *the wicked shall not be unpunished: but the seed of the righteous shall be delivered.*

INTRODUCTORY THOUGHTS

People unite over various causes. Some of those causes are righteous, while others are not. Unity based upon a righteous cause pleases the Lord and leads to righteous acts. Unity based upon ungodly or carnal causes grieves the Lord and leads to the wickedness we find so prevalent in the world today. After the flood, the Lord commanded Noah and his family to *"replenish the earth" (**Genesis 9:1**)*. They could not replenish the earth if they remained together so the Lord wanted Noah's family to spread out across the earth. Yet, the people immediately began settling together and *"Noah began to be an husbandman" (**Genesis 9:20**)*. This may seem insignificant, but it was only the precursor to the unified desire in **Genesis 11:4** to build *"a tower, whose top may reach unto heaven."* Noah's disobedience led to further and greater disobedience and unity in a common wicked cause.

DEVOTIONAL THOUGHTS

- **(For children):** *Mark 2:1-12* tells of four men who worked together for the purpose of bringing their sick friend to the Lord. The Lord forgave the sick man's sins and healed him. He is pleased when we work with other believers to do what is good and right.
- **(For everyone):** How did the Lord feel about the tower of Babel (see **Genesis 11:1-9**)? Why was the Lord displeased with the unity of the people? What came of their unity?
- When did the language barrier between cultures begin? Why did the Lord confound the languages? What does this suggest about the Lord's desire, or lack thereof, for world unity so desired by those willing to accept anyone and everyone?

PRAYER THOUGHTS

- Ask the Lord to help you find unity only in righteous causes.
- Ask God to guide you to others with whom you may be unified.

SONG: *JESUS, I MY CROSS HAVE TAKEN*

Day 318: (Tuesday)
How Good and How Pleasant

*Psalm 133:1 Behold, **how good and how pleasant it is for brethren to dwell together in unity!***

INTRODUCTORY THOUGHTS

The psalmist proclaims: *"Behold, how good and how pleasant it is for brethren to dwell together in unity!"* Unlike the unity of unbelievers and the heathen, the Lord rejoices in the righteous unity of His people. King David was someone who knew and experienced the difficulties of division. He spent a great deal of his life running from a king and those who were against him. Even in the beginning of his reign, the people were divided *(2 Samuel 2:8-11)*. It was not until 7 1/2 years later that the people were united in David *(2 Samuel 5:1-5)*. When the people dwelt in unity, David rejoiced. He likened it to the source of spiritual life for the nation of Israel, the priesthood *(Psalm 133:2)*, and to the source of physical life in the dew of Hermon *(Psalm 133:3)*. In other words, the right kind of unity gave life and hope to the nation!

DEVOTIONAL THOUGHTS

- **(For children):** Read *Genesis 13:5-9*. This conflict could have ended in a fight, but Abraham says in *Genesis 13:8* why that should not happen: *"for we be brethren." Hebrews 13:1* says, *"Let brotherly love continue."* Are you doing your part to make things pleasant in your home, at church, and amongst those you influence?
- **(For everyone):** The anointing of Aaron was a monumental moment in the history of the nation of Israel. Why would David use that as a description of the blessedness of unity *(Psalm 133:2)*?
- The dew of Hermon sustains a great deal of life at its base and throughout the land of Israel. How is that like the time when brethren dwell together in unity *(Psalm 133:3)*?

PRAYER THOUGHTS

- Ask the Lord to make the unity sweet in your local church.
- Ask God to teach you what unity is and how it can be obtained.

SONG: *JESUS, CEMENT OUR HEARTS AS ONE*

Day 319: Church Night

*2 Corinthians 13:11 Finally, brethren, farewell. Be perfect, be of good comfort, **be of one mind, live in peace; and the God of love and peace shall be with you.***

Day 320: (Thursday)
Endeavouring to Keep the Unity

Ephesians 4:1 I therefore, the prisoner of the Lord, beseech you that ye walk worthy of the vocation wherewith ye are called,

2 With all lowliness and meekness, with longsuffering, forbearing one another in love;

*3 **Endeavouring to keep the unity of the Spirit in the bond of peace.***

INTRODUCTORY THOUGHTS

Unity only comes from and through the Lord Jesus Christ, but once it comes, the saints of God must endeavour to keep that unity. One of the reasons why people find unity so elusive is because it requires sacrifice from all those who would enjoy its benefits. Only saints who exercise *"lowliness and meekness, with longsuffering"* will experience unity. No two believers who are using the minds that God gave them will believe every minute detail alike, yet they can enjoy sweet unity and fellowship in the Lord. Obviously, there are times and reasons for believers to divide, but there are also times for believers to forbear *"one another in love"* and endeavour to keep the unity. This unity works by love and can only be bonded through peace.

DEVOTIONAL THOUGHTS

- **(For children)**: Getting along with other children of God is a serious, determined effort that sometimes seems hard because most people want to have their own way. God tells us to put others first *(Romans 12:10)* and do right *(1 Peter 3:8-11)*. Would you be willing to let someone else be the leader or play with a toy first if it avoided trouble and discord?
- **(For everyone)**: What are some of the sacrifices we must make in order to enjoy unity between brothers and sisters in Christ? What might hinder us from enjoying the unity that God wants us to have?
- What does the Bible mean when it says that unity is kept *"in the bond of peace"*? How does peace bind unity? How does the absence of peace cause division?

PRAYER THOUGHTS

- Ask God to help you repent when you hinder proper unity.
- Thank the Lord for the unity you experience in the local body.

SONG: *THE UNITY OF THE SPIRIT*

Day 321: (Friday)
Sowing Discord

Proverbs 6:16 These six things doth the LORD hate: yea, seven are an abomination unto him:

17 A proud look, a lying tongue, and hands that shed innocent blood,

18 An heart that deviseth wicked imaginations, feet that be swift in running to mischief,

*19 A false witness that speaketh lies, and **he that soweth discord among brethren**.*

INTRODUCTORY THOUGHTS

The unity of believers is likened to a cord woven together. Like a threefold cord, unified believers are stronger and better able to endure the attacks from their enemies *(Ecclesiastes 4:12)*. In *Proverbs 6:16-19*, the Lord gives a list of things He hates, one of which is when a man sows *"discord among brethren."* What does it mean to sow *"discord"*? Perhaps the illustration given above sheds the necessary light for an answer. When believers are united, they are like multiple cords woven together. When someone sows discord, he attempts to undo or *"discord"* the threefold cord destroying the unity. Believers void of unity are weaker and more vulnerable to the attacks of the enemy.

DEVOTIONAL THOUGHTS

- **(For children):** One little grain of sand cannot do much by itself. Yet, when it stands together with other grains of sand, *Jeremiah 5:22* says they can hold back the ocean. God's people can likewise accomplish much more work for Him when they are united together.
- **(For everyone):** What are some ways in which you can sow discord among brethren? How does the Lord feel about this work? How can it harm others? How could you make this right with those you have hurt?
- How can believers, like a threefold cord, be stronger when united? How does unity assist in accountability and service for the Lord?

PRAYER THOUGHTS

- Ask the Lord to forgive you for sowing discord.
- Ask God to show you the strength of unity.

SONG: *MAY THIS CHURCH OF THINE*

Day 322: (Saturday)
The Peace of the Perfect Man

Ephesians 4:13 Till we all come in the unity of the faith, and of the knowledge of the Son of God, unto a perfect man, unto the measure of the stature of the fulness of Christ:

INTRODUCTORY THOUGHTS

God's desire is that His people would grow into unity. The *"perfect man"* will experience this unity. The word *perfect* does not suggest a person without sin; but, rather, an individual who has matured in the Lord and been *"furnished unto all good works" (2 Timothy 3:17).* A perfect man is not without error, but is mature enough in the Lord to exercise the lowliness, meekness, and forbearance discussed in the previous devotions. The Bible says, *"Mark the perfect man . . . for the end of that man is peace" (Psalm 37:37).* The will of God is that *"we all"* would come to this *"unity of the faith."* It will only happen as believers grow *"unto the measure of the stature of the fulness of Christ."*

DEVOTIONAL THOUGHTS

- **(For children):** Paul told the church at Thessalonica to *"be at peace among yourselves" (1 Thessalonians 5:13b).* It's not always easy to get along but takes effort on your part *(Psalm 34:14).* It becomes easier as you learn the word of God and as you allow the Lord to help you *(Psalm 119:165).*
- **(For everyone):** Read *2 Corinthians 13:11.* How is being perfect related to being of one mind and living in peace? What does it suggest about your growth when you cannot experience peace and unity?
- Little children fight over foolish things. Young married couples often do the same. How does time and maturity seem to bring peace and unity? How is the same true in the unity of believers?

PRAYER THOUGHTS

- Ask the Lord to help you grow into a *"perfect man."*
- Thank the Lord for His longsuffering in dealing with you.

SONG: *MY FAITH HAS FOUND A RESTING PLACE*

Notes: _____

_____

_____

_____

_____

_____

_____

_____

_____

_____

_____

_____

_____

_____

_____

_____

_____

_____

Quotes from the next volume

(VOLUME 3, WEEK 46)

Subject: Stewardship (con't)

The relationship between the master and the steward is one built upon trust. The master puts all of his possessions into the hands of a steward. He will not do this unless that man has proven himself trustworthy.

As a steward, a man must give himself to a high level of character and morality. After all, he has been entrusted not with his own work or possessions but those of his master.

47

Vanity

Vanity—found 212 times in 189 verses

Variations: vain, vainly, vanities, vanity

Defined: that which is empty, futile, and of no value

First usage: *Exodus 5:9* (vain)

Last usage: *2 Peter 2:18* (vanity)

Interesting fact: The single verse, *Ecclesiastes 1:2*, contains five references to vanity out of only twelve words. This verse by itself contains more references to vanity than fifty-seven of the books of the Bible.

Bible study tip: In order to get a better grasp of a Bible word, try dividing your study into parts and then tying together the whole. For example, you might break a study of vanity into the following parts: *things that can be considered vain* (i.e., words, thoughts, etc.), *companion words of vanity* (i.e., deceived, deceit, falsehood, flattering, lying, etc.), and *various feelings demonstrated toward vanity* (i.e., anger, love, etc.). This will help the Bible student to grasp a deeper understanding.

Sunday, Day 323—Church Day (no devotional)
Monday, Day 324—*All Is Vanity Under the Sun*
Tuesday, Day 325—*Provoking the Lord to Anger*
Wednesday, Day 326—Church Night (no devotional)
Thursday, Day 327—*How Long Will Ye Love Vanity?*
Friday, Day 328—*They Followed Vanity, and Became Vain*
Saturday, Day 329—*Turn from These Vanities*

Day 323: Church Day

Proverbs 30:8 Remove far from me vanity and lies: give me neither poverty nor riches; feed me with food convenient for me:

Day 324: (Monday)
All Is Vanity Under the Sun

Ecclesiastes 1:2 Vanity of vanities, saith the Preacher, vanity of vanities; all is vanity.

INTRODUCTORY THOUGHTS

The book of Ecclesiastes contains documentation of Solomon's life experiment apart from God. He examined the worth of subjects involving happiness, wealth, labour, and death. Ultimately, he concluded that life *"under the sun" (Ecclesiastes 1:14)* was vanity. The word *vanity* means empty or meaningless. Though Solomon wrote extensively concerning vanity, he was not the only person in the Bible to declare the vanity of life. In fact, Solomon's father David declared that *"every man at his best state is altogether vanity" (Psalm 39:5)*. King David added that if both men of high and low degree were laid in a balance together, they would be *"lighter than vanity" (Psalm 62:9)*. Thus, regardless of worldly accomplishments and accolades, a life void of God remains meaningless.

DEVOTIONAL THOUGHTS

- **(For children):** Solomon learned that he could be happy only by trusting in God *(Proverbs 16:20)*. Only through God's word can we understand why the world is full of sickness, sorrow, pain, evil, etc. *(Psalm 119:130a)*. If God left man on the earth without hope of a home in heaven, we would be miserable *(1 Corinthians 15:19)*. Fortunately, He has promised to return for His children *(John 14:1-3)*.

- **(For everyone):** If there were no God, what would be the purpose of things like labour and love? What would be the purpose of life and death? How can we ensure that our life is not vain?
- Read **Revelation 4:11**. For what purpose was man created? What happens when a person fails to do what he was created to do? Are you fulfilling your purpose in life? If not, why not?

PRAYER THOUGHTS

- Ask the Lord to give your life meaning.
- Ask the Lord to show you the vanity of this world.

SONG: *FAREWELL VAIN WORLD*

Day 325: (Tuesday)
Provoking the Lord to Anger

Deuteronomy 32:21 *They have moved me to jealousy with that which is not God;* **they have provoked me to anger with their vanities:** *and I will move them to jealousy with those which are not a people; I will provoke them to anger with a foolish nation.*

INTRODUCTORY THOUGHTS

The Lord redeemed Israel out of Egypt for the purpose of worshipping Him. Instead of willingly serving Him, the nation of Israel turned to vanities. In doing so, they ignited the fire of God's anger *(Deuteronomy 32:21-22)*. Ultimately, God chose to provoke Israel to jealousy with a people *"which are not a people"* – the Gentiles. Since Israel had provoked the Lord to anger with their vanities, He was going to use Gentiles, whom Israel knew to be *"not a people,"* to provoke Israel to anger. The Lord expects the redeemed to flee vanity and give themselves wholly to His work, worship, and will. The Lord has now redeemed Jew and Gentile *"for his name" (Acts 15:14)*, and He expects the same from each of us.

DEVOTIONAL THOUGHTS

- **(For children):** God's will for Uzziah was for him to be king. For the most part, he was a good king. But Uzziah provoked the Lord to anger when he stepped out of God's will and thought he could do the work of the priests. Read what happened to him for his disobedience in *2 Chronicles 26:4, 16-21*.

- **(For everyone)**: The Lord redeemed us with the precious blood of His Son. How could it grieve Him when we seek after vanity and disregard His will for our lives?
- Vanity takes and gives nothing in return. The Lord is able to give far more in return than man could ever give to Him. For what are you giving yourself?

PRAYER THOUGHTS

- Ask God to show you when you are provoking Him with vanity.
- Thank the Lord for His longsuffering.

SONG: *MY SOUL, DEAR LORD, TO THEE ASCENDS*

Day 326: Church Night

*1 Samuel 12:21 And **turn ye not aside**: for **then should ye go after vain things, which cannot profit nor deliver; for they are vain**.*

Day 327: (Thursday)
How Long Will Ye Love Vanity?

*Psalm 4:2 O ye sons of men, how long will ye turn my glory into shame? **how long will ye love vanity**, and seek after leasing? Selah.*

INTRODUCTORY THOUGHTS

The Bible says that vanity is meaningless and empty, yet men love vanity. It fills their imaginations *(Psalm 2:1)*, their thoughts *(Psalm 94:11)*, and their speech *(Psalm 144:8, 11)*. Vanity consumes man so much that he will weary himself for it *(Habakkuk 2:13)*. In comparison to the vanities of this life, most people spend a brief moment in the eternal word of God. Far too many Christians fear to speak God's righteousness but demonstrate boldness as they speak on behalf of their favorite vanities. As men tend to forget to spend time with the Lord, they spend entire days pondering the vanity to be enjoyed later in the day. Is it any wonder why people need so many "pick-me-up" drinks and drugs as they weary themselves in pursuit of vanity.

DEVOTIONAL THOUGHTS

- **(For children):** Children spend much time and strength focused upon the world's heroes that are not real. Do you realize one day we will meet the real heroes of the Bible such as David, Daniel, Moses, Joseph, Noah, etc.? Why not read their stories and pretend to be one of them when at play?
- **(For everyone):** What topics consume your thoughts and your speech? Are these topics vain or do they bring glory to God? How can you turn your vain thoughts into thoughts that are profitable?
- Do you weary yourself for vanity? Do you weary yourself to the point where you cannot find the time and strength to serve the Lord? How does the Lord feel about this?

PRAYER THOUGHTS

- Ask God to help you give yourself to things that are profitable.
- Ask the Lord to convict you about loving vanity.

SONG: *A BANQUET FOR THE SOUL*

Day 328: (Friday)
They Followed Vanity, and Became Vain

*2 Kings 17:15 And they rejected his statutes, and his covenant that he made with their fathers, and his testimonies which he testified against them; and **they followed vanity, and became vain**, and went after the heathen that were round about them, concerning whom the LORD had charged them, that they should not do like them.*

INTRODUCTORY THOUGHTS

When men follow after vanity, they themselves become vain. An individual must make a conscious decision to turn from walking after the Lord to pursue vanity *(Jeremiah 2:5)*. Those who follow after vanity are void of understanding *(Proverbs 12:11)* and end up in poverty *(Proverbs 28:19)*, sometimes both spiritually and physically. David expressed his concern in this area when he said, *"I have not sat with vain persons" (Psalm 26:4)*. He knew the danger of following vanity and declared that he refused even to sit with vain persons. In *Psalm 119:37*, the penman pleaded with the Lord for help in turning away his eyes from beholding vanity. God desires and wills for the saints of God to cease from following after vanity.

DEVOTIONAL THOUGHTS

- **(For children):** Joash served God as long as Jehoiada the priest was alive. But after the priest died, Joash followed vain persons and worshipped idols *(2 Chronicles 24:2, 17-19)*. We should be careful that our friends love the Lord and want us to do right.
- **(For everyone):** Do you follow after vain philosophies, teachings, or entertainment? How have these assisted you in your walk with the Lord? Have they been profitable to you?
- How have you been helped by your time in the scripture? How have you been strengthened by your time in prayer and praise? How is this different from the time spent following vanity?

PRAYER THOUGHTS

- Ask the Lord to help you follow after profitable things.
- Ask the Lord to guard you from vain influences.

SONG: *GIVE ME THY HEART*

Day 329: (Saturday)
Turn from These Vanities

*Acts 14:15 And saying, Sirs, why do ye these things? We also are men of like passions with you, and preach unto you that **ye should turn from these vanities unto the living God**, which made heaven, and earth, and the sea, and all things that are therein:*

INTRODUCTORY THOUGHTS

Paul and Barnabas admonished the heathen to turn from *"vanities unto the living God."* One cannot trust in the Lord and simultaneously trust in anything else. In order for an individual to be saved, he must repent of trusting in anything other than the Lord. One aspect of repentance involves ceasing to trust vanity and turning one's faith toward the living and true God. This saving faith needs to become a living faith following salvation. Believers should consistently turn from *"vain thoughts"* and love the law of God *(Psalm 119:113)*. They should turn from the vain labours that spend their strength for nought *(Isaiah 49:4)* and be *"steadfast . . . in the work of the Lord"* knowing that their *"labour is not in vain in the Lord"* *(1 Corinthians 15:58)*. Additionally, believers should turn from *"vain words"* *(Ephesians 5:6)* and hold *"forth the word of life"* *(Philippians 2:16)*.

DEVOTIONAL THOUGHTS

- **(For children):** Peter was serving the Lord as a fisher of men. Then Peter decided to go back to his old job of fishing. Fishing is not wrong, but Jesus wanted Peter to love Him more than fishing and also expected Peter to do what He had told him to do *(John 21:3, 15-17)*. Even good things can be worthless to us if they are not what God wants us to do.
- **(For everyone):** Have you put your trust in the Lord for your eternal life? From what vanities did you turn in order to do so? From what vanities do you need to turn now that you are saved?
- Are your thoughts, words, and labours vain? What would happen if you stood at the judgment seat of Christ today? Will you *"turn from these vanities unto the living God"*?

PRAYER THOUGHTS

- Ask God to forgive you where you have given yourself to vanity.
Ask God to help your work, thoughts, and speech to glorify Him.

SONG: *MAY I RESOLVE WITH ALL MY HEART*

Notes: _____

_____

_____

_____

_____

_____

_____

_____

_____

_____

_____

_____

_____

Notes: _____

_____

_____

_____

_____

_____

_____

_____

_____

_____

_____

_____

_____

_____

_____

_____

_____

_____

_____

Quotes from the next volume

(VOLUME 3, WEEK 47)

Subject: Temptation

One of the most difficult tasks for every believer involves discerning the difference between the working of God and the working of Satan.

The first step of any temptation is a drawing away. If a man cannot be drawn away, he cannot be tempted.

48

Vengeance

Vengeance—found 106 times in ninety-two verses

Variations: avenge, avenged, avenger, avengeth, revenge, revenged, revenger, revengers, revenges, revengeth, vengeance

Defined: to lay claim to or to punish

First usage: *Genesis 4:15* (vengeance)

Last usage: *Revelation 19:2* (avenged)

Interesting fact: Nowhere in the scriptures is the New Testament believer admonished to take vengeance into his own hands as it pertains to the wrong doings of others. Yet, Christians are twice admonished to or praised for *"revenge"* on our own disobedience *(2 Corinthians 7:11; 2 Corinthians 10:6)*.

Bible study tip: Watch for the use of the words *as* and *so* within a common passage. Oftentimes, the word *as* establishes the pattern and the word *so* presents the parallel. For example, *Deuteronomy 8:5* – *"as a man chasteneth his son, so the LORD thy God chasteneth thee."* The pattern refers to how a man chastens his son which establishes the parallel to how the Lord chastens His children.

Sunday, Day 330—Church Day (no devotional)
Monday, Day 331—*What Is Vengeance?*
Tuesday, Day 332—*The Heathen Understand Vengeance*
Wednesday, Day 333—Church Night (no devotional)
Thursday, Day 334—*To Whom Belongeth Vengeance?*
Friday, Day 335—*For Whom Is Vengeance Reserved?*
Saturday, Day 336—*The Time of Vengeance*

Day 330: Church Day

*Psalm 18:47 **It is God that avengeth me**, and subdueth the people under me.*

Day 331: (Monday)
What Is Vengeance?

*Deuteronomy 32:41 If I whet my glittering sword, and **mine hand take hold on judgment; I will render vengeance** to mine enemies, **and will reward** them that hate me.*

INTRODUCTORY THOUGHTS

A simplistic view of vengeance involves the retribution of an evil deed. The first *(Genesis 4:15)* and last *(Jude 7)* mention of the word *vengeance* substantiates this definition. The Bible uses words like *recompence (Deuteronomy 32:35)*, *reward (Deuteronomy 32:41)*, *punishments (Psalm 149:7)*, *avenge (Jeremiah 46:10)*, *revenge (Ezekiel 25:15)*, and *repay (Romans 12:19)* as descriptive words for *vengeance*. With this in mind, it is clear that vengeance is the just punishment as a consequence upon those who violate the laws of God. It is not the dispensing of wrath without cause but is specific punishment exacted for specific crimes committed.

DEVOTIONAL THOUGHTS

• **(For children):** God punishes evil *(Isaiah 13:11a)*. In Noah's time, God saw that the wickedness of man was great and decided to send a flood *(Genesis 6:5-7)*. Yet, He is so loving, He gave the people 120 years to repent while Noah built the ark and preached. Only eight people made it into the ark *(Genesis 6:8-10; 1 Peter 3:20)*.

- **(For everyone):** How is God just in His execution of vengeance? Why is it so important to note that vengeance is punishment for evil doing? Does God ever mete out judgment to the innocent?
- Why is it dangerous for people to reject the concept that God is to be feared? Why should an understanding of vengeance make the wicked fearful?

PRAYER THOUGHTS

- Ask the Lord to help you tell others about God's vengeance.
- Ask the Lord to keep you from His vengeance.

SONG: *GOD IS A RIGHTEOUS JUDGE BE SURE*

Day 332: (Tuesday)
The Heathen Understand Vengeance

Acts 28:1 And when they were escaped, then they knew that the island was called Melita.

2 And the barbarous people shewed us no little kindness: for they kindled a fire, and received us every one, because of the present rain, and because of the cold.

3 And when Paul had gathered a bundle of sticks, and laid them on the fire, there came a viper out of the heat, and fastened on his hand.

*4 And **when the barbarians saw the venomous beast hang on his hand, they said among themselves, No doubt this man is a murderer, whom, though he hath escaped the sea, yet vengeance suffereth not to live**.*

INTRODUCTORY THOUGHTS

Following a shipwreck, Paul, and those with him, escaped to an island called Melita. The Bible describes the natives as a barbarous people who were not completely void of truth. They demonstrated kindness toward those who had escaped the sea by kindling a fire for them. Paul helped the natives by gathering a bundle of sticks to cast upon the fire. As he cast the sticks on the fire, a viper came out of the heat and fastened on

Paul's hand. Immediately, the barbarians assumed Paul to be a murderer who was being recompensed for his wickedness. Even though these people did not know the Lord, they had some of His laws written in their consciences.

DEVOTIONAL THOUGHTS

- **(For children):** Even if people do not know God, God puts it in their hearts to know the difference between good and evil *(Romans 2:14-15)*. Isaac told Abimelech that his wife was his sister. When Abimelech discovered the truth, he scolded Isaac saying that if someone had taken her for a wife, they would have been guilty *(Genesis 26:10c)*.
- **(For everyone):** If there were no God, there would be no vengeance. Why? How does the understanding of vengeance validate the existence of God?
- How did the barbarians understand kindness and vengeance? How did these truths, that necessitate the existence of God, enter into the understanding of these heathen?

PRAYER THOUGHTS

- Thank God for writing His truth in your conscience.
- Ask the Lord for a deeper understanding of vengeance.

SONG: *STOP, POOR SINNER! STOP AND THINK*

Day 333: Church Night

*Romans 12:19 Dearly beloved, **avenge not yourselves,** but rather give place unto wrath: for it is written, **Vengeance is mine; I will repay, saith the Lord.***

Day 334: (Thursday)
To Whom Belongeth Vengeance?

*Psalm 94:1 O LORD God, **to whom vengeance belongeth;** O God, **to whom vengeance belongeth,** shew thyself.*

INTRODUCTORY THOUGHTS

Sometimes the most difficult and significant tasks involve the simplest truths. For instance, every Christian should quickly learn that vengeance belongs unto the Lord. God confirms as much throughout scripture *(Deuteronomy 32:35; Psalm 94:1; Romans 12:19; Hebrews 10:30)*. This should be understandable as only the Lord has all the necessary information to execute just vengeance 100 percent of the time. When man attempts to execute vengeance, he often does so out of an improper motive or without key information of the evil that appears to have been done. Furthermore, when a believer takes vengeance into his own hands, he robs the Lord of His right and responsibility to exact vengeance at the right time and in the right manner.

DEVOTIONAL THOUGHTS

- **(For children):** Paul *(2 Timothy 4:14)* and Jeremiah *(Lamentations 3:60, 64)* both knew that getting even with their enemies belonged to God. David thanked Abigail for preventing him from getting even with Nabal when David was angry. God got more than even for David *(1 Samuel 25:28d, 30-33, 38)*.
- **(For everyone):** What could go wrong when we take vengeance into our own hands? Have there been times when things appeared one way, but further investigation proved that your thoughts were inaccurate?
- Why did the Lord emphasize that vengeance belonged unto Him? What is our first reaction when someone does us wrong? What is our first desire when we see others wronged?

PRAYER THOUGHTS

- Ask God to help you leave vengeance to Him.
- Thank God for His longsuffering with you.

SONG: *AMIDST THY WRATH REMEMBER LOVE*

Day 335: (Friday)
For Whom Is Vengeance Reserved?

*Nahum 1:2 God is jealous, and **the LORD revengeth**; the LORD revengeth, and is furious; **the LORD will take vengeance on his adversaries**, and he reserveth wrath for his enemies.*

INTRODUCTORY THOUGHTS

The believer's life is loaded with benefits *(Psalm 68:19)*, but one of the greatest of these benefits concerns the area of vengeance. According to scripture, vengeance is reserved for the Lord's enemies *(Deuteronomy 32:41; Judges 11:36)*, or adversaries *(Deuteronomy 32:43; Jeremiah 46:10; Nahum 1:2)*, or the heathen *(Psalm 149:7; Micah 5:15)* but specifically upon *"them that know not God"* *(2 Thessalonians 1:8)*. God does not deal with His people in vengeance, it is reserved for those who reject the gospel of the Lord Jesus Christ *(2 Thessalonians 1:8)*. When the children of God are disobedient, the Lord chastens, but He never takes vengeance upon His own.

DEVOTIONAL THOUGHTS

- **(For children):** Read why God destroyed the cities of Sodom and Gomorrah *(Ezekiel 16:49-50; Genesis 19:24)*. He waited until the two angels removed Lot and his family out of the city *(2 Peter 2:6-7; Genesis 19:16)*. Likewise, God's children are not appointed unto wrath *(1 Thessalonians 5:9)*.
- **(For everyone):** How should believers respond to a greater understanding of God's vengeance (see *Psalm 58:10; Isaiah 35:4*)? Why should believers take comfort from God's vengeance?
- What are some other distinctions you can think of that come with being saved? Write them down and thank the Lord for the benefits of knowing Him.

PRAYER THOUGHTS

- If you are saved, thank the Lord for His salvation.
- Ask the Lord to give you a burden for those who are not saved.

SONG: *TREMBLE, YE SINNERS*

Day 336: (Saturday)
The Time of Vengeance

Proverbs 6:34 *For jealousy is the rage of a man: therefore he will not spare in* **the day of vengeance**.

INTRODUCTORY THOUGHTS

Vengeance is not always executed in a swift fashion *(Ecclesiastes 8:11)*. In fact, believers often grow weary because the wicked seem to prosper in spite of their evil deeds. Yet, the Lord will execute vengeance in His time. The Bible speaks often of *"the day of vengeance"* to come. This day is very likely a thousand year period *(2 Peter 3:8)* which will begin shortly before the second coming of the Lord and will end at the great white throne judgment following the end of the millennial kingdom. It will be a time when the Lord will refuse to spare the wicked *(Proverbs 6:34)* but will set things right for the Jewish people *(Isaiah 34:8; Isaiah 61:2; Isaiah 63:4)*.

DEVOTIONAL THOUGHTS

- **(For children):** Sometimes it seems like the wicked are getting by with their sin *(Psalm 73:3-5)*. But we know that is not the case *(Psalm 11:4; Isaiah 26:21a; Isaiah 59:18)*. God is totally in control *(2 Peter 2:9)*.
- **(For everyone):** What attributes are exemplified when the Lord delays judgment upon the wicked? How can we be grateful for these same attributes even though we know Him?
- Whom do you know that is not saved? How would it grieve you to know that if the Lord were to come right now, they would be forever lost? What can you do to help them?

PRAYER THOUGHTS

- Ask God for a burden for those who are lost.
- Thank the Lord for His righteousness in judgment.

SONG: *LO, HE COMES, ARRAYED IN VENGEANCE*

Notes: _____

_____

_____

_____

_____

_____

_____

_____

_____

_____

Notes: _____

_____

_____

_____

_____

_____

_____

_____

_____

_____

_____

_____

_____

_____

_____

_____

_____

Quotes from the next volume

(VOLUME 3, WEEK 48)

Subject: Temptation (con't)

Man has throughout history battled the idea that he is the only one who has had to endure temptation with a desire to do right *(1 Kings 19:13-14)*. This lie was conceived by the father of lies *(John 8:44)* with the intent of alienating the believer into thinking no one understands his difficulty.

Man never sins apart from his own willingness to do so. Unfortunately, our vocabulary is filled with statements that make sin sound like a horrible accident or mistake; however, in reality, we choose to sin.

49

Warfare

Warfare—found 261 times in 252 verses

Variations: war, warfare, warred, warreth, warring, warrior, warriors, wars

Defined: dispute, conflict, or fighting

First usage: *Genesis 14:2* (war)

Last usage: *Revelation 19:19* (war)

Interesting fact: The Jews are an earthly people, promised an earthly inheritance, who warred an earthly and physical warfare. The church, however, is a spiritual people looking for a heavenly inheritance who fight a spiritual warfare *(2 Corinthians 10:3-4; Ephesians 6:12)*. Failure to understand these basic truths has been the foundational error of a whole host of cults, schisms, and whole religions.

Bible study tip: Pay attention to peculiar wording in scripture. The wording of scripture serves to draw attention to a particular truth. Consider the wording of *1 John 1:10* – *"If we say that we have not sinned, we make him* [Jesus Christ] *a liar."* Is it truly possible to make Jesus Christ a liar? No! This reminds us of the truth taught in *Romans 3:4*, *"let God be true, but every man a liar."*

Sunday, Day 337—Church Day (no devotional)
Monday, Day 338—*The Nature of Our Warfare*
Tuesday, Day 339—*The Enemy Identified*
Wednesday, Day 340—Church Night (no devotional)
Thursday, Day 341—*Weapons of Warfare*
Friday, Day 342—*Amour for the Battle*
Saturday, Day 343—*The Character of a Soldier*

Day 337: Church Day

Psalm 27:2 *When the wicked, even mine enemies and my foes, came upon me to eat up my flesh, they stumbled and fell.*

*3 **Though an host should encamp against me, my heart shall not fear: though war should rise against me, in this will I be confident.***

Day 338: (Monday)
The Nature of Our Warfare

1 Timothy 6:12 *Fight **the good fight of faith**, lay hold on eternal life, whereunto thou art also called, and hast professed a good profession before many witnesses.*

INTRODUCTORY THOUGHTS

Most wars are instigated and then propagated by those with impure and mostly evil motives. Men fight these fleshly wars to satisfy their own lusts, yet the Christian warfare is ordered of the Lord. Unlike carnal wars, this battle is one of faith. The battle plans are given by the Captain seated in heaven, and these directives must be accepted by faith. In fact, the Bible refers to the warfare that is the Christian life as a *"good fight."* At this present time, it is the only war declared with unwavering certainty to be ordered and completely ordained by God. Victories and defeats may not always be as visible, and the toll of wounded or killed will never be reported on the daily news, but the results of this battle have far greater significance than any war fought between two earthly people groups. Every Christian should be willing to fight the good fight of faith.

DEVOTIONAL THOUGHTS

- **(For children):** You are asked to clean your room. You do not want to clean it, but then you remember **Colossians 3:20** and clean it anyway. You just won a good fight because you did what God wanted you to do and refused to disobey like the Devil wanted.
- **(For everyone):** What does the Bible suggest when it calls the Christian life a *"fight of faith"*? How does this identify many of the earthly wars fought in the name of Christianity as unscriptural?
- How can the Christian warfare be called a *good* fight? What makes this warfare good while the vast majority of the wars fought by men are *evil*?

PRAYER THOUGHTS

- Ask God to help you see the faith involved in the believer's fight.
- Ask the Lord to help you fight the good fight.

SONG: *WHO IS ON THE LORD'S SIDE?*

Day 339: (Tuesday)
The Enemy Identified

*Ephesians 6:12 For **we wrestle** not against flesh and blood, but **against principalities, against powers, against the rulers of the darkness of this world, against spiritual wickedness in high places**.*

INTRODUCTORY THOUGHTS

The fact that the Bible describes the Christian life as the good *"fight of faith" (1 Timothy 6:12)* reveals that the believer's warfare is spiritual and never fleshly. In like manner, the enemy lives within the spiritual realm and this battle cannot be seen with the eyes of flesh. The enemy does not simply reside in a country on the other side of the world. In fact, it is no person or people group on this earth. Believers are told that they do not wrestle *"against flesh and blood."* Ultimately, the saints' enemy is the Devil, but his minions include principalities, powers, the rulers of the darkness of this world, and spiritual wickedness in high places. This means that the saints should never look to flesh and blood (mere mortals) for the source of their frustrations or victories. The fight is one of faith; the enemy, the Devil and the Lord our spiritual Captain *(Hebrews 2:10)*.

DEVOTIONAL THOUGHTS

- **(For children):** The Bible is very clear that the Devil is our archenemy *(Luke 22:31; 1 Peter 5:8)*. It is also very clear that through prayer and doing what God says, we have the power to do right *(James 4:7)*. Whether to do right or wrong remains the choice of each individual.
- **(For everyone):** Why is knowing that our enemy is truly spiritual such an important biblical truth? How can identifying the true enemy keep us from expressing our frustrations upon the people that we love?
- Who should be the object of our hate when things go wrong? Who is ultimately the enemy that seeks to destroy us and our testimonies?

PRAYER THOUGHTS

- Ask God to help you realize that your enemy is the Devil.
- Ask the Lord to use this teaching to make you a better Christian.

SONG: *SOUND THE BATTLE CRY!*

Day 340: Church Night

Ecclesiastes 9:18 Wisdom is better than weapons of war: but one sinner destroyeth much good.

Day 341: (Thursday)
Weapons of Warfare

2 Corinthians 10:3 For though we walk in the flesh, we do not war after the flesh:

*4 (For **the weapons of our warfare are not carnal**, but mighty through God to the pulling down of strong holds;)*

INTRODUCTORY THOUGHTS

The Bible clearly emphasizes that the Christian warfare is a *"fight of faith" (1 Timothy 6:12)* against spiritual foes *(Ephesians 6:12)*. With this in mind, it only makes sense that the weapons used in this warfare would also be spiritual in nature. The Christian's fight needs no physical arms, swords, or weaponry of any kind, yet the weapons of this warfare are *"mighty through God to the pulling down of strong holds."* Those religions (and cults) who use physical weaponry to convert others to their "faiths" have never done this at the Lord's bidding or direction. The Christian faith never has nor ever will convert one single person through use of a physical sword or threat. Instead, God's people are completely reliant upon the words of God and the God of those words.

DEVOTIONAL THOUGHTS

- **(For children):** Learn your Bible and use it as a sword *(Hebrews 4:12a)* either to attack error or defend the truth. For example, if someone says you do not have to go to church, quote *Hebrews 10:25a* or *Psalm 122:1*. If someone says a bad word, quote *Psalm 34:13a* or *Ephesians 4:29a*.
- **(For everyone):** What does this teach us about the wars of the past that have been fought with physical weaponry in the name of Christianity with the purpose of converting the enemy "to Christ"?
- How can believers have more success with spiritual weaponry than with physical weaponry? How can this also apply to those who seek worldly methods in converting sinners?

PRAYER THOUGHTS

- Ask God to show you the strength of spiritual weaponry.
- Ask the Lord to help you be faithful in battle.

SONG: *TO ARMS, YE SAINTS, TO ARMS!*

Day 342: (Friday)
Armour for the Battle

*Ephesians 6:11 **Put on the whole armour of God**, that ye may be able to stand against the wiles of the devil.*

12 For we wrestle not against flesh and blood, but against principalities, against powers, against the rulers of the darkness of this world, against spiritual wickedness in high places.

*13 Wherefore **take unto you the whole armour of God**, that ye may be able to withstand in the evil day, and having done all, to stand.*

*14 Stand therefore, having your **loins girt about with truth**, and having on **the breastplate of righteousness**;*

*15 And your **feet shod with the preparation of the gospel of peace**;*

*16 Above all, taking **the shield of faith**, wherewith ye shall be able to quench all the fiery darts of the wicked.*

*17 And take **the helmet of salvation**, and **the sword of the Spirit**, which is the word of God:*

*18 **Praying always** with all prayer and supplication in the Spirit, and watching thereunto with all perseverance and supplication for all saints;*

INTRODUCTORY THOUGHTS

Most battles won have been won because of being equipped with the proper weaponry. Though the substance may be different in Christian warfare, the same theme prevails. No believer is nearly as successful in battle as he is when he dons *"the whole armour of God" (Ephesians 6:11)*. This armour assists the believer as he seeks to stand *"against the wiles of the devil" (Ephesians 6:11)*. This armour defends the loins with truth, the vital organs with righteousness *(Ephesians 6:14)*, the head with salvation *(Ephesians 6:17)*, and the entirety with faith *(Ephesians 6:16)*. The same armour provides the offensive weaponry in the word of God and prayer *(Ephesians 6:17-18)*. Notice that the spiritual weaponry lacks any emphasis upon the physical.

DEVOTIONAL THOUGHTS

- **(For children):** Goliath had better weapons and armour than David *(1 Samuel 17:4-7)*, yet David refused Saul's armour *(1 Samuel 17:38-39)*. He had only a staff, a sling, and five stones, but he was not really depending upon them to defeat the giant. Read on whom David was depending *(1 Samuel 17:45-47)*.
- **(For everyone):** What parts of the body are covered by the armour? Are there any parts left uncovered (i.e., the back, the knees)? Why would these parts need no armour?
- What is the connection between each piece of armour and the part of the body that it covers (i.e., why are the loins girt about with truth, or why is the head covered with salvation)?

PRAYER THOUGHTS

- Thank the Lord for the armour He has given you.
- Ask the Lord to help you put on the whole armour of God.

SONG: *TO ARMS! TO ARMS!*

Day 343: (Saturday)
The Character of a Soldier

*2 Timothy 2:3 Thou therefore **endure hardness, as a good soldier** of Jesus Christ.*

*4 **No man that warreth entangleth himself with the affairs of this life**; that he may please him who hath chosen him to be a soldier.*

INTRODUCTORY THOUGHTS

Dedicated soldiers are a dying breed, especially amongst Christians. Few people endure when the going gets tough or obstacles surface. The average Christian believes that God's will involves no hurdles. In the secular world, drill sergeants, employers, and teachers spend a great deal of time and effort trying to instill discipline into those who grew up lacking character with little desire to succeed. This lack of character affects us all. Good soldiers endure hardness. They do not quit in the service of the Lord because of trials and tribulations. Neither do they allow themselves to be entangled in the affairs of this life. Their main desire is to please the very one who chose them to be a soldier in the first place.

DEVOTIONAL THOUGHTS

- **(For children):** Read about David's mighty men *(2 Samuel 23:8-12)*. They did not quit during hard battles. God does not want us to quit serving Him when we have troubles *(1 Kings 2:2-3; 1 Corinthians 16:13; 2 Thessalonians 2:15)*.
- **(For everyone):** What might be some of the difficulties faced by a soldier in the armed forces? What would a drill sergeant do to prepare a soldier to endure these difficulties? What should we do to be better soldiers?
- How does a soldier who quits lose the confidence of his fellow soldiers? How could you lose the confidence of brothers and sister in Christ when you quit on the Lord?

PRAYER THOUGHTS

- Thank the Lord for calling you to be a soldier.
- Ask the Lord to help you endure hardness.

SONG: *RISE, YE CHILDREN OF SALVATION*

Notes: _____

_____

_____

_____

_____

_____

_____

_____

_____

_____

_____

_____

_____

Quotes from the next volume

(VOLUME 3, WEEK 49)

Subject: Tradition

Many of the traditions of men are in direct opposition to scripture. These traditions cannot be readily accepted by the saints of God who have pledged allegiance to the scripture.

Like in the days of old, God has given the church faithful men who are charged with warning the saints about accepting fables that turn believers from the truth.

The present generation has been handed some wonderful traditions from the previous generations. Those most precious are directly found in scripture while others are founded upon scriptural principles.

50

Watching

Watching—found ninety-four times in eighty-six verses

Variations: watch, watched, watcher, watchers, watches, watcheth, watchful, watching, watchings

Defined: As a verb it means to be alert or awake.

First usage: *Genesis 31:49* (watch)

Last usage: *Revelation 16:15* (watcheth)

Interesting fact: Oftentimes, a person undertaking an action is denoted by simply adding the suffix -*er* to the end of the word; for example, one who *teaches* is a *teacher (Hebrews 5:12)*. At other times, the individual undertaking a task is denoted by adding the word *man* at the end; for instance, one who herds is *"an herdman" (Amos 7:14)*. Interestingly, both suffixes are used in conjunction with *watching*. It appears that the words *watchman* and *watchmen* point to men while at least three of the four references to *watcher(s)* refer to spiritual beings *(Daniel 4:13, 17, 23)*.

Bible study tip: Proper nouns sometimes carry with them meanings that provide deeper understanding or offer an interesting thought. These meanings of places and people's names are not always crucial for biblical understanding. There are times, however, when the meanings are provided within the context of the place or mention of the person. Sometimes, the definition only becomes evident through diligent search. At other times, the Bible uses a phrase such as *"which is by interpretation"* **(John 1:42)** followed by the definition.

Sunday, Day 344—Church Day (no devotional)
Monday, Day 345—*Watch Ye*
Tuesday, Day 346—*In Watchings Often*
Wednesday, Day 347—Church Night (no devotional)
Thursday, Day 348—*The Watchman and Prayer*
Friday, Day 349—*A Circumspect Walk*
Saturday, Day 350—*Could Ye Not Watch One Hour?*

Day 344: Church Day

*Ephesians 6:18 Praying always with all prayer and supplication in the Spirit, and **watching thereunto with all perseverance and supplication for all saints;***

Day 345: (Monday)
Watch Ye

1 Corinthians 16:13 Watch ye, stand fast in the faith, quit you like men, be strong.

INTRODUCTORY THOUGHTS

In Bible times, cities would often build towers to watch the gates to avoid dangers looming from without *(Isaiah 21:8)*. Watchmen would take turns watching the gate. These watchmen were responsible for sounding a trumpet should any danger appear *(Ezekiel 33:6)*. The apostle Paul in his writings applied a spiritual application to this literal act of being a watchman. Just as cities needed men willingly staying awake and alert while others slept or were busy in their daily routines, churches need believers sober and watchful while others might be cumbered about with the cares of this world. Today's watchmen must use their voices like a trumpet to sound the alarm when danger nears.

DEVOTIONAL THOUGHTS

- **(For children):** You would warn others not paying attention if they were about to fall over an object they did not see. God's people can spiritually trip and fall by not paying attention to God's word or by not obeying God. We should be willing to warn them by using God's word to instruct them.
- **(For everyone):** God incorporated specific pronouns to convey His truths. For example, *ye* conveys the plural. When Paul said, *"Watch ye,"* to whom was he speaking? Why is it important that we realize Paul was speaking to a group of believers rather than only to an individual?
- Why does your church, family, and community need you to be a watchman? Are there some people in each group who are sleeping during these times of danger? What should you do?

PRAYER THOUGHTS

- Ask the Lord to make you a faithful watchman.
- Ask the Lord to give you a better understanding of watching.

SONG: *CRY ALOUD, AND SPARE NOT*

Day 346: (Tuesday)
In Watchings Often

*2 Corinthians 11:27 In weariness and painfulness, **in watchings often**, in hunger and thirst, in fastings often, in cold and nakedness.*

INTRODUCTORY THOUGHTS

If ever there was a man in the early church that qualified as a watchman, it would have been the apostle Paul. Paul includes *"in watchings often"* in his testimony about the trials he endured. He also mentioned that these *watchings* approved him as a minister of God *(2 Corinthians 6:4-5)*. We know from the biblical accounts that when many believers were unaware of danger, the apostle Paul stood upon the tower and sounded the trumpet of alarm. While others were spiritually sleeping, the apostle Paul was sober and alert to the needs of the church. No doubt Paul endured sleepless nights, fasted, and went without even the necessities of life because he was watching for the church.

DEVOTIONAL THOUGHTS

- **(For children):** God's man warns God's people with the Bible *(Ezekiel 33:7)*. Paul warned the Ephesian elders to teach the church to watch for false teachers. In fact, Paul warned the pastors for three years *(Acts 20:28-31)*. Following Paul's example, pastors today watch and warn us *(Hebrews 13:17)*.
- **(For everyone):** Can you think of some instances where Paul fulfilled his duty as a watchman? What was the danger? What would have happened if Paul had not sent the warning?
- Why is it important to keep your eyes open in case of danger? What kind of warnings are given by the enemy as to the time and place of his attack?

PRAYER THOUGHTS

- Thank the Lord for the warnings given in His word.
- Ask the Lord to give you a desire to be a watchman for Him.

SONG: *HOLD THE FORT*

Day 347: Church Night

*2 Timothy 4:5 But **watch thou in all things**, endure afflictions, do the work of an evangelist, make full proof of thy ministry.*

Day 348: (Thursday)
The Watchman and Prayer

*1 Peter 4:7 But the end of all things is at hand: be ye therefore sober, and **watch unto prayer**.*

INTRODUCTORY THOUGHTS

Many Bible passages connect watchfulness and prayer. While preaching sounds the trumpet of alarm in the ears of men, prayer sounds the alarm in the ears of God. As a watchman, each believer has a responsibility to his brother or sister in Christ. While some believers are spiritually sleeping, unaware of their present danger, other believers ought to be standing upon the tower of watchfulness and calling upon the Lord. This was the point of Paul's teaching in **Ephesians 6:18** when he said, *"Praying always with all prayer and supplication in the Spirit, and **watching** thereunto with all perseverance and supplication for all saints."*

Devotional Thoughts

- **(For children):** God wants us to watch and pray *(Colossians 4:2)*. Epaphras prayed for his friends that they would do right *(Colossians 4:12)*. When Peter was in prison, the church prayed for him because they knew he had previously denied the Lord *(Acts 12:5)*.
- **(For everyone):** How is praying for others similar to the work of a watchman? When is the last time you acted as a watchman for other brothers and sisters in Christ?
- Who has been standing upon the watchtower on your behalf? Have you thanked them for their labours? What troubles have you avoided because of their faithfulness?

Prayer Thoughts

- Ask the Lord to make you a prayerful watchman.
- Thank the Lord for those who have watched in prayer for you.

SONG: *WAIT ON THE LORD, YE SAINTS*

Day 349: (Friday)
A Circumspect Walk

Ephesians 5:15 See then that ye walk circumspectly, *not as fools, but as wise,*

16 Redeeming the time, because the days are evil.

Introductory Thoughts

Imagine the vulnerabilities of a watchman who refuses to keep his eyes open to every possible angle from which danger could arise. No doubt the enemy would scout the land observing the bad habits of the watchman. If the watchman fails to examine each point of entry, the enemy will attack from the unprotected angle. In like manner, believers are to walk circumspectly. The word *circumspect* means to look all around. Believers are to be sober and vigilant knowing that their enemy, the Devil, *"walketh about, seeking whom he may devour"* *(1 Peter 5:8)*. God's enemies always search for the weak spot where the hedge has been cut down or ignored. This is why there is no angle in the believer's life that can be safely ignored.

DEVOTIONAL THOUGHTS

- **(For children):** Satan hates God and His creation and does not want us to obey God. God wants us to know His word and be circumspect, considering both what He says to do and the consequences if we choose to disobey *(Exodus 23:13a)*. If we despise what God says, the Bible says that we are fools *(Proverbs 1:7b)*.
- **(For everyone):** What are some areas in your life that the Devil could attempt to attack you? What dangers could exist if you fail to walk circumspectly? In what areas of your life are you currently weak spiritually?
- Failing to walk circumspectly is foolish *(Ephesians 5:15)*. Why is this foolish rather than ignorant? What is the difference between foolishness and ignorance?

PRAYER THOUGHTS

- Ask the Lord to give you wisdom to walk circumspectly.
- Thank God for the light He has given you concerning evil.

SONG: *WALK WORTHY OF THE LORD*

Day 350: (Saturday)
Could Ye Not Watch One Hour?

*Matthew 26:40 And he cometh unto the disciples, and findeth them asleep, and saith unto Peter, What, **could ye not watch with me one hour?***

*41 **Watch and pray, that ye enter not into temptation**: the spirit indeed is willing, but the flesh is weak.*

INTRODUCTORY THOUGHTS

Once Judas Iscariot determined to betray the Lord, the earthly ministry of Christ hastened toward the time of His crucifixion. As the time of His death drew near, the Lord Jesus took the disciples to Gethsemane so that He could spend time praying. He asked them to watch while He went to the Father in prayer; however, when the Lord returned from prayer, He found the disciples asleep. He woke them and rebuked Peter saying, *"What, could ye not watch with me one hour?"* What a horrible rebuke as Peter, along with the others, realized that he had failed this one simple request! After everything that the Lord had done for the disciples, they could not force themselves to watch for one hour. In like manner, many believers are going to find out the consequences at the judgment seat of Christ of failing to watch for the Lord.

DEVOTIONAL THOUGHTS

- **(For children):** The Lord is going to return but we do not know when. His warning to watch and pray in *Mark 13:32-37* can apply to us so that we will not be ashamed when He comes *(1 John 2:28)*.
- **(For everyone):** Our lives are certainly a short space of time in the scope of eternity. In light of eternity, how long has the Lord really given us to watch? How much of that time has been wasted?
- What is more important in your life than being obedient to the will of God? What have you chosen above fulfilling your duties as a watchman for the Lord?

PRAYER THOUGHTS

- Ask the Lord to help you see the time of your duty is short.
- Thank the Lord for all the times He has watched for you.

SONG: *LITTLE IS MUCH WHEN GOD IS IN IT*

Notes: _____

_____

_____

_____

_____

_____

_____

_____

_____

_____

_____

_____

_____

Notes: _____

_____

_____

_____

_____

_____

_____

_____

_____

_____

_____

_____

_____

_____

_____

_____

Quotes from the next volume

(VOLUME 3, WEEK 50)

Subject: Tradition (con't)

The Pharisees abused their authority by *"laying aside the commandment of God"* and holding up *"the tradition of men"* (**Mark 7:8**) as more important.

History reveals that many saints of God were severely punished or put to death for rejecting unscriptural traditions such as infant baptism.

Tradition robs men of the blessings only yielded by obedience to the truth.

51

Witnessing

Witnessing—found 191 times in 167 verses

Variations: witness, witnessed, witnesses, witnesseth, witnessing

Defined: To witness can mean to see or know by personal presence, but this study will emphasize the idea of bearing testimony.

First usage: *Genesis 21:30* (witness)

Last usage: *Revelation 20:4* (witness)

Interesting fact: The Bible testifies of a man in hell who had a strong desire that someone would go to his five living brethren and testify to them concerning the truth *(Luke 16:28)*. Unfortunately, it is far too late for those in hell who might desire to see others saved. They cannot help the lost who are yet living. Only a living witness still has opportunity to assist those in need of the Saviour.

Bible study tip: The scripture sometimes uses various names to identify a person or place. For example, the Bible refers to the sea of Galilee as the sea of Tiberias *(John 6:1)*. Sometimes names are changed because of time. At other times, one place or person can be called by two or more names at the same time. Still yet, there are times that someone or something is called by a name merely to make a point. For example, Simon Peter was called Satan to make a point *(Mark 8:33)*. The reader must always consider the context when seeking to determine the purpose of such uses.

Sunday, Day 351—Church Day (no devotional)
Monday, Day 352—*Who Is a Witness?*
Tuesday, Day 353—*To What Should We Give Witness?*
Wednesday, Day 354—Church Night (no devotional)
Thursday, Day 355—*The Purpose of Power*
Friday, Day 356—*To Whom Should We Witness?*
Saturday, Day 357—*The Natural Effect of Faith*

Day 351: Church Day

*Romans 1:16 For **I am not ashamed of the gospel of Christ**: for it is the power of God unto salvation to every one that believeth; to the Jew first, and also to the Greek.*

Day 352: (Monday)
Who Is a Witness?

*Acts 2:32 This Jesus hath God raised up, whereof **we all are witnesses**.*

Introductory Thoughts

A witness is one who testifies to the certainty of an event. As such, the apostles gave witness to the resurrection of the Lord Jesus Christ. By doing so, they were declaring the resurrection to be an absolute truth. The disciples physically witnessed the fact that the Lord Jesus Christ had been put to death, but was alive and well. Although no believer today physically saw the birth, life, death, burial, or resurrection of the Lord Jesus Christ, we can and should still testify to its truthfulness. In order to offer an adequate witness of the Lord's saving grace, an individual must first have experienced the new birth combined with the witness of God's indwelling Spirit *(1 John 5:10)*.

DEVOTIONAL THOUGHTS

- **(For children):** The apostles were excited to tell others about the Lord Jesus *(Acts 4:20)*. They had been with Him. Even though none of us have seen the Lord, Peter said we have something we can trust - the Bible *(2 Peter 1:16-21)*. God's word is pure and true *(Psalm 119:140, 160a)*. Using the Bible, we can tell others about the Lord.
- **(For everyone):** Why would it be difficult for an unbeliever to be a good witness for the Lord Jesus Christ? How does this limit the number of witnesses available to speak for the Lord?
- Though we have not physically seen the resurrected Christ, we can read of Him in the scriptures. How can the scripture lend us authority to be good witnesses for the Lord?

PRAYER THOUGHTS

- Ask the Lord to forgive you for failing to witness for Him.
- Ask the Lord to teach you how to witness.

SONG: *AMAZING GRACE!*

Day 353: (Tuesday)
To What Should We Give Witness?

Acts 4:33 And **with great power gave the apostles witness of the resurrection of the Lord Jesus:** *and great grace was upon them all.*

INTRODUCTORY THOUGHTS

In order to be saved, a person must place his faith solely upon Christ's death, burial, and resurrection for the means of salvation. Paul defined this central body of truth as the gospel of the grace of God *(1 Corinthians 15:1-4; Acts 20:24)*. Though believers may tell what the Lord has done in their lives since being saved, the most important truth when witnessing involves Christ's crucifixion, death, and resurrection from the dead. This truth, the resurrection of the Lord Jesus, became the theme of the early church. A careful study of the evangelistic messages of the early church testifies to this fact. Just as this doctrine historically served as the central truth when dealing with the lost, it should continue to be so today.

DEVOTIONAL THOUGHTS

- **(For children):** Jesus proved He was the Son of God by His resurrection from the dead *(Romans 1:4)*. A person must believe this to be saved *(Romans 10:9)*. Paul was careful in His witness for the Lord to tell about the resurrection *(Acts 17:2-3)*.
- **(For everyone):** Why is it so important to give witness to the death, burial, and resurrection when speaking to the lost about their need for salvation? What happens when we fail to teach this truth?
- How could a personal testimony aid when witnessing to the lost? How could you work the gospel of the grace of God into your own personal testimony?

PRAYER THOUGHTS

- Ask the Lord to show you the importance of the resurrection.
- Ask God to give you boldness to tell the lost about the gospel.

SONG: *I LOVE TO TELL THE STORY*

Day 354: Church Night

*Acts 20:31 Therefore watch, and remember, that by the space of three years **I ceased not to warn every one night and day with tears**.*

Day 355: (Thursday)
The Purpose of Power

*Acts 1:8 But **ye shall receive power**, after that the Holy Ghost is come upon you: **and ye shall be witnesses unto me** both in Jerusalem, and in all Judaea, and in Samaria, and unto the uttermost part of the earth.*

INTRODUCTORY THOUGHTS

The powers demonstrated by the apostles have consumed many Bible teachers who fail to grasp the place and purpose of those powers. These teachers instruct believers to seek the same power that was bestowed upon Peter and Paul and the other apostles. Careful Bible study demonstrates that the motive in this teaching is misplaced. The power given to the apostles was given for the purpose of assisting them in telling a lost and dying world about a risen Saviour. Much of the modern teaching centers upon pride and encourages a selfish Christianity. The biblical power given to the apostles was meant to strengthen their witness to others, not simply to be a self-serving instrument. Modern Christianity focuses on self, while biblical Christianity focuses on the Saviour and others.

DEVOTIONAL THOUGHTS

- **(For children):** Paul said he could do anything the Lord wanted him to do because Christ would give him the strength to do it *(Philippians 4:13)*. God wanted him to witness *(Acts 9:15)*, so the Lord gave him the power to do so *(1 Thessalonians 1:5a; 1 Corinthians 2:4-5)*.
- **(For everyone):** Though there are some differences in the manifestation of power from God, believers should still seek power from the Lord to witness to others. Why is this power important?
- Why are we dependent upon the Lord for help in witnessing? How successful will our methods of evangelism be without the power of God?

PRAYER THOUGHTS

- Ask the Lord to give you His power when witnessing.
- Thank the Lord for the times He has helped you to witness.

SONG: *MUST I GO AND EMPTY-HANDED?*

Day 356: (Friday)
To Whom Should We Witness?

*Acts 22:15 For **thou shalt be his witness unto all men** of what thou hast seen and heard.*

INTRODUCTORY THOUGHTS

The question of an appropriate audience to receive witness of the resurrection may seem quite simple at first. However, the issue is somewhat controversial. Some erroneously teach that believers should only witness to Jews, while others teach that believers should witness to all except for Jews. Others might suggest that believers should not witness to any of the lost because God has chosen some to die and go to hell. These teachings exist for many reasons, none of which are scriptural. The biblical pattern for the New Testament church is that believers should *"witness unto all men."* Everyone needs the opportunity to hear the gospel, despite his or her background or current living conditions. The whole world needs to hear that Christ has risen!

DEVOTIONAL THOUGHTS

- **(For children):** The Lord is not willing that any should perish *(2 Peter 3:9)*. He wants all men to be saved *(1 Timothy 2:4)*. The Samaritans were disliked by the Jews, yet Jesus traveled through Samaria to witness to one of them *(John 4:3-4)*.
- **(For everyone):** What people groups can you name that have been neglected concerning the reception of the gospel? Why have these people been neglected? Are these scriptural reasons for this neglect?
- When is the last time you thanked the Lord for the fact that He did not discriminate against you when it came to His plan to save all those that would believe?

PRAYER THOUGHTS

- Thank the Lord for leading someone to tell you the gospel.
- Ask the Lord to give you a heart to witness to all men.

SONG: *RESCUE THE PERISHING*

Day 357: (Saturday)
The Natural Effect of Faith

*2 Corinthians 4:13 We having the same spirit of faith, according as it is written, **I believed, and therefore have I spoken; we also believe, and therefore speak;***

INTRODUCTORY THOUGHTS

Faith moves a believer to speak on the Lord's behalf. If an individual believed a building would burn to the ground, he would naturally desire to warn those in danger. Believers in like manner desire to tell the lost of the judgment to come. Those who truly believe God's impending judgment to be real and the way of salvation to be unquestionably necessary will naturally desire for their loved ones to learn these truths before eternally too late. If a person claims to have trusted the gospel for salvation but lacks a desire to tell others, that person should examine his conversion to confirm its genuineness.

DEVOTIONAL THOUGHTS

- **(For children):** When we get a new toy, clothes, etc., we cannot wait to tell others. This applies to one's salvation too. It is the most important thing that can happen to anyone *(Mark 8:36)*. Our sins are forgiven and we get to be with God forever *(John 3:16)*. We should desire most of all to tell others this good news.
- **(For everyone):** Why should it be natural for a believer to want others to know the gospel of the Lord Jesus? What does it suggest if that desire does not exist in you?
- Are any of your immediate family members lost? Do any of your friends confess that they have never asked the Lord Jesus to be their Saviour? What are you going to do to help them?

PRAYER THOUGHTS

- Ask the Lord to examine your heart for a desire to witness.
Ask God to work in the hearts of your friends and loved ones.

SONG: *JESUS! AND SHALL IT EVER BE!*

Notes: _____

_____

_____

_____

_____

_____

_____

_____

_____

_____

_____

_____

Notes: _____

_____

_____

_____

_____

_____

_____

_____

_____

_____

_____

_____

_____

_____

_____

Quotes from the next volume

(VOLUME 3, WEEK 51)

Subject: Violence

The excessive presence of violence conveys much about the nature of any time, past or present.

Riches do not take away a man's desire for violence. In fact, riches often promote a man's hunger for violence. Many have suggested that poverty lies at the root of much of the violence in the world; however, the scriptures teach otherwise.

When men cannot fulfil the lusts of their flesh in a righteous manner, they often resort to any means necessary, including violence.

52
Witnessing (con't)

Witnessing—found eighty-eight times in seventy-four Old Testament verses and 103 times in ninety-three verses in the New Testament

Variations: witness, witnessed, witnesses, witnesseth, witnessing

First usage in the New Testament: *Matthew 15:19* (witness)

Last usage in the Old Testament: *Malachi 3:5* (witness)

Interesting fact: God led Paul to implement a new practice that he wrote about in *Romans 1:16*. Paul would first preach to the Jews in each city that he entered. At each stop, after they rejected his message, he would then turn to the Gentiles. Some well-meaning Bible teachers teach that this practice continued even into the present day. Few of these teachers emphasize the truths that Paul also taught saying, *"[t]ribulation and anguish"* would be *"upon every soul of man that doeth evil, of **the Jew first, and also of the Gentile" (Romans 2:9)**.* The whole truth is that the *"Jew first"* principle was both a blessing and a curse and also time-sensitive during the first century.

Bible study tip: At times, in the book of Acts, it can be difficult to determine which people accompanied Paul to the various locations. However, Luke wrote the book of Acts. Always consider the pronouns *we* and *us* in order to locate and understand the times that Luke accompanied Paul.

Sunday, Day 358—Church Day (no devotional)
Monday, Day 359—*Be Ready to Give an Answer*
Tuesday, Day 360—*Praying for an Open Door*
Wednesday, Day 361—Church Night (no devotional)
Thursday, Day 362—*A Threefold Witness*
Friday, Day 363—*I Speak This to Your Shame*
Saturday, Day 364—*Why Christians Fail to Witness*

Day 358: Church Day

*2 Corinthians 4:5 For **we preach not ourselves, but Christ Jesus the Lord**; and ourselves your servants for Jesus' sake.*

Day 359: (Monday)
Be Ready to Give an Answer

*1 Peter 3:15 But sanctify the Lord God in your hearts: and **be ready always to give an answer to every man that asketh you a reason of the hope that is in you** with meekness and fear:*

INTRODUCTORY THOUGHTS

If a believer lives a life to the glory of God, there will come a time when the world wants to know *"a reason of the hope"* that lies within him. Simon Peter addressed this within the context of times of persecution. When believers were known to *"suffer for righteousness' sake" (1 Peter 3:14)*, the world would want to question their hope. Simon Peter reminded them of the importance of knowing how to answer their persecutors. Likewise, believers should know how to answer those curious about the gospel of the Lord Jesus Christ. How shameful is it for believers who do not even know how to explain the need for and plan of salvation?

DEVOTIONAL THOUGHTS

- **(For children):** *1 Timothy 1:1* says the Lord Jesus Christ is our hope. Paul and Silas were beaten and put into prison. Instead of complaining about their circumstances, they chose to pray and sing. The jailor witnessed their unexpected hope and wanted it for himself too. When the jailor asked how to be saved, Paul and Silas were ready with the answer for a man who had already repented. It was to "Believe" *(Acts 16:30-31)*.
- **(For everyone):** Do those around you know that you are saved by the grace of God? When is the last time someone saw something in your life that led them to ask you of the *"hope that is in you"*?
- If someone were to ask you how to be saved, what would you tell him? To what scriptures would you lead him to explain what Christ has done and what that individual needs to do to be saved?

PRAYER THOUGHTS

- Ask the Lord to teach you how to be a better witness for Him.
- Ask the Lord to help you be diligent knowing the scriptures.

SONG: *JESUS SAVES!*

Day 360: (Tuesday)
Praying for an Open Door

Colossians 4:2 Continue in prayer, and watch in the same with thanksgiving;

*3 Withal **praying** also for us, **that God would open unto us a door of utterance, to speak the mystery of Christ**, for which I am also in bonds:*

INTRODUCTORY THOUGHTS

Every unsaved person will have windows of opportunities when he becomes most receptive to the gospel of Christ. The Devil works hard to keep people in darkness and will distract them by every means necessary (i.e., the death of a loved one, a crying child, a ringing phone, busyness, etc.). The salvation of a soul involves a spiritual battle that can only be won by the Lord's intervention. There is a window of time when the lost are most receptive to the gospel, likewise suggesting only a window of opportunity for the saved to speak for Christ. This is the very reason the apostle Paul stressed the importance of the saints of God beseeching the Lord to open to them a door of utterance *(Ephesians 6:19)*.

DEVOTIONAL THOUGHTS

- **(For children)**: When Philip heard the eunuch reading from Isaiah, he asked him if he understood what he was reading. The eunuch admitted that he needed help. A simple question became Philip's "open door" to tell the eunuch about the Lord *(Acts 8:30-38)*.
- **(For everyone)**: Do you remember how the Devil tried to distract you from your need to be saved? What has he done to keep your loved ones from considering their need to be saved? Why is it so important to pray for an open door?
- Paul's prayer was not only for the open door of the hearer of the gospel, but also for the open door of the one giving the gospel. When is the last time you prayed for an open door?

PRAYER THOUGHTS

- Ask the Lord to open a door of utterance for you.
- Ask God to open doors for others to speak to your loved ones.

SONG: *SEND THE LIGHT*

Day 361: Church Night

*2 Corinthians 10:14 For we stretch not ourselves beyond our measure, as though we reached not unto you: for **we are come as far as to you also in preaching the gospel of Christ**:*

15 Not boasting of things without our measure, that is, of other men's labours; but having hope, when your faith is increased, that we shall be enlarged by you according to our rule abundantly,

*16 **To preach the gospel in the regions beyond you**, and not to boast in another man's line of things made ready to our hand.*

Day 362: (Thursday)
A Threefold Witness

Acts 20:20 And *how I kept back nothing that was profitable unto you, but* **have shewed you**, *and* **have taught you publickly**, *and* **from house to house**,

INTRODUCTORY THOUGHTS

The gospel witness involves a message that is narrow in scope, but it can be distributed using a variety of methods. The apostle Paul provided three means by which he ministered the word: he shewed them, he taught them publickly, and he ministered the word from house to house. These same three categories exist even today. Believers can preach the gospel in church services, in publick settings, and from house to house. Even within these areas, the gospel can be spread audibly or by using a printed medium. Every believer should take part in at least some form of witnessing. One very effective means involves the distribution of gospel tracts. Truly, there exists no adequate excuse for a believer not to give the gospel to others.

DEVOTIONAL THOUGHTS

- **(For children):** When Andrew met the Lord, he went and told his brother Simon *(John 1:40-42)*. Philip told his friend Nathanael *(John 1:45-46)*. We need to tell our family and friends about the Lord. Could you invite others to church so they too can hear the word of God?
- **(For everyone):** What purpose does each category serve that Paul implemented into his ministry? Why is it important that believers take part in ministering to others publicly as well as from house to house?
- How many lost people would you estimate visit your services at church on a weekly basis? How many lost people do not even consider attending church services? How can you reach those people with the gospel?

PRAYER THOUGHTS

- Ask the Lord to help you witness in each way.
- Ask God to give you boldness to invite lost people to church.

SONG: *FOOTPRINTS OF JESUS*

Day 363: (Friday)
I Speak This to Your Shame

*1 Corinthians 15:34 Awake to righteousness, and sin not; for **some have not the knowledge of God: I speak this to your shame**.*

INTRODUCTORY THOUGHTS

There are people everywhere who are not saved, no matter where anyone lives. In addition to that, there may also be those who do not even have the knowledge of God. Unfortunately, many believers take for granted that all those who live in certain developed nations of the world have heard the gospel of Christ. This simply is not true. As fewer preach and teach the gospel of God's grace, the number of those ignorant of these truths continues to increase exponentially. In addition to this, those propagating damnable doctrines continue to muddy the message of salvation. These realities increase the responsibility of true believers to be better ambassadors for Christ. Paul expressed these truths when writing to the believers in Corinth. He told them about the ignorance of some in their midst and put the blame squarely upon those who knew the truth and refused to witness.

DEVOTIONAL THOUGHTS

- **(For children)**: Many do not know the true gospel *(1 Corinthians 15:1-4)*. Some consider their good works sufficient to earn them a place in heaven. This is absolutely wrong *(Galatians 1:6-9)*. Find yourself a good gospel tract. Smile and say, "I would like to give you something good to read," as you hand it to someone.
- **(For everyone)**: Who is responsible for sharing the gospel to those in your family who are without God? What about those in your community? How are you accountable, in part, for their ignorance?
- Though many are ashamed of the gospel of Christ, the true shame lies in not sharing the gospel with others. Why is it a shameful thing to be silent concerning the gospel?

PRAYER THOUGHTS

- Ask God to remind you of those that do not know Him.
- Thank the Lord for the time when someone gave you the gospel.

SONG: *HE WAS NOT WILLING*

Day 364: (Saturday)
Why Christians Fail to Witness

*Romans 1:16 For **I am not ashamed of the gospel of Christ**: for it is the power of God unto salvation to every one that believeth; to the Jew first, and also to the Greek.*

INTRODUCTORY THOUGHTS

The average believer when asked about his efforts to share the gospel may offer up several "reasons" why it is not feasible for him or her to tell others about their need for salvation. These reasons often seem spiritual in nature and are sometimes even accompanied by verses of scripture for support. However, the real truth is that believers who do not witness fail to do so because they are ashamed. Those believers who refuse to witness will be offended by this statement, but the apostle Paul confirms its validity. The reason Paul was *"ready to preach the gospel"* to those who were at Rome was because he was *"not ashamed of the gospel of Christ."* Why was he not ashamed? Because he knew that it was *"the power of God unto salvation."* Those who do not witness may offer excuses, but in reality they fail to believe in the power of God.

DEVOTIONAL THOUGHTS

- **(For children):** Read *Psalm 119:46*. Sometimes we fail to speak up for the Lord because we feel the other person will reject what we say. Remember that when some refuse the words of the Bible, they are rejecting God Himself, not you. Consider *1 Samuel 8:7*.
- **(For everyone):** Why did Paul have to admonish Timothy not to be *"ashamed of the testimony"* of the Lord *(2 Timothy 1:8)*? What part might afflictions play in being ashamed?
- Do you worry that others might get angry with you for witnessing to them? Do you worry that persecution might be the response of your efforts to witness? How is this likened to being ashamed in *2 Timothy 1:8*?

PRAYER THOUGHTS

- Ask the Lord to help you know when you are ashamed.
- Thank the Lord for what He did for you on Calvary.

SONG: *ASHAMED, BUT NOT OF JESUS*

Notes: _____

_____

_____

_____

_____

_____

_____

_____

_____

_____

_____

_____

_____

_____

_____

_____

_____

_____

_____

Quotes from the next volume

(VOLUME 3, WEEK 52)

Subject: Violence (con't)

At times it may appear as though the wicked have the upper hand on the righteous, but the LORD knows what is happening in the world. The Bible says of God that His soul hateth *"him that loveth violence."*

As violence increases, the saint's dependence upon the Lord for safety becomes increasingly apparent.

Scripture Index

Genesis 1:27	241	Genesis 12:13	259
Genesis 2:21	236	Genesis 13:5	366
Genesis 2:22	236	Genesis 13:6	366
Genesis 2:23	236	Genesis 13:7	366
Genesis 2:24	236	Genesis 13:8	366
Genesis 2:25	236	Genesis 13:9	323, 366
Genesis 3:4	126	Genesis 14:2	387
Genesis 3:7	237	Genesis 14:21	330
Genesis 3:8	101, 111, 261	Genesis 14:22	330
Genesis 3:9	101, 315	Genesis 14:23	330
Genesis 3:10	101, 237, 315	Genesis 14:24	330
Genesis 3:11	43, 101, 315	Genesis 15:1	97, 102
Genesis 3:12	43, 315	Genesis 15:14	187
Genesis 3:13	315	Genesis 17:17	179, 180
Genesis 3:21	235	Genesis 18:9	180
Genesis 4:5	357	Genesis 18:10	180
Genesis 4:15	379, 380	Genesis 18:11	180
Genesis 4:26	259, 261	Genesis 18:12	180
Genesis 5:22	111	Genesis 18:13	180
Genesis 6:5	339, 341, 381	Genesis 18:14	180
Genesis 6:6	381	Genesis 18:15	180
Genesis 6:7	381	Genesis 19:16	384
Genesis 6:8	381	Genesis 19:24	384
Genesis 6:9	381	Genesis 20:11	343
Genesis 6:10	381	Genesis 21:30	403
Genesis 9:1	325	Genesis 22:2	203, 205
Genesis 9:2	97	Genesis 22:12	102
Genesis 9:20	364	Genesis 24:26	265
Genesis 11:1	365	Genesis 24:27	195
Genesis 11:2	365	Genesis 24:60	163
Genesis 11:3	365	Genesis 24:63	219
Genesis 11:4	325, 365	Genesis 25:8	56
Genesis 11:5	325, 365	Genesis 25:34	38
Genesis 11:6	325, 365	Genesis 26:10	382
Genesis 11:7	325, 365	Genesis 26:24	99
Genesis 11:8	325, 365	Genesis 27:34	25
Genesis 11:9	365	Genesis 28:22	157
Genesis 12:1	325	Genesis 29:20	216
Genesis 12:2	325	Genesis 29:30	163
Genesis 12:3	325	Genesis 29:31	163, 169

Genesis 29:32 169
Genesis 29:33 169
Genesis 29:34 169
Genesis 29:35 . . . . 169, 251
Genesis 31:42 299
Genesis 31:49 395
Genesis 33:14 201
Genesis 35:18 56
Genesis 39:5 140
Genesis 39:6 140
Genesis 41:51 134
Genesis 49:6 363
Genesis 50:17 . . . . 129, 134
Genesis 50:21 134

Exodus 2:2 176
Exodus 2:3 176
Exodus 2:4 176
Exodus 2:5 176
Exodus 2:6 176
Exodus 2:7 176
Exodus 2:8 176
Exodus 2:9 176
Exodus 2:10 176
Exodus 2:13 106
Exodus 4:12 275
Exodus 5:9 371
Exodus 15:1 . . . . 253, 331, 333, 336
Exodus 15:6 253
Exodus 15:11 253
Exodus 15:22 247
Exodus 15:23 . . . . 25, 247
Exodus 15:24 . . . . 243, 244, 247
Exodus 15:25 247
Exodus 15:27 247
Exodus 17:1 247
Exodus 17:2 247
Exodus 17:3 247
Exodus 17:4 247
Exodus 17:5 247
Exodus 17:6 247
Exodus 18:19 65
Exodus 20:20 101
Exodus 23:13 400
Exodus 24:7 . . . . 283, 292
Exodus 24:12 278
Exodus 24:13 227
Exodus 25:2 160
Exodus 28:42 238

Exodus 32:25 237
Exodus 33:16 . . . . 323, 326
Exodus 34:14 167
Exodus 34:28 91
Exodus 36:2 151
Exodus 36:3 . . . . 151, 152
Exodus 36:4 151
Exodus 36:5 151
Exodus 36:7 152

Leviticus 5:5 49
Leviticus 6:2 . . . . 105, 106
Leviticus 16:29 89
Leviticus 18:6 237
Leviticus 18:20 33
Leviticus 19:32 311
Leviticus 19:33 173
Leviticus 19:34 173
Leviticus 27:32 148

Numbers 5:7 51
Numbers 6:1 327
Numbers 6:2 327
Numbers 6:3 327
Numbers 7:1 146
Numbers 7:2 146
Numbers 7:3 146
Numbers 7:4 146
Numbers 7:5 146
Numbers 11:1 245
Numbers 14:1 245
Numbers 14:2 245
Numbers 16:1 248
Numbers 16:2 248
Numbers 16:3 248
Numbers 16:11 248
Numbers 16:32 248
Numbers 16:33 248
Numbers 20:2 247
Numbers 20:8 247
Numbers 21:5 249
Numbers 21:6 249

Deuteronomy 1:27 248
Deuteronomy 2:9 73
Deuteronomy 4:9 278
Deuteronomy 4:10 . . . . 101, 278
Deuteronomy 6:5 204
Deuteronomy 7:7 248

Deuteronomy 7:8 248
Deuteronomy 8:5 379
Deuteronomy 8:17 352
Deuteronomy 8:18 352
Deuteronomy 10:19 213
Deuteronomy 11:19 223
Deuteronomy 16:17 157
Deuteronomy 17:14 284
Deuteronomy 17:15 284
Deuteronomy 17:18 . . . . 284, 288
Deuteronomy 17:19 . . . . 284, 288
Deuteronomy 22:5 . . . . 238, 241
Deuteronomy 28:52 . . . . 347, 357
Deuteronomy 31:11 292
Deuteronomy 31:19 336
Deuteronomy 32:21 373
Deuteronomy 32:22 373
Deuteronomy 32:29 318
Deuteronomy 32:35 . . . . 380, 383
Deuteronomy 32:41 . . . . 380, 384
Deuteronomy 32:43 384

Joshua 1:1. . . . . 200, 229
Joshua 1:2. 200
Joshua 1:8. . . . . 219, 220, 222
Joshua 7:19 . . . . 50, 53
Joshua 8:34 . . . . 285, 286
Joshua 8:35 286
Joshua 9:14 . . . . 65, 68
Joshua 24:14 102

Judges 11:36. 384
Judges 16:4. 209
Judges 20:7. 66
Judges 20:26. 89

Ruth 1:16 349
Ruth 1:20 25
Ruth 2:11 . . . . 63, 349
Ruth 2:12 . . . . 348, 349
Ruth 3:11 63

1 Samuel 1:8 94
1 Samuel 1:9 94
1 Samuel 1:10 . . . . 28, 94
1 Samuel 1:18 94
1 Samuel 2:1 . . . . 253, 260
1 Samuel 2:2 . . . . 253, 260
1 Samuel 2:3 . . . . 253, 260

1 Samuel 2:4 260
1 Samuel 2:5 260
1 Samuel 2:6 260
1 Samuel 2:7 260
1 Samuel 2:8 260
1 Samuel 2:9 260
1 Samuel 2:10 260
1 Samuel 2:23 208
1 Samuel 2:24 208
1 Samuel 2:26 200
1 Samuel 3:13 208
1 Samuel 7:3 52
1 Samuel 7:4 52
1 Samuel 7:5 52
1 Samuel 7:6 52
1 Samuel 8:7 417
1 Samuel 12:14 103
1 Samuel 12:16 302
1 Samuel 12:17 302
1 Samuel 12:18 302
1 Samuel 12:19 302
1 Samuel 12:20 . . . . 103, 302
1 Samuel 12:21 . . . . 302, 374
1 Samuel 12:22 302
1 Samuel 12:23 . . . . 260, 280, 302
1 Samuel 12:24 . . . . 103, 302
1 Samuel 12:25 302
1 Samuel 13:8 344
1 Samuel 13:9 344
1 Samuel 13:10 344
1 Samuel 13:11 344
1 Samuel 13:12 344
1 Samuel 13:13 344
1 Samuel 13:14 . . . . 7, 344
1 Samuel 14:6 . . . . 86, 358
1 Samuel 14:7 86
1 Samuel 16:7 239
1 Samuel 17:4 392
1 Samuel 17:5 392
1 Samuel 17:6 392
1 Samuel 17:7 392
1 Samuel 17:11 100
1 Samuel 17:24 100
1 Samuel 17:32 100
1 Samuel 17:37 100
1 Samuel 17:38 392
1 Samuel 17:39 392
1 Samuel 17:45 392
1 Samuel 17:46 392

1 Samuel 17:47 392
1 Samuel 23:15 197
1 Samuel 23:16 197
1 Samuel 23:17 197
1 Samuel 25:28 383
1 Samuel 25:30 383
1 Samuel 25:31 383
1 Samuel 25:32 383
1 Samuel 25:33 383
1 Samuel 25:38 383
1 Samuel 30:11 177
1 Samuel 30:12 177
1 Samuel 30:13 177
1 Samuel 30:14 177
1 Samuel 30:15 177

2 Samuel 1:12 94
2 Samuel 2:8 365
2 Samuel 2:9 365
2 Samuel 2:10 365
2 Samuel 2:11 365
2 Samuel 3:17 41
2 Samuel 5:1 365
2 Samuel 5:2 365
2 Samuel 5:3 365
2 Samuel 5:4 365
2 Samuel 5:5 365
2 Samuel 12:7 118
2 Samuel 12:9 304
2 Samuel 12:13 304
2 Samuel 12:14 281
2 Samuel 12:16 94
2 Samuel 13:1 209
2 Samuel 18:9 . . . . 116, 241
2 Samuel 18:14 241
2 Samuel 18:15 241
2 Samuel 22:3 350
2 Samuel 22:4 . . . . 252, 253
2 Samuel 22:16 307
2 Samuel 23:8 393
2 Samuel 23:9 393
2 Samuel 23:10 393
2 Samuel 23:11 393
2 Samuel 23:12 393

1 Kings 2:2. 393
1 Kings 2:3. 393
1 Kings 3:9. 191
1 Kings 3:24. 191

1 Kings 3:25. 191
1 Kings 3:26. 191
1 Kings 3:27. 191
1 Kings 8:22. 253
1 Kings 8:23. 253
1 Kings 8:24. 253
1 Kings 8:35. 51
1 Kings 8:54. 265
1 Kings 11:1. 209
1 Kings 11:4. . . . . 45, 110
1 Kings 11:9. 110
1 Kings 12:25. 69
1 Kings 12:26. 69
1 Kings 12:27. 69
1 Kings 12:28. 69
1 Kings 12:29. 69
1 Kings 12:30. 69
1 Kings 15:13. 190
1 Kings 17:13. 150
1 Kings 18:26. 273
1 Kings 18:36. 273
1 Kings 18:37. 273
1 Kings 19:13. 386
1 Kings 19:14. 386
1 Kings 19:19. 229
1 Kings 19:20. 229
1 Kings 19:21. 229

2 Kings 3:11. 228
2 Kings 4:5. 324
2 Kings 4:8. 174
2 Kings 4:9. 174
2 Kings 4:10. 174
2 Kings 5:11. 344
2 Kings 6:15. 358
2 Kings 6:16. 358
2 Kings 6:17. 358
2 Kings 7:5. 192
2 Kings 7:6. 192
2 Kings 7:7. 192
2 Kings 7:8. 192
2 Kings 7:9. 192
2 Kings 7:10. 192
2 Kings 14:26. 26
2 Kings 17:15. 375
2 Kings 22:11. 291
2 Kings 22:16. 291
2 Kings 22:17. 291
2 Kings 22:18. 291

2 Kings 22:19 291
2 Kings 22:20 291
2 Kings 23:1 286
2 Kings 23:2 . . . . 286, 292
2 Kings 23:25 328

1 Chronicles 13:8 337
1 Chronicles 16:9 332
1 Chronicles 16:25 255
1 Chronicles 17:25 262
1 Chronicles 19:4 237
1 Chronicles 19:5 237
1 Chronicles 23:1 331
1 Chronicles 23:2 331
1 Chronicles 23:3 331
1 Chronicles 23:4 331
1 Chronicles 23:5 331
1 Chronicles 23:30 256
1 Chronicles 25:8 276
1 Chronicles 28:3 331
1 Chronicles 28:9 342
1 Chronicles 29:3 161
1 Chronicles 29:9 . . . . 152, 159, 160

2 Chronicles 5:1 331
2 Chronicles 5:13 255
2 Chronicles 7:5 331
2 Chronicles 7:6 331
2 Chronicles 18:7 167
2 Chronicles 19:1 330
2 Chronicles 19:2 . . . . 165, 330
2 Chronicles 20:1 94
2 Chronicles 20:2 94
2 Chronicles 20:3 94
2 Chronicles 20:4 94
2 Chronicles 24:2 376
2 Chronicles 24:17 376
2 Chronicles 24:18 376
2 Chronicles 24:19 376
2 Chronicles 25:14 . . . . 67, 304
2 Chronicles 25:15 . . . . 67, 304
2 Chronicles 25:16 . . . . 67, 304
2 Chronicles 26:4 374
2 Chronicles 26:16 374
2 Chronicles 26:17 374
2 Chronicles 26:18 374
2 Chronicles 26:19 374
2 Chronicles 26:20 374
2 Chronicles 26:21 374

2 Chronicles 30:22 53
2 Chronicles 34:3 328
2 Chronicles 34:33 328

Ezra 4:1 70
Ezra 4:2 70
Ezra 4:3 . . . . 70, 329
Ezra 4:4 70
Ezra 4:5 70
Ezra 7:10 230
Ezra 8:21 95
Ezra 10:1 53
Ezra 10:11 . . . . 51, 52

Nehemiah 2:19 181
Nehemiah 8:3 292
Nehemiah 8:8 . . . . 230, 292
Nehemiah 9:1 . . . . 55, 287
Nehemiah 9:2 . . . . 55, 287
Nehemiah 9:3 . . . . 55, 287
Nehemiah 9:5 257
Nehemiah 9:6 111
Nehemiah 9:20 289
Nehemiah 10:39 4
Nehemiah 12:42 337
Nehemiah 13:11 . . . . 75, 76
Nehemiah 13:15 76
Nehemiah 13:16 76
Nehemiah 13:17 76
Nehemiah 13:18 76
Nehemiah 13:19 76
Nehemiah 13:20 76
Nehemiah 13:21 76
Nehemiah 13:22 76
Nehemiah 13:23 76
Nehemiah 13:24 76
Nehemiah 13:25 76
Nehemiah 13:26 76

Esther 1:10 240
Esther 1:11 240
Esther 1:12 240
Esther 4:16 91

Job 1:21 238
Job 3:1 29
Job 3:20 28
Job 4:14 98
Job 7:11 28

Job 10:1 28
Job 13:15 . . . . 348, 358
Job 15:31 350
Job 17:5 . . . . 113, 117, 121
Job 21:25 28
Job 22:10 98
Job 23:12 295
Job 24:7 237
Job 29:15 173
Job 29:16 173
Job 31:32 173
Job 32:6 311
Job 32:11 311
Job 32:12 311
Job 32:21 119
Job 32:22 119
Job 38:4 332
Job 38:5 332
Job 38:6 332
Job 38:7 . . . . 332, 333
Job 42:1 343
Job 42:2 343
Job 42:6 343

Psalm 1:1 69
Psalm 1:2 . . . . 222, 341
Psalm 2:1 374
Psalm 2:4 185
Psalm 2:11 103
Psalm 2:12 359
Psalm 4:2 374
Psalm 4:4 315
Psalm 5:3 269
Psalm 5:5 164
Psalm 5:9 . . . . 114, 115
Psalm 5:11 359
Psalm 7:17 255
Psalm 9:10 360
Psalm 10:4 . . . . 344, 345
Psalm 10:14 17
Psalm 11:4 . . . . 356, 385
Psalm 11:5 164
Psalm 11:7 . . . . 212, 214
Psalm 12:1 115
Psalm 12:2 . . . . 115, 116, 121
Psalm 12:3 . . . . 115, 116
Psalm 12:4 . . . . 115, 116
Psalm 12:5 17
Psalm 13:5 359

Psalm 13:6 336
Psalm 14:6 17
Psalm 15:1 10
Psalm 15:2 10
Psalm 15:3 . . . . 9, 10
Psalm 16:7 66
Psalm 18:47 380
Psalm 19:7 69
Psalm 19:8 69
Psalm 19:14 . . . . 15, 221
Psalm 20:7 348
Psalm 21:13 255
Psalm 22:3 . . . . 255, 257
Psalm 22:7 181
Psalm 22:8 181
Psalm 25:4 276
Psalm 25:5 276
Psalm 25:6 276
Psalm 25:8 276
Psalm 25:9 276
Psalm 25:12 276
Psalm 26:4 375
Psalm 26:5 167
Psalm 27:1 98
Psalm 27:2 388
Psalm 27:3 388
Psalm 27:4 5
Psalm 27:11 5
Psalm 28:7 . . . . 255, 356, 359
Psalm 30:9 256
Psalm 31:6 167
Psalm 31:19 360
Psalm 32:1 . . . . 118, 130
Psalm 32:2 118
Psalm 32:3 118
Psalm 32:4 118
Psalm 32:5 . . . . 50, 53, 118
Psalm 32:8 289
Psalm 32:10 360
Psalm 33:11 68
Psalm 34:1 256
Psalm 34:8 . . . . 358, 360
Psalm 34:11 210
Psalm 34:13 . . . . 46, 391
Psalm 34:14 . . . . 320, 369
Psalm 35:13 . . . . 92, 94, 95, 268
Psalm 35:28 256
Psalm 36:1 122
Psalm 36:2 122

Psalm 37:13 185
Psalm 37:14 57
Psalm 37:37 369
Psalm 38:1 310
Psalm 38:17 133
Psalm 38:18 . . . . 133, 317
Psalm 39:5 . . . . 122, 351, 372
Psalm 41:1 23
Psalm 44:6 357
Psalm 45:7 164
Psalm 45:17 256
Psalm 47:1 334
Psalm 47:6 334
Psalm 47:7 334
Psalm 48:6 98
Psalm 48:9 341
Psalm 49:6 352
Psalm 49:7 352
Psalm 49:8 352
Psalm 50:7 147
Psalm 50:8 147
Psalm 50:9 147
Psalm 50:10 147
Psalm 50:11 147
Psalm 50:12 147
Psalm 50:14 147
Psalm 50:15 147
Psalm 50:23 . . . . 57, 58
Psalm 51:3 . . . . 133, 304
Psalm 51:4 304
Psalm 51:12 133
Psalm 51:13 317
Psalm 51:14 337
Psalm 54:6 256
Psalm 55:21 115
Psalm 56:3 . . . . 99, 349
Psalm 56:4 349
Psalm 56:5 345
Psalm 58:10 384
Psalm 59:8 185
Psalm 62:9 372
Psalm 62:10 . . . . 351, 352
Psalm 62:11 233
Psalm 63:5 341
Psalm 63:6 341
Psalm 63:7 341
Psalm 64:3 30
Psalm 66:1 337
Psalm 66:2 337

Psalm 66:18 272
Psalm 68:10 17
Psalm 68:19 383
Psalm 69:10 95
Psalm 69:30 . . . . 256, 336
Psalm 69:33 17
Psalm 71:14 258
Psalm 73:3 385
Psalm 73:4 385
Psalm 73:5 385
Psalm 77:6 315
Psalm 77:12 223
Psalm 78:36 124
Psalm 81:1 337
Psalm 83:3 66
Psalm 84:2 7
Psalm 84:4 7
Psalm 85:2 130
Psalm 86:5 131
Psalm 86:7 261
Psalm 86:8 261
Psalm 86:10 261
Psalm 88:1 269
Psalm 94:1 . . . . 382, 383
Psalm 94:11 . . . . 342, 343, 374
Psalm 95:1 333
Psalm 95:2 333
Psalm 95:3 333
Psalm 96:13 190
Psalm 97:10 166
Psalm 99:9 233
Psalm 100:2 336
Psalm 101:1 336
Psalm 101:2 87
Psalm 101:3 167
Psalm 104:1 233
Psalm 104:5 307
Psalm 104:6 307
Psalm 104:7 307
Psalm 104:33 . . . . 256, 334
Psalm 104:34 222
Psalm 106:9 307
Psalm 106:21 247
Psalm 106:22 247
Psalm 106:35 166
Psalm 106:36 166
Psalm 107:1 233
Psalm 107:22 182
Psalm 109:4 270

Psalm 109:24 91
Psalm 111:9 119
Psalm 112:7 358
Psalm 115:4 350
Psalm 115:5 350
Psalm 115:6 350
Psalm 115:7 350
Psalm 115:8 350
Psalm 115:9 350
Psalm 115:11 102
Psalm 115:17 256
Psalm 115:18 256
Psalm 116:3 183
Psalm 116:4 183
Psalm 118:8 . . . . 352, 353
Psalm 118:9 . . . . 352, 353
Psalm 119:6 121
Psalm 119:11 . . . . 223, 288
Psalm 119:15 222
Psalm 119:18 299
Psalm 119:23 222
Psalm 119:24 69
Psalm 119:37 375
Psalm 119:46 417
Psalm 119:48 222
Psalm 119:59 . . . . 225, 318, 341
Psalm 119:63 110
Psalm 119:71 183
Psalm 119:78 222
Psalm 119:97 222
Psalm 119:99 222
Psalm 119:104 167
Psalm 119:105 296
Psalm 119:113 . . . . 167, 376
Psalm 119:115 167
Psalm 119:120 98
Psalm 119:130 372
Psalm 119:140 . . . . 212, 280, 405
Psalm 119:160 . . . . 280, 405
Psalm 119:162 185
Psalm 119:164 257
Psalm 119:165 369
Psalm 122:1 . . . . 7, 391
Psalm 126:1 . . . . 181, 336
Psalm 126:2 . . . . 181, 336
Psalm 126:3 181
Psalm 130:3 132
Psalm 130:4 132
Psalm 133:1 365

Psalm 133:2 366
Psalm 133:3 366
Psalm 138:2 223
Psalm 139:2 343
Psalm 139:3 343
Psalm 139:4 . . . . 12, 44, 343
Psalm 139:14 255
Psalm 139:21 167
Psalm 139:22 167
Psalm 139:23 342
Psalm 140:12 17
Psalm 141:2 265
Psalm 141:3 46
Psalm 141:5 . . . . 118, 310
Psalm 143:5 . . . . 222, 224, 341
Psalm 144:8 374
Psalm 144:11 374
Psalm 145:2 256
Psalm 145:4 224
Psalm 145:5 224
Psalm 145:6 224
Psalm 145:18 262
Psalm 146:3 352
Psalm 148:1 252
Psalm 148:2 252
Psalm 148:3 252
Psalm 148:4 252
Psalm 148:5 252
Psalm 148:6 252
Psalm 148:7 252
Psalm 148:8 252
Psalm 148:9 252
Psalm 148:10 252
Psalm 148:11 252
Psalm 148:12 . . . . 210, 252, 255
Psalm 148:13 . . . . 210, 252, 255
Psalm 148:14 252
Psalm 149:7 . . . . 380, 384
Psalm 150:1 255
Psalm 150:2 255
Psalm 150:3 255
Psalm 150:4 255
Psalm 150:5 255
Psalm 150:6 . . . . 255, 258

Proverbs 1:5 . . . . 67, 277
Proverbs 1:7 400
Proverbs 1:26 185
Proverbs 2:16 . . . . 121, 125

Proverbs 3:5. 357
Proverbs 3:9. 149
Proverbs 3:12. 208
Proverbs 5:4. 26
Proverbs 5:12. 277
Proverbs 5:13. 277
Proverbs 6:6. 22
Proverbs 6:16. . . . . 165, 367, 368
Proverbs 6:17. . . . . 165, 368
Proverbs 6:18. . . . . 165, 368
Proverbs 6:19. . . . . 165, 368
Proverbs 6:20. 124
Proverbs 6:21. 124
Proverbs 6:22. 124
Proverbs 6:23. 124
Proverbs 6:24. . . . . 121, 124, 125
Proverbs 6:34. . . . . 384, 385
Proverbs 7:4. 114
Proverbs 7:5. . . . . 114, 125
Proverbs 7:10. . . . . 238, 239
Proverbs 7:21. 125
Proverbs 8:32. 277
Proverbs 8:33. 277
Proverbs 9:7. . . . . 309, 310
Proverbs 9:8. . . . . 309, 310
Proverbs 10:12. . . . . 212, 216
Proverbs 10:17. 313
Proverbs 10:19. 42
Proverbs 10:27. 98
Proverbs 11:14. 67
Proverbs 11:16. 141
Proverbs 11:21. 364
Proverbs 11:25. 22
Proverbs 11:28. . . . . 351, 352
Proverbs 12:1. 313
Proverbs 12:11. 375
Proverbs 12:15. 67
Proverbs 12:27. 142
Proverbs 13:1. 309
Proverbs 13:18. 277
Proverbs 13:24. . . . . 208, 305
Proverbs 14:12. 316
Proverbs 14:13. 183
Proverbs 15:3. 51
Proverbs 15:8. 268
Proverbs 15:17. 214
Proverbs 15:22. 67
Proverbs 15:26. 344
Proverbs 16:18. 85

Proverbs 16:20. . . . . 360, 372
Proverbs 16:29. 198
Proverbs 16:31. 311
Proverbs 17:17. 215
Proverbs 18:8. 9
Proverbs 18:9. 140
Proverbs 18:19. 88
Proverbs 19:17. . . . . 20, 23
Proverbs 19:18. 208
Proverbs 19:20. 321
Proverbs 20:5. . . . . 65, 66
Proverbs 20:18. 67
Proverbs 20:19. 123
Proverbs 20:27. 315
Proverbs 21:17. . . . . 140, 141
Proverbs 21:20. 140
Proverbs 21:31. 357
Proverbs 22:9. 23
Proverbs 23:5. 141
Proverbs 23:7. 342
Proverbs 23:9. 310
Proverbs 23:22. 311
Proverbs 24:1. 166
Proverbs 24:6. 67
Proverbs 25:23. 14
Proverbs 26:4. 98
Proverbs 26:5. 98
Proverbs 26:22. 9
Proverbs 26:28. 117
Proverbs 27:2. 254
Proverbs 27:5. . . . . 305, 308
Proverbs 28:4. 78
Proverbs 28:7. 110
Proverbs 28:13. . . . . 50, 51
Proverbs 28:16. 167
Proverbs 28:19. . . . . 22, 375
Proverbs 28:23. . . . . 118, 303
Proverbs 28:26. 351
Proverbs 28:27. 23
Proverbs 29:5. . . . . 117, 121
Proverbs 29:15. 305
Proverbs 29:25. 99
Proverbs 30:5. . . . . 50, 286
Proverbs 30:8. 372
Proverbs 31:28. 253
Proverbs 31:29. 253
Proverbs 31:30. 351

Ecclesiastes 1:2 . . . . 371, 372

Ecclesiastes 1:14 372
Ecclesiastes 2:1 183
Ecclesiastes 2:2 .... 180, 183
Ecclesiastes 3:1 .... 94, 166
Ecclesiastes 3:2 166
Ecclesiastes 4:12 368
Ecclesiastes 5:1 6
Ecclesiastes 5:2 6
Ecclesiastes 5:3 .... 6, 42
Ecclesiastes 5:4 6
Ecclesiastes 5:5 6
Ecclesiastes 5:6 6
Ecclesiastes 5:7 .... 6, 42, 44
Ecclesiastes 7:3 183
Ecclesiastes 7:5 .... 300, 312
Ecclesiastes 8:11 384
Ecclesiastes 9:18 390
Ecclesiastes 12:1 210
Ecclesiastes 12:12 .... 283, 291, 296
Ecclesiastes 12:13 100

Isaiah 1:16 60
Isaiah 3:16 240
Isaiah 3:17 238
Isaiah 5:24 289
Isaiah 8:12 .... 98, 99
Isaiah 8:13 .... 98, 99
Isaiah 9:6 65
Isaiah 11:3 190
Isaiah 13:11 380
Isaiah 14:7 337
Isaiah 21:8 396
Isaiah 26:21 385
Isaiah 29:24 246
Isaiah 30:1 355
Isaiah 30:2 .... 355, 357
Isaiah 30:3 .... 355, 357
Isaiah 30:9 122
Isaiah 30:10 122
Isaiah 31:1 .... 355, 357
Isaiah 31:3 34
Isaiah 34:8 385
Isaiah 34:16 .... 284, 285
Isaiah 35:4 384
Isaiah 38:15 28
Isaiah 38:17 26
Isaiah 40:22 356
Isaiah 41:10 100
Isaiah 41:28 66

Isaiah 42:1 .... 203, 204
Isaiah 45:5 233
Isaiah 47:1 238
Isaiah 47:2 238
Isaiah 47:3 238
Isaiah 49:4 376
Isaiah 50:2 307
Isaiah 53:1 184
Isaiah 53:2 184
Isaiah 53:3 184
Isaiah 55:8 .... 18, 118, 183, 340
Isaiah 55:9 .... 18, 118, 183, 340
Isaiah 58:3 .... 89, 95
Isaiah 58:6 94
Isaiah 58:7 237
Isaiah 59:2 264
Isaiah 59:4 348
Isaiah 59:7 344
Isaiah 59:18 385
Isaiah 61:2 385
Isaiah 61:8 214
Isaiah 61:10 333
Isaiah 63:4 385
Isaiah 66:1 356
Isaiah 66:2 291

Jeremiah 2:5. 375
Jeremiah 4:14 342
Jeremiah 4:18 28
Jeremiah 5:22 368
Jeremiah 7:3. 349
Jeremiah 7:4. 349
Jeremiah 7:5. 349
Jeremiah 7:6. 349
Jeremiah 7:7. 349
Jeremiah 7:8. .... 348, 349
Jeremiah 9:1. .... 76, 77
Jeremiah 9:2. 77
Jeremiah 9:3. 77
Jeremiah 9:9. 77
Jeremiah 13:25 349
Jeremiah 16:17 55
Jeremiah 17:5 353
Jeremiah 17:6 353
Jeremiah 17:7 353
Jeremiah 20:9 78
Jeremiah 29:31 349
Jeremiah 31:34 134
Jeremiah 33:3 262

Jeremiah 46:10 .... 380, 384

Lamentations 1:4 26
Lamentations 3:40 .... 189, 318
Lamentations 3:60 383
Lamentations 3:64 383

Ezekiel 16:15 351
Ezekiel 16:49 384
Ezekiel 16:50 384
Ezekiel 25:15 380
Ezekiel 33:6 396
Ezekiel 33:7 398

Daniel 3:14..................... 79
Daniel 3:15..................... 79
Daniel 3:16..................... 79
Daniel 3:17................. 79, 348
Daniel 3:18................. 79, 348
Daniel 4:13..................... 395
Daniel 4:17..................... 395
Daniel 4:23..................... 395
Daniel 6:3.................. 62, 117
Daniel 6:4.................. 62, 117
Daniel 6:5..................... 117
Daniel 6:6..................... 117
Daniel 6:7..................... 117
Daniel 6:8..................... 117
Daniel 6:9..................... 117
Daniel 6:10.................... 269
Daniel 7:10................ 227, 228
Daniel 9:4..................... 53
Daniel 9:20.................... 53
Daniel 11:21 .... 113, 125
Daniel 11:32 113
Daniel 11:34 .... 113, 121

Amos 3:3 .... 106, 111
Amos 4:4 339
Amos 4:5 339
Amos 5:10 .... 168, 303, 308
Amos 6:1 357
Amos 7:14 395

Jonah 3:5 94

Micah 5:15..................... 384
Micah 7:5...................... 353

Nahum 1:2.................. 383, 384
Nahum 1:4..................... 307

Habakkuk 2:2 291
Habakkuk 2:13 374

Zephaniah 3:12................. 355
Zechariah 2:8................. 215
Zechariah 3:2................. 302
Zechariah 3:4................. 236
Zechariah 7:5................. 93
Zechariah 8:17 165
Zechariah 8:19 215

Malachi 1:9 267
Malachi 2:11 211
Malachi 2:12 276
Malachi 3:5 411
Malachi 3:7 147
Malachi 3:8 148
Malachi 3:11 307
Malachi 3:16 342

Matthew 3:17................ 203, 211
Matthew 4:1................... 195
Matthew 5:16................. 313
Matthew 5:17................. 339
Matthew 5:33................. 42
Matthew 5:34............... 42, 43
Matthew 5:35............... 42, 43
Matthew 5:36............... 42, 43
Matthew 5:37................. 42
Matthew 5:44................. 267
Matthew 6:2................ 61, 136
Matthew 6:5................ 61, 270
Matthew 6:6................. 270
Matthew 6:7................. 272
Matthew 6:8................. 218
Matthew 6:9.............. 260, 272
Matthew 6:10................ 272
Matthew 6:11................ 272
Matthew 6:12.............. 130, 272
Matthew 6:13................ 272
Matthew 6:16............... 91, 92
Matthew 6:25................ 339
Matthew 6:26................ 339
Matthew 6:27................ 339
Matthew 6:28................ 339
Matthew 6:29................ 339

Matthew 6:30. 339
Matthew 6:31. 339
Matthew 6:32. 339
Matthew 6:33. 339
Matthew 6:34. 339
Matthew 7:1. 188
Matthew 7:3. 189
Matthew 7:4. 189
Matthew 7:5. 189
Matthew 7:6. 310
Matthew 8:26. 307
Matthew 9:15. 90
Matthew 10:24. 275
Matthew 10:25. 275
Matthew 10:28. 100
Matthew 11:29. 110
Matthew 12:3. . . . . 285, 291
Matthew 12:18. . . . . 203, 204
Matthew 12:21. 355
Matthew 12:25. 343
Matthew 12:34. . . . . 30, 86, 234, 244
Matthew 14:23. 270
Matthew 15:9. 280
Matthew 15:14. 196
Matthew 15:19. . . . . . . 86, 244, 341, 411
Matthew 15:32. 91
Matthew 16:18. 1
Matthew 17:21. 94
Matthew 17:25. 340
Matthew 18:6. 210
Matthew 18:10. 210
Matthew 18:12. 340
Matthew 18:14. 210
Matthew 18:20. 215
Matthew 18:28. 105
Matthew 18:29. 105
Matthew 18:32. 135
Matthew 18:33. 135
Matthew 19:4. . . . . 241, 294
Matthew 20:26. . . . . 228, 229
Matthew 20:27. . . . . 228, 229
Matthew 20:28. . . . . 228, 229
Matthew 21:12. 309
Matthew 21:13. 309
Matthew 21:15. 210
Matthew 21:28. 340
Matthew 22:29. 285
Matthew 23:9. 119
Matthew 23:23. 121

Matthew 24:20. 90
Matthew 25:35. 232
Matthew 25:36. 232
Matthew 26:31. 357
Matthew 26:33. . . . . 122, 357
Matthew 26:34. . . . . 122, 357
Matthew 26:35. 122
Matthew 26:40. 400
Matthew 26:41. . . . . 34, 400
Matthew 26:47. 115
Matthew 26:48. 115
Matthew 26:49. 115
Matthew 26:57. 195
Matthew 27:2. 195
Matthew 27:31. 195

Mark 1:35. 270
Mark 2:1. 365
Mark 2:2. 365
Mark 2:3. 365
Mark 2:4. 365
Mark 2:5. 365
Mark 2:6. 365
Mark 2:7. 365
Mark 2:8. 365
Mark 2:9. 365
Mark 2:10. 365
Mark 2:11. 365
Mark 2:12. 365
Mark 2:20. 92
Mark 4:37. 312
Mark 4:38. 312
Mark 4:39. 312
Mark 4:40. 312
Mark 5:40. 181
Mark 6:7. 107
Mark 7:8. 402
Mark 7:34. 184
Mark 8:8. 143
Mark 8:32. 311
Mark 8:33. . . . . 311, 404
Mark 8:36. 409
Mark 10:24. 352
Mark 10:25. 352
Mark 12:41. 147
Mark 12:42. 147
Mark 12:43. 147
Mark 12:44. 147
Mark 13:11. 220

Mark 13:32. 401
Mark 13:33. 401
Mark 13:34. 401
Mark 13:35. 401
Mark 13:36. 401
Mark 13:37. 401
Mark 16:7. 216

Luke 1:2 227
Luke 3:19 78
Luke 3:20 78
Luke 4:1 95
Luke 4:2 95
Luke 4:16 . . . . 2, 292
Luke 4:29 195
Luke 5:1 205
Luke 5:2 205
Luke 5:3 205
Luke 5:4 205
Luke 5:5 205
Luke 5:6 205
Luke 5:22 343
Luke 6:8 343
Luke 6:21 . . . . 182, 185
Luke 6:25 182
Luke 6:38 150
Luke 6:45 223
Luke 8:27 239
Luke 8:35 . . . . 235, 239
Luke 8:39 47
Luke 9:46 339
Luke 9:47 . . . . 339, 343
Luke 9:48 339
Luke 10:20 182
Luke 10:30 177
Luke 10:31 177
Luke 10:32 177
Luke 10:33 177
Luke 10:34 177
Luke 10:35 177
Luke 10:38 312
Luke 10:39 312
Luke 10:40 312
Luke 10:41 312
Luke 10:42 312
Luke 11:17 343
Luke 12:16 345
Luke 12:17 345
Luke 12:18 345

Luke 12:19 345
Luke 12:20 345
Luke 13:34 184
Luke 15:13 138
Luke 15:14 138
Luke 15:17 319
Luke 15:18 319
Luke 15:19 319
Luke 15:20 319
Luke 16:1 139
Luke 16:28 403
Luke 18:9 357
Luke 19:8 60
Luke 19:11 139
Luke 19:12 139
Luke 19:13 139
Luke 19:14 139
Luke 19:15 139
Luke 19:16 139
Luke 19:17 139
Luke 19:18 139
Luke 19:19 139
Luke 19:20 139
Luke 19:21 139
Luke 19:22 139
Luke 19:23 139
Luke 19:24 139
Luke 19:25 139
Luke 19:26 . . . . 137, 139
Luke 19:27 139
Luke 19:40 258
Luke 20:19 123
Luke 20:20 123
Luke 20:21 123
Luke 22:31 390
Luke 22:32 198
Luke 23:34 . . . . 30, 216, 270
Luke 23:39 132
Luke 23:40 132
Luke 23:41 132
Luke 23:42 132
Luke 23:43 132
Luke 24:17 43
Luke 24:25 44
Luke 24:38 341
Luke 24:45 299
Luke 24:52 3
Luke 24:53 3

John 1:1 65
John 1:3 221
John 1:12 206
John 1:14 65
John 1:20 . . . . 49, 50
John 1:38 275
John 1:40 415
John 1:41 . . . . 231, 415
John 1:42 . . . . 231, 396, 415
John 1:45 415
John 1:46 415
John 3:2 275
John 3:6 34
John 3:16 . . 147, 188, 207, 214, 294, 409
John 3:33 233
John 4:3 408
John 4:4 408
John 4:24 35
John 5:22 187
John 5:23 187
John 5:39 . . . . 288, 339
John 6:1 403
John 6:5 315
John 6:6 315
John 6:11 . . . . 271, 324
John 6:12 . . . . 138, 142
John 6:37 294
John 6:43 245
John 6:61 247
John 6:63 34
John 7:7 168
John 7:24 . . . . 189, 191
John 8:11 52
John 8:14 190
John 8:15 190
John 8:42 196
John 8:44 . . . . 196, 386
John 11:16 . . . . 105, 329
John 11:35 184
John 12:3 241
John 12:27 184
John 12:43 254
John 12:48 190
John 13:1 216
John 13:34 . . . . 213, 232
John 13:35 . . . . 213, 232, 363
John 14:1 373
John 14:2 373
John 14:3 373

John 14:6 65
John 14:7 65
John 14:8 65
John 14:9 65
John 14:10 65
John 14:11 65
John 14:13 263
John 14:14 263
John 14:15 . . . . 147, 205
John 14:16 64
John 14:21 114
John 14:26 289
John 15:9 206
John 15:15 262
John 15:16 263
John 15:18 168
John 15:19 326
John 16:23 262
John 17:11 363
John 17:17 190
John 17:21 363
John 17:22 363
John 17:23 . . . . 206, 363
John 17:26 206
John 20:16 275
John 20:24 4
John 20:31 288
John 21:1 197
John 21:2 197
John 21:3 . . . . 197, 377
John 21:7 238
John 21:15 377
John 21:16 377
John 21:17 377
John 21:20 211

Acts 1:8 . . . . 81, 325, 406
Acts 2:32 404
Acts 2:42 107
Acts 2:46 . . . . 2, 4
Acts 2:47 2
Acts 3:6 18
Acts 4:18 75
Acts 4:19 75
Acts 4:20 . . . . 75, 405
Acts 4:29 75
Acts 4:31 75
Acts 4:33 405
Acts 4:34 145

Acts 4:35 145
Acts 6:1. 230
Acts 6:3. 230
Acts 6:4. 229, 230
Acts 7:38 1
Acts 7:58 79
Acts 7:59 79
Acts 7:60 268
Acts 8:1. 325
Acts 8:22 341
Acts 8:30 . . . . 230, 289, 414
Acts 8:31 . . . . 230, 414
Acts 8:32 . . . . 195, 230, 414
Acts 8:33 . . . . 230, 414
Acts 8:34 . . . . 230, 414
Acts 8:35 . . . . 230, 414
Acts 8:36 414
Acts 8:37 414
Acts 8:38 414
Acts 9:15 407
Acts 9:31 81
Acts 10:34 187
Acts 10:35 187
Acts 10:36 187
Acts 10:37 187
Acts 10:38 . . . . 175, 187
Acts 10:39 187
Acts 10:40 187
Acts 10:41 187
Acts 10:42 187
Acts 11:26 4
Acts 11:29 157
Acts 12:5 399
Acts 12:12 270
Acts 12:21 119
Acts 12:22 . . . . 119, 254
Acts 12:23 . . . . 119, 254
Acts 13:1 . . . . 279, 329
Acts 13:2 . . . . 108, 233, 329
Acts 13:3 . . . . 94, 329
Acts 13:22 . . . . 7, 221, 345
Acts 13:27 292
Acts 14:11 350
Acts 14:12 350
Acts 14:13 350
Acts 14:14 . . . . 119, 350
Acts 14:15 . . . . 119, 350, 376
Acts 15:10 281
Acts 15:14 373

Acts 15:21 292
Acts 16:25 336
Acts 16:30 . . . . 316, 413
Acts 16:31 . . . . 316, 413
Acts 17:2 406
Acts 17:3 406
Acts 17:11 294
Acts 17:21 267
Acts 17:31 187
Acts 18:24 279
Acts 18:25 279
Acts 18:26 279
Acts 19:18 50
Acts 20:7 2
Acts 20:20 . . . . 279, 415
Acts 20:24 . . . . 231, 405
Acts 20:27 . . . . 165, 235
Acts 20:28 398
Acts 20:29 398
Acts 20:30 398
Acts 20:31 . . . . 398, 406
Acts 20:35 18
Acts 21:13 217
Acts 22:15 407
Acts 27:22 361
Acts 27:23 361
Acts 27:24 361
Acts 27:25 361
Acts 27:33 90
Acts 28:1 . . . . 176, 381
Acts 28:2 . . . . 175, 381
Acts 28:3 . . . . 176, 190, 381
Acts 28:4 . . . . 176, 190, 381
Acts 28:6 176

Romans 1:4 406
Romans 1:8 47
Romans 1:14 231
Romans 1:16 . . . . 404, 411, 417
Romans 1:28 15
Romans 1:29 15
Romans 1:30 15
Romans 1:31 15
Romans 1:32 15
Romans 2:1 . . . . 188, 189
Romans 2:2 188
Romans 2:3 188
Romans 2:9 411
Romans 2:14 382

Romans 2:15 382
Romans 2:16 187
Romans 2:21 . . . . 189, 281
Romans 2:29 254
Romans 3:4 . . . . 352, 387
Romans 3:13 . . . . 114, 115
Romans 3:14 30
Romans 3:20 303
Romans 3:23 214
Romans 4:6 133
Romans 4:7 133
Romans 4:8 133
Romans 5:8 214
Romans 5:10 . . . . 231, 330
Romans 5:11 131
Romans 7:14 . . . . 33, 34
Romans 7:15 163
Romans 8:5 36
Romans 8:6 . . . . 33, 36
Romans 8:7 . . . . 34, 36, 37
Romans 8:8 34
Romans 8:15 100
Romans 8:26 263
Romans 9:20 241
Romans 10:1 268
Romans 10:9 . . . . 51, 406
Romans 10:13 131
Romans 10:17 294
Romans 12:6 158
Romans 12:7 158
Romans 12:8 158
Romans 12:9 261
Romans 12:10 . . . . 173, 367
Romans 12:11 173
Romans 12:12 . . . . 173, 269
Romans 12:13 . . . . 19, 171, 173, 175
Romans 12:19 . . . . 380, 382, 383
Romans 14:12 12
Romans 14:19 82
Romans 14:21 84
Romans 15:2 20
Romans 15:14 303
Romans 15:25 20
Romans 15:26 . . . . 20, 21, 160
Romans 15:27 . . . . 20, 21, 33
Romans 16:7 105
Romans 16:17 . . . . 327, 328
Romans 16:18 328
Romans 16:21 105

1 Corinthians 1:9 106
1 Corinthians 2:4 407
1 Corinthians 2:5 407
1 Corinthians 2:14 289
1 Corinthians 2:15 . . . . 187, 191
1 Corinthians 3:1 . . . . 12, 33, 34, 35, 191
1 Corinthians 3:3 37
1 Corinthians 3:9 111
1 Corinthians 3:10 319
1 Corinthians 3:11 319
1 Corinthians 4:17 278
1 Corinthians 5:11 328
1 Corinthians 6:1 193
1 Corinthians 6:2 193
1 Corinthians 6:3 . . . . 187, 193
1 Corinthians 6:4 193
1 Corinthians 6:5 193
1 Corinthians 6:6 193
1 Corinthians 6:7 193
1 Corinthians 6:8 193
1 Corinthians 7:3 17
1 Corinthians 8:1 85
1 Corinthians 8:13 83
1 Corinthians 9:1 321
1 Corinthians 9:11 33
1 Corinthians 10:1 245
1 Corinthians 10:2 245
1 Corinthians 10:3 245
1 Corinthians 10:4 245
1 Corinthians 10:5 . . . . 37, 245
1 Corinthians 10:6 245
1 Corinthians 10:7 245
1 Corinthians 10:8 245
1 Corinthians 10:9 245
1 Corinthians 10:10 . . . . 245, 246
1 Corinthians 10:11 245
1 Corinthians 10:12 . . . . 245, 317
1 Corinthians 10:13 245
1 Corinthians 10:14 245
1 Corinthians 10:23 83
1 Corinthians 10:31 12
1 Corinthians 11:3 196
1 Corinthians 11:14 241
1 Corinthians 11:15 241
1 Corinthians 11:31 . . . . 192, 313
1 Corinthians 13:3 158
1 Corinthians 14:5 87
1 Corinthians 14:15 334
1 Corinthians 14:26 87

1 Corinthians 14:40 6
1 Corinthians 15:1 . . . . . . 316, 405, 416
1 Corinthians 15:2 . . . . . . 316, 405, 416
1 Corinthians 15:3 . . . . . . 316, 405, 416
1 Corinthians 15:4 . . . . . . 316, 405, 416
1 Corinthians 15:19 373
1 Corinthians 15:22 330
1 Corinthians 15:33 . . . . 44, 46
1 Corinthians 15:34 416
1 Corinthians 15:47 330
1 Corinthians 15:48 330
1 Corinthians 15:49 330
1 Corinthians 15:58 376
1 Corinthians 16:2 . . . . 146, 157
1 Corinthians 16:13 . . . . 393, 396
1 Corinthians 16:15 232

2 Corinthians 1:9 . . . . 353, 356
2 Corinthians 1:10 353
2 Corinthians 1:12 60
2 Corinthians 4:5 412
2 Corinthians 4:13 408
2 Corinthians 4:17 217
2 Corinthians 5:3 237
2 Corinthians 5:17 59
2 Corinthians 5:18 231
2 Corinthians 5:20 231
2 Corinthians 5:21 184
2 Corinthians 6:4 397
2 Corinthians 6:5 397
2 Corinthians 6:14 . . . . . . 106, 110, 166,
. . . . 328, 329
2 Corinthians 6:17 324
2 Corinthians 7:11 379
2 Corinthians 8:1 . . . . 145, 160
2 Corinthians 8:2 . . . . 145, 160
2 Corinthians 8:3 . . . . 145, 160
2 Corinthians 8:4 . . . . 145, 160
2 Corinthians 8:5 . . . . 145, 160
2 Corinthians 8:9 152
2 Corinthians 8:12 158
2 Corinthians 8:23 105
2 Corinthians 9:6 23
2 Corinthians 9:7 . . . . 149, 152, 156, 160
2 Corinthians 10:3 .38, 39, 342, 387, 390
2 Corinthians 10:4 . . . . 39, 342, 387, 390
2 Corinthians 10:5 . . . . 342, 345
2 Corinthians 10:6 379
2 Corinthians 10:14 414

2 Corinthians 10:15 414
2 Corinthians 10:16 414
2 Corinthians 11:13 227
2 Corinthians 11:14 227
2 Corinthians 11:15 227
2 Corinthians 11:23 217
2 Corinthians 11:24 217
2 Corinthians 11:25 217
2 Corinthians 11:26 217
2 Corinthians 11:27 . . . . 89, 92, 217, 397
2 Corinthians 12:20 . . . . 9, 11
2 Corinthians 12:21 11
2 Corinthians 13:5 316
2 Corinthians 13:10 82
2 Corinthians 13:11 . . . . 366, 369

Galatians 1:6 416
Galatians 1:7 416
Galatians 1:8 416
Galatians 1:9 416
Galatians 1:13 59
Galatians 1:23 59
Galatians 2:6 328
Galatians 2:7 328
Galatians 2:8 328
Galatians 2:9 . . . . 108, 328
Galatians 2:11 76
Galatians 2:12 76
Galatians 2:13 76
Galatians 2:14 76
Galatians 2:20 207
Galatians 3:24 351
Galatians 4:11 320
Galatians 4:15 145
Galatians 5:12 364
Galatians 5:13 232
Galatians 5:15 . . . . 13, 232
Galatians 5:17 34
Galatians 6:1 . . . . 301, 317
Galatians 6:3 122
Galatians 6:6 155
Galatians 6:10 . . . . 18, 232
Galatians 6:14 . . . . 166, 323

Ephesians 2:3 59
Ephesians 2:8 316
Ephesians 2:9 316
Ephesians 2:10 320
Ephesians 2:13 264

Ephesians 2:18. 264
Ephesians 2:19. 105
Ephesians 3:6. 105
Ephesians 3:19. 85
Ephesians 4:1. 366
Ephesians 4:2. 366
Ephesians 4:3. 366
Ephesians 4:11. 84
Ephesians 4:12. 84
Ephesians 4:13. . . . . 84, 363, 369
Ephesians 4:14. 84
Ephesians 4:15. . . . . 84, 168
Ephesians 4:16. 84
Ephesians 4:22. 59
Ephesians 4:26. . . . . 14, 27
Ephesians 4:27. 27
Ephesians 4:29. . . . . . .13, 42, 45, 86, 391
Ephesians 4:31. 29
Ephesians 4:32. . . . . 30, 135
Ephesians 5:4. 181
Ephesians 5:6. 376
Ephesians 5:11. . . . . 109, 166, 329
Ephesians 5:15. . . . . 399, 400
Ephesians 5:19. 337
Ephesians 5:25. . . . . 204, 207, 215
Ephesians 5:26. . . . . 288, 293
Ephesians 6:1. . . . . 196, 311
Ephesians 6:2. 311
Ephesians 6:6. 61
Ephesians 6:10. 76
Ephesians 6:11. . . . . 391, 392
Ephesians 6:12. . . . . . .387, 389, 390, 391
Ephesians 6:13. 391
Ephesians 6:14. . . . . 391, 392
Ephesians 6:15. 391
Ephesians 6:16. . . . . 391, 392
Ephesians 6:17. . . . . 39, 392
Ephesians 6:18. . . . . . .268, 392, 396, 398
Ephesians 6:19. 414

Philippians 1:4. 260
Philippians 1:20 79
Philippians 1:27 61
Philippians 2:2. 364
Philippians 2:5. 229
Philippians 2:6. 229
Philippians 2:7. 229
Philippians 2:8. 229
Philippians 2:14 . . . . 244, 245

Philippians 2:15 . . . . 245, 313
Philippians 2:16 . . . . 245, 376
Philippians 2:25 105
Philippians 3:3. 355
Philippians 3:4. 351
Philippians 3:5. . . . . 351, 356
Philippians 3:6. 351
Philippians 3:7. 351
Philippians 3:8. 356
Philippians 3:10 . . . . 108, 111, 361
Philippians 3:20 60
Philippians 4:3. 105
Philippians 4:6. 260
Philippians 4:8. . . . . 222, 340, 341
Philippians 4:14 155
Philippians 4:15 155

Colossians 1:14 131
Colossians 2:13 . . . . 132, 133
Colossians 2:16 90
Colossians 2:17 90
Colossians 3:8 . . . . 30, 45, 46
Colossians 3:13 . . . . 30, 135
Colossians 3:16 . . . . 335, 336
Colossians 3:17 12
Colossians 3:18 196
Colossians 3:20 . . . . 225, 300, 389
Colossians 3:23 61
Colossians 4:2 . . . . 399, 413
Colossians 4:3 413
Colossians 4:6 30
Colossians 4:11 105
Colossians 4:12 399
1 Thessalonians 1:5. 407
1 Thessalonians 2:3. 127
1 Thessalonians 2:4. 127
1 Thessalonians 2:5. . . . . . 113, 115, 116,
. . . . 123, 127
1 Thessalonians 2:6. 127
1 Thessalonians 2:19. 320
1 Thessalonians 3:2. 105
1 Thessalonians 4:9. 213
1 Thessalonians 4:11. 291
1 Thessalonians 4:13. 56
1 Thessalonians 4:17. 126
1 Thessalonians 5:9. . . . . . 116, 126, 384
1 Thessalonians 5:13. 369
1 Thessalonians 5:14. 303
1 Thessalonians 5:17. 269

1 Thessalonians 5:25. 268
1 Thessalonians 5:27. 292

2 Thessalonians 1:8. 384
2 Thessalonians 2:9. 113
2 Thessalonians 2:15. . . . . 280, 393
2 Thessalonians 3:6. 328
2 Thessalonians 3:10. 21
2 Thessalonians 3:11. 21
2 Thessalonians 3:12. 21

1 Timothy 1:1 413
1 Timothy 1:2 280
1 Timothy 1:4 81
1 Timothy 2:1 268
1 Timothy 2:2 268
1 Timothy 2:4 408
1 Timothy 2:8 . . . . 264, 270
1 Timothy 2:9 . . . . 235, 240
1 Timothy 3:2 . . . . 171, 172, 173
1 Timothy 3:4 199
1 Timothy 3:5 199
1 Timothy 3:11 354
1 Timothy 3:15 6
1 Timothy 4:6 280
1 Timothy 4:11 . . . . 280, 281
1 Timothy 4:12 . . . . 62, 224, 281
1 Timothy 4:13 . . . . . . 224, 225, 287, 292
1 Timothy 4:14 224
1 Timothy 4:15 . . . . 219, 224, 225
1 Timothy 5:1 . . . . 109, 310
1 Timothy 5:2 109
1 Timothy 5:8 22
1 Timothy 5:9 174
1 Timothy 5:10 . . . . 172, 174
1 Timothy 5:17 308
1 Timothy 5:18 308
1 Timothy 5:19 308
1 Timothy 5:20 308
1 Timothy 5:23 48
1 Timothy 6:8 19
1 Timothy 6:12 . . . .39, 74, 388, 389, 390
1 Timothy 6:14 313
1 Timothy 6:17 . . . . 156, 348, 352
1 Timothy 6:18 . . . . 41, 155, 156
1 Timothy 6:19 156

2 Timothy 1:7 100
2 Timothy 1:8 417

2 Timothy 1:16 232
2 Timothy 1:17 232
2 Timothy 1:18 232
2 Timothy 2:2 . . . . .85, 230, 278, 279
2 Timothy 2:3 393
2 Timothy 2:4 393
2 Timothy 2:15 . . . . . .283, 287, 295, 297
2 Timothy 2:19 320
2 Timothy 3:16 . . . . 286, 296
2 Timothy 3:17 369
2 Timothy 4:1 187
2 Timothy 4:2 . . . . 299, 300
2 Timothy 4:3 300
2 Timothy 4:4 300
2 Timothy 4:5 398
2 Timothy 4:7 184
2 Timothy 4:10 209
2 Timothy 4:14 383

Titus 1:8. . . . . 171, 173
Titus 1:12. 301
Titus 1:13. 301
Titus 1:14. 301
Titus 2:1. 279
Titus 2:2. . . . . 279, 354
Titus 2:3. 279
Titus 2:4. . . . . 205, 279
Titus 2:5. 279
Titus 2:6. 279
Titus 2:7. 279
Titus 2:8. 279
Titus 2:15. . . . . 299, 303
Titus 3:2. 13
Titus 3:8. 320

Philemon 6 46

Hebrews 2:10. 389
Hebrews 2:12. 336
Hebrews 2:13. 353
Hebrews 4:12. . . . . .68, 343, 391
Hebrews 4:16. . . . . .39, 261, 264
Hebrews 5:12. . . . . 279, 395
Hebrews 6:10. . . . . 73, 232
Hebrews 7:25. 263
Hebrews 8:11. 134
Hebrews 8:12. 134
Hebrews 9:10. 33
Hebrews 10:25. . . . . 3, 391

Hebrews 10:30. 383
Hebrews 11:3. 111
Hebrews 11:6. 149
Hebrews 11:7. 103
Hebrews 11:17. 359
Hebrews 11:18. 359
Hebrews 11:19. . . . . 102, 359
Hebrews 11:25. . . . . 55, 124
Hebrews 11:36. 73
Hebrews 11:37. 73
Hebrews 11:38. 73
Hebrews 12:5. . . . . 302, 312
Hebrews 12:6. 312
Hebrews 12:15. 27
Hebrews 12:16. 38
Hebrews 12:28. . . . . 101, 103
Hebrews 13:1. . . . . 216, 366
Hebrews 13:2. 174
Hebrews 13:6. 100
Hebrews 13:7. 58
Hebrews 13:15. . . . . 233, 256
Hebrews 13:16. 41
Hebrews 13:17. 398

James 1:6 271
James 1:7 271
James 2:15 19
James 2:16 19
James 3:1 198
James 3:5 10
James 3:6 10
James 3:8 . . . . 11, 46
James 3:13 58
James 3:14 26
James 4:7 390
James 4:9 179
James 4:11 . . . . 10, 13
James 5:12 43
James 5:13 336
James 5:16 53

1 Peter 1:15 61
1 Peter 1:18 59
1 Peter 1:23 188
1 Peter 2:1 12
1 Peter 2:2 . . . . 12, 36, 295
1 Peter 2:3 12
1 Peter 2:5 314
1 Peter 2:12 58

1 Peter 2:13 196
1 Peter 2:14 196
1 Peter 3:1 58
1 Peter 3:2 58
1 Peter 3:3 240
1 Peter 3:4 240
1 Peter 3:5 240
1 Peter 3:7 271
1 Peter 3:8 367
1 Peter 3:9 367
1 Peter 3:10 367
1 Peter 3:11 367
1 Peter 3:12 111
1 Peter 3:14 412
1 Peter 3:15 412
1 Peter 3:20 381
1 Peter 3:22 196
1 Peter 4:4 326
1 Peter 4:7 398
1 Peter 4:9 . . . . 171, 172
1 Peter 5:8 . . . . 296, 390, 399

2 Peter 1:11 227
2 Peter 1:13 339
2 Peter 1:16 405
2 Peter 1:17 405
2 Peter 1:18 405
2 Peter 1:19 405
2 Peter 1:20 405
2 Peter 1:21 405
2 Peter 2:6 384
2 Peter 2:7 . . . . 59, 384
2 Peter 2:8 59
2 Peter 2:9 385
2 Peter 2:18 371
2 Peter 3:3 185
2 Peter 3:4 185
2 Peter 3:8 385
2 Peter 3:9 . . . . 131, 408
2 Peter 3:11 . . . . 57, 61
2 Peter 3:16 48
2 Peter 3:18 303

1 John 1:3. 110
1 John 1:6. 111
1 John 1:7. . . . . 105, 111
1 John 1:8. 317
1 John 1:9. . . . . 51, 52, 132, 133, 317
1 John 1:10. 387

1 John 2:1 . . . . 129, 263
1 John 2:2 263
1 John 2:12 . . . . 129, 133, 135
1 John 2:15 . . . . 209, 326
1 John 2:28 401
1 John 3:12 326
1 John 3:13 . . . . 168, 326
1 John 3:17 212
1 John 3:20 44
1 John 3:22 271
1 John 4:7 . . . . 204, 212
1 John 4:8 . . . . 164, 206
1 John 4:11 206
1 John 4:18 98
1 John 4:19 . . . . 212, 285
1 John 4:21 . . . . 109, 215
1 John 5:3 217
1 John 5:7 262
1 John 5:10 404
1 John 5:14 271
3 John 7 330

3 John 8 . . . . 105, 329
3 John 14 347

Jude 3 74
Jude 7 380
Jude 9 73
Jude 16 243
Jude 19 323
Jude 24 263

Revelation 1:3 . . . . 283, 293
Revelation 1:12 283
Revelation 1:13 283
Revelation 1:17 97

Revelation 1:18 97
Revelation 1:20 284
Revelation 2:5 316
Revelation 2:6 165
Revelation 2:13 73
Revelation 2:15 165
Revelation 2:20 275
Revelation 3:5 49
Revelation 3:18 . . . . 65, 237
Revelation 3:19 . . . . 250, 299, 304
Revelation 4:11 373
Revelation 5:4 283
Revelation 5:9 333
Revelation 7:17 195
Revelation 8:1 251
Revelation 8:4 259
Revelation 10:10 25
Revelation 13:10 195
Revelation 15:3 331
Revelation 16:15 395
Revelation 18:2 163
Revelation 19:2 379
Revelation 19:5 251
Revelation 19:13 187
Revelation 19:19 387
Revelation 20:4 403
Revelation 20:11 227
Revelation 20:12 . . . . 227, 228
Revelation 20:13 . . . . 187, 227
Revelation 20:14 227
Revelation 20:15 227
Revelation 21:4 185
Revelation 21:8 97
Revelation 22:3 227
Revelation 22:15 203
Revelation 22:16 1